Vox intexta

Vox intexta

Orality and Textuality
in the Middle Ages

Edited by

A. N. Doane and Carol Braun Pasternack

THE UNIVERSITY OF WISCONSIN PRESS

The University of Wisconsin Press
114 North Murray Street
Madison, Wisconsin 53715

3 Henrietta Street
London WC2E 8LU, England

5   4   3   2   1

Printed in the United States of America

Library of Congress Cataloging-in-Publication Data
Vox intexta: orality and textuality in the Middle Ages / edited by
  A. N. Doane and Carol Braun Pasternack.
  304 pp.   cm.
  Includes bibliographical references and index.
  ISBN 0-299-13090-8   ISBN 0-299-13094-0 (pbk.)
  1. Literature, Medieval—History and criticism.
  2. Oral tradition—Europe.   3. Transmission of texts.
  I. Doane, Alger Nicolaus, 1938–   II. Pasternack, Carol Braun.
PN671.V69   1991
809'.02—dc20   91-3573

Contents

Acknowledgments

The editors wish to thank all those who made possible the 1988 Con-Texts conference at the University of Wisconsin–Madison—for which most of these essays were originally prepared—above all the participants themselves, most of whom are represented in this book. Funding for Con-Texts was provided by the Anonymous Fund of the University of Wisconsin–Madison, the Brittingham Foundation, the Hewlett Committee, the Humanistic Foundation, the Knapp Bequest, the Departments of English, of French and Italian, and the Medieval Studies Program. We are grateful to all those who attended the conference and made it such a pleasure and success. More personally, thanks are due to Professors Eric Rothstein, Christopher Kleinhenz, and Frank Gentry, the chairs of the sponsoring departments, for their enthusiasm and support as the conference was being planned. We thank Kathy Dauck and Susan Youngs of the English Department, University of Wisconsin–Madison, whose labors and concerns for a long time, before, during, and after its meeting, made the conference a smoothly running reality.

While "Con-Texts" was taking shape as *Vox intexta* we incurred many debts and owe many thanks: to the contributors for their continuing cooperation and patience during the long editorial process; to Janice Grossman, funded by the Interdisciplinary Humanities Center at the University of California, Santa Barbara, for editorial assistance; to Matthew Livesey for compiling the index; to Yvonne Schofer for saving us from many errors in the French citations and titles; to Martha G. Blalock for work on the citations; to Barb Gaffney, for retyping many of the essays; and to Angela G. Ray, the copy editor for the University of Wisconsin Press, who brought a diversity of manuscripts into consistent style. Finally, the editors thank each other for the energy, collegiality, and rethinkings—and the friendship—sustained over many months and miles.

Contributors

John Dagenais is Associate Professor of Spanish at Northwestern University. He is currently working on a book entitled *The Larger Gloss: The Ethics of Reading the* Libro de Buen Amor.

A. N. Doane is Professor of English at the University of Wisconsin–Madison and the author of *Genesis A: A New Edition* (1978) and *The Saxon Genesis* (1991).

John Miles Foley is William H. Byler Professor in the Humanities in the English Department of the University of Missouri–Columbia and Director of the Center for Studies in Oral Tradition. He is the editor of the journal *Oral Tradition* and author of many books on oral theory, including *The Theory of Oral Composition: History and Methodology* (1988) and *Traditional Oral Epic: The Odyssey, Beowulf, and the Serbo-Croation Return Song* (1990).

Dolores Warwick Frese is Professor of English at the University of Notre Dame. She is the author of *An Ars Legendi for Chaucer's* Canterbury Tales: *Re-Constructive Reading* (1991).

Sylvia Huot, Associate Professor of French at Northern Illinois University–Dekalb, is the author of *From Song to Book: The Poetics of Writing in Old French Lyric and Lyrical Narrative Poetry* (1987).

Robert Kellogg, Professor of English at the University of Virginia, is the author of *A Concordance to Eddic Poetry* (1988), with Robert Scholes, of *The Nature of Narrative* (1966), and with E. U. Crosby and Julian Bishko of *Medieval Studies: A Bibliographical Guide* (1983).

Laurence de Looze is Assistant Professor of Comparative Literature at Harvard University. He is writing a book on "pseudo-autobiography" in the fourteenth century.

ix

Tim William Machan, Associate Professor of English at Marquette University, is the author of *Techniques of Translation: Chaucer's Boece* (1985) and editor of the Old Norse *Vafþrúðnismál* (1988). He is currently writing a book on "textual criticism and the medieval text."

Stephen G. Nichols is Edmund J. Kahn Professor of Humanities in the Department of Romance Languages at the University of Pennsylvania. He is the author of many books and collections, including *Romanesque Signs: Early Medieval Narrative and Iconography* (1984), and is currently working on a book, *Voices in the Text: Writing and Orality in Troubadour Lyric Poetry.*

Ward Parks, Associate Professor of English at Louisiana State University–Baton Rouge, is author of *Verbal Delivery in Heroic Narrative: The Homeric and Old English Traditions* (1990).

Carol Braun Pasternack is Assistant Professor of English at the University of California–Santa Barbara. She is completing a book entitled *Shaping True Words: The Textuality of Old English Poems.*

Ursula Schaefer of the Englisches Seminar in the Albert-Ludwigs-Universität, Freiburg im Breisgau, Germany, is the author of *Höfisch-ritterliche Dichtung und sozialhistorische Realität: Literatursoziologische Studien zum Verhältnis von Adelsstruktur, Ritterideal und Dichtung bei Geoffrey Chaucer* (1977) and is currently writing a book on "vocality" in Old English literature which will appear in Fall 1991.

Dennis Tedlock is the James H. McNulty Professor of English in the Poetics Program at the State University of New York at Buffalo. He is the author of *Finding the Center: Narrative Poetry of the Zuni Indians* (1972), *The Spoken Word and the Work of Interpretation* (1983), is editor and translator of *Popul Vuh: The Mayan Book of the Dawn of Life* (1985), and has recently published a book of original poetry, *Days from a Dream Almanac* (1990).

Hanna Vollrath is Professor of Medieval History at the Ruhr-Universität, Bochum, Germany. She is the author of *Die Synoden Englands bis 1066* (1985) and "Deutschen Geschichte im Mittelalter" in *Rassow Deutsche Geschichte,* ed. M. Vogt (1987).

Alois Wolf is Professor of German Literature at the Albert-Ludwigs Universität, Freiburg im Breisgau, Germany. He is the author of many articles and books on medieval German and Romance literature, including *Deutsche Kultur im Hochmittelalter* (1986) and *Gottfried von Strassburg und die Mythe von Tristan und Isolde* (1989).

Introduction

The dilemma is inescapable: either the anthropologist clings to the norms of his own group, in which case the others can only inspire in him an ephemeral curiosity in which there is always an element of disapproval; or he makes himself over completely to the objects of his studies, in which case he can never be perfectly objective, because in giving himself to all societies he cannot but refuse himself, wittingly or not, to one among them.

—Lévi-Strauss, *"A Little Glass of Rum"*

The essays in this volume began as papers invited for a conference at Madison, Wisconsin, in April 1988, "Con-Texts: Orality and Textuality in the Middle Ages." Each participant was asked to address the problems implied in the title: How did medieval textuality intersect with language production that was actually oral or pretended to be oral? How adequately can postmodern notions of textuality deal with medieval oral production in its medieval and/or modern textual forms? The aim was to elicit work that would unite two of the most exciting fields in current medieval studies, oral theory and postmodern criticism, testing work that has been done, discovering gaps and oversights, and striking out in new directions. The resultant papers covered a range of the literatures of medieval Europe (and modern Central America) and a diverse array of theoretical approaches. What marks them is an openmindedness of approach to the medieval phenomena and a skeptical attitude to the critical past and present. Though little will be found that resembles classical "oral-formulaic theory" or conventional deconstruction, Parry and Derrida, *fort* and *da,* haunt the pages of the book. Every essay recognizes that at the heart of the oral phenomena is a presence now absent that cannot be recaptured by statistical methods or exorcised with a wave of the Derridean wand, while the present absence we call text is here received less as deferral and more as invasive presence.

Orality and Textuality compresses the gap that is habitually maintained between two seemingly mutually exclusive and sequential epistemes. In the West, the conjunction has been resisted (Augustine), negativized (Plato), deplored (Lévi-Strauss), elided (Derrida), with the result that the text has always been privileged over the voice. But there is no way for the conscientious student of ancient textuality to do without the *and* which both joins and maintains the separation. Since Parry the conjunction has been historicized, thematized, and disciplined, resulting in a dual or paradoxical status for that large body of data known to be or imagined as orally originated, performed, or (in the case of indubitably authored works) projected. This has given rise to a heightened sense of complexity, not to say confusion and paradox, in discussions of origins and modes of production in the various literary, linguistic, and musical spheres of medieval studies.

On one side, the inevitably textual status of all medieval orality has seemed to dictate a textualist approach. The "Parry/Lord" school has always capitalized on the ethnographic fact of oral origins but in spite of this is less historicist than structuralist: "oral-formulaics" was one of the first bastions of structuralism and has remained one of the last. As in any structuralist project, the empirical details have tended to be supplanted by virtualities that bring out invisible patterns inferred from great masses of data. Captured on recordings (which are texts insofar as they are fixed and indefinitely replicable if not recuperable), the oral phenomena have been transferred to edited and regularized written formats which have always been more "there" than the long-since breathed-out songs themselves. The South Slavic model, based on living performances gathered in rural areas of modern Yugoslavia, has given this school a certain epistemological hegemony. Its data, jealously guarded and tended by the oral-formulaicists, have ironically assumed the status of ancient and medieval texts: their aural reality has been succeeded by hypertexts dissected into concordanced formulas, systems, themes, etc.[1] Once the songs became texts, stripped of their sonic component and location within and between bodies, the "written residue" was endowed with all the prestige that has traditionally inhered in the texts studied by classicists and medievalists. For practical purposes, *oral-formulaic* has in fact become equivalent to *text-formula*.

On the other side, it is known—though rarely is the knowledge effective—that nearly all vernacular texts and many Latin ones (e.g., saints' lives, liturgy) preserved from the Middle Ages down to the thirteenth century and beyond are merely traces of an existence that was normally vocalized. Texts were written to be heard—whatever the mechanisms of their original production. Recognizing this, a newer trend, associated by medievalists with Paul Zumthor, but not restricted to him, has been remembering the "beauty of the voice" that the text effaces when it is read in a milieu of silence. Whether an ethnographer remembering something heard, or a literary scholar projecting back what never can have been heard again, or a medievalist (like Zumthor) insisting on the echo of the voice, however irrecuperable the voice itself, this looser grouping demands that the phonics, the breathings, the stalls, the timbre, the gestures, and the communal surroundings be taken somehow into account, however uneffaced this stubborn textuality may remain. Unsettling to traditional philology, such approaches necessarily privilege the remembrance of performance, the unique, the peculiar, the *proper,* as opposed to text, with its virtualities, authorization, and individualized intention and reception.

Students of the "oral texts" of earlier ages are forced by the nature of the case to project. They have their texts, products of written manuscripts, and they have the stories they've made (which they have reason to believe to be true ones), telling that some of these texts were once not writing, but speech. They must explain these texts by stories of orality; that is, their understanding of the text's orality is always metonymic, the writing standing for a voice, and hence always/already figural.[2]

Scholars have tended to paint the picture of orality in black and white, either/or, "us and them" terms. The dichotomy "orality/literacy" has been widely influential through the work of Walter Ong and Jack Goody. And at first and for a long time the oral-formulaicists denied the reality of the "transitional text," so that a given production had to be seen either as oral or "literate." Ethnographically and historically, past societies have been seen in ideal terms, as either "primary oral" or "literate." The sense of lack, of the primitive and imperfect, that seems to linger in the term *oral* used of cultures and societies coexists uneasily with a nostalgic notion that orality is somehow original, pure, forceful. But medievalists such as Clanchy, Stock, Bäuml, and many others have been resisting the naturalness of the opposition, showing not only that primary orality is forever inaccessible to us (if it is not merely mythical) but also that in all the forms of writing from the Middle Ages until at least the later thirteenth century, orality and writing interpenetrate and influence one another in active and vital ways, sometimes cooperatively, sometimes conflictively. This book develops the realization of this symbiosis of orality and textuality, as theoretical nexus, as historical probability, as the fictions and stratagems of medieval people themselves, and as textualization and projection in the work of modern critics and editors.

A. N. D.

Notes

1 The "oral-formulaic" school has not only captured the recordings but has also attempted thereby to control the definition of what is *oral,* tending on one ground or another to exclude contemporary and Third World examples which have been of-

fered that don't conform to the South Slavic / Homeric paradigm of "formulaically-improvised, metrical, heroic song." See Gary Miller's review and comments on the "New Orthodoxy," a not entirely ironic term in his usage (1–8). He shows by argument and example how most of the writing of the oral-formulaic school keeps folding back on itself and its previous avatars as if to protect itself from intrusive heresy.

2 This is what the following observation by Zumthor seems to mean: "Formally speaking, I would describe *poetry* as a group of utterances organized more or less rigorously in a sort of vast discourse that globally set itself up as a metaphor for all the everyday discourses enunciated within a social group" ("Spoken Language" 194). But *metonymy* seems preferable to *metaphor,* because the relation of text to lost voice is seen by most medievalists not as a relation of becoming but as a relation of replacement or representation. This of course does not apply to Zumthor himself. As used here, *metonymy* means a replacement made by later *readers* who because of disjunction of time and place cannot hear a text. It thus differs from Foley's use of the term in this volume; he sees metonymy as inherent in the tradition itself, regardless of the mode of reception.

PART ONE
ORAL PERFORMANCE
AND ORAL TEXT

Introduction

What does it mean to write about oral performance and make it the object of scholarship, especially when, as is true for the Middle Ages, the performances survive only as written texts? The subject of orality in the Middle Ages is plagued by this problem of lost performances, the problem of trying to understand something that no longer exists, of relying by necessity on letters drawn on vellum, and then of relying for the sake of convenience on lines of poetry printed in the modern fashion in books. Dennis Tedlock, John Miles Foley, and Ward Parks agree that these written texts cannot transparently represent oral performances. When we look at letters on a page, we have to concentrate on determining exactly what sort of hybrid we are studying and what kind of interference our presuppositions about texts and about oral performances impose on our experiences of those texts. Significant difficulties rise up before us: the loss of voice and dialogic response that characterize performances, the difficulties of acquiring understanding of the contextual traditions that contribute to a text's meaning when it is produced, and the fact that the written text has come to represent a specific kind of textuality, very different from what this volume argues existed in medieval manuscripts. Tedlock brings to this set of problems the insights of one who struggles to transcribe and understand varieties of contemporary Zuni performances; Foley, of one who compares Greek and Anglo-Saxon texts with Serbo-Croatian texts and performances; and Parks, of one who examines our writings about medieval texts against modernist and postmodern literary theory.

Dennis Tedlock's printed performance of "The Speaker of Tales Has More Than One String to Play On" transports us out of that medieval trap to contemporary Zuni performances of the story of "when newness was made." (We asked him to be keynote speaker for the conference that generated this book because he could share with the other, medievalist participants his experiences with performances not captured by the text and with an ongoing debate about how to present these performances to the textualized world of scholars.) In the text he has created for this book, Tedlock tries to maintain a sense of the voices audiences hear, the voices of storytellers and of his own performance. His article talks—in its style and in its printed form that maps pauses and to some degree intonation as well. In doing so, it illustrates how much the normal for-

3

matting of words on the page evens out voice. He talks us through two performances of the story of newness, one memorial and ritually uniform in performance, the other spoken, improvised, multivoiced. Through his scoring and his
running analysis, he attempts to keep the specificity of the performances. He
also shows the generic range of oral performances and the need to recognize
in our theories that not all orality is epic or metric or formulaic in phrasing.
He undermines Derrida's and Bakhtin's assumptions that epic is the archetype
of orality, imposing an originary monologism, and adopts the terminology
Bakhtin developed for the novel to analyze the multivoiced telling of a tale.

While Tedlock shows us what has been lost, John Miles Foley copes with
what medievalists do have—texts from cultures that practice written and oral
circulation of story and knowledge, cultures that are "hybrid." Modifying
Milman Parry and Albert Lord's work and drawing on Wolfgang Iser's, Foley
theorizes in "Orality, Textuality, and Interpretation" how traditional forms
preserved in medieval texts generate meaning (*traditional* correctly replaces
oral as the descriptive name for these texts). A comparatist himself, Foley,
like Tedlock, insists on distinguishing genres, traditional culture, and individual performances. He also insists that each of these has its "traditional rules"
that structure not "fossilized" phraseologies but a fluid idiom within which
poets compose and audiences understand texts. These rules, then, facilitate a
certain kind of extratextual meaning different from meanings generated by
nontraditional texts and participate in a different aesthetics. He proposes using
the texts we do have to determine these rules and to advance our methods of
interpretation.

Texts stand in the place of voice and presence, providing words that allow
us to imagine some ways performances made meaning. Ward Parks takes us
back from the texts to performances and argues that our own modern textuality stands between us and those performances. We have textualized orality
as we have textualized the world, from the perspective of our book-lined studies. Parks, asking that we recognize our textuality, calls for a dialogics of oral
and literary theory. He asks that we question the assumptions of literary theorists about the relationship of orality to writing, specifically critiquing New
Criticism, Derrida, and Bakhtin. In effect, Parks asks that the oral theory
question the literary and vice versa. Finally, reworking Bakhtin, he shows
what is present in the dynamics of a performance that is lost in a textual
transcription and must be fictionalized into presence in the novel—the dialogue between performer and tradition (here his work intersects with Foley's)
and between performer and present audience (here his work complements
Tedlock's). The problematics of orality and those of textuality, then, can be
two sides of the same coin. We know our modern possibilities and limitations
more fully by trying to know this otherness of traditional performance.

C. B. P.

Dennis Tedlock

The Speaker of Tales Has More Than One String to Play On

Reading the Score

Pausing: Lines beginning at the left margin are separated by pauses of at least half a second each, but no more than a full second; indented lines are run on without a pause. A strophe break with a dot (•) indicates a pause of two or three seconds.

Amplitude: **Boldface type** calls for a relatively loud voice; small type calls for a soft voice.

Intonation: A period, even when it falls within a line or ends a non-sentence, indicates a marked drop in pitch that completes an intonational contour. A lack of punctuation at the end of a line indicates intonational enjambment, which is to say an incomplete contour. The sound of a vowel is held at a steady pitch for a full second or two when it is followed by a lo————ng dash.

Chanting: Passages written on two different registers, ruled off with horizontal parallel lines, are rendered in something close to a singing voice but with only two pitches, two or three halftones apart. The higher pitch falls on syllables or words written in the higher register.

Score for a Talk on Storytelling

My texts for today
come from the Zuni Indians of New Mexico
one of them taken down in dictation a century ago
the other taken down by tape recorder a little over twenty years ago
and both dealing with a time so remote
that newness itself was being made then.
One of them, "The Word of Kyaklo"
which is recited every four years or so
is the official, canonical version of the story of newness
not produced by oral-formulaic composition
but repeated verbatim
by a masked performer who studies for the part for a year.
The other is a hearthside interpretation of the story of newness
partly given by tradition
and partly redrawn, or resounded, edited, and elaborated
by a particular narrator
Andrew Peynetsa
on a particular occasion.
I have compared these two texts before
in The Spoken Word and the Work of Interpretation
but I've tuned my ear differently here
among other things you'll notice that I've been reading Bakhtin.
Later you may want to check the translations I'll be reading from here
against the ones I've published before.
Translations are not authoritative
every time I return to a text
I find myself involved in what some of you call mouvance.
You will also notice, I hope
without my having to make every point fully explicit
that I have some difficulties
to put it mildly
with received notions about so-called oral cultures
in particular with epic-centered notions
verse epic in particular.
There are hundreds of living oral traditions
in Africa, in Oceania, in the Americas
in which people pray, make speeches
cite proverbs, pose riddles
sing songs, chant chants, and speak stories
and they do so

just as the ancient Hebrews did
without counting out feet
by tens or any other number.
They transmit some things verbatim
typically songs, more often lyric than narrative
and they compose others by means of oral formulas
typically orations rather than narratives
and when they tell stories
myths, tales, legends, anecdotes
they move into regions where they are finally no more formulaic
than human speech in general is.
Spoken narrative is not really
a genre among other genres.
Typically it is replete with quotations from the characters
and can therefore contain examples of all other genres.
I don't know why Bakhtin fails to acknowledge the existence of
ordinary spoken folk narrative
but he, like so many others, Derrida among them
sets up the Homeric epic as the archetype of oral narrative
which then becomes a story told with the voice of authority
a monologue beyond questioning.
If that's the kind of voice we're seeking in an oral tradition
we can certainly find it
and we won't do much better than "The Word of Kyaklo."
It purports to be nothing less
than an eyewitness account of the story of newness
told through the mouth of the mask of the god named Kyaklo.
Here are just a few of Kyaklo's lines
more or less as they sound in Zuni:

		ya		
Nomilhte ho'n chimiky'anapkya te			a	

	ia	
Awiten tehwu	a	

	la	
Annohsiyan tehwu	a	

ye
Ho'na lilha aateya   e

na
Ho'naawan tacchu pi'lha shiwani te'o   a

lha
"Imati el   a

kya
Yam yu'yaanam on'ak   a"

and here are the same lines, plus a dozen more in English translation:

ma
In truth this is how our newness is   ade

wor
The fourth inner   rld

wor
The soot inner   rld

li
Here is where we all   ive

Bo
Our father who is the Priest of the   ow

be
"Perhaps this need not   e

lear	
By means of what he has	rned

foun	
This light of day could be	nd

en	
Worries could come to an	nd"

cal	
To his own younger brother he	led

ca	
Right away running he	ame

he	
"Yes you have called me	ere

be	
Might it then	e

mu	
Someone will speak just short of too	uch

kno	
That is what you will let me	ow

tho	
That will be my only	ought

da	
As I live day by	ay"

wa
His younger brother is who this   as

spo
These were the two who   oke

and Kyaklo goes on like this for hours.
Whether he speaks as narrator
or quotes the characters in his story
(he quotes two of them in this passage)
it all sounds the same.
Even leaving aside Kyaklo's mode of delivery
his monotone chant with one auxiliary tone
there is still a sense in which the characters are all alike
and like the narrator himself:
in their choices of words, idioms, metaphors
they all stay on the same high level of formality.
The masked performer does not impersonate the characters in the story
he only impersonates Kyaklo
and Kyaklo only sounds like himself.
Now, when this same story is
spoken
rather than chanted
interpreted
rather than reproduced
told on some quiet evening at home
rather than proclaimed on a holy day in that holy chamber
known as the kiva
then the voice divides
the narrator speaks with many voices
not only by shifts in his choices of words, idioms, metaphors
but by shifts in the way he sounds.
Indeed
he spends most of his time sounding quite un-
like himself.
Even so
Andrew Peynetsa
on a chilly evening in early spring
by the hearth in his farmhouse with his family
with me there, too

and my tape recorder
does sound like himself at first.
His first words are,

Well then

words that could be heard in any conversation
he's just talking with us, so far
not asking our permission to take us into another time
we only know that something will follow
and this is what follows,

this

he says, with a pause on both sides
he's doing what speakers of many languages do with demonstratives
holding us back
fixing our attention
before he lets us know what "this"
will be, and "this"

is when **newness was made.**

He speaks a little louder here
"when newness was made" is how you say "at the beginning" in Zuni
he's telling his audience,
"You'll be hearing the story of the beginning,"
the origin story. We're no longer in conversation
or at least not ordinary conversation,
and he goes on,

While newness was in the making
when the earth was still soft

and those two lines form a couplet
or at least we could speak of couplets if he went on and on like that
couplets not because there's meter here
not because there's a measured rhyme of sounds
the two lines don't even have the same number of syllables
whether in Zuni or in translation
but because there's a rhyme of meanings.
This is a semantic couplet.

But we've got to beware of any act of scansion
it seems to have a dulling effect on the senses
produces a sort of
interpretive inertia.
The rhyme of meanings here is at best a slant rhyme
the second half of the couplet
"when the earth was still soft"
is not a case of mere
reiteration
not a mere filling out of pattern, not a case of
oral-formulaic pleonasm.
"When the earth was still soft" tells us something about
"while newness was in the making," tells us
what the earth was like then, and when it was still soft,

the first people came out
the ones who had been living in the first room beneath.

Here's a bit of parallelism again
the second slant rhyme of meanings in a row
it tells us the "first people" are in the
"first room beneath," and he goes on,

When they came out they made their villages
they made their houses a————ll around the land.

And there we have two parallel statements again
"villages" and "houses," but then
they made them "a————ll around the land," and I don't know how
that "a————ll" could scan, whether metrically
or parallelistically
or how well it could be sung to an instrument
it makes for a Doppler effect
we don't know where one village ends and the next begins
or exactly how many there are
and notice that this is not onomatopoeia
not an imitation of a sound made by villages
but an icon, through an intersense modality
of their visible continuity, their countlessness
or the sweep of a gaze across a wide landscape
well populated.
It is the eyes that are given voice here.

And the narrator, having broken his chain of couplets
after producing just three of them
and none too tightly constructed at that
lets the villagers go on making houses, he says,

They were living this way
but it was the Sun's thinking
that this

and here's our "this" before a pause again,
"this"

was not right
not the way to live.

A parallel couplet again, but what is more interesting
is that despite the tendency
in oral narrative
to use direct discourse
when quoting what the characters say, or
even what they think, this narrator tells us
what
"the Sun's thinking" was, and not
exactly what the Sun thought.
Here Andrew Peynetsa is double-voiced
as Mikhail Bakhtin would put it
speaking as narrator
and speaking (or thinking) as Sun
at one and the same time
and he goes on that way for another line
one more line about what was "not the way to live" :

They did not offer him feathered wands, jeweled cornmeal.

Apparently the Sun is thinking rather formally.
At least a part of this new line scans as a parallel couplet again
it's two sorts of things the people are failing to offer him
but the narrator doesn't fill out all the boxes, he doesn't say,
"They did not offer him feathered wands" and
"They did not offer him jeweled cornmeal," but rather
"They did not offer him feathered wands, jeweled cornmeal,"
he's not looking for a missing half-formula

not filling out a form.
Now
without any warning
except that he changes his voice
raises it
just a little above the ground of his narrative
he goes ahead and quotes the Sun after all
just at the point where the Sun's thinking reaches a conclusion
concerning what to do about the people who came out on this earth
from the first room.
What the Sun says (or thinks) is,

"Well, perhaps if the ones who live in the second room come out, it will be
    good."

So the narrator gives his own opening word,
"well"
to the first person who speaks within his narrative.
This person is the Sun Father
the Supreme Deity of the Zuni
but his voice could not be more different from the Voice we're used to.
His first word is "well"
and his second is "perhaps."
His statement is not a command, nor even a declaration
but a speculation.
This is all the more surprising when we consider the notion
the received notion
that oral tradition bends its will to the task
focuses its supposedly agonistic energies on the task
the always somewhat desperate task
of transmitting important words, important themes
by means of measured and memorable formulas.
But what if the thing we were trying to transmit
was some kind of uncertainty?
And notice it's not just the narrator, in his own voice, who's
keeping us in suspense
but the narrator speaking in the Sun's voice.
Now he makes a bridge from the Sun's voice back to the action
saying,

When he had said
                this

---

he splits this phrase between two clear pitches
sounds like he's chanting.
As Michael Riffaterre might put it
he awakens the memory of a verbal precedent
calls up an intertext even though he does not quote it.
Even in his mode of delivery he stops a little short of quoting Kyaklo
since he doesn't save his higher pitch for the end of the line.
But he does sound as if he weren't just
speaking to a few people by the fireside, he's almost
making an announcement
sounding a fanfare
for the people who were still in the second room below
when the Sun started thinking about them, but then
he drops right back to the intimate ground of his narrative, saying,

the ones who lived in the second room came out.
Their lightning smell
killed the ones who had already come out.

So he doesn't get very far before something rises
from the narrative ground again:
it's got a pause on both sides of it
even though it's just a noun phrase, and it's
louder than the lines before and after, it's
"their lightning smell."
Smell of electric arcs, smell of ozone, smell of stink bugs.
And for the people who were already here when the second people came out
back "when newness was made"
it was the smell of death.
And in case we might wonder about survivors,

All of them died

the voice of death, once it has happened
even to "all of them"
is a small voice
the quietest voice that has yet been heard
it drops below the ground of the narrative
or recedes behind the picture plane.
The people from the first room give place
to the ones whose lightning smell killed them,

and the second people lived o———n for some years

we won't be bothered with whatever happened during those years
it's the Doppler effect again
lack of scansion again
only this time it's not our vision that's blurred
but our sense of time,
"o———n for some years" they lived,

but they did not think of anything, it was not right.

So these second people
who "lived o———n for some years"
were something like the first people
who "made their houses a———ll around the land."
Now it's time for the people who are still down in the third room to come out.
If we were all Zunis we would know there were four rooms in all
numbered from the top down
and sure enough,

Those who lived in the third room beneath were summoned.

The narrator doesn't bother to have the Sun thinking again
doesn't bother to fill in all the boxes, but instead
he makes explicit something that wasn't clear before
tells us the people in the room beneath "were summoned."
Apparently
when the Sun talked (or thought) to himself before, saying,
"Perhaps if the ones who live in the second room come out,"
this was as good as a summons, so
the Sun has some authority after all, but it's masked.
As for "those who live in the third room,"

When they came out
the second ones were all killed by the lightning smell of the third ones.

Again we get a summary treatment
with no special attention paid to "their lightning smell" this time
but again there is something added:

Their ruins are all around the land
as you can see.

All around Zuni are ancient ruins
the traces of villages abandoned long ago

"as you can see."
The narrator goes into the second person here
abandons his role for a moment
almost reopens the conversation he took over at the beginning of all this
though he's not really inviting someone else to speak.
What he is doing is making a direct appeal to common experience
he's marking something that is otherwise implicit, namely
the fact that his discourse refers to something outside of itself.
And for those who know the ruins he refers to
the landscape will never be the same
the story is now inscribed in the landscape
can henceforth be read
in the ruins that are a———ll around.
A person will not be able to see one of these ruins
to see the traces of masonry walls
potsherds and charcoal, chipped obsidian scattered on the ground
without thinking of this story, of the people
who came out on the earth before the people of the present day.
Now the narrator goes on inscribing the landscape, saying,

Around the mountains where there is no water today, you could get water
    just by pulling up clumps of grass
because the earth was soft.

Now the "you" is so broad it includes anyone, includes the narrator
it's something like saying,
"one could get water" instead of "you could"
it's double-voiced
the third person overlaid with the second person
and this whole statement departs from the narrative voice in another way,
    too.
It is spoken in an
interpretive voice
in this case a reasoning voice
putting together the fact that the earth was soft and wet then
with the fact that there were villages all around then, even
"around the mountains where there is no water today"
where no one would build a village today.
In the chanted version of the story
"The Word of Kyaklo"
there is no interpretive voice.
You either get what Kyaklo says or you don't.
But now

after this message from Andrew Peynetsa
it's time to get back to our story:

This is the way they lived, when newness was made.

Notice that he's not really back to a full narrative voice yet
he's picking the story up again by referring back
to what he said before his digression.
Only now is he ready to move forward again, and again
we hear the echo of a chant in his voice
if only for a single line:

Sun	thinking
The	was

that they did not think of anything.

Here we have two voices in two lines
the chanting voice that announces the Sun's thinking
and the conversational voice that describes what the Sun is thinking
the one appropriate to the Sun's authority
sounding a little bit like Kyaklo
and the other sounding the way people would sound
the people who "did not think of anything"
who never said (or thought) anything important
and both of these voices are at the same time the voice of the narrator
moving along through a third-person narrative.
The story continues:

The ones who were living in the fourth room
were needed
•
but
the Sun was thinking
•
he was thinking
that he did not know what would happen now.
•

The words of the narrator are as hesitant
as the Sun's thoughts are inconclusive

and who knows how much time
was going by
in these lo———ng pauses
in the midst
of the Sun's thinking.
But something was slo———wly happening:

The clouds, the clouds were swelling.
The clouds were getting better aaaa**aaaaAAAAH THE RAIN CAME**
fine drops came, it rai—————ned, it rained and rained
it rained all night.

Here we have an echo
and an icon
a diagram in sound.
The narrator gives voice
to a gathering and breaking rainstorm.
There were "the clouds, the clouds"
and "it rained and rained"
which is to say there were visual and auditory rhythms
but also
"the clouds were swelling," some things were building
stea———dily
some things didn't scan,
"the clouds were getting better," a crescendo was coming,
*"aaaa**aaaaAAAAH THE RAIN CAME**"*
and finally "fine drops came"
after those big splatters that announce a thunderstorm
and once that had happened
"it rained all night"
water was running everywhere, and:

Where there were waterfalls
the water made foam.
Well, you know how water can make foam

here's another switch to the second person
another appeal to common experience

certainly
it can make foam
•

certainly, that water
made suds.

These are the suds made by alkaline water
water muddied by a rainstorm.
The speaker has dwelt on this point
wanting to make sure we get it before he returns to his narrative voice:

It was there
where the suds were made
that the twin Priests of the Bow
sprouted.
There the Ahayuuta twins
received life.
Their father brought them to life.
They came out of the suds.

Having moved the story forward by just one event
the narrator hovers again
constructing parallel statements.
The movement is interpretive again, rather than narrative:
the metaphorical statement that the twins "sprouted"
which belongs to sacred language
is translated into the statement that they "received life"
which belongs to everyday language.
Now the suds at the bottom of a waterfall have been inscribed
much as the ruins were inscribed.
The next time we see suds at the bottom of a waterfall
struck by sunlight
hints of iridescence in the bubbles
we can read something there
the sprouting, the coming to life
of the Ahayuuta twins.
Now it's back to the story:

When they came out, "Aha———
so **we've sprouted.**" "Yes yes."

Here, for the first time, someone speaks out loud
rather than merely thinking
and we hear not one voice but two.
This is a dialogue

a dialogue between twins.
Note that the twins put the metaphor of sprouting back in play.
Or else the narrator, when he said "sprouted"
was anticipating their kind of language
and telling us in advance how to interpret it.
The twins, having tried out their capacity for speech, now try out
their legs:

Then they stepped forward a little and stood there.
•

And they go on standing there while the narrator pauses
longer than usual
this is a metonymical pause
it's only a couple of seconds
but it stands for a hesitation that could've been much longer.
It is not the narrator who is wondering what to do next
but the twins, he gives voice, as it were
to their hesitation.
And when one of them does break the silence
his first word is shot through with a sigh:

"Well
what's happening?
What will our **road** be?"
"Well I don't know."

The voices of the twins are differentiated here
one of them is bold enough to pose a question
giving emphasis to the "road" metaphor
while the other says, in a soft voice
that he doesn't know the answer.
The narrator puts in another long pause after their exchange
and then adopts
as his own
the soft voice of not knowing the answer:

•
At midday
when it was about midday

having said plainly, if in a soft voice
that it was "midday"

he backtracks a little and makes the voice of not knowing more explicit
saying it was "about midday"
and he keeps his voice small even when the action gets under way again:

their Sun Father came down
near where they stood
and stepping forward a little
he came to them where they stood.

Here, as in a later passage where strangers meet
the narrator gives a quiet voice to shyness
in this case the shyness of the freshly sprouted twins
about to meet the noontime Sun, their father, in person.
In the next line the narrator's soft voice becomes the twins' own voice
as they greet their father
but rises once their father begins his reply.
In Zuni the exchange goes like this:

"Ko'na, tacchu, ko'na to' tewanan teyaye?" "K'ettsanisshe, hom chaw 'aa**chi.**"

And in translation:

"How, father, how have you been passing the days?" "Happily, children of **mine.**"

The twins are double-voiced here
their quietness does not fit the highly formal greeting they have chosen
which is normally delivered in a full voice
and on top of that they seem uncertain about their choice of words.
When they first start the phrase, "Ko'na to' tewanan teyaye?"
or, "How have you been passing the days?"
they backtrack and insert the word "tacchu"
or "father"
which in fact should've come sooner.
Indeed, if they had said the correct words in the correct order
and delivered them with the full high seriousness of a ceremonial occasion
they would have split them into two separate lines
each with the strongest stress saved for the final syllable
and each sounding like a complete utterance in itself:
*"Ho'n aan tac**chu.***
*Ko'na to' tewanan teya**ye?"***
Or in translation,
*"Father of **ours.***
*How have you been passing the **days?"***
But instead they say,

"How, father, how have you been passing the days?"
The Sun starts off his reply gently
echoing their own soft voice
but only long enough to say, *"K'ettsanisshe,"*
"Happily,"
then he changes voices
(it's not only narrators who change voices but characters too)
adopting the high seriousness that was lacking in the twins' speech
saying,
"hom chaw aa**chi.**"
Or, "children of **mine.**"
But in the next line he meets the twins halfway:
he doesn't return all the way to a soft voice, but he does
for the time being
abandon the ceremonial mode of delivery.
Note the conversational turn-taking in this line.
Zuni narrators often represent turns as taking place without any pause
and here it happens twice:

"Have you sprouted now?" he asked them. "Yes we've sprouted."
  "Indeed."

Here it is the Sun who is double-voiced:
he stays on a high level by using the "sprouting" metaphor
but the question into which he puts this metaphor
recalls one of the most ordinary of Zuni greetings, which is,
"Have you come now?"
The insertion of sprouting into such a greeting
comes dangerously close to being funny.
In a couple of earlier lines
the ones that sounded almost like a chant
we had an implicit intertext from above the level of our story.
In the case of the Sun's greeting
the not-quite-quoted intertext is from a lower level.
The twins answer the Sun in kind:
they recall the ordinary reply to a greeting, which is,
"Yes we've come," by saying,
"Yes we've sprouted."
Then they continue as follows:

"What's your reason for having us sprout?
Is it because something is going to happen?
Or is it because of

talk that stops just short of too much, something that's going to be said:
is that why you
brought us to life?"

Again the Ahayuuta twins fall short of high seriousness
at least where the sheer sound of these lines is concerned
but they do use a ceremonial phrase,
"talk that stops just short of too much,"
a Zuni circumlocution that refers
gingerly
to discourse of the kind that brings news of grave importance
so grave you're almost afraid to hear it.
But when the twins precede this dread phrase with,
"Is it because something is going to happen?"
and when they follow it with,
"something that's going to be said,"
they are, in effect, glossing it
surrounding it with interpretation
even though the Sun
unlike a couple of people in the narrator's audience
(one of them being myself)
knows perfectly well what it means.
In effect, Andrew Peynetsa's interpretive voice
the voice that sometimes addresses us, the audience,
in the second person
has entered into the voice of the Ahayuuta twins.
No such joining of voices occurs in "The Word of Kyaklo."
The god says what he says
and the anonymous man behind the mask adds nothing.
As for Andrew Peynetsa
having produced this interpretive quotation
he now attributes it to the Ahayuuta
then goes straight on to the Sun's reply.
The Sun returns to the ceremonial mode for his first two lines:

That's what the Ahayuuta asked the Sun. "**Yes,** without any **doubt.**
Children of **mine.**
All these, our daylight, our people
have emerged, have come. When I summoned the ones in the first room
they came out and stood in my daylight.

There is some parallelism here
but again it works in an interpetive way

the narrator demystifies the Sun's words in the very act of quoting them:
"daylight," a figure of speech for people who live in the daylight
is translated into "people," and
"have emerged" is translated into "have come."
Now the Sun tells the twins what happened when the people emerged
repeating a story the narrator has already told.
Some of the Sun's wording and phrasing is familiar
but as for his lines
not a single one is identical to any earlier line.

I thought of them but they never offered me jeweled cornmeal.
They never offered me feathered wands.
Because of this I summoned the ones in the second room beneath.
The ones who came out first
made their houses all around, made villages.

At this point, for just one line
he chants just a little like Kyaklo
and keeps his voice loud for a second line before he goes on:

se	light
The cond ones out, because of their ning smell	

did away with the first ones.
The second ones made villages when they came out.
And because I thought,
'The way they are living is not what I had in mind,'
I summoned the ones who lived
in the third room.
The second ones were killed by the lightning smell of the third ones.

And now
as he comes to the brink of what he wants to happen next
he chants for just one line again:

fourth	down
The ones in the room are still there	

and because I know I will need them
I have **given you life.**
You will **go inside.**

You will bring them out, and **perhaps then**
as I have in mind

and then, as he comes to his last line
he relaxes his voice, almost sounds like someone saying,
"They all lived happily ever after."
But what he says is,

they will offer me jeweled cornmeal."
That's what the Sun
told his two children. "So.
So, is this why you brought us to life?" "Yes, this is why I brought you to
   life."

Now the twins will give a full reply to the sun's oration
going into the full ceremonial mode for the first time
and even keeping it up for more lines than he did:

"Very well **indeed.**
We will **try.**
This place where they may or may not live is **far.**
There in the room full of **soot.**
The ones who live in the fourth room," the Ahayuuta **said.**

Note that in the last of these ceremonial lines
the heavy emphasis that marks the end is displaced:
instead of falling on the final word spoken by the Ahayuuta
it waits for the narrator's own last word,
*in "the Ahayuuta **said.**"*
Which is to say that once again we have a double voice.
Next
after another one-line chant
this one from the narrator
the Ahayuuta twins take their leave of the Sun
still speaking in the ceremonial mode:

When they had said
                        it:

"Now we will **go.**
Father of **ours.**

Have good **thoughts.**
Whatever happens when we enter upon their roads, it will be," they said.

The Sun replies in a similar manner, for one line
but then, rejecting the twins' expression of uncertainty
he foregrounds his own determination by making a whole line loud:

"By all means may you also have good **thoughts.**
Certainly you will bring them out with you," so their father said. "Very
    well."

Now the narrative of the twins' actions
begins with the same boldness with which the Sun finished speaking:

The twins went on
until they came to the place of emergence.
A hole was open there.

In the next line their uncertainty returns for a moment
but it is quickly and boldly followed by action:

"Well, **here,** perhaps."
They entered.

As they descend through three rooms and on into the fourth
each room turns out to be darker than the one before
and the narrator gives voice to this process
describing the lighter rooms quietly
then using a full and even a loud voice
complete with a couple of chanted phrases
when he gets to the darker rooms:

When they entered, entered the first room
it was full of a light like dawn.
The second
room they entered
was full of yellow light.

---

	third
In the	**room they entered**

they could hardly make anything out.

	fourth	
There in the	**room**	

when they entered
it was full of darkness, nothing could be seen
nothing could be made out.
They got their footing
when they came to the bottom.
•

*That loud "**nothing could be seen**" is in the third person*
but it gives voice to the adventure of the twins.
After getting their footing they get a
breather
if only a couple of seconds long
before they go for a walk in a totally dark world.
The narrator knows perfectly well what's going to happen next
but he gives voice to the uncertainty of his characters
even while staying in the third person:
he constructs his next sentence awkwardly
dangles its fragments over the brinks of multiple pauses
uses words like "some" and "perhaps" and "someone"
and repeatedly revises his description of what the twins encounter
(or what they think they've encountered)
before he lets it come into focus.
Now we have come just about as far as we can
from the formulaic fulfillment of metrical requirements.
Here's how it goes:

Then they went some distance
toward the west and came upon two
•

who perhaps **lived** there, **villagers**
someone was close by, a **deer**
someone was going around hunting, following a **deer,** and they met him.

Then begins the description of this meeting
in the soft voice of shyness
just like the meeting of the Sun and his newly sprouted children:

He came right up to them:
they didn't see him until he came right up to them.

Next comes their conversation, in which this hunter
a mere human being
opens with a colloquial expression of surprise, followed immediately
by the most ordinary of all Zuni greetings
the one the Sun paraphrased when he said, "Have you sprouted now?"

"He———y, have you come now?" he said. "Yes.

As the conversation continues
the twins speak their lines with condescension
not using the ceremonial mode even though they know it now
and speaking with a tension that betrays impatience
or perhaps a certain nervousness at being in the dark.
The hunter speaks his lines with a gentle, even weak voice
without any marked changes of amplitude.
Whether he knows the ceremonial mode or not
he doesn't use it:

What are you doing going around here?" the Ahayuuta twins asked him.
"I'm following a deer, have you seen him?"
"Well, it's full of darkness here, how could we see a deer? We can't see
    anything.
Where do you live?" they asked him.
"This way
toward the west:
that's where we live." "Indeed.
That's where we're going," so said the Ahayuuta twins. "Indeed. Well,
    I'll take you along."
"**All right, but we can't see.** How can we find the way?" "Even so, we can
    find the way quite well."
"All right, but we still can't see. Wait
let us do something," and they made **cedar-bark torches.**
When they had made cedar-bark torches they
made them blossom

there's a metaphor in "blossom" but it's glossed immediately:

lit them
and the one who had been in the dark could hardly see.

In that last loud line
the narrator shifts from doubling his voice with that of the twins
to doubling it with that of the hunter they've met in the darkness.
The light of the torch is as alarming to this poor human
as the darkness of the fourth room was to the divine twins.
Now the hunter almost abandons his weak voice
managing to emphasize some words over others
but still not adopting the ceremonial mode
not saving his emphasis for line-final syllables:

"Have **mercy**
put those things out, **I can't see,**" so he said.
"**If you would just follow me,** we could go."

And now we are plunged back into the darkness of his world
where people move along quietly:

They put out their cedar-bark torches.
He took them along toward the west, they went on, went on

and Andrew Peynetsa said, "they went on, went on" in a gravelly voice
he could smooth and roughen his voice at will, and
when "they went on, went on," their road wasn't a smooth one
at least not for the twins.
As for the hunter, remember that he had already said,
"We can find the way quite well."
Anyway, they all went on

until they arrived at a village.
"**This** is where we **live.**"

At this point the turn-taking is not immediate.
It takes the twins a moment to answer:

•

"So this is where you **live.**

And then the narrator gives the twins a hesitant mode of speech
something like the one he used for their encounter with the hunter
only now
instead of being uncertain as to what they've found in the darkness
the twins are uncertain as to just how to ask the hunter
this person they've already treated with condescension
whether he might take them to someone who is

unlike himself
important:

Are there
perhaps
people who live, are there people who live by the sacred things, do they
    have
a house here?
Isn't there
•

that sort of
household around here somewhere?" they said. "Well perhaps I
might know why it is you came.

The hunter is speaking in his weak voice here, but
once again, as in the matter of finding the way
he turns out to be smarter than the twins think he is.
He continues,

Well, **let's go,**" he said, and **they went toward the plaza** and entered it.
•

The priest's
the Word Priest's house was the one they approached.
They went up and entered where the Word Priest
lived, that must have been the way it was.

Here, the narrator speaks in an interpretive voice
but this time, instead of marking it with the second person
saying something like, "Well, you know,"
he claims to be stating an obvious probability
something that "must have been" the way he describes it.
In the matter of the Word Priest
there is plenty of room for interpretation.
The various published versions of the narrative of newness
including "The Word of Kyaklo"
make it clear that Zunis have never settled on one clear answer
to the question of how, when, and where
the Word Priest should enter the story.
In this version he is already there in the fourth room
living in a house on the plaza of a village
and so,

They entered his dwelling.

And the narrative goes o———n
with further voices and double voices.
We've only heard the first ten minutes or so
of a story that lasted the better part of an hour
and wasn't finished even then.
Andrew Peynetsa preferred to save the other parts
for other nights.
And he knew how to speak a lot of other stories, too
tales of a more secular sort
stories of things that happened long ago
but not all the way back when newness itself was made.
Many of these tales are about the Ahayuuta twins
who, for all their closeness to the Sun Father
sometimes take the lead role in parodies.
Tales have no canonical versions
no Kyaklo who recites them verbatim.
They exist only
in the form of interpretations
and it takes a multiplicity of voices to tell them.
Andrew Peynetsa was skilled at telling tales, and that's why
he was able to change the monotonous chant of Kyaklo
into a decent story.
Now I have to say
that for all the complexities of voice in spoken narratives
there is something profoundly ordinary about them.
Ordinary because there are storytellers everywhere
and not only among the Zuni
who time their pauses
who hesitate here and leap ahead there
proclaim some things and whisper others
giving shifting shades and colors to their words.
The liberation of the heteroglossic potential of language
from the authoritative, monological voice of the epic
does not wait for the coming of written prose fiction.
There is Yellowman
out there in Montezuma Canyon
telling stories in Navajo to Barre Toelken.
And Susie James
up there in Sitka, Alaska
telling stories in Tlingit to Nora and Richard Dauenhauer;
Francisco Ortigosa Tello
down there in the Sierra de Puebla of Mexico
telling stories in Nahuatl to Tim Knab;

Alonso Gonzales Mó
clear down in Ticul, Yucatán
telling stories in Yucatec Maya to Allan Burns;
Ma Winifred Kisiraga
all the way over near Lake Victoria in Tanzania
telling stories in Haya to Sheila Dauer and Peter Seitel;
Mohammed Ya Sin
high up in the Afghan province of Herat
telling stories in Persian to Margaret Mills;
Banjo Wirrunmarra
somewhere in the Australian outback
telling stories in Ungarinyin to Stephen Mueke and Alan Rumsey;
and then indeed there is Wilmot McDonald
not so far away in Glennwood, New Brunswick
telling tales to Sandy Ives
old tales about Jack in plain English.

Notes

In keeping with the spirit of Paul Zumthor's *mouvance,* this text is somewhat changed from the one I read aloud beside the choppy waters of Lake Mendota in Madison, Wisconsin, on Friday morning, 15 Apr. 1988. In particular, having heard Michael Riffaterre's address "The Mind's Eye: Memory and Textuality" on the evening of that same day, I have noted instances of what he called "the awakening of the memory of the intertext." Also, I have changed my translation of the Zuni term *k'oli* from "electric smell," which various hearers in Madison found anachronistic, to "lightning smell."

The scoring and translation of the excerpt from "The Word of Kyaklo" are my own, based on the partial Zuni text published by Stevenson in "The Zuñi Indians." The excerpt from "When Newness Was Made," as performed by Andrew Peynetsa, is a revised version of the translation in Tedlock, *Finding the Center,* 221–98. For various discussions of the transcription, translation, and interpretation of oral performances, including the ones discussed here and others from the Maya Quiché of Guatemala, see Tedlock, *Spoken Word.* When I refer to M. M. Bakhtin in the present paper, the particular essays I have in mind are "Epic and Novel" and "Discourse in the Novel," in *Dialogic Imagination.* Jacques Derrida's views on the epic and orality are set forth in the first part of his *Of Grammatology.*

For transcripts of spoken narratives similar to the one excerpted here, see (for example) Toelken and Scott; Dauenhauer and Dauenhauer; Knab; Burns; Seitel; Margaret Mills; and Mueke, Rumsey, and Wirrunmarra. For narratives performed in English, see Titon. Except in the case of Mueke, Rumsey, and Wirrunmarra, the makers of these transcripts are innocent of the editorial vice, most common among linguists, of eliminating any pauses that fail to march in step with clauses or sentences, as if they were errors of punctuation.

2 John Miles Foley

Orality, Textuality, and Interpretation

For some time medievalists and classicists alike have been aware that the standard Parry/Lord approach to oral literature has significant but limited applicability to the texts with which they are most familiar. The reason is simple: the Yugoslav oral epic tradition—especially the Muslim tradition on which Milman Parry and Albert Lord founded their analogy—may in important ways reflect the dynamics of, for example, the Anglo-Saxon and ancient Greek traditions, but it differs in that it arose and developed in a nearly "textless" environment.[1] Whereas many of the Serbo-Croatian singers thus carried on their age-old epic tradition entirely without the intercession of the written word, all medieval and classical works have of course reached us only in textual form. In the atmosphere of exuberance that accompanied early studies of formulaic and thematic structure, comparatists tended to overlook discrepancies among traditions, genres, and documents in favor of stressing similarities and deriving "proofs" from these demonstrated congruencies. Equally disappointing has been the overreaction against the arguments of the oralists. Many literary scholars, true to their modern refraction of what Homer or the *Beowulf* poet must, after all, have been about, have wanted to preserve their poems' art by denying their oral traditional roots, by seeking to bring such works comfortably within the sphere of purely literary traditions.

This essay attempts to show, first, that both of these approaches must lead to misinterpretation of works like *Beowulf* and the *Odyssey*, primarily be-

34

cause each takes an untenably monolithic position on the fundamental nature of the received texts. After a brief consideration of the complexity of traditional style and idiom that is so much a part of these oral-derived works, I then go on to study the unique phenomenology of a text that nonetheless has clear (and nourishing) oral roots.

The Case against Extreme Positions

Comparative investigation of what has too loosely been called "oral literature" has provided contemporary critical theory and scholarship with radical new insights and enormous new challenges. Whatever opinion or position one holds, it is undeniable that we have not read Homer or Old English poetry in quite the same way since Parry. The number and variety of entries in the interdisciplinary bibliography continue to grow, now comprising well past two thousand books and articles, written chiefly since 1960. Again whatever version of the argument one approves, it has become a commonplace that many of the ancient Greek and Anglo-Saxon poems that have reached us as manuscript texts are related in some way to a prior or ongoing oral tradition. On that much there seems to be general agreement.

But beyond this modest consensus one soon encounters the not-so-shiny *næssas* of what Ruth Finnegan has called, with appropriate disapprobation, the "Great Divide." Here the scholar interested in elucidating various ancient and medieval poems must, in effect, predetermine what he or she will conclude by opting for membership in the "oral" or the "written" camp. If the pure oralist side is chosen, then one must pledge allegiance to formulas and themes that exist primarily because they are useful, whose major reason for being is to provide the poet with a special language that enables, or even promotes, composition in performance. Aesthetics is not a plank in this party's platform (or is a very minor one at best), because this quality of verbal art smacks too much of the literate and literary author, the very antitype of the preliterate, orally composing figure they are supporting as their candidate for poetic office.

The only alternative for most scholars faced with this dilemma has been the "written" camp, which takes the position that our modern conception of what is true and beautiful in verbal art supersedes any details of provenance, structure, and so on. For many, and with good reason, membership in the second group has been not so much a refusal to acknowledge oral roots but rather a defense against the abrogation of aesthetics that such an acknowledgment seemed to demand. So, as the scholarship bears witness, a great deal of the activity in this interdisciplinary field amounted to an almost political standoff between two extremist parties: the pure oralists claiming nonliterary origins and, effectively, nonliterary character for some of our most cherished texts and the "written" caucus defending the literary quality of these texts against what they viewed as a dangerous attack.

Such extremist positions, as improbable as they may *a priori* seem, are especially precarious in relation to Old English and ancient Greek poetic texts, for a number of reasons. First, and most fundamentally, the Parry/Lord theory is an approximation founded on analogy, not an externally supported proof; one can no more champion unalloyed orality for manuscript texts on the basis of formulaic density than one can proscriptively deny that such an observed phraseological texture affects the meaning of a text. If a certain type of theme occurs or does not occur in a narrative work, that presence or absence alone cannot prove the text originally oral or originally written. Life, and the traditional poetries with which I am familiar, are more complicated than that.

As I see it, comparative studies as a whole need to break camp from either end of the "Great Divide" and create a spectrum of possibilities that more nearly corresponds to the reality of what we have found in the field and in the archive. We must be willing to calibrate our comparisons and our conclusions by taking account of differences in at least three areas: the tradition (whether Native American, Turkish, medieval English, or whatever), the genre (as closely as one can track this aspect across traditions), and the nature of the documents. It is remarkable, for instance, that we sophisticated moderns have usually failed to ask ourselves whether our formulaic analyses or thematic parsings have been performed on "texts" that were recorded acoustically, written down from dictation, edited from such dictation, or whatever. Surely such simple attention to the nature of the document is but the "gross anatomy" in our learning the biology of oral and oral-derived texts, but almost always this prerequisite has been ignored.

Furthermore, the ancient and medieval texts present a special problem in that writing and textualization figured in various ways in their production. If we are to insist, as we should, on the oral traditional aspects of such works, then we must also not fail to acknowledge the other side of the coin: the situation in these periods is not as simple and straightforward as has been assumed by either camp, and in many cases we are no doubt dealing with hybrid or transitional texts.[2] Walter Ong and Brian Stock have made us aware of the "cultural diglossia" that permeated medieval Europe, and without a chronology or certain attributions for all but a few Old English poems, it would be as presumptuous to eliminate literacy from our considerations as it would be to deny the effects of orality.

The key concept in further development of this field must then be *complication*. We can no longer afford to settle for either side of the Great Divide model, for to do so is to turn away from the complex reality of our ancient and medieval texts. And in turning away from that reality we also preclude a faithful interpretation of works that—variously, of course—owe a debt to both the oral and the written word. Instead of attempting a meek and finally false compromise between our two major parties, then, I would advocate clearing the air and evolving a theory or model that explains the complex, hybrid nature of the work rather than seeks to reduce it according to the artificial dictates of one or the other school. For the truth is that both extremist positions "murder to dissect," and both can affirm their ideas only by exclusion of the other. We shall be seeking a comprehensive theory of textual interpretation that not only allows but actually takes active account of both the oral and the written dimensions of such texts. The goal is to reinvest the textual artifact with something approximating its original complexity in the transitional world from which it comes.

The Complexity of Oral Traditional Style

It is an irony not unexemplified in other areas of scholarly investigation that the key to unlocking the riddle of traditional phraseology and narrative has also been the single greatest obstacle to its further growth. I speak principally of the major source statements by Milman Parry on the formula (*Epithète, Formules,* "Studies, I and II"), in which he studies the formulaic structure of the Homeric texts. As brilliant and as groundbreaking as these writings have been for generations of scholars, overliteral adherence to what were after all only first approximations has handicapped consequent analysis and explanation.

To begin, we recall that Parry focused in the 1928 French theses almost solely on the noun-epithet formulas in the *Iliad* and *Odyssey,* a very limited and specialized arena in which to conduct what was meant as a global demonstration. Second, when in 1930 and 1932 his Harvard essays moved from documentation of *traditional* structure to the argument for a necessarily *oral* poet and poems, he greatly enlarged the field of diction examined without enforcing the same rigorous criteria for *formula* and *formulaic system.* In the two later essays, in other words, he sought to analyze Homeric diction by example only; that this prominent change in methodology is to be assigned to convenience of demonstration is evident in his own admission that "a full description of the technique [of formulaic composition] is not to be thought of, since its complexity, which is exactly that of the ideas in Homer, is altogether too great. One must either limit oneself to a certain category of formulas, and describe their more frequent uses, as I have done in my study of the noun-epithet formulas, or one must take a certain number of formulas of different sorts that can be considered typical" ("Studies, I" 307). The problems that leap to mind are obvious: How typical of the diction as a whole is the chosen category? How uniformly will the different categories obey the strictures of a single definition and conception?[3]

In fact, as I have shown at some length elsewhere, neither of these two sampling techniques will penetrate to the root of oral traditional diction, since in either case one soon outruns the original Parryan conception of "formula" and the underlying assumption that manipulation of fixed and substitutable units constituted the chief mode of poetic composition.[4] Speaking more positively, we may say that an oral traditional diction is not a collection of relatively static, largely equivalent parts but rather a continually developing "wordhoard" whose heterogeneous contents are the product of what I call *traditional rules*. Under these rules, and over time, a traditional phraseology evolves and serves generations of poets as an idiom, and like any idiom it is used not in a fossilized, lockstep routine but in a fluent compromise among idiolect, dialect, and language as a larger entity. Such a specialized language may appear—at a first and necessarily preliminary level of investigation—to consist, as Arnold van Gennep described the process, of "cards" that can be tectonically "shuffled," but that appearance results from the subtler and more fundamental organization of the diction by rules.

Anything more than a brief discussion of traditional rules would be inappropriate here, but we should at least take note of the obvious (but often ignored) facts of the natural divergences among languages and the consequent heterogeneity of formulaic phraseologies.[5] Anglo-Saxon poetic diction, for example, exists in symbiosis with a prosody that depends on the stressed alliterating cores of words for its most fundamental substance—not on feet or metra or even syllables but rather on patterns of stressed morphemes. Any attempt to translate the notion of "formula" from its mother-language definition in ancient Greek to the milieu of Anglo-Saxon poetry should have involved a consideration of the enormous differences between the metron- and colon-based Homeric hexameter and the stress-based alliterative line. To search for a Homeric Greek syllabic regularity in Old English verse is to seek what does not, and cannot, exist; thus, to search for a Homeric phraseology in *Beowulf* or other Anglo-Saxon poetry is futile.[6] The concept of traditional rules that necessarily take their shape from the linguistic idiosyncrasies of the particular language offers a way out of this overgeneralization by insisting on a tradition-dependent set of criteria for each phraseology. Comparison among dictions can then go forward without the disabling reduction of all languages and all linguistic registers to a single group of defining characteristics.

A similar kind of differentiation between and among genres can aid the comparatist in establishing a realistic grasp of the range of formulaic structure across traditions. While this aspect of variation may not be so obvious in Old English poetry, since versions of the same alliterative prosody constitute the metrical foundation for most surviving poems, it can be a crucial consideration in traditions like the Yugoslav, where, for example, the lyric "women's songs" (*ženske pjesme*) are sung in symmetrical octosyllables while the heroic epics are sung in decasyllables or long-line *bugarštice* meters. Which of the Yugoslav genres do we summon as the authoritative comparand? In the past the answer furnished by comparatists has been, without exception, the Muslim subgenre of epic narrative; all else has been ignored (Foley, "Literary Art"). A far more reasonable answer would involve matching genres as closely as possible across traditions, thus comparing apples with apples and oranges with oranges to the extent that such an ideal alignment can be made.[7] Of yet more immediate and obvious relevance to Old English is a third criterion for differentiation: that of the nature of the actual text before us. Is this a transcription and, if so, from what source? Do we have any reason to assume we know the poet's identity? Can we ascertain any facts or construct any reliable hypotheses about the history of transmission or the authority of the given manuscript? To what extent can we suppose Latin learning might have played an active role in the creation of a given text? These and numerous other questions will help to distinguish the Old English poems from manuscript texts of Homer and even more from the performance-texts recorded, whether by dictation or acoustically, in Yugoslavia. Once again, the key word must be *variety,* and we must avoid at all costs a simplistic, leavening perspective that only too conveniently purchases an illusory uniformity by erasing distinctions among traditions.

In addition to distinguishing among the various phraseologies by appeal to linguistic and other differences, traditional rules also defeat the charge of "mechanism" *within* a given individual idiom. For while formulaic theory can account for only a certain percentage of the poetic lines in a sample text, an analysis from traditional rules explains every line and its traditional structure. In terms of the epic poetries mentioned above, for example, Homeric Greek and Serbo-Croatian reveal the quality of "right justification" in their phraseological makeup: metrically more extensive elements seek line- and colon-end according to a definite set of layered criteria. That this phenomenon is possibly an Indo-European characteristic can be argued from the available comparanda in other language families (Foley, *Traditional Oral Epic,* chap. 3). The "odd prosody out" in this regard is the Old English alliterative line; apparently because of the Germanic stress shift and redefinition of the prosodeme from the syllable or position to the stress, right justification did not survive as a feature of the Old English traditional idiom. Nonetheless, rules like this one—such as the "word-type placement" that informs all three poetries (but of course in singular ways)—govern the creation and maintenance of traditional phraseology at a level much more fundamental than that addressed by the concept of *formula.* To put the same matter in another way, traditional dictions are ever-changing collections of inequivalent phrases that come into being, are preserved, and are discarded—all under the aegis of traditional rules.[8] There is nothing inherent in a traditional idiom, in short, to damn it irrevocably to mechanism; just as important, that idiom is fundamentally different from a nonformulaic, nontraditional idiom.[9]

This is likewise true regarding the "theme" or "type-scene," elements in what I like to think of as a narrative phraseology. Once again the specific nature of traditional narrative patterns will differ markedly from one poetry to another, and even within a single tradition there will be significant variation in the kind, size, and texture of thematic units. It has long been observed that the narrative patterns found in Old English poetry differ from those reported in Serbo-Croatian and ancient Greek epic, particularly in the amount of actual verbal correspondence among instances of a given theme. But it is not well appreciated that the South Slavic poets themselves employ patterns with widely varying verbal correspondence and that the phraseological texture of the units is in part a function of whether one adduces as evidence the songs of one *guslar,* the repertoire of the singer's district, or the pandialectal tradition as a whole (defined synchronically, diachronically, or in both ways).[10]

But if the search for an archetypal theme must in the end be as fruitless as the search for an archetypal formula, this means only that the narrative diction is as plastic and responsive as the phraseology that serves as its most immediate medium. Far from simply "playing with cards," sorting the pieces of the jigsaw into a virtually foregone attitude and shape, the oral poet—and the transitional poet who employs the oral traditional idiom—combines personal artistic resources with an inherited poetics. Having learned the special language, a poet may, according to his or her personal gifts and aspirations, use it with great and memorable fluency or compose the oral traditional equivalent of Dr. Johnson's also quite memorable doggerel about his hat and the Strand. The point is that the inheritance itself is not a mechanistic shorthand that imprisons the poetic inspiration but a wonderfully complex and echoic idiom that can bear the weight of genius and, in its own inimitable way, conjure its deepest insights. Just how the oral traditional idiom accomplishes that task will be the subject of the third section of this essay.

Aesthetics and Phenomenology

To this point we have been content to lay the ground work for consideration of the aesthetics of oral and oral-derived poetry by making some basic distinctions. The evolution of scholarship in this field has made it only too clear that the Great Divide model distorts more than it clarifies, and the conventional ideas of formula and theme, while necessarily preliminary to more sophisticated conceptions of phraseology and narrative structure, must now be radically reinterpreted to take account of the complexity of the world's oral traditions and those texts with roots in oral tradition. Complementarily, we have found that the oral traditional texture of the diction and narrative appears to be much less a matter of manipulating a Lego-set collection of substitutable parts than of learning to speak an idiom that is the issue of traditional rules and processes operating on phraseology and thematic structure.

Having attempted to alleviate a few of the more popular and lasting problems in studies in oral tradition (structure "versus" aesthetics, orality "versus" literacy, and so forth), we may now pass on to the most significant item on the contemporary agenda in this field: the matter of interpretation. Just what difference does it make, scholars have asked since before Parry and Lord, whether a work is oral (or oral-derived)? Do we read such works any differently if we know or can say with some confidence that they owe something to oral tradition? To my mind this is both the most challenging and the most rewarding problem that confronts all of us interested in orality and textuality.

It is only too easy to dismiss the question out of hand, maintaining, for example, that any work that presents itself to us modern readers as a text automatically creates a modern audience for whom orality, or even its residue, is quite irrelevant. This view would leaven the work and its parts into a smooth surface, with all features and dynamics to be explained according to the modern, posttraditional dispensation. Of course, as soon as one eliminates by fiat any dimension of aesthetic meaning—of textual activity, if you like—it *is* gone and will not continue to be troublesome. The question begged, just as obviously, is whether such wrenching from context is a defensible exordium to the scholarly and critical peroratio. The very fact of this collection of essays would argue against the legitimacy of such a procedure, and I would further argue that by stripping a work of its oral traditional character we must immediately and finally falsify whatever else we may wish to say about it. One might as well decide that Laurence Sterne's pictorial representations in *Tristram Shandy* are to be interpreted only orally and, having thus hit upon a "reason" not to admit them to consideration, pass on to the next irrelevancy.

If we can agree that oral traditional features demand interpretation *sui generis,* then the question arises about how to cope with them. Perhaps a specific quandary, well known to all who have wrestled with these problems, will offer a place to start. Anglo-Saxonists, and with them Hellenists, Slavists, and numerous others, have often balked at just how to interpret a repeated phrase. Is the poet making a particular point? Is irony involved, or perhaps the kind of literary echo we so admire in, for example, the classical allusions of the Neoclassicals? To this point in the development of the field we have but two possible answers to these questions: the poet is attempting a special effect, whether ironic, allusive, or whatever; or the poet is not attempting a special effect but merely using the formulaic turn of phrase (an epitomized expression conveying an "essential idea," as Parry construed it).

On the basis of comparative work in the three traditions mentioned above, I would suggest a third alternative. Instead of assuming a poetics that owes its existence and contribution only to the poet, so that everything depends on his or her *conferral* of meaning to the phrase, should we not consider the traditional meaning that *inheres* in that phrase? What can *tradition* possibly denote if we ascribe referentiality solely or chiefly to the individual composing the poem, for no matter how brilliant an artist he or she may be, the poetic tradition remains more than a silent partner in the artistic enterprise. The phraseology and narrative structure that are the bequest of generations of poets cannot be merely a kind of elaborate Morse code that enables composition in performance; surely the traditional idiom resonates with "extratextual" meaning, makes necessary (because institutionalized) reference to situations, characters, and deeper strata shared with other poems, and in short presents any individual poet and poem with a natural context that, while always unspoken, is ever-present. Indeed, to put it most strongly, that referentiality must be so much a part of the poetics of oral and oral-derived poems that a poet simply could not avoid tapping into its wellsprings: certain phrases and scenes will bear certain traditional meanings whether or not the poet consciously intends them to do so.

In the South Slavic epic, for example, the most ordinary of phrases or scenes bears an inherent meaning that can be at least in part recovered through reference to a group of texts in the tradition. Thus "Mustajbeg of the Lika" connotes more than the mere name plus topographical specification; the Lika is a liminal territory between Christian and Turkish lands, and its partly geographical and partly mythical liminality images Mustajbeg's often duplicitous behavior. Other heroes are similarly conjured, whether by relation to a place-name or, in many cases, by a single typical detail. As with the Homeric epithets that were the basis for Parry's original demonstrations, such a designation summons not just the single detail but the entire heroic personality for which it stands, *pars pro toto*. The operative dynamic is *metonymy*—with access to extratextual meaning guaranteed by institutionalized associations within the tradition.[11]

The same fundamental process underlies the poet's composition by theme, or typical narrative pattern. Once again automatic reference to the larger world of the song (instanced nominally in a single performance or text) and of the tradition as a whole is assured by the metonymic identity of the pattern. Whether we summon as evidence the characteristic texture of the "Shouting in Prison" theme in South Slavic epic, wherein the action of the female intermediary is played off against definite expectations set up by the mere use of this traditional form, or some other example, we shall find that the narrative metonym commands a whole world of referentiality. We may think here of the Homeric feast scene, whose ritual wholeness is broken by the arrogant presumptuousness of the suitors in *Odyssey* 1, or of the riddle of the description of Andreas's first night in the Mermedonian prison. In the latter case, the inexplicable addition of the passage that seems to make the hero-saint another Seafarer or Wanderer proves to be an occurrence of the well-known figure of Exile (Greenfield). If we have learned to listen attentively to the highly metonymic idiom of Old English poetry, then we understand that the poet is explaining just how miserable Andreas is by explaining just how much of an exile figure he has poetically become—in traditional terms.

Such richness of meaning derives from the simple fact that any performance or text—whether oral or oral-derived—is not "the whole story." Its elements have life outside the narrow confinement of any given configuration, and that life is a matter not only of compositional utility but also of aesthetic content. The metonyms of phraseology or narrative pattern collectively constitute a kind of anaphora, or epiphora, in which the repeated element occurs not in a contiguous line or stanza but in a "contiguous" performance or text in the poetic tradition or, ultimately, in the contiguous yet unspoken tradition. And just as the more usual conception of anaphora is of bridging the gap from one individualized or particularized situation to another, with the different sections of the lines involved being unified by the repeated phrase, so these traditional metonyms invoke an immediate traditional context for the story-specific, or performance- or text-specific, action at hand. When we "read" or interpret any traditional performance or text with attention to the metonymic meaning it necessarily summons, we are, in effect, recontextualizing that work, bridging Iserian "gaps of indeterminacy" (e.g., *Implied Reader*), reaffirming contiguity with other performances or texts, or, better, with the ever-immanent tradition itself. We are solving the equivalent of the line-to-line anaphora, only not in the here-and-now of the single text but on the immensely larger canvas of the tradition as a whole.

But how shall we recapture the extratextual meaning of classical and medieval texts that present themselves to us without the prior or ongoing oral traditional contexts from which they derive? This is a serious problem, not entirely susceptible to solution, but one which any commitment to the most faithful interpretation possible must deal with. I suggest a three-step approach that follows the trajectory from philology to aesthetics.

First, we must have a reliable "grammar" of oral traditional features specific to the tradition involved. This will mean setting aside clumsy comparative approximations and penetrating to the traditional rules under which the highly resonant phraseology and narrative idiom are negotiated over generations. With this information in hand, it will be possible to discuss elements and patterns with some authority, because we will be examining them with some precision.

Second, we can learn from well-collected, living oral traditions something more valuable than what an archetypal formula might look like. We can learn just what resonance phrases and typical scenes have as one moves within the repertoire of a single singer, a single local tradition, or, for example, an epic poetry as a whole. Consulting the South Slavic epic poems collected by Parry and Lord, for example, soon disabuses one of the notion that resonance in such a medium is solely, or even primarily, textual.[12] The arena for anaphora, in other words, must be extended from the text to (as much as is recoverable of) the tradition. Once that is accomplished, some sense of the metonymic range of oral traditional elements can be gained, if only by analogy.

Third, with this sense in hand, we must pay full attention to recurrence in the canon (a highly textual term, but appropriate for the extant transitional body of poetry in Old English), and even within the individual poem. The object here would not of course be to generate unsupportable contentions about provenance but to recover, in whatever degree we can, the resonance of phraseological and narrative patterns. Alain Renoir's work on oral-formulaic—that is, traditional—context (e.g., *Key*) has been especially valuable in this regard, and one hopes for more attention to such dimensions.

Implementation of these three steps will promote more meaningful study of classical and medieval texts that owe allegiance to both the oral and the written word. In regard to incipient textuality, as in the Old English period, we shall be most accurate in our interpretations only when we proceed from a hybrid poetics, an aesthetics that places the enormous significance of oral roots alongside the more familiar, more modern implications of textuality. By taking account of the rich traditional resonances of this special idiom, that is, by realizing its metonymic character and extending our notion of anaphora beyond the line, passage, and even text to the larger context of the tradition, we will find that such oral-derived works will yield up the wellsprings of meaning that cannot be tapped by a strictly textual analysis.[13]

Notes

1 For a history of the Parry/Lord approach to date, see Foley, *Theory;* relevant bibliography is available in Foley, *Oral-Formulaic Theory,* with updates in *Oral Tradition.*

2 Note Lord's recent admission of "transitional texts" into the canon ("Perspectives" 478–81).

3 The classic definition of the formula is, of course, "a group of words regularly employed under the same metrical conditions to express a given essential idea" (Parry, "Studies, I" 272).

4 See "Traditional Phraseology in the *Odyssey*," chap. 4 of Foley, *Traditional Oral Epic.* As Arnold van Gennep, an influence on Parry's work, put the matter in relation to the South Slavic tradition: "The poems of the guslars consist of a juxtaposition of clichés, relatively few in number and with which it suffices merely to be conversant. . . . A fine guslar is one who handles these clichés as we play with

cards, who orders them differently according to the use he wishes to make of them" (52; my translation).

5 See Foley, *Traditional Oral Epic*, for such discussion, especially chaps. 3 ("Comparative Prosody") and 4–6 (on traditional phraseology in ancient Greek, Serbo-Croatian, and Old English).

6 Worse yet, when one conducts such a Pyrrhic expedition and, on the basis of having failed to find the expected (but necessarily unfindable) evidence, then rules out the contribution of oral tradition, the original sin of misapprehension becomes confounded by a second transgression that proceeds from a false premise. See Benson, "Literary Character," and Foley, *Traditional Oral Epic*, chaps. 3, 6.

7 Even where only an approximate fit is possible, that inexact but general correspondence will be far superior to some of the matches forced upon various works in the past.

8 This also means that what are apparently "nonce" phrases can be created, again under the aegis of traditional rules, and may be used only a single time even in an extensively recorded repertoire. Such phrases are nonetheless traditional, since they are formed according to the same rules that structure phraseology repeated many times.

9 A related point, and one left completely out of account by the Great Divide theorists, is the possibility—nay, observed certainty—that mechanistic oral poets can and do exist. Just as in the literary sphere, one encounters in a living oral poetic tradition a very few people who are excellent at their craft, a large number who compose with indifferent results, and some who are quite limited and unsuccessful members of the tradition.

10 See Foley, *Traditional Oral Epic*, chap. 8.

11 Naturally, not all phrases harbor the same degree of connotative meaning. Some will have more general, or less focused, referents; and some will be associated with larger complexes of meaning (such as narrative patterns). Just as the structure of traditional phraseology is best understood as a spectrum of inequivalent forms, so the levels and kinds of meaning these forms generate must vary. See Foley, "Formula," on differences in metonymic reference.

12 One thinks here of the infamous argument over whether Homer "intended" to balance one instance of the scene of "Ransoming a child" in Book 1 of the *Iliad* (Chryses and Chryseis) with another in Book 24 (Priam and Hector). Instead of having the discussion degenerate into puerile estimates of the length of the Homeric audience's attention span, it would seem best to posit that—as with so many other patterns in Homer—these are two instances of a pattern much larger than a single (albeit very large) text.

13 Certain of the fundamental ideas in this essay are developed at length in Foley, *From Structure to Meaning in Traditional Oral Epic*.

3 *Ward Parks*

The Textualization of Orality in Literary Criticism

Literary scholars today are living in the age of the text. The sheer quantities of textual material already available to us have never been equaled, and torrents of new publications swell our bibliographies and swamp our desks. This proliferation on the material level is matched by the growing theoretical centrality of writing, text, intertext, and other pivotal concepts referring to the world of print and documents. Indeed, *text* has become perhaps the leading general term for a production in the verbal arts, whatever the genre or original medium of dissemination. The textualization of criticism has reaped a rich harvest: it has made possible the enormous diversification and growth in theoretical sophistication that has marked literary studies in recent decades. Yet it brings its hazards as well. For unless the partiality of the textualized outlook is clearly recognized, it becomes the author of crude and violent reductions, especially when confronted with subject matter that is innately, intractably nontextual. Nowhere does this problem emerge more dramatically than in the case of oral "literature." So long as it is viewed *sub specie litterae,* oral discourse will inevitably come out looking like an inferior breed of writing. And the oral poet, despite the euphemisms and accolades that more text-minded exegetes intermittently feel moved to bestow upon him, will remain, in the end, a kind of second-class writer.[1]

The difficulty in expostulating on this problem of textual bias is that, in the current climate of opinion, it is simultaneously assumed as obvious and denied. On the one hand, anthropologists, folklorists, oral-formulaicists, and others have been coping with this issue since the birth of their disciplines. On the other hand, literary scholarship rarely acknowledges the reductionism involved in characterizing as a "text" what may have been originally an oral communication, much of whose life as a spoken utterance is necessarily purged from any textual redaction. The reason why so obvious a point is so routinely overlooked is that literary scholarship as a whole is vitiated by what are, finally, vocational class prejudices. It is hard to renounce the sense of superiority that highly developed literacy affords. In consequence, generations of critics have, perhaps unintentionally, propounded aesthetic and interpretive theories that presuppose reading and writing, that could not function in an oral context. This longstanding problem has been enormously aggravated in recent years, however, by critical theories that virtually mythologize the text and the grapheme, to the point at which, among those in the umbra of these trends, the orality of a spoken communication can hardly be discussed at all. Instead of investigating orality/literacy relations in particular literary texts, then, in this essay I will try to point out the self-blinding to this issue that is a precondition and enabling move for some of the most influential current textualist theory. In particular, I will critique the treatments of orality, first in the differential monologics of Derridean deconstruction and then in the textual dialogics of Bakhtin.

Deconstructive Textualism against the World

Despite its self-representation as a revolutionary movement, deconstructive textualism perpetuates a devaluation of orality that was evident, in the American scene at least, even in theories that it sought to replace.[2] What has remained constant is a failure to recognize that the text-centered or even the text-decentered mindset represents a particular limited outlook, one alternative in a larger world of possibilities. While literacy in no way prohibits scholars from approaching the world of primary orality in a percipient and nonreductive manner, they do need to adjust their perspectives in light of realities that purely textual models cannot accommodate.

For an illustration of the problem, consider the New Criticism, with the return to the text itself as its theme and battle cry.[3] Whatever the merits of this approach—and they were many, particularly in light of the era in literary criticism out of which it came—it could hardly be said to articulate the sensibility of any oral society. Kinneavy in a well-known book, *A Theory of Discourse* (1980), represented communication acts as triangles with four parts: the encoder, decoder, and reality (or referent) correspond to the points of the triangle, and the signal to the space enclosed. While one might wish to revise or elaborate on this scheme, it is plain that a participant in an oral performance could not fail to be aware of the general dimensions of interaction to which these terms refer. The encoder or speaker, for example, is insistently, visibly, and audibly present, the explicit source of the spoken message and object of group attention. The decoders are similarly undeniable as the human beings to whom the singer is singing. The tale as a shared domain of imagined reference, whatever might be the complexities in the "mimetic" relationship between fiction and the world, is another important aspect of the interaction. Oral societies often take their tales quite seriously, as the ancient Greek attitude toward Homer shows. And without the spoken word as signal, communication could not even begin. In such a setting, then, what sense does it make to "get back to the text" when the entire interaction has been completed without recourse to anything of the kind? Are the oral auditors guilty of the "intentional fallacy" when they try to understand what the singer is trying to say? Should one bring along a notepad to catch the ambiguities that surely could not be unraveled to the New Critic's satisfaction in the half second between one word and the next? The New Criticism, practically by definition, banished what is oral from the canons of what it could treat as "literary" art.

Though they represented the vanguard in a subsequent critical wave, structuralism and semiotics accentuated this orientation both by making the linguistic and textual modeling more systematic in certain respects and by generalizing it beyond the field of literary criticism per se. Now the world became a text, or at least a structure susceptible to linguistic (and thus, by the methods of the day, potentially textual) analysis; and even where the textual metaphor did not explicitly obtain, the codes and structures informing and/or derived from analysis were implicitly conceived in visual and static terms, frozen, like a text, in visual space.[4] Yet in the evolution of textualism all these were merely prologues to deconstruction, especially as Jacques Derrida has formulated it in his epoch-making volume *Of Grammatology* (1974), which has probably enunciated a denigration of orality in favor of an absolutely privileged *écriture* more radically than any other theoretical outlook has ever done. Derrida is quite clear in his order of priorities: writing, he tells us, far from merely representing oral speech, is its very precondition. For writing epitomizes that displacement that is inherent in all language as a differential system.[5] Voiced utterance brings with it the illusion of signification, meaning, reference, all of which are, in their real formal essence, a logocentric, metaphysical presence. But that "transcendental signified" to which the signifier is supposed to refer is itself a signifier, not a terminus to the signifying process, not a self-contained plenitude of meaning, but a trace defined precisely by what it is not; and thus meaning is deferred on down a chain of signifiers in a never-ending dissemination. Since all verbal articulation presupposes this trace borne of the differential nature of language, orality is itself "preceded" by an archewriting, in which it is comprehended and culminated. Thus the unpleasant fact of orality can be done away with since it is, in the end, just another form of writing after all.

As Derrida and his followers would have it, writing becomes the champion in a battle against logocentrism and metaphysics that oral-based thought has been imposing on humanity for several millennia. Yet as Ong points out, Derrida's account of the history of orality/literacy relations is enormously oversimplified and distorted; the kind of thinking that can properly be called logocentric and metaphysical, for example, is not at all typical of primary oral cultures but arose with writing.[6] Nor do deconstructionists seem to have given sufficient consideration to some of the uses which literacy and writing have actually served. Through much of its history in ancient Greece or the early Middle Ages, for example, writing—or at least those uses of writing that stand in the clearest line of relationship to current critical discourse—was largely the preserve of an intellectual or priestly elite whose aims were anything but egalitarian. More recently, as Ananda Coomaraswamy has argued, literacy and the institutions and technologies that it supports have been instrumental in the progress of Western imperialism, economic as well as ideological. In literary history, the reification of literary discourse through the print revolution made it possible for a burgeoning capitalistic economy to appropriate the verbal arts into the world of commodities, productions over which it could exert its control.[7] We should note also the longstanding association between literacy and male dominance. Again, throughout the Middle Ages and for some time after, formal academic training in reading and writing centered on texts in Latin, which was taught to boys only.[8] My aim here is certainly not just to turn the tables, making orality over into the apostle of social justice and writing into the scapegoat. Frankly, I can't see that either orality or writing exhibits any innate ideological proclivity at all; rather, each adopts the ideology of its present user. My point is this: how do those who, denying the ideological nonalignment of writing, are anxious to credit it with virtue and enlightenment, explain the many black marks on its pedigree? For the deconstructive mythologizing of writing seems to mandate an averting of the eyes from many of the uncomfortable realities in writing's actual history. Writing has not consistently gravitated toward the oppressed underclasses, nor they toward it. To the contrary, it has frequently—even regularly—been co-opted by dominant institutions and privileged elites, in Western civilization and others as well.

There is an eminently simple reason for these curious distortions and partisanships where the subject of writing is concerned; indeed, the reason is so obvious that the extent to which it is ignored in critical discussions is one of the surest indicators of its truth. The Derridean privileging of writing "triumphed" as it did because of its appeal to the prejudices of the literary/scholarly class.[9] We humanists have long been a beleaguered tribe. We commonly perceive ourselves as underpaid and undervalued by society at large and disregarded (or at best patronized) by our colleagues in the sciences.[10] How many times have I found myself at a loss for a situationally appropriate reply to that embarrassing question so often put to me by perplexed friends and relatives, What exactly is it that you do? Unfortunately I don't invent medicines, computer technology, bombs, or other undeniably useful social commodities. What I *can* do—and this is probably the only specialization that I share with all my departmental colleagues—is read and write. In dialogues (real or imagined) with unsympathetic nonhumanists, a philosophy or critical theory that takes writing as its cornerstone, that makes knowledge itself a function of this skill, would come indeed as the answer to a prayer.

Deconstruction celebrates a concept of language that replicates in philosophical terms the daily research habits of the literary humanist; but since deconstructive theory banishes the agents of signification, one can assert it as a general truth (or nontruth or truth-under-erasure) without acknowledging the extent to which it is invested in a particular point of view. Let us suppose that I am inquiring into some term or passage or idea or construct. How would I proceed? I would embark on a foray into the library in search of a good book on the subject. This book would be filled with graphemes that do nothing if they do not signify. But through in-text allusions and other "traces" I find that my current text (A) articulates its own position by differentiating itself from text B. Thus its meaning has been disseminated, as it were; in pursuit of that will-o'-the-wisp (i.e., "meaning") I follow through the line of footnotes to text B, which, like text A, signifies and disseminates its meaning further. And so on and on, for the rest of my life, or until I quit the business. But in my real-life experience as a human being the play of signification is cut short, not once and definitively, but over and over again, each time I sit down to write. Derrida's appeal is in part that he plays right into the hands of the researcher who wants to promote this life experience as the surest—indeed, the only— basis for knowledge. The privileging of writing privileges the writer—and especially the academic writer. And so, "By a slow movement whose necessity is hardly perceptible, everything that for at least some twenty centuries tended toward and finally succeeded in being gathered under the name of language is beginning to let itself be transferred to, or at least summarized under, the name of writing" (Derrida, *Of Grammatology* 6). To allegorize this in a rather crude and un-Derridean spirit: twenty centuries' worth of books, arrayed before me not temporally but spatially across the library shelves in linguistic (and now we can proclaim it: grammatological) codes decipherable by me, culminates in that writing and scholarly publication that brings me employment, promotion, and kudos. By characterizing textual meaning in Derridean terms, I am simply describing what I do. Hermeneutics as autobiography: the critic inscribes his own story into every text. A seductive theory indeed for the literary scholar!

But this theory is altogether committed to the literary scholar's point of view: it does not work nearly so well for anyone else. Would you want to entrust your life to an airplane pilot newly converted to Derridean views on the impossibility of cartographic and radiographic reference who intends to put those views into practice for the first time on your particular flight? If, dying of thirst in a desert, you were to greet some stranger with the entreaty Water! would you not prefer an interlocutor who holds the kind of "naive" theory of linguistic reference that would induce him to bring you some, rather than one who responds, say, with edifying discourse on water and its properties, since, after all, the word-thing distinction is only another logocentric fallacy. For as we all know (when we are not theorizing), there is a substance referred to by the English word *water* that plays a crucial role in the biology of life forms and would do so even if the first rudiments of language had never been.[11] In fact, most language use has more in common with these examples—in the sense that they engage real-life problems—than with the contexts in which deconstructionists like to view it. The domain of praxis can endure just so much language play. Yet the world in which people do and act is precisely what deconstruction ignores.[12]

What this example calls attention to is deconstruction's inability to cope with language problems that, by one means or another, muster the rhetorical wherewithal to dislodge it from its usual, privileged vantage point. Deconstruction is indeed a highly subjective affair, though its subjectivity is of a corporate variety. For it is not in the particularities of the individual experience that the deconstructive vision is grounded, but in that key relationship common to all in our profession, between "me and my text(s)." *Text(s)* here carries a double meaning: the text(s) that I am reading, and the text(s) that I am writing, with the former sense culminating in the latter, as we have seen. Once this starting point has been admitted, once we have established our imaginative vision in a space where texts are the first things to greet it, then all else follows. "Reality" becomes so problematical that it is virtually banished from hermeneutical discussions.[13] For texts, by the rules and research habits we have established, refer only to other texts, and reality reimposes itself on our awareness only when we have locked up the office for the day. But within this critical discourse reality is never given its moment. History is detemporalized, though in compensation it has been given spatial extension; yet twenty centuries can be spanned by bringing two books together from different corners of the library. Even historical authors fade like debunked superstitions behind the concrete reality of letters in black and white. Me and my texts: by according absolute institutional privilege to this relationship, we en-able ourselves to assert mastery over the fields of knowledge spread out before us in textual form. We may not have read every book; but who could know more about textuality itself (or intertextuality, with me as the unacknowledged mediator) than those who have devoted their lives to it?

The textualizing of orality is just one movement, then, in the textualizing of the world, a happening to which current critical discourse gives continuing testimony. And all of this is an expression of the collective interests of those controlling the modes of discourse in which discussion of these matters is carried on. Disengaging from this hermeneutical program will not be easy. For the textual standard of measure is repeatedly reinforced in academic circles by a range of socially normative mechanisms. Most professional evaluations, for example, concentrate on publication records. And in less formal ways one is frequently "tested" by colleagues (through name-dropping, etc.) about what one has read. All of this is natural and much of it necessary. Yet it does not have to follow that we apply these same standards to all literature, particularly oral "literature." Unfortunately the textualizing reduction seems to do away with any need to detach and distance ourselves from the object of study. For as "text," literary discourse seems "always already" to fit into that world in which we always already know so well how to operate.

I would like to conclude this section with a tale from black American folklore as retold by Sterling Brown, professor and raconteur. Out for a pleasant paddle one fine day, Sister Goose was grabbed by Br'er Fox, who accused her of swimming on his lake. When she denied his pretensions to ownership and insisted, "I got just as much right to swim on this lake as you got!" Br'er Fox simply reasserted that the lake was his and declared that he would execute her and pick her bones. Sister Goose refused to buckle under, however, and took the matter to court.

And in the court the Sheriff was a fox, the jurymen were foxes, everybody who came to see the trial—all were foxes. The prosecuting lawyer was a fox, and the defending lawyer was a fox.

So they tried her. They gave her a fair trial. They executed her. And they all sat around and picked her bones. (Sterling Brown 43)

While texts may be the scholar's sustenance, they are an oral tradition's dead bones. If we want to be more than just the bone-pickers of what we have killed, we will have to learn to face the limitations of our own literacy.

Orality and the Dialogic

Despite its celebration of the differential trace as that which is neither oral nor written in the ordinary sense but constitutes the opening that makes both speaking and writing possible, Derridean textualism remains nondialogic, imprisoned in the tortuous corridors of its own grammatological liberation, hermetically sealed off from the living world of communication between persons. The "middle voice" of *différance* winds up preempting both the activity and recipience of real human exchange in favor of a monology of the intertext.[14] Confronted with the problematic of oral tradition, a theory such as this has no choice but to deny the very existence of what it has been asked to explain.

Yet there are other currents active in the world of contemporary literary criticism that offer better prospects. Particularly apt to the uses of an oral criticism is the recent turn toward dialogics, catalyzed by the Anglo-American discovery of the work of Mikhail Bakhtin. Bakhtin was himself very much the textualizer: "The text is the unmediated reality. . . . Where there is no text, there is no object of study, and no object of thought either" (*Speech Genres* 103). In this and many of his views he was far removed from effective sympathy with oral-based thought, though he plainly conceived of his formulations as extending to utterance of all kinds. Yet the fecundity and depth of his writings single out dialogics nonetheless as one channel through which orality and textuality might productively engage one another.

Oddly enough, the word *dialogue* evokes the image of oral, not written, interaction; when applied to written communication, it takes on a metaphoric quality. Derived from the Greek *dia*, "through, between, one with another," and *legein*, "to talk" (from the Indo-European *leg-*, "to gather; speak"), it calls to mind two human beings conversing. The word does not in itself suggest *text*. Language in dialogue does not have the opacity of texts; it does not displace people but goes between them. The human beings in an actual dialogue are real, bound together pragmatically in a context of face-to-face encounter. Thus dialogue harks to the domain of human concourse. Language is indeed innately dialogic in this sense. While the field of person-to-text may provide the crucible from which we fashion the tools of intellectual inquiry, we must not forget that the person-to-person dynamic has primacy as the "context" in which language originates phylogenetically and ontogenetically, both in the evolution of species and in the becoming of the individual through the course of infancy. At last as at first, texts will never matter to people as much as other people do.

Rooted while it may be in human interaction, dialogics cannot be limited to settings of direct oral exchange. The person-to-person paradigm retains its primacy as a mental and imaginative background against which dialogic meaning configures itself. Yet even oral traditions invoke echoes and resonances that do not derive from the immediate, present performance as a synchronic event. But writing is the author of innumerable displacements, immeasurably enriching the selection of potential avenues of dialogic movement. Derrida and other textualists have established this much at least, that writing is not a mere representation of speech, a mere moment of arrest on its journey from speaker to addressee, but rather possesses a dynamic of its own. In view of media differences, then, it would be helpful, in trying to articulate relations between the oral and the written in literature, to construct a rough typology of dialogic types. This could be done in many ways. Yet in response to the current dominance of textualist and theoretical approaches, I will choose an opening strategy that is both oral and pragmatic. That is, I will assume that ultimately human beings stand at the beginning and end points of any dialogue and that oral dialogic patterns provide the most important models with the deepest psychological appeal. Other dialogic elaborations unfold within spaces containable in the context of pragmatic exchange between humans.

The question I would like to pose, then, is this: what are the possible relations, spatial and temporal, between the originator of an utterance and its recipient in an oral setting, or, let us say, in the context of an oral tradition? Of course the progress of a message from speaker to addressee is only one movement in a dialogue, albeit a necessary one. Yet even a single transmission contains dialogic implications. For as receptional theory has set forth in detail, the act of construal entails far more than a simple passive mirroring of a form received from without. If an audience does not rise to greet a message, the message never fully lives. And so the best performers are those who can best "read their audiences." An oral utterance is as much a product of the ear as of the tongue.

In an oral setting, the primary form of transmission is between a speaker and hearer present to each other in time and space.[15] We will call this primary dialogue and primary transmission. Primary dialogue is relatively synchronic and unilocal. Of course, time is always required in the articulation of any utterance, dialogic or otherwise, and a short temporal gap divides its actual speaking out from its perception and interpretation in the mind of a hearer.[16] Nonetheless, in a primary transmission the consciousness of performer and audience has to be concentrated at virtually the same point of articulation at the same moment of time; if a hearer falls, let us say, five or ten seconds behind, he will lose the thread of discourse. From this standpoint, then, an oral audience is limited in the number and type of interpretive maneuvers that it can perform consciously on any given passage while the performance is still going on; in-depth hermeneutics must be reserved for those "textual" features that are recorded in the long-term memory.[17] These limitations may not always please the textualized critic, since they undercut many cherished close-reading practices. Yet what is lost poetically on one account is compensated for in another. For while performers and audiences may lack the time and habit to incorporate lengthy, multistep interpretive operations into the *conscious* process of encoding and decoding, they can draw, consciously and preconsciously, on present realities in the actual scene of poetic articulation. A physical performance setting, perhaps a common mood and sense of occasion, an awareness of specific present individuals—all these a speaker/audience group can share in a way that writer and reader cannot. Such intangibles, sources that undoubtedly are of great poetic power in an oral traditional setting, vanish entirely in any textual redaction.

Yet such primary, synchronic dialogue is only one form of oral transmission. The other principal form is *diachronic,* or interperformative, that takes place not within the individual performance but between performances. Diachronic transmission is a second-order phenomenon in that it is brought about through a series of primary, synchronic transmissions. Nonetheless, it provides the mechanism by which oral cultures keep their lore alive and pass it on to succeeding generations; since this function of preservation cannot be accomplished in any other way, oral societies consistently display a keen interest in this, the "traditional" aspect of their "literatures." Diachronic transmission, at least in the longer narrative genres, often presupposes "textual" multiformity. Let us suppose, for example, that storyteller A recounts tale T^1 to an audience that includes future storyteller B. This primary and synchronic narrative transmission provides the basis for B's subsequent retelling of the tale, now in a version that we will call T^2, to an audience that includes another potential storyteller, C; and so forth. Thus diachronic transmission enables poets to "speak through" (*dia-legein*) to individuals whom they have never met, indeed, who live perhaps centuries after their own time. What they transmit is not a text, reified, absolute, Bakhtin's "unmediated reality" and "object of study," but an art of telling that comes into manifestation only in performance, that can accommodate itself to changing conditions and can pick up colors of the outside.[18]

Though participants in the synchronic performance group are oriented toward the diachrony of tradition, the two forms of transmission, primary and secondary, remain distinct: for the constituents in the primary dialogue are directly perceptible through the senses, whereas those of the second order can only be recollected through the memory or inferred from formulaic resonance. The configuration of the two types, however, is radically revised by writing, to the point at which the distinction loses much of its force. "Primary" transmission now becomes that from writer to reader; "secondary" transmission becomes the influence which one literary work exerts on another. Yet the correlations of space and time have been disrupted. For the writer-to-reader dialogue is not confined within a single temporal and spatial circumference; its life is indefinitely extendable through the medium of the text, which may still be able to find readers thousand of miles and years from the point of its creation. The text has seemingly made utterance "autonomous" and "context-free" (see Ong, "Writing," esp. 152), in that it is no longer tied to any particular set of human articulators or interpreters. Primary and secondary transmission have become coparticipants in tradition, which no longer offers itself to human consciousness only through the memory but has been reified, displayed in visually perceptible graphemes inscribed between book covers. What used to be the "synchronic" and "diachronic" in dialogue has become converted to the "textual" and the "intertextual."

It is here that the work of the textualists and the textualizing dialogists comes to bear. Let us consider, for example, Bakhtin's notion of "heteroglossia," as it is set forth in two early essays, "Epic and Novel" and "Discourse in the Novel," in *The Dialogic Imagination*. Etymologically suggesting "other-tongued-ness" or linguistic dialogization, *heteroglossia* seems to designate for Bakhtin the contextuality of any utterance which permits it to mean only through the co-voicings of all those conditions or presences that as silent partners environ its articulation, *conditions* here comprehending anything from the generic to the sociological to the material. Thus conceived, heteroglossia would seem to lend itself splendidly to the study of oral tradition. Yet Bakhtin is emphatic in linking its entrance into literary expression with the rise of the novel (though it is sometimes evident much earlier in forms that are essentially, to Bakhtin, protonovelistic); the epic, by contrast, is to Bakhtin monologic and univocal.[19] Here and elsewhere Bakhtin seems to me to be animated by a peculiar pronovelistic generic chauvinism, although this partiality needs to be read against the intellectual background of the era out of which these essays grew. Nonetheless, I do find a certain validity in his distinction. For the forms of heteroglossia which his analysis brings to light— the "personal" multiple voicings through author or narrator or character as well as the "impersonal" stylizations of multiple social languages—do indeed seem to define a province that the novel genre has made it its special task to explore. Such dialogized speech modes as "double-voicing" or "hybridization"—and here we might mention as well "unreliable narrators" and other cognate devices studied over the last two decades by narratologists—do indeed attain prominence and become objects of explicit artistic development far more in novelistic discourse than in the texts of epics.

More than in the *texts* of epics—that is the point. The novel has *textualized* heteroglossia. Invented in the age of print, disseminated through a medium of written exchange whereby author and reader need not and usually do not know each other directly, conveying verbal discourse in spatialized typographic form divested of most nonverbal concomitants, the novel is probably the most textual of all major "literary" genres. But since language utterance is most insistently dialogic, since the image of person speaking to person cannot be eradicated from the human psyche in its relationship to language use, the novel has reified dialogue, has allegorized dialogue through the modalities of typography, has rendered dialogue into visibility in codes interpretable only within the medium of dialogic exchange that the novel has cultivated. This has been one of the distinctive *genii* of the novel form. And to a literary criticism that has blossomed within the same textualized conditions, such a mode of artistry might seem like the natural and inevitable consequence of the creative impulse unfolding within the verbal medium. And so textualized dialogization becomes the standard, the perfection, the *telos* of artistic evolution. And by the same token, prenovelistic genres, in Bakhtin's representation of them, seem unripe and premature. Or perhaps to others unable to countenance this obvious ethnocentrism, oral and oral-derived genres might be better read (viz., textualized) in such fashion that their fundamental otherness (with respect to communication medium) as against the world of text-utterance can be glossed over and concealed from view.

Yet to claim that an oral performance is undialogized is a patent absurdity; what one means is that it is undialogized in the textual sense. But an oral performance is far more than a text; even the performance itself exists in dialogue with its tradition, as we have already explained. Why should a singer of tales disregard his present audience so that inter- and intratextual dialogues may remain uncontaminated by the extratextual and extralinguistic, when the text has for him no phenomenological reality at all? Why should he try to reify the oral language *event* that he is in the very process of enacting in collaboration with his audience, when his performance is already contextualized by a world full of perfectly good things (*res*)? Why should he try to imprison a dialogue with active beings and presences within codes interpretable only inside that field that extends between the reader and his text, when his poem is not a text at all but a song for hearers? The fact is that oral poets are engaged in forms of dialogue that readers find difficult to imagine. And the reason for this difficulty is that the texts through which we approach most oral "literary" discourse have effaced all that is most distinctly oral.

How then are we to construct a means of understanding dialogue within oral tradition? The synchronic modality is more easily grasped: the singer is conversing with a real audience in an actual physical setting. Yet there is more than this: we still need to account for the dialogue with diachrony. And this can be interpreted as a dialogue with memory. When Homer said, "Sing, O Muse," to the goddess daughter of Memory (Mnemosyne) or when Old English poets said "I heard," thereby summoning the recollection of what they heard into the discourse at that moment being formulated, they were relating themselves to a domain in which the memories of the performer/audience group could meet and interact, enter into "dialogue," as it were.[20] And this traditional dialogue occurs not through the intertextual but through the inter-mnemonic. It is a dialogue of memories. John Miles Foley has used the term *metonymy* to describe the relation between an expressed feature (such as a formula) in the synchrony of oral performance and the traditional context on which it draws.[21] The song-text, defined as a specific verbal rendering, is the stimulus that activates those lines of association in the memories of the performance group by which the song acquires its resonance. This one-half of the traditional dialogue—the singer's words—may be textually recuperable. But the silences are not; and it is in the silence that the play of memory unfolds. Without these answering voices from the silence, oral "literature" becomes as sterile as a raga melody plucked on a sitar whose drone strings have been cut off.[22]

Memory is the living medium of an oral tradition. In a certain sense texts are at war with memory, as Plato observed, since they take over its function. Text displaces memory, but the conflict between them arises because of their very kinship. My act of writing this essay at this moment is environed by the books in my personal library around me in a fashion not unlike the memories and echoes that inform the oral rendering. Yet textuality has given to utterance a materiality that memory does not have. I can open and read my books as a human being acting on the material plane, and what I find there has an objective existence and extension of its own that may stand fully at variance with my recollection of it. The "book of memory," by contrast, never fully separates itself from the mind of the one who remembers. Yet both memory and the text present their contents to human consciousness through a kind of knowing-by-seeing. Early rhetoricians, who cultivated memory as one of the principal branches of the rhetorical art, used visual images as mnemonic devices: items one wishes to remember should be configured on a mental representation of some memorable scene, such as a temple.[23] Writing extends this process: in my personal mental world, bits of discourse that I wish to refer to have particular places, perhaps in books whose covers and colors and sizes I know, perhaps under certain call numbers in a familiar corner of the library. Whereas in a former age I would have searched my memory, today I search the bookshelves. From the literate person's standpoint, then, memory might indeed be defined as Derridean archewriting constituted as archetext, never fully materialized as text until actual manual or typographic writing came into play, always half-immersed in the unconscious and known as text only in the becoming into consciousness. From an oral culture's standpoint, the written text could be defined as memory concretized, memory torn out from its native soil in human experience but in the process fixed in durable form that frees it, apparently, from the effects of time.

To us today, oral tradition is usually a book and not a memory, and this is the root of our misunderstandings. The challenge that orality poses, and it does so more for scholars than for any other segment of the contemporary population, is to learn to respond to it on its own terms without abandoning the intellectual modalities that textuality has created for us. For if one cannot enter into sympathetic attunement with the object of study, one's knowledge of it remains barren and superficial. On the other hand, if one abandons one's own frame of reference, naive projections and facile syncretisms ensue. We must try to maintain ourselves in a state of genuine dialogue with oral tradition, a dialogue in which we are perhaps responsible for upholding the continuity and rigor of argument, yet in which we try nonetheless to create spaces in which we efface ourselves, so that the image and echo of what is truly *other* can begin to appear. Only thus can we do our subject justice. For we must never forget that our partner in this dialogue has, in the world of our discourses, become a silent one.

Notes

I would like to express my appreciation to the Louisiana State University Council on Research for the 1987 Faculty Summer Research Stipend that supported the research and writing of this paper.

1 Lord, in *Singer of Tales,* comments extensively on the inadequacies of conventional literary criticism in the face of oral tradition. A vast scholarly literature now addresses problems of orality and oral tradition; for excellent introductions to oral-formulaic scholarship, one important line of approach to this subject, see Foley, *Oral-Formulaic Theory,* and Foley, *Theory.*

2 In *Of Grammatology,* Derrida badly misrepresents the history of criticism and linguistics when he imputes to it a fear and rejection of writing; on Derrida's misconstruction of the significance of Saussure in this regard, see Ellis 19–20. On the character of the French intellectual scene out of which deconstruction grew, see Ellis 83–86. The early deconstructive penchant for representing deconstruction in revolutionary terms may in part be explainable, according to Ellis, against the background of the conservatism of the French literary establishment of the time, which interacted with a longstanding disposition among certain coteries of French intellectuals to *épater la bourgeoisie.*

3 For a fine treatment of the New Criticism in the context of the historical movement from orality to literacy, see Ong, *Interfaces.*

4 Both structuralism and semiotics, for example, rely heavily on the notion of the sign. As Ong points out, however, the reduction of language to signs (derived from *signum,* meaning a standard or banner) appeals to chirographic and typographic mentalities as it would not to oral folk (*Orality* 75–77). As Tyler argues in *The Unspeakable* (see esp. 3–59), Derrida does not succeed in escaping from a visualist orientation.

5 Derrida's point of departure in this, of course, is Ferdinand de Saussure. For a critique of these attempts to represent language as a system of pure differences, see Scholes (esp. 86–110). Derrida's prioritizing of writing over speech bounds without argument over objections of the most obvious sort (see Ellis 21–28). For example, speech plainly precedes writing historically and psychologically, since writing is a relatively new invention, and since all infants exhibit a disposition to speak as they do not to write. Nor does Derrida make it clear exactly why writing is an appropriate term for *différance* or *trace,* which, if they are valid concepts at

all, pertain to oral contexts as much as to written ones, as Derrida himself insists. To assume that *trace* is characterizable in terms of "writing" rather than speech—a dominant theme in much of Derrida's scholarship—is to slip an extremely loaded and preemptive metaphor through without critical examination.

6 See Ong, *Orality* 165–70; see also Kelber.

7 For a fascinating discussion of the impact of print as it came to be felt more and more profoundly over the course of the eighteenth century, see Kernan.

8 On the role of Latin as a male "puberty rite" in the Renaissance era, see Ong, "Latin Language Study."

9 For a proclaimation of theory's "triumph," see J. Hillis Miller.

10 The eminent sociobiologist Edward O. Wilson, for example, claims that natural selection can ultimately be made to explain "ethics and ethical philosophers, if not epistemology and epistemologists, at all depths" (3). So much for philosophy. Yet can philosophers endure this reduction of their field into a mere esoteric sidebranch of biology? Scientists like Wilson seem to have all the hard facts—and, in an age of budgetary constraints, the money too. Perhaps our critical fashions are more determined (no doubt largely on a subconscious level) by rather mundane sociological and economic considerations like this than we would like to admit.

11 See, again, Scholes 74–110, for a critique of the rather over-hasty dismissal of reference in post-structuralist theory.

12 Deconstruction has come under recent fire, particularly from Marxists, for its exclusion of the world from its critical discourse. For a forceful and highly readable version of this argument, see Eagleton 127–50. J. Hillis Miller's 1987 article is in part a deconstructionist's answer to such charges.

13 Thus J. Hillis Miller stresses the problem of the "material base." Granted; but why is it always the world that gets problematized? Why do we not problematize that act, that arbitrary choice, of approaching the world through texts and writing? It is not true, incidentally, that hermeneutics—interpretation—is by nature a textual activity. On this matter see Ong, "Writing," and particularly Ong, "Before Textuality."

14 See Derrida, "Différance," esp. 137. Derrida's characterization of *différance* in terms of the middle voice is part of his critique of origins and ends; it implies, in terms of the communication process, a deconstruction of speaker/author and listener/reader. *Différance* promotes textuality and undoes people. Such a philosophy is not only antihumanistic but also antihuman.

15 The following distinction between primary and secondary (or, in the oral context, synchronic and diachronic) transmission is one that I have amplified upon variously in Parks, "Interperformativity," "Orality," "Traditional Narrator and the 'I Heard' Formulas," and "Traditional Narrator in *Beowulf*."

16 Much of this interpretation—phonemic construal, for example—must be done quickly, since sensory memory can retain an imagistic or "echoic" impression for only a brief duration, measurable in milliseconds. On sensory memory and other perceptual matters, see John Anderson 36–72.

17 Again, on the relations between short-term and long-term memory and for a review of theories in cognitive psychology on the mnemonic storage and retrieval of meaning, see John Anderson, esp. 73–197.

18 The modalities of this art have been a principal subject of study for oral-formulaic criticism; for a seminal treatment, see Lord, *Singer.*

19 See Bakhtin's exposition on the distinction between these genres in "Epic and Novel: Toward a Methodology for the Study of the Novel" (*Dialogic Imagination* 3–40). For an excellent review and elaboration on Bakhtin's distinction between the monologic and the dialogic, see Kristeva, esp. 47–59.

20 On these formulas and the cognate traditional narratorial construct in Old English and ancient Greek poetry, see Parks, "Interperformativity," "Traditional Narrator and the 'I Heard' Formulas," and "Traditional Narrator in *Beowulf.*"

21 See Foley, "Editing Oral Epic Texts," "Tradition," and "Reading the Oral Traditional Text." See also Foley's essay in this volume.

22 See Foley "Editing Oral Epic Texts," esp. 82–85, for a fine statement of the endemic limitations of typographic representations of the oral-traditional multiform.

23 For a classic study of this tradition, see Yates.

PART TWO
ORAL-WRITTEN INTERFACES:
EVENTS IN HISTORY

Introduction

When people in medieval Europe, England, and Scandinavia were making the change from oral to written modes of expressing and remembering, what was involved—in political relations, in preserving traditions, in developing new modes of thinking? Alois Wolf, Robert Kellogg, and Hanna Vollrath all deal with the complexities of the bicultural societies of the European Middle Ages, societies in which Latin and then vernacular literacies interacted with vernacular orality. They each discuss different specific circumstances: Vollrath compares three eleventh-century texts, each concerned with ecclesiastical disputes in the German part of the Imperium; Kellogg analyzes the textuality of the Elder Edda as it is presented in a manuscript of thirteenth-century Iceland; and Wolf contrasts various interrelations between oral and literate productions in diverse areas of Europe, England, and Scandinavia, focusing on texts related to the Burgundian army's defeat in 437 and texts related to the Goths' history, Ermanaric's death in the fourth century, and Theodoric's reign in the sixth. On one thing they agree: extant texts do not represent pure states of orality, although certain distinctions between the oral and the written do help in analyzing these hybrids.

Alois Wolf relies on distinctions between the heroic and Germanic and the Christian and Roman, keeping his concept of oral matter within the narrow, conservative sphere of stories preserving the distant past and showing no Christian or Roman influence. He finds that stories and ideas move not only from oral to literary productions but also from literary to oral, in a complex interaction. The different specificities of the textual complexes he studies show that one cannot separate textual traditions from politics and geography. Even similar beginnings do not lead to the same sorts of relations between the oral and literate: the German traditions keep a sharp separation, the French merge the Christian and the heroic, and the Anglo-Saxon and Icelandic differ again from each other and from the German and French.

Robert Kellogg concentrates less on the matter of the texts and more on the form, attempting to come to terms with the sort of hybrid represented by the Elder Edda. He finds traces of earlier oral productions in these poetic texts—formulas, themes, and myths—and also elements of literacy—titles of poems, headnotes to them, consciousness of difference between the old stories and the present—and so believes these texts to be the product of thirteenth-century scholarly interests. Using Saussure's concepts of *parole* and *langue,* Kellogg asserts that oral versions differed in being specific events, nonrepeatable performances within the vast competence of story that was epic. While someone authored the manuscript that presents the Elder Edda, selecting and ordering the poems and writing the notes that introduce them, no authors existed for epic or for performances of the tradition. Each kind of production is specific to its time and place: the productions of epic, however, no longer exist, while the Edda does, exhibiting one time when oral and written coexisted and the author of a manuscript could attempt to mediate between them.

Hanna Vollrath deals with mentality, staying surprisingly and revealingly with Latin texts. She follows Brian Stock in her concentration on the role written texts played in society, especially in those societies struggling to define the institutions of law, religion, and the state. She takes issue, however, with Stock's analysis of medieval histories and their interpretive language. Using Jack Goody's distinctions regarding the tendency of literate religions to generalize or decontextualize their formulations, Vollrath locates within the oral mentality the tendency to treat a text as an object with a fixed and single meaning and within the literate the tendency to treat it as something which can be abstracted and to which reasoning can be applied. Eleventh-century chronicles allow her a double view of oral and written differences: they show historical situations within which oral customary laws and written canon law clashed, and they show the ways the chroniclers within their accounts used texts to mediate the conflict. Although throughout the eleventh century written law comes to dominate oral, the chroniclers show in their interpretations that they still understand texts as entities to be used rather than writings to be analyzed for general principles that can be applied to various situations. Thus, in their Latin writings they continue to exercise an oral mentality.

C. B. P.

Alois Wolf

Medieval Heroic Traditions and Their Transitions from Orality to Literacy

The European Middle Ages were a period of privileged literacy, a literacy that was based on the Holy Scriptures and on Latin, which was no longer anyone's mother tongue but which guaranteed universal communication and access to the treasures of classical learning and literature. Literacy means not only writing but also extensive and intensive reading; here again the particular nature of Christian medieval literacy must be taken into account. Reading in monastic education was conceived of as ruminating and aimed at piercing the superficies of the letter. Writing and reading under these circumstances provided unique perspectives which did not necessarily become operative in any given case, but the probability of their effectiveness was high and often worked in ways not apparent to a modern mind. At the same time, the Middle Ages were also a period of privileged orality, not only because of the overwhelming number of illiterates but also because orality was an essential feature of medieval society. Orality and literacy may well seem extreme opposites—their respective qualities and shortcomings have already been treated at some length in recent years, and theories have been produced—but in the Middle Ages orality and literacy, it is generally agreed, merged and supported each other.[1] The truth of this is apparent if we only think of the importance of religious ceremonies in which sacred literacy is at its highest when combined with orality—the spoken word with the whole impact of acoustic and visual phenomena. There existed many forms of literacy in Latin and in the vernacular and many forms of orality, comprising storytelling and memorized or improvised poetic traditions. Oral recitation of written hagiographic texts was an experience of everyday life in monasteries: the psalms learned by heart became part of a secondary oral culture, and orality and literacy could meet when monks or clerics tried to take advantage of the possibilities offered by vernacular oral traditions.

Literacy in the Middle Ages was not available to everyone at every time and place. There could be no literacy without a scriptorium with all its requirements that could only be found in a monastery, a bishop's see, or the residence of a powerful lay ruler. Literacy, under these circumstances, was a precarious enterprise, always subject to changing local conditions. This makes it difficult, if not impossible, to assert anything apart from the fact that religious writing must have been of importance, a fact that can hardly be overestimated in its far-reaching consequences concerning writing, letters, and literature. Although literacy was entrusted to the medieval Church—an institution both centralized and universal—the "literarization," if I may use this term, of the vernacular idioms nevertheless turned out to be an extremely complex process, producing an astonishing variety of texts, which seems to elude any theoretical approach. This process becomes particularly puzzling when we turn to heroic traditions and their transitions—I insist on the plural—from orality to literacy.

In recent years the interest in the problems of orality and literacy has increased, numerous studies have been published, and we live under the threat of being drowned in the waves of fashionable theories. Modern linguistics and approaches based on the results achieved by ethnologists, not to mention the highly speculative contributions of certain philosophers, pretend to offer the key to overall solutions. Only recently the eminent scholar Paul Zumthor published an article in one of the leading German newspapers (*Frankfurter Allgemeine Zeitschrift* 26 Nov. 1987) pretending that literature is a postmedieval phenomenon and that to understand the problems of literacy and orality in the Middle Ages one has to start from the results provided by the investigations done on primitive illiterate societies of our time. Without denying that investigations of that sort may certainly enlarge our horizons—Dennis Tedlock's essay in this book is a brilliant and enlightening example—I disagree firmly with the general pretensions of Zumthor's new Rousseauism as far as the European Middle Ages are concerned. Theories based upon isolated observations of exotic material cut off from the singular historical context can give only a limited number of elementary, even banal, insights and fail to explain the unique situations in medieval Europe. And it is precisely this uniqueness that rightly deserves our full attention. To me the task of literary research in this field seems to be to describe carefully the phenomena of orality and textuality in specific cultural contexts. That is the purpose of the following pages.

Heroic Traditions about Burgundians and Goths
in the Migration Period

Allusions to Old Germanic lore found in the writings of classical authors prove only the existence of *carmina*, be it songs of praise or heroic songs, among the Germanic peoples, but unfortunately they cannot be substantiated by heroic legends of the Middle Ages.[2] The Roman historiography of late antiquity provides the first allusions to events that took place in the premedieval period of migrations that gave birth to powerful heroic traditions attested later on in medieval written tradition.

One nucleus of these events is formed by the disastrous defeat of a Burgundian army in 437, entailing the death of the male members of the royal family. To the same nucleus, although originally not attached to it, belong the circumstances of Attila's death in 451. Another nucleus involves the history of the Goths, the death of Ermanaric in 375, and the reign of Theodoric in the first half of the sixth century. The reign of the Ostrogothic king Theodoric, who ruled over parts of the western half of the ancient Roman empire, offered the possibility of an interaction between Germanic traditions and Roman historiography and policy; in contrast, the destruction of the Burgundians was of no importance to the Romans, and Attila's death was an event outside the confines of the empire. The reactions of late Roman historians to these events may give valuable insights into the relations between literacy and oral tradition.

Regarding the first nucleus, we only have a casual notice which seems to owe nothing to the parties involved or to legendary oral tradition. Prosper Aquitanus, living in the first half of the fifth century and writing contemporaneously with the events, only mentions the fact of the defeat of the Burgundians.[3] The same applies to the earliest information about Attila's death, but there the beginning of a legend, which must have taken shape soon after the event, can be observed.[4]

Concerning the other nucleus, the allusions in Latin sources of Ostrogothic history include casual mention and important literary reactions as well as oral traditions; in the case of Theodoric in particular, there might be even more to it. The account given by Jordanes in his *De origine actibusque Getarum* and the lost works of Cassiodorus must have accorded with the official opinion of the Gothic court. The pro-Gothic bias of these historians may well have changed the nature of the relations between oral traditions and court historiography from mere casual recording of parts of oral legends to conscious interpretation.

Ammianus Marcellinus, the Roman officer and historian, writing at the time of the events, was the first to mention the death of Ermanaric, presenting it as the suicide of a despairing king in the face of the Hunnish attack on his kingdom.[5] A century and a half later Jordanes, following Cassidorus, gives a well-known and entirely different version of the same event.[6] Until the new and convincing analysis of this version proposed by Andersson ("Cassidorus"), this famous passage was read as an immediate and faithful reflex of oral heroic tradition in Latin historiography and seemed to support the generally accepted theory that in its early stage Germanic heroic legend contained a strong historico-political element, which was to disappear only as time went on. The so-called privatization, which constitutes an essential feature of Germanic heroic poetry, implying the reduction of political conflicts to human problems within related clans, would have to be considered as a secondary phenomenon. According to Andersson the political aspect in Jordanes's account of Ermanaric's death is due to the old Roman idea of treachery (*Rosomonorum gens infida*) found in Roman historiography. The application of this pattern to the circumstances of Ermanaric's death aligned this famous king and ancestor of Theodoric's with important figures of Roman history, and accordingly his enemies came into the anathematized category of typically barbarian traitors.

In this imperial context, one of Jordanes's passages which is usually overlooked gains additional weight. When introducing Ermanaric, Jordanes does not hesitate to compare him with Alexander the Great. To give more authority to that judgment Jordanes pretends to follow the example of *nonnulli*. He mentions not only that Ermanaric "perdomuit multas gentes" but also that he "suisque parere legibus fecit," which gives a typically Roman touch.[7] The later Old Norse poems about Ermanaric's death, *Ragnarsdrápa* and *Hamðismál*, which do not show any trace of political motivation, would then be closer to the authentic oral tradition than Jordanes's account. If this explanation is right, then the cornerstone of the older theory of the evolution of Germanic heroic traditions is removed. The biased historian Jordanes, interested in investing already early Ostrogothic history with an imperial Roman touch, would have resorted to oral traditions only insofar as they provided elements of an explanation of Ermanaric's death which dispensed with the rather embarrassing suicide of this otherwise powerful and impressive ancestor of Theodoric.[8] The execution of the traitor's wife, Sunilda, although it seems an act of gratuitous cruelty to modern minds, would appear as a legal measure that was severe but just and in accordance with the crime committed.[9] The pro-Gothic historian might have intended to present this execution in such a light as to foreshadow the justification of Theodoric's attitude toward Odoacer and Odoacer's wife, Sunigilda. This interpretation of the circumstances of Ermanaric's death based on literary historiographic models did not influence the oral traditions dealing with the same facts; in the Old Norse, Anglo-Saxon, and German texts, no evidence for the existance of the *Rosomonorum gens infida* can be found.

The crucial point about these orally transmitted legends is the disappearance of Odoacer, seemingly because of changes in the role of Ermanaric. But before tackling this difficult problem, we must discuss the most striking aspect of the presentation of Theodoric himself in heroic legend, namely the theme of Theodoric's exile. To my knowledge, the flagrant contradiction between the historical facts (for nearly thirty years Theodoric reigned successfully over Romano-Gothic Italy) and the version of the oral heroic traditions (he was expelled from his kingdom, exiled at Attila's court, and thwarted in his desperate attempts to reconquer Italy) used to be explained by a natural inclination of heroic legends toward tragedy.[10] This is not wrong, but insufficient.

The question arises how the fortunate ruler Theodoric could enter into heroic legend in the first place; his less fortunate successors would have been more propitious candidates for such a heroic career. Apart from Vidigoja-Witege, a figure into which two personalities—one of early Gothic history and one of the time after Theodoric—seem to have merged, the orally transmitted legends do not tell anything, for example, of Totila or Teja. Beginnings of legends of that sort, if they existed, apparently could not compete with the powerful story of Theodoric. But what was this story like, and how did it come into existence? The very fact that this successful king could become the center of heroic legends might be explained by the influence of an extraheroic, extraoral, even literate impulse rather than by that of a primary oral heroic one. I do not think that the rise of the exile legend can be the result of a purely autochthonous development within an already existing heroic tradition. After all, such a tradition cannot have grown out of nothing. The mere fact that Theodoric, coming from the east, invaded Italy is not sufficient.

The exile legend can be better understood when the possible influence of official policy at Theodoric's court is taken into account. Consequently Theodoric's situation would be quite different from that of Ermanaric, especially as far as orality and literacy are concerned. The current view of a one-way road from orality to literacy in this case would have to be reversed, when an official and learned literary tradition at the basis of court policy could become the source of oral heroic legends.

When Theodoric invaded Italy and fought Odoacer, he acted in agreement with the eastern Roman emperor. Notker Labeo, for instance, who might well have had knowledge of the German orally transmitted exile legend, gives the historically correct account in the prologue to his Boethius.[11] From the imperial Roman point of view Theodoric's invasion of Italy presented itself as a legal *reconquista*. The successful Theodoric, the new ruler of Italy, practicing a policy of Roman restoration and appearing in Roman attire, tried cautiously to present himself as the legal successor of the Roman sovereigns. His invasion of Italy, seen against this Roman background, could be interpreted as a return, especially since Roman history contained a famous example of a heroic and difficult, but eventually successful, return from the east, the return of Aeneas. Gilbert Highet's hint that attempts were made at Theodoric's court to set up a Trojan pedigree for the Gothic king could lend support to our argument.[12] After all, the Franks, who did not have political or military ambitions in Roman Italy, later on claimed Trojan ancestors. It seems quite natural that the Goths, once they had conquered Italy, preceded the Franks in this claim.

The change in official historiography brought about by the execution of Boethius and Symmachus and the rapid decline of Gothic supremacy in Italy might have put an end to the further elaboration of Trojan ancestry and the analogy with the return of Aeneas. But by that time basic elements of the literary Trojan-Aeneas parallel, supported by real historical memories about Theodoric's roaming in the Balkans, could already have made their way into vernacular oral tradition, where they became reshaped according to heroic patterns and were integrated into existing heroic Gothic lore. The tragic touch necessary for this evolution was provided by the downfall of the Gothic power soon after Theodoric's death. Once detached from the control of learned court literacy and following the inherent laws of epic evolution, the idea of a return from the east made it possible to associate Theodoric with Ermanaric, with Attila, and, by this detour, eventually with the Nibelungen. The fact that the early Attila and Ermanaric legends as preserved in the north do not show any trace of a Theodoric legend could strengthen the hypothesis of a secondary and literate origin of the exile legend. Originally unassociated with Ermanaric and Attila, it developed later and no longer spread out over the whole of the Germanic area.

The rise of Theodoric's power in Roman Italy, according to this hypothesis, exposed older Ostrogothic heroic legends about Ermanaric at least partly to the influence of official historiography. On the other hand, the same learned opinion favored at the court might have rendered, via exile legend, the untragic and successful king Theodoric capable of entering into heroic tradition and playing an important part in it. With the collapse of Gothic power this influence ceased to work, and these traditions as they spread out were subject to varying cultural conditions and different modes of literarization. The Old Norse poetic records and the few allusions in Anglo-Saxon poetry represent a state of evolution of the Ermanaric legends which does not seem to have been affected by these newly developed traditions about Theodoric.

In medieval Germany these legends took a different turn. Particularly in the southeast of the German area, the old and well-established stories about Ermanaric merged with traditions concerning Theodoric, which proved to be even more powerful. Ermanaric became subordinated to Theodoric, who, following a typically medieval perspective, turned out to be Ermanaric's nephew.[13] Contrary to the Old Norse and Anglo-Saxon texts, the Old High German *Hildebrandslied* (c. 830) does not mention Ermanaric but puts Theodoric in a central position, making him the victim of Odoacer's malice. A century later the Latin *Quidlinburg Chronicle* report the same story, with the only difference that Ermanaric is mentioned too. The words of *Hildebrandslied* 18, *Otachres nid,* correspond exactly to the Latin wording *instigante Odoacro.* It is obvious that the author of the Latin text draws directly on oral tradition but that tradition itself is likely to have been created by literate circles at Theodoric's court. By that time the Theodoric legend must have been firmly rooted in southern German oral tradition. Flodoard, in his *Historia ecclesiastica Remensis,* also of the tenth century, alludes to Ermanaric's same cruel actions against his family and relatives; referring to a written tradition, he pretends to have taken his information from *libris teutonicis.*[14] Flodoard is a serious historian, but we are reluctant to accept the existence of heroic poetry written down on a large scale in the vernacular at that time. From then on the name of Odoacer disappears in the continental sources and is replaced by Sibiche, a name that can be traced back to the earlier history of the Goths. The texts of Flodoard and of the *Quidlinburg Chronicle* show the historical figures of Ermanaric, Odoacer, and Theodoric completely integrated into the archaic and purely heroic pattern of the family revenge story. It is interesting to note in contrast that in continental vernacular literacy we do not find important traces of the Ermanaric legend. Even the Middle High German *Kaiserchronik,* although dealing exhaustively with Theodoric, does not mention Ermanaric. There is no trace of him in the *Nibelungenlied,* in which Theodoric after all manages to acquire a very honorable epic position. It is not until the literarization of the Dietrich cycle later on in the thirteenth century that Ermanaric emerges from the oral tradition which must have existed all along in southern Germany.

The Impact of the Carolingian Empire
on Continental Heroic Traditions

The transition of heroic traditions into literacy in early medieval Germany must be seen within the literarization of the vernacular as a whole, a process extending over centuries and offering changing aspects as it went on. If we consider heroic poetry, nearly four hundred years separate the written version of the *Hildebrandslied* from the written version of the Nibelungen legends, but *written* does not have the same meaning in both cases, since the literary character of the *Hildebrandslied* is very different from that of the *Nibelungenlied.* Old High German monastic literacy to a large extent was only a by-product of the imperial policy of assuring a higher intellectual standard for clerics. In the same pragmatic vein it made accessible to the nonliterate the basic requirements of the Christian faith in the vernacular on a local or regional scale. Only a few religious texts composed in traditional alliterative lines, such as *Muspilli* and the *Wessobrunner Hymn,* exceed the limits of elementary religious instruction. All the more surprising is the recording of the *Hildebrandslied,* which was, moreover, done in a highly artificial *koine* combining Low German and Upper German linguistic features. It is tempting to establish a link between the curious fact that of all heroic lore only the Hildebrand-Theodoric legend was committed to writing and the fact that Charlemagne took an interest in the Ostrogothic past. (Walahfrid Strabo's hostile attitude toward the heretic king Theodoric in his poem *De imagine Tetrice* is informative in this respect.) If this assumption is reasonable, the mere existence of the written form of the *Hildebrandslied* in Carolingian Germany, where otherwise the bulk of heroic traditions did not pass the threshold of literacy (for Charlemagne's famous collection of old songs probably concerned texts of a different genre), would underline once more the possibility of ties between court literacy—Ostrogothic or Carolingian—and the incorporation of Theodoric into heroic legend. Ties of that sort would help to explain the peculiar position of the Theodoric legends within the Old Germanic heroic traditions.

The Carolingian *Hildebrandslied* takes its heroic matter very seriously; this attitude is even enhanced by the Christian and "modern" touches which characterize the written text. It is interesting to notice that in Carolingian Germany Old Germanic poetic matter with no bearing on Theodoric attained literacy only in the Latin epic *Waltharius*. But contrary to the *Hildebrandslied,* the Anglo-Saxon *Fight at Finnsburg,* or later Eddic poems, the *Waltharius* does not take the heroic traditions seriously; this distinctive feature remarkably enough gains weight because it seems closely related to the high degree of stylistic elaboration which distinguishes this work and thus conveys an additional message of some importance about the cultural-historical background. The text of the Latin epic has nothing in common with the text of the *Hildebrandslied,* although the orally transmitted legends which are behind it must have been comparable to the oral versions behind the *Hildebrandslied* or the Eddic poems. Latin cannot have been the only reason why the *Waltharius* was something absolutely new when we consider the heroic traditions. After all, Latin could have been used in quite a different way, as we shall see later on.

The *Waltharius*-poet drew largely on Roman and early Christian stylistic models, while having in mind heroic Germanic traditions, and in my opinion he knew quite a lot about the rudiments of *chansons de geste* and was probably familiar with the *moniage* traditions. In his literary approach to the legends of Walter and Attila and to the Nibelungen-matter, he left virtually no stone of the heroic traditions unturned. In a carefully studied introductory chapter, he elegantly dismisses the concept of a heroic age which is the keystone of the underlying legends, and he goes on to disassemble Germanic heroic legends and epic patterns in order to reassemble them in a sophisticated way into new units, literary units which form a short epic poem, possibly in the tradition of a classical epyllion. The traditional grandeur of leading figures is cut down to size or ridiculed. One of the most brilliant items of heroic legend, the refusal to hand out the fabulous treasure, is deprived of its fascination and subordinated to the allegorical concept of *avaritia*. Heroic legends, by means of a highly elaborate Latin literacy, are reduced to a divertimento of connoisseurs.[15]

Before going further, it is important to highlight the term *Carolingian*. The establishment of the Frankish kingdom which was to become the Carolingian empire changed the cultural landscape of Europe; these fundamental and unpredictable changes probably had repercussions also on heroic traditions. The Carolingian empire became a sort of melting pot, and although later on Germany and France drifted away from each other, the common basis was strong enough to survive the early partitions. Carolingian culture provided new conditions for the transmission of old heroic lore, not least by giving birth to the new heroic poetry which was to culminate in the *chansons de geste*. These new French traditions, based on the conflict between Christians and Muslims or Vikings, necessarily had strong ties with religion. These traditions developed in Old French, that is to say in the new vulgar language which emerged beside the existing Germanic idioms in the ninth century and which was closely related to Latin and its literary heritage. The fact that this new tradition had to institute a new poetic diction seems to have facilitated its transition from orality to literacy. The literarization of the new French heroic poetry that took decisive shape in the *Chanson de Roland* precedes that of the legends of the Nibelungen by nearly a hundred years. The great French epic can even be considered almost as a primary phenomenon, if we neglect the few religious texts existing before in French, whereas the passage from orality to literacy in the case of Old Germanic lore in Germany is definitely of secondary order, to a large extent due to a literary situation strongly under French influence.[16]

In the ninth century, end rhyme began to overthrow the existing metrical systems and to hold sway over poetry written in the vernacular; even medieval Latin came under its influence. End rhyme for orally transmitted Germanic lore meant a rupture in tradition, whereas the newly developed heroic poetry in French grew up with it.

Twenty years after the Franconian monk Otfrid had dedicated his ambitious end-rhyming biblical epic to Louis the German, the *Ludwigslied* was composed. This song celebrates the victory of the West Frankish King Louis III over the Vikings at Saucourt in 881. The *Ludwigslied* (in Braune 136) has been preserved in a manuscript of about the year 900 written in northeastern France, probably by a bilingual scribe: it is immediately preceded by the first poem existing in French, *The Song of Saint Eulalia*. Although the *Ludwigs-lied* does not deal with ancient heroic lore, its subject matter, the fight be-tween Franks and Vikings, must nevertheless be considered.

The historical event which is at the base of the *Ludwigslied*, the Franks fighting the heathen Vikings, could have inaugurated an Old German equiva-lent of the French *chansons de geste*.[17] It is true that the *Ludwigslied* cele-brates a victory, and victories are not propitious for the rise of heroic legends, but the same event later on gave birth to the French *chanson de geste* of Gor-mont and Isembart. Nothing of that sort appears in Germany. As a literary work, the *Ludwigslied* does not emerge from oral traditions fermenting for at least a number of years or perhaps a few decades; neither did it create a tradi-tion. It follows the event immediately as a literary text and aims clearly at glorifying the king, presenting him as the Christ-like savior who leads the chosen people, the Franks, to victory over the Philistines, the Vikings.

The poem is also devoid of all stylistic devices that are characteristic of Germanic heroic poetry.[18] In adopting the new end-rhyming verse couplet, the poet made it clear that he did not want this new Christian heroism to be con-fused with the Old Germanic heroic traditions which had no relevance to the Christian faith. In France there was no such break with the developing heroic traditions. There the new Carolingian heroic matter developed rapidly and soon gained high literary prestige, as can be seen in the *Chanson de Roland,* a poem I believe to be nothing less than an elaborate literary coronation of orally transmitted heroic poems and legends. In Germany, the much older he-roic traditions remained within the confines of orality until about 1200. (This does not mean, of course, that these traditions could not have been influenced by literature.) The fact that a text like the German *Ludwigslied* came into being seems to me of high significance if compared with what happened in France. After all, we must not forget that we are dealing with the same reli-gious, cultural, and even political setting, which has its roots in a common Merovingian and Carolingian past. In the German area, we observe a cleavage between what we could call the authentic heroic traditions and the new, reli-giously inspired ways of dealing with martial events. The former did not sur-face into literacy, apart from the *Hildebrandslied;* on the other hand, the *Lud-wigslied,* a monument to the Christian heroic attitude, did not create a new heroic tradition in early German literature. It is quite different in France. As Menéndez Pidal puts it (473), we observe parallel to the emergence of French as a distinct Romance language the constitution of a new heroic style, capable of combining genuine heroic attitudes with a Christian interpretation of fight-ing, attitudes which still furnished the material basis for the new heroic tradi-tions. This newly developed heroic poetry in France from its very beginning seems to have been close to literacy.

Already as early as in the panegyric poem *In honorem Hludowici* by Ermoldus Nigellus (d. c. 835), oral traditions about the spectacular actions of Guillaume d'Orange emerge in highly literate Latin distichs. Zado the Saracen, taken captive by the Franks, tries to deceive them: "Hoc vero agnoscens Vilhelmus concitus illum / percussit pugno, non simulanter agens" (Ermold le Noir 525–26). Being extremely choleric and dealing out blows like that are the typical marks of Guillaume d'Orange, as can be seen from the *chansons de geste* of the Guillaume cycle. From there Guillaume's blows crossing the linguistic frontiers penetrate even into the legends of the Nibelungen: Rüdeger, killing a Hunnish warrior at Attila's court in Guillaume's manner, is not part of old Nibelungian heritage. It was certainly not Ermoldus Nigellus who invented this blow, nor did he follow any model in classical literature.[19] This interpretation of the passage of Ermoldus's poem lends support to Menéndez Pidal's opinion that oral legends about Roland's death gradually but irresistibly forced their way into the official Latin historiography of the Carolingian court (Menéndez Pidal 263). The fact that we know nothing about the form in which these legends were transmitted does not say anything against their existence.

Two other, unfortunately fragmentary, texts, the *Fragment of La Haye* and the *Nota Emilianense,* confirm that oral heroic traditions could be reflected in literary medieval Latin. The *Fragment of La Haye,* written between 980 and 1030, probably in Normandy, deals with a heroic event in the legendary history of southern France (Aebischer). The Latin prose text is a copy of a Latin poem in hexameters, and to that extent it is comparable to the *Waltharius*. In the *Fragment* we meet a number of heroes of the Guillaume d'Orange cycle, who appear a century later in the *chansons de geste.* The Latin text, quite unlike the *Waltharius,* respects the heroic tradition and in its outlook seems to keep close to orality. The same applies to the other fragment, the *Nota Emilianense,* which dates from about 1065 and is of Spanish origin (Menéndez Pidal 390). This prose text, written in nonclassical Latin, gives a version of Roland's death which must be a fairly faithful reflex of an oral vernacular tradition, already enlarged if compared with Einhard's report in his *Vita Caroli magni.* These Latin texts come close to a recording of orally transmitted legends, which seem to be respected by the authors, probably because they refer to the fights against the Arabs and appear to fit in easily with medieval Christian ideas, whereas the *Waltharius*-poet had to cope with legends of quite a different stamp. In France the barrier separating this sort of Christian heroic orality from literacy must have been rather low, because fairly soon and apparently without any cultural problems oral heroic traditions could be transformed into the grand epic of the *Chanson de Roland.* It is particularly striking that in France the great heroic literary epic could be attained directly without being preceded by biblical book-epics. Unlike early Christian Latin and Anglo-Saxon and Old Low German literature, there is no great biblical epic in early France; the 129 stanzas of the *Passion de Clermont* do not fall in line with the works of Juvencus or Avitus, with *Heliand* or *Genesis*.

Only three centuries or so separate the battle in the Pyrenees from the *Chanson de Roland,* but there is a gap of seven hundred years between the collapse of the Burgundian kingdom and the *Nibelungenlied.* It seems therefore to be a reasonable assumption that, from the beginning, literacy and oral heroic tradition were much closer to each other in Old French than in German, where these oral traditions went back to a remote past and were of a different nature. The relations between orality and literacy in Old French are not only those of a transition from an oral to a written state but, as already implied, also those of mutuality.

This interaction of orality and literacy and the fact that the separating line between orality and literacy could easily be crossed explain certain features of Old French epic which are absent from Germanic heroic poems as far as we can judge by the *Hildebrandslied* and the Eddic songs. The extant *Chanson de Roland* as a text then would bear the marks not only of a literary mind working on a rich oral tradition but also of a tradition that itself might have been exposed to literary influence. Parallel with the evolution of oral heroic poetry in France, hagiographic texts written in the vernacular began to emerge. One of them, the *Chanson d'Alexis,* even resorts to the decasyllabic verse which was to become the usual heroic meter. All of them avoid continuous narrative lines, preferring to conceive a tale not as an epic flow but rather as a succession of fairly independent little units, stanzas or passages of varying length, the *laisses.*[20] Common ground between hagiography and the *chansons de geste* is also to be found on the level of the tale itself, if one thinks, for example, of the links between the story of Ganelon and the *Vita Sancti Amandi* (Ohly, "Zu den Ursprungen"). The final integration of the sacred into the heroic at its best, in the scenes dealing with Roland's death, was achieved by the literary genius of the author, but the ground had been prepared in the traditions, including the oral ones, on which he could rely.

Medieval Latin hagiography itself could not keep away from the influence of classical literature and Roman mannerism. The same seems to apply to the French heroic traditions throughout their evolution. This influence is manifest in the descriptions of fights, in the exaggerated use of numbers of warriors, in the multitude of names, in the insistence on the crude details of wounds, and in the handling of the arms. Occasionally, classical models and manneristic techniques of description merge with genuine medieval phenomena, as can be seen in the use of the lance and in the way blows are dealt with the swords (Ross 135). An interesting example of a combined literary influence which probably goes back to the oral stage of the development of the *chansons de geste* is offered by the numerous and almost formulaic indications of time. Lines of the type "tresvait le jur, la noit est aserie" (*Chanson de Roland* 717), occurring over and over again, have a long literary past. Homer and Virgil offer passages in which the theme of nightfall and daybreak is a favorite item of description. The Old French wording of this theme, however, is not classical but clearly biblical: "quoniam advesperascit et inclinata est iam dies" (Luke 24.29). Nothing of that sort occurs in Germanic traditions (Wolf, "Der Abend wiegte" 190).

The contrast between the transitions from orality to literacy in the *Chanson de Roland* and in the Middle High German *Nibelungenlied* is instructive. The *Nibelungenlied* comes on the scene roughly a century after the appearance of the *Chanson de Roland* in its full epic form. Both works are grand vernacular literary epics based on oral traditions, and both works are the products of the same medieval civilization. Yet it must be emphasized that the conditions of the transitions from orality to literacy are not identical in each case, and the same applies to the results of the transition. By 1200 German as a literary language had already achieved a very high standard and was capable of articulating complicated issues, as shown in the works of Gottfried and the Minnesänger. The poet and compiler of the *Nibelungenlied* had no use for these subtleties, but subtleties like these were not yet even within reach of Old French at the time of the *Chanson de Roland*. The *Nibelungenlied*-poet also had at his disposal the whole range of great literary epic genres which had not existed a century earlier. This leads to a structural problem when we consider the *Nibelungenlied* as a literarization of various Nibelungen legends. The *Chanson de Roland* is more or less the well-balanced elaboration of a simple heroic pattern—heroic hubris, triumphant death, and revenge. The poet of the *Nibelungenlied*, although respecting the traditional simple stanzaic style, was bold enough to rearrange most of the inherited matter by pouring it into different molds and by applying different epic patterns. In doing so, he created in his own way a new epic genre (Wolf, "Literarische Leben"). Seen only as a simple fact of literacy, the *Nibelungenlied* can be compared with *Beowulf* or the *Chanson de Roland*. But if we consider the situation in the Germany of about 1200, we realize that this is literacy of a quite different quality.

The Anglo-Saxon "*Chansons de geste*"

Closely tied to Christian literature as it is, Anglo-Saxon heroic poetry cannot be put on the same level with Old French, though there are points of contact. On the other hand, in Anglo-Saxon Britain the transition from orality to literacy differed widely from that in Germany, in spite of a common Germanic basis. In England, oral heroic matter even attained the dignity of a great literary book-epic in *Beowulf*. This process necessitated a thorough reshaping of the matter which was at the poet's disposal and a decisive change of perspective. The *Finnsburg Fragment*, however, tells us that in Anglo-Saxon, traditional heroic matter could also pass from orality to literacy without any apparent substantial changes. Compared with the Finnsburg episode in *Beowulf*, the *Finnsburg Fragment* seems to represent a fairly genuine echo of orally transmitted heroic tradition (Wolf, "Verschriftlichung von europäischen Heldensagen" 311). Two other Anglo-Saxon poems, the *Battle of Brunanburh* and the *Battle of Maldon*, although dealing with contemporary martial events rather than traditional heroic matter, are relevant to our discussion.

The *Battle of Brunanburh* invites comparison with the Old High German *Ludwigslied*, the *Battle of Maldon* with the Old French epic. In both sets the given facts are nearly identical. In the first, Christian rulers, King Aethelstan and King Louis III, respectively, gain glorious victories over the heathen Vikings. But while the poet of the *Ludwigslied* takes a resolute step away from the inherited Germanic poetic tradition in replacing the alliterative line with the new end-rhyming verse and the traditional stylistic devices with the new clerical style and a biblical perspective, the Anglo-Saxon poet, whose text was inserted into the *Anglo-Saxon Chronicle*, has no scruples about following the Old Germanic verse tradition and combining it with new aspects, which point to a clerical outlook and indicate that the apparent oral Germanic verse tradition, seen from our point of view, is maintained only as a surface phenomenon. Oral performance of this poem is by no means excluded, but the guiding principle in its composition seems to have been literacy, with no gap separating the two modes of expression. When the poet in the final passage underlines the uniqueness of the battle, he refers to books and to old, erudite men. The subject matter is arranged in a regular succession of parallels and opposites—Aethelstan's army, his enemies—which has a tinge of the schoolroom. Metaphors, at first sight appearing to be composed and employed in a traditional way, seem to reveal a more bookish character when looked upon more closely; the reader of the rather chroniclelike narrative, for example, is suddenly confronted with a cluster of kennings dealing with the battle (*Battle of Brunanburh* 49), the beasts of the battlefield appear (61), or, abruptly and not in accordance with the general stylistic line of the poem, the classical epic image of the sun is displayed in medieval Christian terms (13). This image, moreover, is preceded by an equally well-known epic formula: *feld dœnnede secga swate*. The scanty scaldic evidence has *fold* [or *völl*] *rjóða*, whereas the Latin writers prefer *terra madet*, which comes nearer to the Anglo-Saxon poem (Andersson, "Blood" 15).

Exulting at Aethelstan's victory, the poem accords a central position to the place of the battle. The exposition of the poem working with the incantatory power of the naming of the glorious proper names, placing them always in the first hemistich, culminates in the naming of Brunanburh (5). Naming of places is no primary phenomenon in Old Germanic heroic tradition, as can be seen from the *Hildebrandslied* and the Eddic poems (King 23). Even the scalds do not insist on it; the *Hrafnsmál,* celebrating Harald Fairhair's victory, mentions the place of the triumph only in the seventh stanza, without any apparent emphasis on it. On the other hand, in hagiographic tradition the place where a martyr was tortured and killed could acquire spiritual significance. In this literary tradition, the name of Roncesvalles in the *Chanson de Roland* assumed the function of a leitmotiv, thus giving an additional structure to the text. The same applies to the name of Alischanz in the Guillaume cycle. Although the *Battle of Brunanburh* does not celebrate the exemplary death of a Christian warrior, the naming of the place of the victory has to be understood as part of the same tradition. Comparable to the *Chanson de Roland,* to the *Ludwigslied,* and to Otfrid's biblical epic, but contrasting with oral heroic tradition in Old Germanic, the *Battle of Brunanburh* is steeped in patriotism, king, Christianity, and territory, forming a new and promising unit. Orality in this text seems to be only one element among others in what is fundamentally a literary composition.

The other Anglo-Saxon heroic text dealing with a contemporary event, the battle fought near Maldon in 991, shows a remarkable resemblance to the *Chanson de Roland* written a century later. The inauguration of the new Christian heroic tradition seems to have been centered on France, from there radiating into Spain and to a lesser degree into Britain. Germany apparently had no share in this new development, apart from the *Ludwigslied.* In Britain the evolution toward a powerful literary genre comparable to the French *chansons de geste* was probably stopped by the suppression of Anglo-Saxon after the Norman conquest.

The *Battle of Maldon,* preserved without its beginning and ending, still represents a medium-sized epic of 325 alliterative lines. This fact is not without relevance for the prehistory of the *Chanson de Roland* and has not caught the attention of Romance philologists. After all, this epic poem furnishes the proof that the link between short narrative poems, Heusler's *Ereignislieder,* and the great book-epic exists not only in the imagination of literary historians. The poet, working at least sixty years after the poet of the *Battle of Brunanburh,* still follows the same traditions, which had their roots in Old Germanic poetic technique, although now and then end rhyme and assonance creep in. Only a short span of time separates the event from the redaction of the poem, not long enough for the creation of a strong oral tradition about the death of Byrhtnoth. (The same applies to the *Battle of Brunanburh.*) This is not without serious implications for my argument. If we also take into account the considerable scope of the poem, it seems reasonable to assume that the *Battle of Maldon* cannot be a recording of an orally composed and recited work but must be considered as a literary effort by a poet familiar with traditional Anglo-Saxon verse technique. He might have had at his disposal a short orally transmitted poem about Byrhtnoth's heroic death and about the reaction of one or some of his faithful retainers. Even such poems, if they existed, would probably have shown the marks of Christian influence.

On the other hand, the existing epic poem does not dispense with the traditional heroic outlook. In this case, orality means not only traditional verse and style but also the capacity to preserve attitudes which were essential to Old Germanic heroic traditions, now placed in a Christian context. The agreement with the later *Chanson de Roland,* even in the details, is striking: refusal of the enemy's proposals, the hubris of the Christian hero provoking the disaster, the existence of disloyal cowards, the fidelity of the majority of the retainers culminating in Old Byrhtwold's heroic words, which correspond exactly to Roland's triumphant assessment of the desperate situation, the theme of purely heroic revenge combined with a keen sense of gratitude toward a generous lord.[21] An indication that the *Battle of Maldon* is closer to orality in the sense just mentioned is seen by the fact that the *Chanson de Roland* achieves a much higher degree of integration of the hagiographic into the heroic. It suffices to refer once more to the pathetic scenes of Roland's death, where, in a fascinating metamorphosis, heroic brag turns into confession of sins ending up in prayer; even the sword participates in this movement.[22]

But the *Battle of Maldon* marks only the beginning of that evolution; the religious/hagiographic aspect combined with the authentic heroic structure is not yet the guiding principle. It is only present in isolated passages, for the conscious integration of the religious into the heroic does not yet seem to be an issue. Characteristically, it is again the hero's death which offers the starting point for the introduction of the religious theme. This is evident in Byrhtnoth's prayer, when he realizes that he is mortally wounded (*Battle of Maldon* 178–80). This short prayer remains rather conventional, dealing only in a general way with the situation of the soul after death. Unlike Roland's prayer, Byrhtnoth's does not refer to the precise situation of the warrior, and there is no need for the hero to show any contrition about his disastrous hubris. The mere insertion of that interchangeable prayer indicates the lower degree of literary complexity in this text as compared with the *Chanson de Roland.* The description of Byrhtnoth's fight and death nevertheless seems to offer an example of an interesting interaction between traditional oral technique and literacy inspired by procedures peculiar to hagiography. Byrhtnoth's death is effected in three stages, with increasing gravity of the wounds. The fight itself is described in a way that follows the traditional line and could be regarded as a fairly true mirror of an orally conceived heroic poem, although it is surprising that Byrhtnoth does not accomplish extraordinary feats of arms before he is killed; on the contrary, the description of his entry into the battle is also the description of his death. Behind the heroic surface the hagiographic pattern emerges now, a pattern that shows the death of a martyr, usually effected in stages. Byrhtnoth, as he grows weaker and becomes increasingly defenseless, begins to resemble a martyr who exposes himself to the blows of his slayers. Byrhtnoth raises his eyes to heaven before he is killed by the heathens (*Battle of Maldon* 172).[23] Byrhtnoth differs from Saint Stephen only in that he does not pray for his enemies.

What follows is purely heroic, which to me excludes an overall allegorical explication of the poem.[24] In this last part of the poem orality becomes apparent again in the details, in the individual alliterative lines, even if these lines were composed in a scriptorium. But the episode as a whole is conceived according to the classical literary pattern of the enumeration of heroes, leading up to the final heroic outburst in the triumphant words of old Byrhtwold: "Hige sceal þe heardra, heorte þe cenre, / mod sceal þe mare, þe ure mægen lytlað," and so on (*Battle of Maldon* 312–13). In eleventh-century England oral heroic poetry must still have been deeply rooted in the memory of the people and their poets, crossing easily the threshold of literacy.

Heroic Traditions and Literacy in Iceland

What can medieval Iceland teach us about the transitions from orality to literacy? Iceland, though part of medieval Christian Europe, is a unique case. Settled from about 870 onward, mostly by emigrants from Western Norway, and Christianized in the year 1000 by public consent, Iceland, with its accumulation of an active, intelligent, and fairly homogeneous population that took a keen interest in its Norwegian history, became the storehouse of oral Germanic traditions, both inherited and more recently developed. In addition, Iceland also became the center of new literary activities in the north. Even more important and with no parallels elsewhere in medieval Europe, orality and literacy in Iceland form a powerful unity, thus defying modern theories of a supposed incompatibility of the two cultures. Snorri Sturluson, one of the greatest Icelandic writers, was at the same time a poet and narrator in virtually full possession of the oral traditions of the north; the same is true for his nephew Sturla and many others. A century and a half after the conversion, in 1156, an Icelander was consecrated bishop; in 1133 the first monastery had been founded. A few years earlier, the Icelanders, following the southern, mostly Anglo-Saxon example, had just begun to appreciate the advantages of literacy. Law, genealogies, and religious information were committed to writing. The text which tells us about it contains no allusion to any mythological or heroic lore.[25]

This was not a situation very different from that found in other parts of the medieval world. It must have answered to certain basic social and spiritual necessities. But within less than a century the development of vernacular literacy in Christian Iceland took a turn of its own, so that by the beginning of the thirteenth century the situation differed fundamentally from that in the other Germanic-speaking countries under the rule of Christian literacy. We find existing side by side, apparently without any problems, miracle tales, saints' lives, various other religious literature, historical writing of great value, texts recording mythology and old heroic traditions, and, increasingly, accounts of the lives and deeds of simple Icelandic, mostly pagan, farmers who had lived only about two centuries or so before. Heroic traditions of different sorts passed into literacy on a large scale and in a quite natural way, being part of a great and unparalleled movement toward vernacular literacy.

To a large extent, it seems to me, this movement owes its existence and force both to the keen interest of many Icelanders in their Norwegian past and to the fact that Norwegians and Icelanders had developed the art of scaldic poetry, a genre unknown elsewhere in the Germanic area. This sophisticated art began to flourish in the ninth century. It was transmitted by faithful memorizing, and only from about 1170 onward was it committed to writing. Scaldic poetry, being unepic by nature, was strongly attached to historical persons and events and enjoyed high prestige, yet at the same time it cannot be separated from mythological and heroic traditions. These traditions provided the raw material for the metaphors and for the highly artificial kennings, one of the glories of the form. Scaldic poetry was a pillar of Old Norse historiography, as we know from Snorri. The high esteem scaldic poetry enjoyed must have had a strengthening effect on vernacular oral poetry as a whole, not excluding inherited heroic poetry of simpler make.

Analogous to the word-by-word transmission of scaldic poetry, the traditional and anonymous Eddic poems in Old Norse might have begun to move away from an originally freer form of transmission and reciting to strict memorization, in a technique of preservation similar to that used by scalds.[26] The prestige of scaldic poetry may also be responsible for the absence of any attempt to produce great verse epic in Old Norse. This means that in Iceland the transition from orally transmitted heroic lore and poetry to literacy came to pass without the help of Virgil, although Virgil was known to the lettered people in the north. This absence of great verse epic increased the chance of great prose writing. Icelanders, like the Old Greeks, must have been great storytellers, but the outcome was quite different. The strong historical feeling which stimulated literacy in Iceland had its roots in the attachment of the Icelanders to their own past and its traditions, which reached far back and comprised mythology as well as heroic subject. The same interest in the past may well have increased the prospects of storytelling, which turned out to be an important requisite for the later saga writing and which was not without influence upon Icelandic historiography, as can be shown for instance in Snorri's version of the history of Saint Olaf (Fidjestøl; Hofmann 168).

The varied literary production of the first half of the thirteenth century in Iceland may be considered a result of this strong historical interest. Literary activities included putting into writing heroic traditions; the prime example, of course, is the activity of an unknown writer who about 1220 compiled the collection of the Eddic poems, a copy of which (c. 1270) has come down to us in the Codex Regius. This compiler subordinated a number of mythological and heroic poems under a guiding principle taken from literary composition, but apparently he recorded faithfully the individual poems so that in this case the transition from orality to literacy is almost identical with simple recording. In the *Völsungasaga* only a few years later, the same heroic matter passed from orality to literacy in a quite different way. The compiler in that case did not hesitate to break with the oral traditions of individual poems and tried to merge them into coherent prose. In doing so, he placed the old heroic poetic tradition on the level of the newly developed medium of Icelandic historiography (Wolf, "Altisländische" 184). About the same time, a Norwegian author did the same thing with a huge bulk of medieval heroic matter mostly of southern origin; the outcome was the so-called *Thidrekssaga,* which differs considerably from the *Völsungasaga,* not only in its structure and pretension but also in the way in which oral traditions are taken up.

These particular Icelandic ways of dealing with heroic traditions in the thirteenth century can also be studied conveniently in the work of a single author, Snorri Sturluson. Snorri's work is of special significance because it shows that the same writer who put the history of St. Olaf into the center of his historiographic achievement and who possibly even wrote the saga of his ancestor Egil could deal with oral traditions from the heathen past, whether mythology or heroic matter. Iceland, thanks to the cultural and political circumstances prevailing at the time of its Christianization, was the only place in medieval Europe where heathen mythology was recorded on a large scale along with the old heroic traditions. The early Germans and even the Anglo-Saxons, converted much earlier and possessing the art of writing well before the Icelanders, could not or did not care to record mythological lore. The absence of this process of selection and reduction in Iceland provided quite a different context for the heroic traditions when they passed from orality to literacy. In his *Edda,* Snorri combines word-by-word recording of lines, stanzas, and sequences of stanzas with the reshaping of the same matter in contemporary prose. Snorri must have been convinced that all these oral traditions, even the mythological ones, presented a valuable cultural heritage, comparable to that which by the medium of Latin was handed over from classical antiquity to medieval Christianity. What applies to Snorri is true of many of his contemporaries, and this may help us to understand the unique Icelandic contribution to the process of transition from orality to literacy.

Notes

This essay is a revised and enlarged version of the thirty-minute talk I gave at Madison in 1988. I am indebted to my American colleagues who kept a benevolent eye on my manuscript.

1 The idea of an irreconcilable opposition between an oral culture and a literate one as maintained by a school of modern scholars neglects the decisive historical conditions which are nowhere the same. Applied to certain cases this idea may yield some basic insights. Its generalization, however, is completely inadequate to a consideration of the European Middle Ages and impedes the advancement of research.

2 Tacitus, *De origine et situ Germaniae,* cap. 2: "celebrant carminibus antiquis, quod unum apud illos memoriae et annalium genus est, Tuistonem deum terrae." In his *Annales* (2.88), Tacitus writes about Arminius: "dolo propinquorum cecidit. Liberator haud dubie Germaniae et qui non primordia populi Romani, sicut alii reges ducesque, sed florentissimum imperium lacessierit, proeliis ambiguus, bello non victus, septem et triginta annos vitae, duodecim potentiae explevit, caniturque adhuc barbaras apud gentes, Graecorum annalibus ignotus, qui sua tantum mirantur, Romanis haud perinde celebris, dum vetera extollimus recentium incuriosi." The expression *dolo propinquorum* has to be kept in mind!

3 Prosper Aquitanus, in his *Chronicle,* writes about negotiations between the Romans and the Vandals and continues: "eodem tempore Gundicarium Burgundionum regem intra Gallias habitantem Aetius bello obtinuit, pacemque ei supplicanti dedit, qua non diu potitus est; siquidem illum Hunni cum populo atque stirpe sua deleverunt" (PL 51.596).

4 Prosper Aquitanus notes of Attila's death only: "Attila in sedibus suis mortuo magna primum inter filios ipsius certamina de obtinendo regno exorta sunt" (PL 51.604). A hundred years later Marcellinus Comes, working at the court of Byzantium, knows details which bear the marks of oral tradition: "Attila rex Hunnorum Europae orbator provinciae noctu mulieris manu cultroque confoditur, quidam vero sanguinis rejectione necatum perhibent" (*Chronicon,* PL 51, 929). Jordanes, writing at the same time in Italy and referring to the report of Priscus, ambassador at Attila's court, gives another version which introduces the important theme of Attila's marriage: "Qui, ut Priscus istoricus refert, exitus sui tempore puellam Ildico nomine decoram valde sibi in matrimonio . . . socians eiusque in nuptiis hilaritate nimia resolutus, vino somnoque gravatus resupinus iaceret, redundans sanguis, qui ei solite de naribus effluebat, dum consuetis meatibus impeditur, itinere ferali faucibus illapsus extinxit . . . sequenti vero luce cum magna pars diei fuisset exempta, ministri regii triste aliquid suspicantes post clamores maximos fores effringunt inveniuntque Attilae sine ullo vulnere necem sanguinis effusione peractam puellamque demisso vultu sub velamine lacrimantem" (Jordanes 123). Jor-

danes still holds the sober and medically realistic opinion of Attila's death: "sine ullo vulnere!" The *Quidlinburg Chronicle* of the tenth century gives another version: "Attila rex Hunorum et totius Europae terror, a puella quadam, quam a patre occiso vi rapuit, cultello perfossus interiit" (Grimm 10). This story is nearly identical with the Old Norse *Atlakviða:* the drunken Attila is killed by a woman who took revenge. Dronke conveniently assembles the evidence of the Latin sources (34).

5 In his *Chronica* (31.3) Ammianus writes: "Huni . . . Ermenrichi late patentes et uberes pagos repentino impetu perruperunt, bellicossissimi regis et per multa variaque fortiter facta vicinis nationibus formidati, qui vi subitae procellae perculsus, quamvis manere fundatus et stabilis diu conatus est, impendentium tamen diritatem augente vulgatius fama magnorum discriminum metum voluntaria morta sedavit."

6 "Nam Hermanaricus, rex Gothorum, licet, ut superius retulimus, multarum gentium extiterat triumphator, de Hunnorum tamen adventu dum cogitat, Rosomonorum gens infida, quae tunc inter alias illi famulatum exhibebat, tali eum nanciscetur occasione decipere. Dum enim quandam mulierem Sunilda nomine ex gente memorata pro mariti fraudulento discessu rex furore commotus equis ferocibus inligatam incitatisque cursibus per diversa divelli praecipisset, fratres eius Sarus et Ammius, germanae obitum vindicantes, Hermanarici latus ferro petierunt; quo vulnere saucius egram vitam corporis inbecillitate contraxit . . . inter haec Hermanaricus tam vulneris dolore quam etiam Hunnorum incursionibus non ferens grandevus et plenus dierum centesimo anno vitae suae defunctus est" (Jordanes 91–92).

7 "Nam Gothorum rege Geberich rebus humanis excedente post temporis aliquod Hermanaricus nobilissimus Amalorum in regno successit, qui multas et bellicosissimas arctoi gentes perdomuit suisque parere legibus fecit" (Jordanes 88).

8 Gschwantler (202) provides sufficient evidence that Jordanes knew Ammianus's account and deviated consciously from it, preoccupied as he was with the idea of ruling out Ermanaric's suicide.

9 Ohly's enquiry into the theme of sundering by horses opens new perspectives, particularly when he remarks that as a rule "ist die Zerreissung des Verräters . . . als verdient und angemessen anerkannt worden, darum als solche auch stets ungesühnt geblieben" ("Zerreissung" 561). Jordanes, however, combined the theme of sundering as a legal procedure with the heroic theme of revenge, a further indication of the instructive heterogeneity of Jordanes's report. The later vernacular sources do not speak of the quartering of the woman but of her trampling to death by horses; here the idea of revenge is appropriate.

10 As Schneider (1: 230) puts it: "Das Los des glücklichsten aller Völkerwanderungskönige nach zweieinhalb Jahrhunderten Gegenstand einer altenglischen Elegie—dieser Wandel ist nur erklärlich, wenn man mit dem Eindruck rechnet, den das tragische Ende seines Volkes allen germanischen Stämmen hinterliess." Schneider's theory seems to presuppose that Germanic heroic memory worked in terms of the political history of the great tribes instead of the narrow and powerful perspective of family ties and elementary emotions. For a detailed survey of the material concerning Theodoric, see "Dietrich von Bern" in Hoops (5: 425–30).

11 "Tô uuárd táz ten chéiser lústa, dáz er dioterichen uríuntlicho ze hóve ládeta, tára
    ze dero mârun constantinopoli, únde ín dâr mít kûollichen êron lángo hábeta, únz
    er ín dés bîten stûont, táz er îmo óndi mít ótachere ze uéhtenne; únde úbe er ín
    úberuuúnde, romam ióh italiam mít sînemo dánche ze hábenne." Alfred the Great,
    in his translation of Boethius, gives the same account.
12 Highet (54), referring to Hodgkin, *Italy and her Invaders* (3: 294), says: "We are
    told that Cassiodorus actually provided a Trojan family tree for the executioner of
    Boethius, Theoderich the Ostrogoth."
13 The typically medieval theme of the importance of being someone's nephew points
    to Carolingian origins. In the early *chansons de geste* and the traditions preceding
    them, this theme began to grow luxuriantly.
14 There may be some doubt about the exact meaning of *teutonicus,* whether it refers
    exclusively to the language or also to the political aspect, indicating books ori-
    ginating in the eastern part of the old empire and even written in Latin.
15 This is at least the conclusion of my two papers on *Waltharius.*
16 I tried to defend this view in several articles on the *Nibelungenlied.*
17 Wehrli (84) was the first to draw attention to that possibility.
18 In this respect I disagree strongly with Harvey (8).
19 The example in classical literature (*Iliad* 2: 246–70, Ulysses beating Thersites)
    which comes close to our passage is lacking the essential feature, the blow with
    the fist.
20 See my paper on "Frühmittelalterliches Erzählen."
21 *Battle of Maldon,* 312: "Hige sceal þe heardra, heorte þe cenre, mod sceal þe
    mare, þe ure mægen lytlað." Cf. *Chanson de Roland* 1087: "Nus i avum mult
    petite cumpaigne. Respunt Rollant: Mis talenz en engraigne." While sensible of
    allegorical interpretations, I nevertheless disagree with Robertson (*Preface* 165)
    and Brault (180) in their evaluations of Roland's refusal to blow the horn. Both
    scholars try to rule out purely heroic elements and thus neglect Olivier's reproach
    and Roland's remorse.
22 The elaborate description of Roland's death provides ample evidence that there is a
    literary procedure at work which paradoxically uses what seem to be formulas in a
    nonformulaic way, lines or hemistichs not being interchangeable, as the oral-
    formulaic theory would have it, but rather part of a brilliant composition leading to
    a climax.
23 There are points of contact between the *Battle of Maldon* and the Old French *Vi-
    viens* epic, i.e., the martyrlike death and the promise not to budge an inch.
24 On the other hand I cannot follow C. Clark, who claims that the poet of the *Battle
    of Maldon* played down Christianity "in order to depict Germanic heroism with the
    more purity" (292).
25 "Sem nú tidisk á þessu landi, bæði lög ok ættvisi eða þydingar helgar" (Hau-
    gen 12).
26 See in this volume Kellogg's discussion of this same issue in slightly different
    terms.

5 *Robert Kellogg*

Literacy and Orality in
the Poetic Edda

The oldest vernacular literary texts that survive from medieval Europe are the products of two cultures. First, they are marked by the characteristics of oral-formulaic composition, pointing back to origins in preliterate societies. But they are also the products of literacy, coming to us as they do in written manuscripts. In some cases, such as the text of *Beowulf* or of *Hildebrandslied,* scholarly convention has proposed a period of two or three hundred years as the probable time between an "original" composition of the work and its having been written down in the manuscript form in which we have it. In other cases, such as the *Chanson de Roland* or the *Nibelungenlied,* the lapsed time is usually seen as shorter. In any event, these early vernacular works have come down to us with stereotyped elements of diction, narrative style, and structure that are typical of poetry composed orally in performance.

In addition to the formal signs of oral composition, many of these works, especially the Germanic heroic poems, also share a common body of legend that refers to people and events as far back as the fifth and sixth centuries. Only by means of oral tradition could material of this antiquity have been preserved in vernacular tradition. In fact, it may be the age of such myths and legends that led scholars in the past to believe that the poetic texts are considerably older than the manuscripts in which they are preserved, older even than writing itself in the case of Scandinavia. The same scholars who have written that certain of the Icelandic eddic poems probably date as far back as the ninth century have also in general been unwilling to acknowledge obvious signs of oral extemporaneous composition in them. This conventional view is more often an implied assumption than an explicit argument, but it is one in need of examination. It holds that some eddic poems, while they must have been originally composed long before writing was used in Scandinavia—even before the settlement of Iceland—went into oral tradition as fixed texts of the sort we are accustomed to in modern literate cultures.

As formulaic and traditional as these early vernacular texts are—as directly, in other words, as they point to oral-formulaic techniques of composition—they are also in some sense the products of writing, not of some hypothetical pagan, preliterate writing, but of the literacy that produced the thirteenth-century manuscripts in which they have survived. Like the *Iliad* and the *Odyssey*, early vernacular European texts are at times even a bit bookish, betraying not just the technology of literacy but some of its organizing and cognitive habits as well. These texts have, after all, been preserved in written codices that exploit the book's ability to organize and preserve a single, unified, stable text of considerable length. We find in some texts—again *Beowulf* comes to mind—an acknowledgment of the historical past, of a time when men believed and behaved differently from men today. When the Danes in *Beowulf* make offerings to idols, the narrator says, "Such was their custom, the hope of heathens" (178b–179a). His awareness of the discontinuity between the beliefs and the events of the past and those of the present is not a trait of orality but of literacy.[1]

Rather than to argue for the exclusively oral or the exclusively literate nature of early European vernacular texts, it is more reasonable to concede that they represent a collaboration between two contemporaneous cultures, one essentially oral and the other essentially literate. For several hundred years after the introduction of writing to northern Europe, a spectrum of possibilities existed in most societies between orality at one extreme and literacy at the other. Identifying in their oldest literary texts the boundaries, even the contradictions and tensions, between their allegiances to oral and to literate culture is one way of understanding more fully the nature of their art and thought.

I will try to illustrate this idea with an extended example from thirteenth-century Iceland. In the body of poetry that we call the poetic or Elder Edda (the Icelandic term is *eddukvæði*), traditions are preserved that developed in northern Europe many centuries before the earliest manuscript texts were written.[2] Like *Beowulf, Widsiþ, Deor, Hildebrandslied,* and *Heliand,* the poems of the poetic Edda derive important features of their meter, diction, and story from what appears to have been a common preliterate Germanic tradition of heroic and mythological song (Heusler). Even some of the imagery that has survived in Icelandic eddic poetry was inscribed on stones in Sweden as early as the seventh century (Hauck). The evidence, in other words, that eddic poetry is grounded in ancient myth and heroic tradition is a scholarly commonplace and accounts in some measure for the high value we place on it.

The principal manuscript containing eddic poetry, Codex Regius 2365, 4^0, is now happily in Iceland, after a long residence in Denmark that began in the Royal Library, from which its name was derived. Codex Regius 2365 was written in Iceland about 1270 and is a well-conceived book. It is written in a single hand throughout and bears a complex and essentially unrecoverable relationship to a number of other surviving manuscripts and literary texts. Codex Arnamagnæan (abbreviated AM) 748, 4^0 in Copenhagen, for example, contains slightly variant texts of seven of the poems in Codex Regius. As many as twenty of the Codex Regius poems are quoted whole or in snippets, or are very closely paraphrased, in a number of other texts, including Snorri Sturluson's prose *Edda* and the prose legendary narrative *Völsunga saga*. From the existence of these closely variant versions and from such internal evidence as spelling conventions that vary from poem to poem, we must assume that Codex Regius has been compiled from a variety of older written sources (Lindblad). Our manuscript would seem to be, considering the body of other works to which it is related, but the tip of a thirteenth-century antiquarian iceberg, the main body of which has disappeared, making a detailed linkage impossible among the works that have survived.

Although Codex Regius is an anthology of poems on what were even in the thirteenth century considered to be old, traditional subjects, it has been organized with understanding and taste. It begins with an unnamed poem that, fifty years before the manuscript was written, Snorri Sturluson in his *Edda* had called *Völuspá*. The poem tells of the creation of the world and the gods, and it prophesies their destruction. Following *Völuspá* are ten more poems associated with gods and other supernatural beings. Then come legendary/mythological poems about the Völsungs, which make up the balance of the book.

To help the reader understand the poems in their context, someone (the "Compiler" of Codex Regius 2365, we could call him) has written some prose notes and comments. A few of these prose passages are also in AM 748, indicating that they did not entirely originate in Codex Regius and that the Compiler is therefore not the scribe of the manuscript, but rather a more abstract anterior figure.[3] Nevertheless, the Compiler of Codex Regius is a presence in the work in a way that neither its scribe nor the author is; the Compiler's voice, like the poems themselves, is shared in places with Codex AM 748, and the voice must be thought to have developed at some time prior to the writing of either manuscript. This presence in the work functions as both the guiding organizer and the speaker (both the *histor* and the *rhetor*). We are chiefly indebted to the Compiler for the succinct prose summaries of background information that he provides for the short eddic poems, information that is occasionally indispensable to our understanding. In most of what follows I will be interested in focusing attention not on eddic poetry itself but on this voice or presence through which it is presented.

The Compiler's work is of two kinds. In the first type, he adopts a voice identical to that of the narrator of the poems, telling enough of the story in prose to lead seamlessly into the verse, either a whole poem or a part of a poem. He does not even mention the poem as such, but just moves the narrative back and forth from his prose to the poetry that he has presumably inherited from oral tradition. Here is a typical example from his headnote to the important mythological poem that is called *För Skírnis* in Codex Regius and *Skírnismál* in AM 748. The note's only purpose is to assist in telling the story clearly.

> Freyr, the son of Njörðr, sat in Hliðskjálf and saw over the whole world. He looked into Jötunheim, where he saw a beautiful maiden as she went from her father's house to the women's quarters. From this he suffered great inward pain. Skírnir was the name of Freyr's servant. Njörð asked him to speak to Freyr. Then Skaði [Freyr's mother] said:

The poem then follows. It is a series of speeches by six different characters in forty-two stanzas, which are held together in a comprehendable narrative by two more short prose links from the Compiler. The main outlines of the story of *Skírnismál* had been told by Snorri in *Edda* (*Gylfaginning* 37), so that even without the Compiler's contributions we would, with Snorri's help, have no difficulty piecing it together from the poem alone. In other cases, however, such as the story about Helgi Hjörvarðsson, which has not survived outside of Codex Regius, the poem would be completely baffling without the Compiler's narratives.

The Compiler's second voice speaks to us from outside the fiction, in the role of a thirteenth-century scholar, referring to the poems as poems. At the beginning of a poem that is without a title in Codex Regius but is called *Oddrúnargrátr* in later paper manuscripts, he briefly identifies Oddrún and her circumstances and then adds, "About this story it is here told in verse." Similarly, he writes before the poem *Atlakviða* that Guðrún Gjúkadóttir had avenged her brothers, "svá sem frægt er orðit" ("as has become well known"), and then adds a few words later, "About that, this poem is made." The two voices, one from inside the fiction and the other outside it, may of course derive ultimately from two separate sources, but that is something we are never likely to know. The second, scholarly voice has several shadings, from the kind of Compiler's note I have just quoted to the expression of a greater ideological remove from the old material.

Neither Snorri in *Edda* nor the Compiler in Codex Regius can be completely identified intellectually with the world of mythic and heroic narrative. Snorri's work is especially complex, self-conscious, and sophisticated in its uses of traditional poetry and has been much studied by scholars (Margaret Clunies Ross). He was no doubt an exceptional individual, and yet he may in some respects also be representative of the antiquarian movement of which his work is a part. He organizes and rationalizes mythic narratives in his concise retelling of them with the ostensible purpose of explaining how traditional poetic language and imagery should be interpreted literally, and to a certain extent also ethically. Snorri's method is that of the historian and storyteller, and his sympathy with the old mythic and poetic traditions is implicit in his deep knowledge of them, even when he tells a story for the purpose of explaining an image or metaphor. He is not an allegorist, and he does not use the old traditions against themselves, attempting instead a synthesis of the old pagan literary culture and the contemporary world of Christian scholarship. Even if Snorri was a conservative intellectual, he lived in and derived his mentality from the thirteenth century in Iceland, not from pagan antiquity in Norway or Denmark.

Similarly, the poems that the Compiler collects and edits in Codex Regius can be thought to derive from pagan antiquity, and yet they are also an important constituent of the thought and language of his own contemporary culture. While he has less scope to demonstrate Snorri's intellectual complexity, the Compiler does occasionally reveal, like Snorri, a consciousness of the discontinuity between the worlds of ancient story and the present more rational, scholarly, literary time. He does this primarily by referring to "heathen times" or "antiquity" (the word is *forneskja* in Icelandic) and to "old stories" (*fornar sögur*).[4] The reader begins to notice this, for example, in the Compiler's short narrative called *The Death of Sinfjötli*, where he writes concerning the Völsungs, "Sigmundr and all his sons greatly surpassed all other men in strength and size and spirit and abilities. Sigurðr, however, was foremost and everyone in old literature [*fornfræði*] calls him superior to all other men and the noblest of warrior kings."

There is no irony here, no lack of conviction or sympathy, simply a scholar's appeal to the authority of old knowledge. The Compiler is slightly more Snorri-like in a note appearing between two of the poems that editions now call *Reginsmál* and *Fáfnismál:* "Sigurðr concealed his name because it was their belief in heathen times that the word of a doomed man had great power if he cursed his enemy by name." In scholarly fashion he identifies a custom that may no longer be familiar to his audience, a move he feels necessary in explaining the appearance at this point in the poem of a stanza which hides Sigurðr's identity in a riddle. In specifying a "then" and "now" he moves a little further back from his material rhetorically than he did in merely referring to *fornfræði*.

The Compiler shares with some of the writers of Icelandic family sagas a stylistic device designed to enhance the impression of a story's substance, by reporting that "some people say this, while others say that." The following is a passage from a narrative entitled *On the Death of Sigurðr* that appears between two poems in Codex Regius about the killing of Sigurðr by his brothers-in-law, the sons of Gjúki:

> Here in this poem [by which the Compiler refers either to the *Sigurðarkviða,* which has gone before or the *First Guðrúnarkviða,* which follows] is told about the death of Sigurðr, and it indicates that they killed him outdoors, but some say that they killed him sleeping in bed. The Germans say that they killed him out in the woods, and in the old *Poem of Guðrún* [a later poem in Codex Regius] it says that Sigurðr and the sons of Gjúki had ridden to the Thing, where he was killed. But everyone also says that they betrayed his trust and attacked him lying down and unprepared.
>
> Guðrún sat over the dead Sigurðr. She did not cry like other women, but she was ready to die of grief. Both women and men went to comfort her, but it was not easy. People say that Guðrún had eaten of Fáfnir's heart and that she understood the language of birds. This is said further about Guðrún [the poem follows].

The work of the Compiler is here as rich and literary as it gets, citing poems by title, correctly reporting on various versions of the legend—including the South Germanic tradition preserved in the *Nibelungenlied,* that Sigurðr (Sifrit) is killed out in the woods on a hunting expedition—and then, in a simplicity of style as fine as the best of Snorri's *Edda* or the *fornaldarsögur,* doing justice to Guðrún's inexpressible pain before she was able to cry.

The Compiler does not succeed in arranging the poems in Codex Regius neatly according to whether they are about gods or heroes. The ninth poem after *Völuspá* is not about a god exactly but about Völundr the smith, whose poem, *Völundarkviða,* may have earned its place among the supernatural beings because he was still thought of as a powerful elf (Grimstad). Völundr had also lived for seven years with a Valkyrie. Several other legendary heroes, including Sigurðr, had adventures with Valkyries, associating them with Óðinn and powers beyond the merely human. These Valkyrie stories serve as a transition between the fictions of the gods and elves and giants and poems about the more nearly historical personages in the courts of the Burgundians and Huns.

Two of these transitional heroes who were beloved of Valkyries were named Helgi. They come ultimately from Danish legend rather than Burgundian, and although in Codex Regius they are said to be Völsungs (Helgi Hundingsbani is Sigurðr's half-brother), they are elsewhere not considered Völsungs at all. Their three poems come before the history of the Völsungs proper. At the end of the second poem of Helgi Hundingsbani, the Compiler reveals a division of allegiances that we have noticed before. He wants both to tell the story and, in this instance, to dissociate himself from it: "It was a belief in heathen times that men could be reborn, but that is now called old women's foolishness. Helgi and Sigrún are said to have been reborn. He was named Helgi, Prince of the Haddings, and she was Kára, the daughter of Hálf-dan, as is told in the poem *Káruljóð*, and she was a Valkyrie." (Neither the poem *Káruljóð* nor any other tradition of Kára has survived.) It may not be immediately clear what motivates this particular critique of traditional fantasy, since the Compiler had already mentioned without comment, in a prose link between the fourth and fifth stanzas of the poem, that Helgi's Valkyrie lover Sígrún had already been reborn once. She was the earlier Helgi Hjör-varðsson's Valkyrie lover Sváva reborn.

Regardless, for the moment, of why this remark is made, we see here the conflict between an allegiance to old traditions and the claims of a new scholarly rationalism as clearly as anywhere in Codex Regius. In the long run, however, it is not the antithesis in allegiances that matters, but rather the remarkable cultural synthesis that is achieved by means of this tolerant acknowledgment of contradiction. In fact, constructing the synthesis was most likely the motive—here, in Snorri's *Edda,* and in *Beowulf*—for mentioning the beliefs of the pagans. Doing so brings the conflict between old and new, myth and history, fantasy and empiricism, out into the open and allows the purely heroic, dramatic, and ethically exemplary elements to be contemplated and valued apart from any pagan "taint." More subtly, the Compiler's characterization of the transmigration of souls as being an old wives' tale focuses our attention on the possibility of an allegorical, genetic, or metaphorical sense in which we can in fact understand that the continued presence of the ancient heroes and lovers in subsequent generations explains their nature.

The assignment of titles to poems and prose narratives is probably a feature of thirteenth-century literacy. When stories are in oral tradition, a distinction is felt more strongly between the *events* being told and the *telling* of them than is the case in a literate culture, where we almost need to be taught the distinction beween "story" and "discourse." In Icelandic, the Compiler's usual distinction is between *saga* (events) and *kvæði* (poem) or *kveðja* (to compose). A name might be applied more naturally to the events than to any particular telling of them, and even by the thirteenth century the names of eddic poems tend to be of the sort "A Poem about X" or "The Sayings of Y." With the possible exceptions of the two poems *Hávamál* and *Oddrúnargrátr,* which could be said to name themselves,[5] the eddic poems (as distinct from the comments of their thirteenth-century collectors) do not refer to particular poems by name. Snorri Sturluson, the greatest of the cultural synthesizers, knew three of the poems in Codex Regius by name, *Völuspá, Alvíssmál* (although he calls it *Alsvinnsmál*), and *Grímnismál,* as did some other writers in the thirteenth century. In addition to *Völuspá,* the Compiler in Codex Regius omits a title before the texts of *Völundarkviða* and eleven of the heroic poems. In compensation, he gives titles to his prose pieces, some of which, like *Frá Völundi ok Níðaði* (*Concerning Völundr and Níðaðr*) might have been intended to serve as names of poems. Aside from the titles written at the beginnings of poems, he mentions four titles within his prose: the *Old Poem of the Völsungs,* the *Greenland Lay of Atli,* the *Old Poem of Guðrún,* and the *Old Poem of Hamðir.* This last comes as an appropriate symbol of his antiquarian tidiness. At the end of the final poem, the conclusion of the whole vast myth, Guðrún's sons Hamðir and Sörli (the products of her third marriage) lie dead. The last words of Codex Regius are the Compiler's note: "That is called *The Old Poem of Hamðir.*"

As many as fifteen of the Codex Regius poems are paraphrased or quoted in *Völsunga saga,* one of the best known of the legendary sagas, which was written in Iceland at about the same time as Codex Regius. We cannot say what relationship exists between the particular texts in Codex Regius and *Völsunga saga.* The similarities are close, but neither work is copied from the other. As a genre, the legendary sagas (*fornaldarsögur*) are closely related to eddic poetry. They are in many respects the prose equivalent. Like eddic narrative, they tell stories from the heroic and legendary past of the Germanic world. Unlike the great family sagas (*Íslendinga sögur*), they do not deal with Icelanders. To what extent the mentioning of Icelanders in a prose narrative, or the not-mentioning of them, was felt in the Middle Ages to be an absolute generic attribute we cannot be sure. A similar prohibition against mentioning Englishmen in Anglo-Saxon epic narrative would suggest that it may have been taken seriously and, conversely, that the cultivation of narrative in prose and verse about native heroes (e.g., the Anglo-Saxon Chronicle and the Icelandic family sagas) was even then understood to be a distinctly different literary activity from telling mythic and legendary stories of the prenational Germanic past.

The Compiler of Codex Regius 2365 was not alone in his consciousness of a significant historical break between the world of the old stories and the present. This kind of consciousness and the serious effort made at synthesizing the two worlds is also one of the features of Snorri's thought that makes him most interesting. Where Icelandic literary art is most traditional, with its clearest debt to orality, it is also deeply scholarly, which is to say deeply literate. As the aristocratic and ruling groups in a society turn from orality to literacy, the oral traditions might be expected to begin the long slide from sacred myth and epic to ballad and märchen. This doubtless happened in Scandinavia as elsewhere. But the antiquarian movement of thirteenth-century Iceland that is represented in Snorri's *Edda,* in Codex Regius 2365, and in the written texts of the legendary sagas was able to save a remarkable body of myth and legend from perishing altogether. It is with some brief description of the oral-formulaic heritage of this scholarly movement that I will conclude.

In an oral tradition, poetic narratives of the eddic sort exist as "texts" only at the moment of performance. Like any other utterance, they exist in the silence between performances not as texts but only as an abstract cultural *competence*—the ability of some members of society to produce poems in performances. This distinction between a text of a poem and the competence to perform a poem is parallel to, and derives from, Saussure's distinction between utterance (*parole*) and language (*langue*). The text is *parole*, an actual event; the competence is *langue*, an abstract system, in terms of which the event is intelligible.

There are many references in the family sagas, kings' sagas, and the collection known as *Sturlunga saga* to literary performances, both extempore and as entertainments at courts and assemblies. Jeff Opland has collected and commented on a number of similar references made by English writers of the Anglo-Saxon period. What we cannot assume about the Icelandic examples—there has always been less tendency to do so about the English ones—is that the *texts* that were performed on these occasions enjoyed either a prior or a subsequent existence, beyond the fleeting moment of their performance. The fact that later writers in England and Iceland do seem to suppose that preliterate oral performers had memorized their texts ought to count for very little. The question for us is unavoidable: where did Snorri and the other Icelandic collectors—or for that matter the scribes of the *Beowulf* manuscript—get their traditional poetic texts?

This question cannot be answered with certainty, but it can be approached in terms of the classic Parry/Lord model of oral tradition, in which the memory of fixed texts plays little or no role.[6] A number of scholars have documented the presence in eddic poetry of the formulaic diction that in the Parry/Lord hypothesis is the primary evidence of oral composition (Harris, Lönnroth, Pàroli, Meletinsky, Gurevi, Sigurðsson). Such formulas make it possible for a performer to sing or recite verse with the same fluency that a speaker might deliver a speech in prose. Many of the formulas in eddic poetry simply move the narrative forward and would scarcely be considered formulaic in any significant sense were it not for the fact that they satisfy the rules of poetic meter and alliteration. For example, *einu sinni*, "once," makes a good half-verse and is used that way five times in a *b*-verse (e.g., "Á leit Guðrún   einu sinni") and four times in an *a*-verse (e.g., "einu sinni   af öllum hug"), always, of course, as in these examples, with vowel alliteration. Only slightly less frequent are *öðru sinni* and *þriðja sinni*. Another example of a simple narrative formula is the alliterating pair *einn*, "one," "only," "alone," and *allir*, "all," in the sense "one is *X*er than all," for example, "Varð einn borinn   öllum meiri" (Vsk 14), "One was born greater than all," and "eitt er þeirra   öllum betra" (HHj 8), "one of them is better than all."[7] This formula occurs seventeen times in eddic poetry.

The study of formulas becomes more interesting when we move from colorless structural idioms of this sort toward culturally specific ideas. For example, another very common formula type in eddic poetry, as in Old English narrative poetry, is the whole-line formula naming the speaker and his or her father (e.g., "Vaknaði Brynhildr   Buðla dóttur"; "Brynhildr awakened, the daughter of Buðli"). Brynhildr is identified as Buðli's daughter seven times in this way and one time when the epithet *dóttur Buðla* appears in an *a*-verse. Sigurðr goes by the epithet *burr Sigmundar* or *Sigmundar burr* five times. Related to these very common patronymic epithets is a fixed formula of introduction combining the words *ek heiti*, "I am named," with the phrase *hét minn faðir*, "my father was named":

Hrímgerðr ek heiti,	Hati hét minn faðir	HHj 17
Andvari ek heiti,	Óinn hét minn faðir	Rgn 2
Sigurðr ek heiti,	Sigmundr hét minn faðir	Ffn 4
Vindkaldr ek heiti,	Várkaldr hét minn faðir	Fls 6
Svipdagr ek heiti,	Sólbjartr hét minn faðir	Fls 47

More mythic is a set of epithets applied to gods and kings in their roles as "lords." Formulas with *dróttinn* can be made to fill a *b*-verse: *hafra dróttinn*, "lord of he-goats" (twice), *þursa dróttinn*, "lord of giants" (four times). Sigurðr is called *seggja dróttinn* and Gunnarr *gumna dróttinn*, both meaning "lord of men" but varying to provide the appropriate alliteration. Gunnar is also *Gotna dróttinn*, "lord of the Goths." The attraction between two words cannot always be explained as a matter of alliterative convenience as the association here of Gunnarr with *Gotar* and *gumnar*. In some cases the frequency of a pairing suggests an inherited image. For example the association of *drekka*, "to drink," and the adjective *dýrr*, "precious," "noble," in *dýrr mjöðr*, "precious mead," and *dýr veig*, "precious drink," suggests that *dýrr* might not work in free variation with just any word beginning with a *d* but is more precisely bound to the image of drink:

drykk ins dýra mjaðar	Háv 105
ok ek drykk of gat ins dýra mjaðar	Háv 140
Vel skulum drekka dýrar veigar	HHu II 46
Hann skal drekka dýrar veigar	Hnd 34
drekka ok dæma dýrar veigar	Hlð 16

Similar traditional images do not even involve alliteration in associating one word with another in a formula. Like Óðinn, the raven (*hrafn*) is associated with the high (*hár*) gallows (*meiðr* or *galgi*):

hrafn kvað at hrafni, —sat á hám meiði	HHu I 5
hrafn af meiði hátt kallaði	Sgk I 9
Hrafn flýgr austan af hám meiði	Hlm 8
Horskir hrafnar skulu þér á hám galga	Fls 45

Another of the culturally specific formulaic images familiar to students of Old English heroic poetry is the giving and receiving of "rings." Of the more than thirty occurrences of the word *baugr*, "ring," nearly every one is involved in some kind of formula. A conspicuous half-line formula is *baugar rauðir*, "red, that is, golden rings."

rauðir baugar ok in ríkja mær	HHu I 56
—bíðk-a ek þess bót,— bauga rauða	Vln 19
þér býðr bróðir bauga rauðar	HHu II 35
Bitt þú, Sigurðr, bauga rauða	Ffn 40
bauga rauða burar Sigmundar	Sgk II 39
Buðu þeir árla bauga rauða	Odg 21
Buðum vit þegnum bauga rauða	Odg 26

In addition, there are *ljósir*, "bright," and *fagrir*, "fair," *baugar* in less frequent formulas. These few examples may suffice to illustrate the densely formulaic quality of eddic verse. More detail is likely to be tedious to the nonspecialist.

The Parry/Lord model was developed to describe orally composed epic poetry, and the eddic lays are too short and episodic to be called epic. But from the work of Parry and Lord the possibility has arisen of considering the relationship between epic and eddic poetry in a new way. Rather than conceiving of oral epic as a text, a thing accomplished in a single performance, it is more reasonable to consider it as an especially rich cultural competence. Epic, like other oral traditions, is *langue*, not *parole*. It is a narrative form that depends for its creation upon an oral tradition that is supported by an aristocratic and heroic culture. And yet the epic poem as we habitually conceive it cannot be *experienced* as a single unified and coherent whole until its generative culture has given way to a later stage of development, namely, one in which writing is used in the recording of texts.

Medieval Scandinavia did not produce a written form of epic that we know of. Writing, when it came, was used for things more attuned to the stable, learned, ecclesiastical and courtly cultures that sponsored it. Decisive in this matter was the Icelanders' emphasis on developing a narrative prose fiction that grew out of their own national history. The old preliterate epic did not die altogether, however. Contemporaneously with the family sagas, a more modest place was given to the ancient Germanic myths and legends in eddic poems and legendary sagas. In the mind of the Compiler of Codex Regius, the eddic poems were very much like epic episodes in the mind of an oral performer. They existed for him and could be fully comprehended and appreciated only in a much larger world of story. This fact alone, without considering in a more particular way the character of the poems themselves, suggests that they are survivals of something much larger—calcareous deposits, crystallizations that have been precipitated from a large solution of myth and legend. It is clear, in other words, that the eddic poems are late, not early—relics, not progenitors. Like the closely related legendary sagas, the poems of Codex Regius assumed a literary form that was congenial to the tastes of a people whose imaginations no longer dwelt in epic but who were nonetheless capable of acknowledging, tolerating, even creating new fictional forms out of the contradictions between myth and history, both of which they understood the importance of preserving.

Notes

1 Klaeber's text reads, "Swylce wæs þeaw hyra, / hæþenra hyht." The whole project of distinguishing between the habits of mind associated with orality and those associated with literacy, including this one of continuity or discontinuity with the past, received an important impetus with the publication in 1963 of Jack Goody and Ian Watt's article "The Consequences of Literacy." Since then, the work of Havelock and of Ong has been widely influential, with more specialized medieval situations being the province of Bäuml.

2 I will use the terms *edda, poetic edda,* and *eddic poetry* interchangeably to refer to the poems in the Codex Regius 2365, 4^0 (which, by the way, does not call itself edda) and to similar poems found in other manuscript collections and in the legendary sagas (*fornaldasögur*). These terms have arisen through association with an imaginary poetic "edda" that tradition attributed to Sæmundur the Wise. The only actual book entitled *Edda* in the Middle Ages was a quite different work, the very important prose treatise on myth and poetics by Snorri Sturluson, to whom I will refer a number of times in this essay. For the texts of eddic poems, I will cite the normalized-spelling edition of *Eddukvæði* by Guðni Jónsson, although I am much indebted also to the standard edition, entitled *Edda,* edited by Gustav Neckel. The translations are mine.

3 There is much of value about "authors," "scribes," "compilers," "editors," and so forth in thirteenth-century Icelandic historical writing in Tómasson, 180–194 and throughout.

4. This in itself is actually a familiar epic topos in the poems, where it is not a signal of quite the same type of belatedness as may be attributed to it in thirteenth-century prose. The epic form is illustrated in Old English *in gear-dagum* and Icelandic *í árdaga*. The very idiomatic Icelandic phrase is found, incidentally, thirteen times in eddic poetry and, except for once in *Völuspá,* always (as in the opening of *Beowulf*) at the end of the line.

5 *Hávamál* could be said to name itself in the final stanza (164): "Nú eru Háva mál kveðin / Háva höllu í" (Now are the sayings of Hávi [the High One, Oðinn] recited / in Hávi's hall). The case of *Oddrúnargrátr* is similar but more interesting. The poem ends with Atli's sister Oddrún saying, "nú er of genginn / grátr Oddrúnar," by which she means "Now the weeping of Oddrún is over." Mistaking *event* for the *telling* of it, later scribes and editors thought she was saying her poem was over

(as the *Hávamál* announced the simultaneous conclusion of event and telling) and have called the poem *Oddrún's Weeping*. Recognizing the error, Guðni Jónsson entitles the poem *Oddrúnarkviða* (*The Poem of Oddrún*) in his edition.

6 Since Magoun's "Oral-Formulaic Character," a vast literature applied the ideas of Milman Parry and Albert B. Lord to all of the vernacular literatures of medieval Europe, the most convenient guide to which is John Miles Foley's *Oral-Formulaic Theory and Research*. The most detailed and scholarly discussion I have seen recently on the oral background of edda is Harris, "Eddic Poetry as Oral Poetry." Lars Lönnroth, too, has a series of articles on the topic, especially "Iorð fannz æva né upphiminn: A Formula Analysis."

7 The abbreviations of titles of eddic poems are the ones I used in my *Concordance:* Ffn (Fáfnismál), Fls (Fjölsvinnsmál), Háv (Hávamál), HHj (Helgakviða Hjörvarðssonar), HHU I, II (Helgakviða Hundingsbana I, II), Hlð (Hlöðskviða), Hlm (Hjálmarskviða), Hnd (Hyndluljóð), Odg (Oddrúnargrátr), Rgn (Reginsmál), Sgk (Sigurðarkviða), Vln (Völundarkviða), Vsk (Völuspá in skamma).

6 *Hanna Vollrath*

Oral Modes of Perception in Eleventh-Century Chronicles

The question of the transition from memory to written record in the Middle Ages is very much the question of the dynamics of this period. If we come to understand what it really means—the transformation of a society that functions through the physical presence of the spoken word into one that relies on impersonal media—then we will be better able to understand the fundamental changes not only in medieval European society but also in many societies of the Third World of today, because "the appearance of literacy in a society formerly dependent on oral communication can contribute to the way in which individuals perceive issues, frame them in language, and evolve systems of interpretation" (Stock 5). Brian Stock relates the transformation of medieval society from around the year 1000 onward to a change in the role of written texts in this society, claiming that "after 1000, oral discourse increasingly functioned within a framework of legal and institutional textuality" (10). Stock is very convincing when he treats this change in the area of social organization, of reform movements and scholarly theology and philosophy, and in the rise of heresies, but less so, in my opinion, when he treats the use of metaphors and other interpretive devices by some medieval historians.

I will start from the same basic point Stock does. I will first render his theoretical assumption in my own simpler words: I start with the hypothesis that literate knowledge is of a different type and structure than that transmitted orally and that true familiarity with book knowledge will affect the way people perceive their own world. The question is, how exactly does it do that? In regard to religion, the anthropologist Jack Goody maintains that literate religions influence the normative structure of a social system toward universalism, because "written formulations encourage the decontextualization or generalization of norms" (*Logic* 12). But exactly what kind of mental operation is necessary for decontextualization on the one hand and for the fitting of general norms into a given context on the other?

I have selected three chronicles written in the eleventh century by ecclesiastics or monks living and working in the German part of the Imperium. The oldest of them, Thietmar von Merseburg, finished his chronicle shortly before his death in 1018. Hermann the Lame finished his chronicle in 1054.[1] Frutolf von Michelsberg wrote up to the year 1099. Times had changed considerably in the course of the century in which these historians were writing. Thietmar stands as a witness to an unperturbed coexistence and cooperation of *regnum* and *sacerdotium* (royal—or rather lay—and clerical power) within an all-embracing *ecclesia*.[2] Around the middle of the century the sources reveal the first phase of the movement for Church reform. From the mid-fifties onward a more radical faction established itself within the reform movement.[3] It later crystalized around Gregory VII, who became pope in 1073. The Gregorians claimed that all bad customs ultimately stemmed from lay intervention in Church affairs. Consequently they worked toward an ecclesia which was to be run solely by the anointed agents of the hierarchy. That amounted to nothing less than the overthrow of the old order (see Tellenbach, *Libertas*). The Gregorians claimed to be reestablishing the primitive Church that Christ himself had founded on Peter the Rock, and they used canon law as an instrument to achieve this end.

It has long been noticed that the Gregorians substantiated their convictions by a more literary use of the old texts, thus transforming "the basic skill of reading and writing into instruments of analysis and interpretation" (Stock 11). This transformation is, I think, equivalent to an act of abstraction: people no longer just read or copied letters, words, and sentences; they treated them not as fixed, self-contained entities with a kind of hermetic reality of their own in manuscripts and scriptoria but as instruments conveying meaning. Meaning, however, is never an entity in singularity; something is only meaningful in a context, as part of a reference system. The distinction between the very word and the meaning that word conveys allows the gap to be bridged between a normative Latin text and the lived reality, which, of course, was experienced and talked about in the vernacular. Only texts that are analyzed for their meaning can be made an integral part of decision-making in the lived world. It was this analytic approach to the old texts that enabled the Church reformers to notice the discrepancies between the ancient legal rules and the prevailing customs and uses in the Church, which were orally transmitted and which, when seen in the light of the texts, appeared as bad customs, as abuses.[4]

What the Church reformers from the second half of the eleventh century onward tried to do was to integrate the venerated old texts into the world they lived in. They overcame the texts' seclusion and singularity by establishing their meaning as the normative point of reference in concrete experiences, thus superseding a reference system that consisted of orally transmitted customs. This was really a new way of experiencing and judging that part of the world affected by the new use of the texts. How far across the intellectual spectrum did it go? Was it restricted to the intellectual avant-garde, or did the "normal" historians like the ones under discussion participate in that change of perception? Does Frutolf, who was a scholar, show different modes of perceiving and evaluating the events he relates from Thietmar and Hermann, who lived before the texts of the ecclesiastical tradition acquired that different quality? The test cases will be decisions that lead to conflicts either among ecclesiastics or between ecclesiastics and the lay powers, including the king. How did these three historians perceive decisions and the ensuing conflicts? Do they give judgment, and if so, what is their point of reference?

I will start with a letter written in 1085 by the papal legate Odo of Ostia, a Frenchman, who became Pope Urban II in 1088 (see Vogel; Becker). Odo undoubtedly belonged to the intellectual elite of his age. His letter is an example of the analytic and interpretive approach to tradition that allowed the integration of an old ecclesiastical normative sentence into a given situation. The background of the letter is as follows: From about 1070 a conflict between the German emperor Henry IV and the papacy had been building over the question of episcopal investitures; Henry claimed the traditional right of investiture. This conflict coincided with a struggle between Henry IV and Saxony, part of Henry's kingdom. The Saxons virtually ended Henry's rule in their province by expelling him and his followers (see Leyser). It must be stressed that the Saxon uprising was quite distinct from the investiture contest in its underlying causes. We have two battlefields in the second half of the eleventh century—one, in which Henry had the pope and the pope's ecclesiastical party for his enemies, and the other, in which the Saxon magnates were fighting Henry for "Saxon" reasons. When Pope Gregory VII banned Henry IV in the year 1076, the Saxon opposition advocated the election of a new king, saying that they could not accept someone as the anointed of the Lord who had been cut off from the body of the Church by the pope's ban. This meant that the ecclesiastical and the lay enemies of Henry IV combined forces (see Fenske). Although Henry managed to free himself from the papal ban by begging forgiveness for his sins from Gregory at Canossa, a new king was nevertheless elected by his German enemies in March 1077. There were ups and downs for both sides in the following years, but in the main the constellation of the seventies prevailed in the eighties: the pope renewed the ban in 1080, the Saxons and their allies in other German duchies remained hostile, and civil war disrupted large parts of the kingdom. "Therefore," as a contemporary writer of King Henry's party put it, "it was decided with the approval of the bishops of both sides, that, since this long fought-over case could not be decided by swords, it should be ended by books" ("terminaretur libris").[5] By the authority of the holy canons, it was to be judged on which side justice lay (Frutolf 100). Both sides elected learned ("litterati") and eloquent men and convened for a disputation at Gerstungen and Berka.[6] The papal legate Odo was present. He wrote what we would call an open letter shortly after the conference to quell rumors that Henry's party had won the disputation by their arguments.[7] Although it is obvious that the legate Odo was far from being a neutral observer, it is worth considering his version of the debate to find out how he deals with the books that were supposed to end the conflict.

According to his letter, the rebel party first defended the pope's right to excommunicate Henry by quoting and interpreting Christ's words to the apostles in Matthew 16.9: "Whatever you bind on earth shall be bound in heaven, and whatever you loose on earth shall be loosed in heaven." To this the Henricians responded that their lord had not been excommunicated, because he could not be excommunicated. To prove their point, they quoted a passage from the introduction of Pseudo-Isidore which Odo fully includes in his letter: "According to canonical legislation, no one deprived of his belongings or ousted from his episcopal see by force or terror can be accused, summoned, judged, and sentenced unless full legal restitution has been made allowing him to enjoy his rights freely and peacefully" (cf. *Decretales Ps.-Isidorianae* 18). The sentence that follows in Pseudo-Isidore applies the same procedure to a woman who had been repudiated by her husband under the suspicion of adultery— restitution first and then the answering of charges. From this the Henricians drew the conclusion that this sentence applied to everybody and not just to bishops. "For the rude and illiterate," as Odo put it, the Henricians argued that, since their lord had been ejected from Saxony by rebellious force, any legal action against him—such as the pope's excommunication—was against canon law and therefore without force.

It is obvious that the Henricians took the procedural rule literally, at face value. We will return to their method of treating the text in a moment. What is of immediate interest is the analytical and interpretive treatment of the text by which Odo refutes their argument. He accuses them of perverting the meaning of the quotation by false interpretation. If this doctrine, he says, should spread in the Church, anyone deprived of a horse, an ox, or a donkey could not be made to answer for perjury, incest, or any other spiritual matter in an ecclesiastical court. Odo arrives at a distinction between the sentence and its meaning by reflecting on the *method* of argumentation, which is clearly an act of abstraction. He finds fault with the formal structure of their argument, which runs that anybody deprived of something cannot be made to answer any charge. In this, he says, they treat as an absolute law that which was meant as a *discreta interpositio* by Pseudo-Isidore, that is, valid only in a corresponding context. To shorten Odo's rather long exposition, let us condense his version of Pseudo-Isidore even more than he does: if someone has a charge against somebody and takes by way of force what he considers his right, the accused is not obliged to answer any charge in the appropriate court until the *status quo ante* has been restored. Odo does not state it so briefly, but he undoubtedly is looking for the legal principle, the meaning of the text, and treats the bishop expelled from his see and the woman repudiated by her husband as examples to elucidate the underlying principle. He distinguishes between the legal rule and the diversities of situations in which it might be applied. This way of treating a text is equivalent to taking the text of the canon law out of its isolation and considering the relevant circumstances.[8]

Now that we have seen how a member of the intellectual avant-garde in the late eleventh century treated a text, let us turn to Thietmar von Merseburg of the early eleventh century and see what he does with texts. In the third book of his *Chronicle* (chaps. 12–15, pp. 98–108), Thietmar relates an incident that took place in 981 and concerned his own bishopric of Merseburg. The emperor Otto the Great had founded Merseburg in 968 as the fulfillment of a vow taken in 955. As the worldly endowment of the new foundation was to come from the neighboring bishoprics and as canon law required the consent of the bishops in such cases, Otto spent time and trouble to get that consent. The bishop of Halberstadt remained adamant, however. He never gave his approval of the diminution of his see.[9] As far as we know, the breach of canon law that occurred when Otto went ahead anyway had no legal consequences for many years, until, in fact, a disputed election to the archiepiscopal see of Magdeburg created a situation in which this legal fault of the past came in handy.

Adalbero, archbishop of Magdeburg, had made it very clear that he did not want one Ohtric for his successor; Ohtric nevertheless got elected after Adalbero's death by the "clergy and the people," as Thietmar put it in order to indicate that he considered the election canonical. A delegation from Magdeburg was dispatched to Emperor Otto III, who resided in Rome at the time, to obtain the emperor's approval and investiture. To achieve this end it tried to engage the support of Giselher, then bishop of Merseburg, who was a favorite of the emperor. It soon turned out, however, that they had picked the wrong person, as Giselher himself wanted to become archbishop. This would have meant a translation from one see, Merseburg, to another, Magdeburg, a thing forbidden by canon law. Thietmar relates how Giselher achieved his end anyhow:

There was a universal synod held in Rome. The wisest of men convened so that the prophecy of Jeremiah might be fulfilled: "How the bright gold is obscured and its best color changed." The pope told the judges that Giselher did not have a regular see, as his [Merseburg] had been unjustly taken from Halberstadt. When the pope asked the judges whether Giselher could be promoted to the archbishopric of Magdeburg, they affirmed with canonical authority, giving words and examples that this could lawfully be done, not minding David's admonition: "Judge rightfully, ye sons of men," and the other saying: "A corrupt judge cannot discern that which is right."

It is evident what the pope's argument was: Merseburg's foundation had involved a breach of canon law so, legally, it never existed and so it does not exist now and so Giselher is not its bishop and hence no translation is necessary for him to become archbishop. Thietmar goes on to say that this meant the end of the bishopric of Merseburg for several years.

Thietmar makes it clear beyond dispute that he considered the whole transaction illegal. Like the legate Odo, he is convinced that canonical authority was falsely applied, but unlike Odo, he does not give any arguments to substantiate his conviction. He could have argued that the factual existence of Merseburg for as many as thirteen years had established rights or that Giselher's episcopal unction was not invalidated by the fact that it was given on false grounds. But he does not do anything of the sort. He has the vague feeling that the reference to canon law was a mere pretext to legitimize something that had been decided on quite different grounds—which it certainly was. But he is helpless in dealing with the problem intellectually. He experiences canonical authority as the quotation of a text that he can either accept or deny, God forbid. So he accepts it, but he also accepts Merseburg's right to exist. Both are right for him. The trouble is that they contradict each other.

Thietmar experiences the canon law text as an intruder into his own legal world, and he has no means of establishing it as an integral part of the world he lives in. Biblical quotations and a reference to the undiscernible judgment of God, sometimes obscure but never unjust, have to make up for the deficiency. Thietmar comes to regard the whole affair as the punishment for the sins of "all of us," as he says. This explanation has a distinct function: it gives meaning to a situation that Thietmar experiences as being devoid of meaning because it is contradictory. There is a striking difference in Odo's approach. For Odo it is the meaning of the text that was established through analysis and interpretation, while for Thietmar it is the meaning of the situation. The one allows for the integration of the text into the given legal situation; the other sees the two as separate entities and plasters up the gap between them by an appeal to higher, supernatural wisdom. The one is particular in its arguments, the other takes refuge in universal truths.

The second case is similar in structure to Thietmar's story. Hermann the Lame relates an event that took place in 1032 and concerned his own monastery of Reichenau, which ended up losing a privilege that Hermann considered to be its rightful possession. This is what he has to say:

Abbot Bern of Reichenau sent the privileges of his monastery to Rome and received in return a privilege together with episcopal sandals from Pope John, allowing him to celebrate mass in episcopal garments. This aroused the bishop of Constance, who accused the abbot before the emperor of having infringed upon his office and his honor. Both—the emperor and the bishop—kept bullying the abbot until he gave up both the privilege and the sandals to be burnt publicly in the bishop's synod on March 30. That same year the monastery of Buchau burnt down, on January 12. (666–67)

We know from a papal privilege of Gregory V (996–99) that the abbot of Reichenau had received the right to celebrate mass in episcopal garments as far back as 998 (Böhmer-Zimmermann, no. 825). It must have been one of the privileges the abbot had sent to Rome to be confirmed and for which he received a confirmation charter in return. Apparently the abbots of Reichenau had not exercised this old right of theirs in the meantime. The monks of Reichenau might not even have known about it until Bern, renowned for his learning, rediscovered the old document. The bishop of Constance, to whose diocese Reichenau belonged, regarded the abbot's renewed honor as an infringement upon his own rights. Evidently his criterion for legitimacy was oral customary law, in which right and wrong depended on legal memory. Right was what people remembered to have always been the way it was. A right the owner stopped exercising would soon fall into oblivion and thereby cease to be a right. Written law, on the other hand, does not depend on continual practice. When the abbot of Reichenau reactivated his old right to wear episcopal garments and corroborated it by papal charters—both ancient and recent—he clashed with an oral legal system in which continued practice functioned as a point of reference for establishing legitimacy. The oral system prevailed, and the written document was eliminated, not just mentally, as in Thietmar's case, but physically, by cremation.

And again, Hermann, like Thietmar, is unable to cope with the situation, although he is in a better position than Thietmar was, who had been confronted with the problem that canon law had been employed to contradict what he believed to be right. In Hermann's case, the papal privilege as the written legal text and his own legal convictions nicely corroborate each other, yet Hermann is at a loss to understand just why the bishop with the support of the emperor was able to deprive Reichenau of its right anyhow. So, like Thietmar, he takes refuge in the idea of supernatural justice. He mentions the burning of the monastery of Buchau right after relating the burning of the papal privilege and sandals at the episcopal synod, although the monastery burnt several weeks *before* the synod. By stressing that it happened "the same year," he clearly connects the two incidents, letting the burning of Buchau appear as God's revenge for the bishop's wrongdoing. Once again, we see superhuman justice having to right a wrong that had arisen because two different legal systems had clashed and legal texts could not be integrated into the legal system based on orality.

Let us return to the first case that was mentioned, the conference at Gerstungen and Berka in 1085. The bishops of the two opposing parties met—the Henricians and the combined parties of the rebellious Saxons and the Gregorians. They came together to discover truth and justice through books of canon law. The papal legate's interpretive treatment of the canon law text was quite different from that of the Henricians, who quoted a passage from Pseudo-Isidore that said nobody who had been deprived of his belongings could be summoned, judged, or sentenced. The papal legate Odo declared this to be a perversion of the meaning of the text, which must not be understood absolutely, that is, literally, but read in its proper setting.

Frutolf von Michelsberg included an account of the debate in his chronicle:

The Archbishop of Mainz, who was the spokesman of King Henry's party, said that the emperor had been wronged both by the pope and by the princes of the kingdom, adding that he had been driven out of Saxony and deprived of his regnal power by the Saxon upheavals and that therefore canon law forbade his being summoned or judged or sentenced. The Archbishop of Salzburg, the spokesman of the rebels, tried to prove this to be false, saying that nobody was absolved—*absolutum*—from divine law, least of all the king, who did not hold Saxony as a personal possession, but as a realm of the Lord God, who gives it to whomever he wishes, as is testified by Daniel and by King Nebuchadnezzar. Also Henry had refused to give satisfaction to the pope *before* he had lost Saxony. (100–101)

Frutolf's report contains the same argumentative elements as Odo's letter, and yet Frutolf has a completely different way of perceiving the legal arguments and hence the whole situation. Frutolf renders the canon law text from Pseudo-Isidore quoted by the Henricians, and he obviously knows that the opposing party has argued that it should not be understood "absolutely"—*absolute*. But he or whoever told him the story missed the point: Frutolf does not relate the word *absolute* to the understanding of the text, as Odo had done, but to humans not being absolved (*absolutum*) from divine law, which he holds as synonymous with the will of God. Least of all is a king so absolved, because God gives and takes kingdoms as he wishes. Whereas Odo tried to get at the legal *principle* of the canon law text to refute the literal understanding of the

Henricians, Frutolf makes both sides treat and understand the text literally. In letting the Gregorians argue that the text could not be applied to Henry because a kingdom was not just any kind of property, he indirectly admits that the canon law text would apply if it *were* a normal kind of property. In the given situation this would mean that if the Saxons had deprived Henry of a couple of horses instead of part of his kingdom, the excommunication by the pope would have been considered illegal.

Let us try to visualize the situation to get a little further. After many years of civil war, both sides agreed to find out in the books which side was favored by the authority of the canons. So on both sides, one may presume, learned men got busy to find ammunition in the books with which to fight for their cause. It must have been a happy find for King Henry's men when they hit upon the canon laid down in Pseudo-Isidore and quite an unexpected one for the rebel party. The papal legate Odo wrote his letter after the conference to squelch rumors about the other side's success. Many of those present, denounced as rude and illiterate by Odo, seem to have been convinced by the canon and hence regarded King Henry's excommunication as illegal. It might very well have been that the Gregorians had little to say contrary to the canon at the moment it was presented. It looks to me as if Odo had to step in with his analytical and rationalizing refutation of the Henricians' interpretation of the text because his companions had not known how to cope with the quotation and had muddled the whole affair. It might very well have been, in fact, that Odo himself, who had been present at the conference, had not known how to reason against the Henricians immediately and that only after reading and reflecting upon the canon law text later, "at his desk," had he been able to develop the categorizing concepts that allowed him to refute his opponents. Jack Goody's observation is very much to the point: "Reading permits a greater distancing between individual, language, and reference than speech, a greater objectification which increases the analytic potential of the human mind" (*Logic* 142). In any case, at a time when an intellectual like Odo of Ostia could discern the meaning, the sense, and the underlying principle of a text and discuss it rationally, under whatever circumstances it might be applied, the majority of his contemporaries still used the text as a ready-to-serve weapon very much as they would have used a club to bang their truth into the heads of their enemies. For them the world functioned according to the rules of an oral legal system in which a text remained a stranger. It was accepted when it corroborated what everyone already knew, and it was eliminated when it disturbed prevalent convictions.

If we presume oral perception that is *not* governed by abstract notions embodied in a text to be essentially singular and concrete, then we may very well say that Frutolf, just like Thietmar and Hermann, treats a text "orally," as a single entity, as a kind of thing, in fact as an instrument or weapon. The text is as little a part of the decision-making and judging process as in earlier times. When Brian Stock says that "after 1000, oral discourse increasingly functioned within a framework of legal and institutional textuality," we will have to add that the change must have escaped the absolute majority of the population, as even a learned monk at the end of the century was unable to integrate a text into his world.

Notes

1 The standard edition of Thietmar von Merseburg's *Chronik* is Holzmann's; here page references are to Trillmich's edition, based on Holzmann's. References to Hermann the Lame's *Chronicle* are to Buchner's edition in *Quellen,* which is based on Pertz's edition.

2 For a discussion of the Ottonian *Reichskirche,* see Fleckenstein, *Grundlagen* and "Begriff"; cf. the critical assessment of Fleckenstein by Reuter, and Fleckenstein's reply, "Problematik."

3 The movement of Church reform and the ensuing investiture contest is not particular to any one country but is essentially part of the history of Latin Europe as a whole. For a general introduction, see the Cambridge Medieval History, and Southern, *Making of the Middle Ages.* For the problem in the context of German history, see Tellenbach, *Westliche Kirche;* Keller; and Haverkamp.

4 Schieffer, *Entstehung,* stresses that the Church reform movement of the eleventh century was essentially a matter of changing perception, that is, of a growing awareness of incongruities that had previously existed for centuries without causing much discomfort; see also Schieffer, "Priesterbild."

5 *De unitate ecclesiae conservandae,* 2.18 (MGH, Lib. de lite 2, 234).

6 For a discussion of the sources concerning this meeting, see Meyer von Knonau 3–9, and Robinson, 105–9.

7 The letter is edited in Erdmann and Fickermann 375–80.

8 In some Saxon narrative sources, namely the "Annalista Saxo" and the "Annales Magdeburgenses," another "Gregorian" account has survived that follows an argumentative procedure very close to that in Odo's letter. Erdmann (204) attributes this account to the polemical anti-Henrician Bernhard of Hildesheim.

9 For the founding of Halberstadt, see Beumann 103.

PART THREE
STAGING THE POET'S PRESENCE

Introduction

Oral poets stand in front of their audiences, audience and poet physically present, the performance shaped by that double presence. But what happens to the "performance" when sounds become letters? Again we face the fact that medieval words survive only in writing. Here we see how extant texts show traces of the profound change from orality to writing and present the stresses and conflicts involved in that transition. Once again we face events. These events take place in the tenth through the fifteenth centuries and involve the different ways the poets are present before their audiences and the role writing plays in those relationships. The poet's presence is always meaningful, but technology alters the means for staging that presence, and the meaning of that presence changes in relation to the technology. The tensions reverberate between tradition and the individual poet and between the physicality of performance and the disembodied, decontextualized potential of reading.

By the tenth century in Anglo-Saxon England, vernacular poems exist in manuscripts, divorced from the poets who would have performed them in a purely oral culture, but still ready to be voiced and heard. Ursula Schaefer theorizes the semiotics of this transitional situation, in which performing and hearing remain vital elements of communicating meaning, even while essential elements of that situation have been cut loose—the poet and a unitary context for creation and performance. This change requires a compensation, a fictional first person. Schaefer distinguishes, however, this "conditional fictionality" from a fully literary textuality, which operates in a manner relatively autonomous from the context in which one reads it, because of its autoreferentiality. In contrast, medieval "vocality" (Schaefer uses Zumthor's term) is not autonomous at all, nor is it a fictional equivalent for reality; it is anchored through the nature of its formulaic language to its cultural contexts and traditional truths. The poems stored up in manuscripts must stay within this semiotics, and to do so, they include the language to create the speaker or "knower" for the poem—they stage the poet's presence. The situation that writing created of removing the poet from the performance was something

115

new, a site of struggle and innovation. Schaefer shows us its traces in the poetry of Cynewulf, perhaps the most lettered of Old English poets.

Stephen G. Nichols discusses a more learned struggle in twelfth-century France, again over the presence of the poet and the voice of the body. In the milieu of the troubadour's performance, the written text does not disappear. Against Zumthor's theory, Nichols argues that the poet's presence is double, that the body is an instrument for writing as well as singing, and that troubadour songs exhibit the tension between voice and letter that reverberates in the Middle Ages. By the twelfth century, vocalized poetry is thoroughly lettered, and it participates in a long-standing philosophical argument about the relationship between speech and writing. Discussing Augustine and his relation to Plato and Aristotle, Nichols reveals the position troubadour performances assume in this argument, using Guillaume IX as his example. Here he sees a "battleground" in which Augustine's distrust of the body and its sensuality is countered by the troubadour's use of the body both as an instrument of performance based on and subsuming writing and as a trope for the transference of sexual to verbal power. Contra Augustine but following Aristotle, the body is the source of textual authority.

Names of poets—Guillaume IX and Cynewulf—are attached to the vernacular texts both Nichols and Schaefer discuss. Their signatures gesture toward the poet's presence in spite of his or her absence from the manuscript and toward the poem's reperformance through a reader. Laurence de Looze moves our attention to this innovative textuality per se, theorizing the shifting relation between reader and author implicated in changing strategies of "authorial self-naming." He examines terms for the author used from the twelfth through the fifteenth centuries in France to discover changing ideas about what an author does in relation to text and audience. He studies their methods of signing, from Turoldus's straightforward insertion of his name at the end of the *Chanson de Roland* to Machaut's complicated anagrams and Christine de Pizan's directions for voicing her name. In this process, de Looze reveals that a "new complicity between author and reader" transpires as writing becomes more thoroughly infixed. Knowledge of the author becomes so important that the readers must know the author's name before they can unravel an anagram; conversely, the signature has no definitive meaning without the reader's participation. The author's name, then, motivates a culturally significant, hermeneutical activity, which, as de Looze makes clear, complicates considerably Foucauldian analyses of the author function.

C. B. P.

Hearing from Books: The Rise of Fictionality in Old English Poetry

It is widely contended that medieval poetry lacks the autonomy which is the main characteristic of modern literary (i.e., fictional) discourse. Umberto Eco, for instance, has seen the reason in the *analogia entis* of the Scholastics, a "conception of the cosmos as a hierarchy of fixed, preordained orders" (*Role* 57). While true enough, there were other complementary circumstances that restricted the degree of autonomy that was achieved in modern texts. I see them in the use of and access to the written and the vocal medium and hence in the particular way in which poetry was typically communicated throughout the Middle Ages.

Particularly in the early Middle Ages, these circumstances must have been determined by what Paul Zumthor simply but insistently calls "le fait de l'oralité" (*Lettre* 17). Although in varying proportion, orality and literacy/writing existed side by side throughout the Middle Ages, with the oral-aural medium the prevailing mode of transmission, regardless of whether the message had an oral source or existed in writing and was subsequently voiced again. In *La lettre et la voix* (1987) Zumthor has introduced yet another term which pays tribute to the specificity of medieval poetic communication: *vocality.*

The term implies a whole concept of medieval poetic communication. Zumthor makes the point that throughout the Middle Ages poetry was almost exclusively transmitted in what he has called "performance," the temporal coincidence of communication and reception (21). In 1983 he was already insisting on it: "The *performance* is the complex action through which a poetic message is simultaneously transmitted and perceived, here and now. Speaker, receiver(s), circumstances (no matter whether or not the text, by the way, through linguistic means represents them) are concretely confronted and are undeniable. In the performance the two axes of social communication intersect: the one that links the speaker to the author and the one through which situation and tradition are united." [1] The coincidence can obviously only occur in the oral-aural medium. In *La lettre et la voix* Zumthor definitively explains *vocality* as the realm in which the "physical aspect of medieval texts, their mode of existence as objects of sensorial perception" unfolds (21). To my mind vocality is thus the term, as well as the concept, by which medieval poetic communication can much more adequately be grasped than with the dichotomy "orality versus literacy."

Thus this specific "mode of existence" of medieval poetic communication as "objects of sensorial perception" may further account for its lack of autonomy compared with modern literature. Because medieval poetry was transmitted in vocality it was subject to the semiotics of orality. Oral signs do not "decay" into *signifiant* and *signifié*. [2] This holds for all speakers at any period in time, and for any language that is not confined to the realm of the written. Along these lines, Hans-Martin Gauger remarks about *Bedeutung* that the German word actually covers two things, namely *das Bedeuten,* the act of signifying, and *das Bedeutete,* the signified "thing": "Bedeutung ist also— als Bedeuten—etwas Akthaftes: das benennende Gerichtstsein des Wortes auf ein Ding." [3]

We tend to neglect this double orientation of language even when dealing with medieval poetry, because we usually approach literary phenomena with a fully literate conception of poetry. But an awareness of the prevailing vocality of the Middle Ages obliges us to conceive of its poetic discourses as sharing with all other (oral) utterances the dynamics of the extralinguistic world. [4] This is the semiotic reason for the lack of autonomy in medieval poetry.

This point obviously needs further substantiating. I will try to support it in four different steps, the first three of which are theoretical. I will briefly outline some major points of reception theory regarding the status of the literary text in order to show that this theory was developed on and for written material; it is indeed dealing with *literary* texts in the strict sense of this term. If nothing else, this short survey may have as its result the mapping out of some theoretical suppositions with which we should *not* approach texts originally received in vocality. My second step, also theoretical, will be to ask how reception in vocality may have functioned; I will refer to modern findings on oral signification, at the same time not denying that analogous conclusions must be drawn very cautiously. It should become obvious from the discussion as a whole, however, that vocal poetic communication is, to a large degree, context-dependent, thus differing in important ways from reading reception in general. My third and final theoretical step will be to concentrate on the phenomenon of the "poetic I."[5] I want to especially pursue a point made by Franz H. Bäuml in his receptionalist approach to the question of the share and the impact of orality and literacy in and on medieval poetry.[6] In this section it will become obvious that the special situation of medieval vocalized poetic communication leads to a seemingly paradoxical conclusion. The prevailing vocality both excludes fictionality and simultaneously re-creates it.

My fundamental argument, it suffices to say at this point, is that, by definition, vocality uses a voice. If the original voice was separated from the hearer because writing interfered, this voice had to be inscribed in the text as a fiction that could be actualized "as if" it were present at the time of the performance.

In the last part of this essay, I will illustrate my theoretical arguments with a discussion of Cynewulf, an Anglo-Saxon author who has repeatedly been cited as evidence both for and against the "Oral-Formulaic Theory." My aim will be to show how this conspicuously literate poet whom we call Cynewulf made use of his specific situation for poetic communication. I will subsequently suggest what, intentionally or not, has been the result of this use.

Literary Referentiality

To begin with, we should reconsider our notion of *text* and thus the phenomenological status of (poetic) discourse in writing and in vocality respectively.[7] In "From Utterance to Text: the Bias of Language in Speech and Writing," David Olson has suggested a distinction between *text* and *utterance* that actually returns him to the older use of the term *text* as referring exclusively to written discourse. Such a distinction is heuristically useful in order to keep us from approaching medieval poetry with questions that are phenomenologically not pertinent. Examining the modern theory of reception in its various manifestations in order to see how inseparable it is from writing helps one to realize how reception in vocality can *not* function.

Take for instance Michael Riffaterre's statements on how meaning is created in a text. In his fundamental book *Text Production,* he phrases it as a question: "Might it be that the text is its own referential system?" (34). It comes as no surprise that the answer is positive. Speaking of the semantics of a poem, Riffaterre a little later emphatically states that "the axis of significations is horizontal" (35). The autonomy of the literary text is phenomenologically sketched by him in the observation that with a piece of literature "the signified is deduced from the text" (15), that is, the signified cannot be found outside and independent of the text. Moreover, when Riffaterre speaks about "the textual nature" of the "literary verbal message," he characterizes literature as a "kind of message [which] is known only through texts" (2).

This coincides with other scholars' concepts of literary phenomenon, particularly of literary fictionality.[8] Riffaterre's claim that the literary text is its own referential system, or his dictum of the horizontal axis of significations in such a text, corresponds to what has been phrased by Karlheinz Stierle as "autoreferentiality of language in the form of pseudoreferentiality."[9] Fictional texts, Stierle argues, use language in a pseudoreferential way, which means that in such texts linguistic referentiality neither asks nor allows for extratextual verification. For Stierle the main characteristic of fiction is its "Charakter einer Setzung" ("nature of a nonverifiable assertion"; 356). And his argumentation eventually completely coincides with Riffaterre's when Stierle further qualifies the notion of "pseudoreferentiality" as the use of language where the "Referenzbedingungen nicht einfach als aussertextuelle Vorgaben übernommen, sondern durch den Text selbst erst erzeugt [werden]" ("conditions of reference [are] not taken over from extralinguistic givens but [are] rather produced by the text itself"; 362).

Given that the phenomenological and thus also the semiotic status of the text in vocality are necessarily different from the text to be read, Stierle has another important observation. While Riffaterre marks the "textual nature" as a "particular characteristic of the literary verbal message" (2), Stierle contends that autoreferentiality is not limited to fictional texts alone. In his view "systematic texts" share this characteristic of autoreferentiality. Stierle defines a "systematic text" as a text which "der Klärung der Verwendungsbedingungen seiner Termini dient" ("[itself] serves to clarify the conditions for the use of its own terms"; 363). Arguing in very much the same direction, David Olson has advanced the even more extreme position that for *all* (written) texts "the meaning [is] in the text" (264). This closure of the written text, its autoreferentiality and thus also its autoreflexivity, creates a relative autonomy, which in literary texts is pushed to the extreme of almost absolute autonomy.

Traditionality, Context, and Conventionality

In contrast with the written and read text, vocalized discourse presents itself to the hearer as open.[10] But it isn't sufficient to argue *ex negativo,* as my dealing with text theory may suggest. We have to seek for a positive delineation of how meaning is created and thus conferred in vocality. Because we are dealing with a culture long past, we have to look for evidence in an indirect way by seeing how far we can go in drawing analogous conclusions when we take our insights in contemporary auditive reception as the heuristic basis.

A number of features of medieval poetry have, up to now, been interpreted as indications of oral composition because they do indeed display similarities to (modern) spoken language. Among these features are, for instance, the prevalence of paratactic construction and what appears to modern readers to be highly ambiguous syntax when subordination does occur. Moreover, oblique pronominal references have been seen as paralleling the "restricted code" of dominant orality (largely untouched by written language).[11]

The strongest argument for oral composition—or at least residues of such a compositional process—has usually been seen in the "formulaicness" of medieval poetry.[12] I am skeptical about the cogency of the "argument from formulaicness" with regard to compositional origin.[13] If, however, we put the features seemingly indicating oral composition into the larger context of vocality, then we may reinterpret them as language use which was meaningful for the receivers. Hence these features should be considered as indicators not of composition but of successful communication on behalf of the receivers. Moreover, if we can account for these features as being characteristics of a specific semiotic procedure in contemporary oral communication, it should be legitimate to conclude that they worked in very much the same way in medieval poetic vocality.

With poetry in vocality (which is regarded here as a special case of orality), meaning was generated for the medieval receivers by their inferring a referential tie between text and context. Early medieval poetic discourse was thus taken as indexical, as pointing at the receivers' lifeworld. To elaborate on David Olson's observations, for the contemporary audience the meaning of the discourse was supposed to be found not in the text but in the context. The term *context*, it should be noted here, does not refer to the contiguous linguistic context. Rather *context* in this usage is meant to grasp all that is not intratextual.

Turning to concentrate on one of these features which are usually taken as evidence for oral composition, formulaicness, I must be more specific about what I mean.[14] I turn again to a definition from Zumthor: "In that [medieval] society formulaicness refers to everything within the discourses and the modes of utterance which has the tendency of being resaid continuously in a manner hardly diversified, of reproducing itself with minimal and [yet] countless variations."[15] Obviously this is a much broader concept of formula and formulaic expression than Parry/Lord's. In particular it is not restrictively seen from the point of view of the poetic composer but defined from the more general stance of society and its (active as well as passive) use of formulaic diction.

As Olson has pointed out, the very rationale of formulaic diction is that it refers to "shared experiences and interpretations, that is, to a common intuition based on shared commonsense knowledge" (277). Deborah Tannen gives an obvious example of such a "reference to shared interpretation" in present-day colloquial English: "It does not really matter whether one says 'I could care less' or 'I couldn't care less.' The expression is, in either case, a handy way to make reference to a familiar idea" (2). In textual language, however, the presence or absence of the negation often makes all the difference. Formulaicness in everyday speech as well as in poetic diction has the function of evoking a certain norm as unquestioned reference. This becomes immediately obvious with proverbs and sayings. Hence, without doubt, formulaicness can be ideologically functionalized.

Yet does this also hold for other formulaic expressions? Can we infer that the formulas of medieval poetry were context-dependent? This would seem to have been the case for gnomic formulas; the difficulty is deciding whether a certain formula in a medieval poem is gnomic or not. While within gnomic diction the propositional, that is, communicative, aspect of (formulaic) language use still functions at least as much as does the metacommunicative (see Tannen 2 f.), however, poetic formulas seem to have existed which communicatively were almost empty.[16] Unless we are willing to classify those formulas as simple metrical fillers, we could see their function mainly on the metacommunicative level, the message of that metacommunication being "traditionality." The potential of formulaicness to carry traditionality may, I contend, also be functionalized to give a poetic discourse a traditional guise. I will later on cite Cynewulf as an example for this use of formulaicness.

Poetic traditionality, in its turn, may eventually end up as a convention. There is, however, a basic phenomenological difference between conventionality and traditionality in poetry, in that the latter is perceived as signaling that the discourse is about something which exists or is supposed to exist outside the poetry itself. Traditionality as a metacommunication thus works as an indicator of extratextual referentiality. Conventionality, on the other hand, may be perceived as signaling that the text is a specimen of all texts sharing that convention and thus be understood as indicating intertextual referentiality.

Obviously this distinction between traditionality and conventionality is a heuristic construct. In reality the two may well coexist within the same phenomenon, since linguistic traditionality seems always to have the potential of turning into conventionality. Peter Koch has recently suggested the term *Diskurstradition* ("discourse tradition"), which could be applied to this very phenomenon. Hence in primary orality a certain type of formula (poetic formulas in a very limited sense of the notion) undoubtedly indicates internal referentiality between discourses availing themselves of these very formulas. But we must not forget that already the immediate performance alone ties these discourses to their context outside the discourse. In other words, discourse and context are inseparable. It would seem that in contemporary oral cultures poetic discourse is strongly embedded in specific contexts. Thus, internal references between poetic discourses which signal conventionality are a redundant feature as long as the discourses themselves only occur in contextual situations that are defined to begin with. It seems that a turning point is reached when there is a decrease in the importance of the context of such traditional/conventional discourses. In primary oral cultures the tradition itself is then prone to being forgotten, while societies with access to literacy may further avail themselves of the traditional element, though of course using it mainly as a convention.[17] If I understand Jauss correctly, this is what he means by claiming that the medieval genres emancipated themselves gradually from their initially cultic, religious, and social functions, a process which he then calls "*Prozess* einer allmählichen Literarisierung" ("Theorie" 352; his emphasis).

In all likelihood, certain types of formulaic expressions may have a prevailing conventional function in primary orality too. Thus, they can be regarded as harbingers of the aesthetization, that is, the emancipation, of poetic discourse. Yet in the Middle Ages, this disconnection from the extratextual world could only be brought about by extensive as well as intensive literacy. In that literate climate formulaicness can become an aesthetic device proper, contributing to the tendency of poetic texts to set signals which function as demarcations of the extratextual world.[18] Conversely, it seems that no formula, as conventional as it may be, completely loses its intrinsic characteristic of establishing traditionality and thus of depending on orality/vocality to remain meaningful. This is why Zumthor can observe a decreasing frequency of formulaic expression as the Middle Ages were drawing to their end. As a consequence of the spreading of writing, he says, poetic language saw a "deformulisation" and has, ever since, adopted an "orientation autoreflexive" (*Lettre* 217).

Formulaic expression and the contextuality maintained by this mode of expression can, as I will later show, also be functionalized by a medieval poet who writes his text. This formally presented contextuality, in the sense of reference to shared knowledge, finds its expression in the poetic use of the first-person plural pronoun. Embedded in formulas in the Parry/Lord sense, the *we* occurring in medieval poetry indicates not informational discourse (i.e., the presentation of something unexpected) in the sense of information theory but rather confirmational discourse falling back on something "we all know." Walter Ong, elaborating on an observation of Eric Havelock's, has pointed repeatedly to the fact that one of the consequences of literacy is the separation of "the knower from the known" (*Orality* 105; see also "Writing"). The deictic value of the first-person plural pronoun is that it includes the speaker and those to whom he or she speaks. Hence this pronominal reference may indeed be interpreted as the manifestation of the unity of the knower(s) and the known, comprising the text—or rather, utterance—and the whole (potential) context.

The results thus far can be summed up briefly: First, the contextuality of medieval poetic discourse in vocality is mainly to be seen in its semiotic orientation, which is directed externally. In contrast with this, the written and subsequently read text may, indeed must, be largely autonomous from its non-linguistic context in order to be meaningful to the recipient. Second and conversely, if poetry in vocality is subject to the semiotic conditions of orality, then this poetry, in order to be successfully received, cannot be its own referential system. The continued use of formulaic expressions is a strong indication for this semiotic condition, because such expressions tie the poetic discourse to the extratextual world and thus depend on this extratextual world for their "referential system." This is why it remains context-dependent. So third, texts in vocality cannot and must not function as messages which are "known only through texts" (Riffaterre, *Text Production*). On the contrary, they have to be messages everyone is familiar with as of old, or so they have to pretend.

Conditional Fictionality and the Staged Utterance

If there was pretense—and we will shortly see that indeed there was—it was the author's task not to produce *figmenta* or *mendacia;* at least he or she had to take good care not to be detected in having done so. The early Middle Ages were not yet prepared to tolerate the "Aristotelian option" of the verisimilar, except for one phenomenon: the "poetic I."

In view of *performance,* the poet who was writing down a composition, or had it written down, was forced to build into the text "a vicarious voice." Even if we consider some of the preserved poetry to be "transcripts" of sorts from oral poetry, the simple act of writing down had already transformed the "singer's" existence onto parchment which had to be brought to life again by somebody who usually was not this singer. This transformation of the living individual into a merely "potential voice" meant that until the "performance" it was waiting, as it were, to be revived by somebody else (or even by the same individual). This was the consequence of the moment of performance being separated from the moment of composition. While with the "singer of tales" the sung composition and the reception by listening were one, as soon as the writing medium interceded, composition and performance were separate events. Once poetry became captured on parchment, the narrator, or, more generally, the "poetic I," was brought into being. Rainer Warning argues that all (literary) fiction is a "staged discourse." For the Middle Ages the technical need for that staging was created because each performance was a seemingly "live report." In comparison with this, reception via reading can leave the narrator as an *être de papier* (Barthes, "Introduction" 19) on the page, having no need of a live voice.

It would seem that once medieval vernacular poems were inscribed on parchment, they had become *texts* in the sense of something "fixed, boxed-off, isolated" (Ong, *Orality* 53). But did the poems not go through a re-transformation with every performance, in that a live voice, *viva vox,* translated what was fixed into a flux again, folding down the sides of the box, taking the agglomeration of words out of their isolation into what at least *appeared* as live communication? In the light of Warning's pragmatics of fiction as a "staged discourse" and of the present discussion of the semiotics of vocal poetic communication, we may think of the text in performance as a *staged utterance.* The part to be staged is what the author provides, and we may even figure that a scribe did the very same thing by just retaining the "I" which delivers what is to be told. The ensuing utterance, in its turn, is what the audience receives.

Hence, due to the semiotics of the act of poetic communication in the early Middle Ages, we arrive at this seemingly paradoxical situation: prevailing vocality excluded fictionality and, simultaneously, re-created it. Fictionality was excluded because a text in vocality semiotically functioned for the receivers like, an utterance, with the discourse being extrareferential rather than autoreferential. Its meaningfulness was context-dependent rather than arising from the text itself as its "own referential system" (Riffaterre, *Text Production*).[19] Moreover, as soon as writing interceded, whether as a poetic discourse "just" written down like a transcript (if ever something like that was feasible) or as a written composition to begin with, a specific setup became necessary in order for the poetic discourse to be suitable for communication. While characteristics such as formulaicness (and all those "oral features" mentioned above) came naturally, so to speak, in order to abide by the semiotic rules of vocal communication, the creation of the "poetic I," although also complying with the demands of vocality, could be considered as constituting the visible, or rather audible, phenomenological leap. Making use of the semiotics of vocality/orality can be regarded as an unintended (or sometimes even ideologically geared) deception in order to produce messages that were meaningful to the contemporary audience. This is what I call "conditional fictionality" (Schaefer, "Instance" 47 ff.). The new, "staged" reunification of the "knower and the known" in the figure of the narrator, be he or she a first-person singular *I,* or even more fictitiously merging in the communal *we,* worked on the basis of what Iser has called a tacit contract between the audience and the author ("Feigning" 214 f.). And it is this very acceptance of the contract which gave rise to fictionality in early medieval poetry.

Fictionality in Cynewulf

The tacitness of the contract Iser speaks of presupposes that the author/poet and the prospective recipients do not enter into direct contact. Due to this mutual absence, writing authors fictionalize their recipients as much as they create the fictitious speaker (see Ong, "The Writer's Audience is Always a Fiction"). An author must inscribe himself or herself into the text with this vicarious voice which may then be staged when the poem is meant to be communicated in vocality. The "singer of tales" has no need to undertake any of these efforts: the singer is present, and the audience is immediately addressed. Nevertheless, this presence shared by the two parties also demands that the communication of the singer be marked off from other types of discourse. Apart from the "framing" circumstances which may have accompanied the appearance of the singer (I am thinking here of particular situations like festivities, the possible announcement of the singer, etc.), there were "internal signals" to make the singer's communication stand out against other types of discourse. With the Germanic singer, versification must have been such a signal. Moreover, formulaicness could have had this demarcating function.[20] Yet it cannot be formulaicness as such, but specifically poetic formulas to which we may assign this quality. As I have said, certain formulas must have carried two metamessages at the same time, one of traditionality and another of conventionality. Such formulas seem to have appeared in strategically prominent moments of the poem, in particular at the very beginning (see Zumthor, *Lettre* 231).

Witnessing to this type of formulaicness are the beginnings of two Old English poems, both of which have come down to us in codices of the tenth/ eleventh centuries.[21] The first passage introduces the remaining 3179 alliterative long lines recounting the story of the Scandinavian hero Beowulf, while the second is the introduction to Cynewulf's *Fates of the Apostles* of 95 lines.

> HWÆT WE GARDEna   in geardagum
> þeodcyninga   þrym gefrunon
> hu ða æþelingas   ellen fremedon
> (*Beo* 1–3)
> Lo! We got to know, in old days, of the Speardanes,
> of the tribeskings' glory,
> how the noble ones developed courage

> HWÆT Ic þysne sang   siðgeomor fand
> on seocum sefan   samnode wide
> hu þa æðelingas   ellen cyðdon
> (*FAp* 1–3)
> Lo! I, weary of traveling, found this song,
> in feeble spirit, and gathered from (far and) wide
> how the noble ones displayed courage

In both cases *hwæt* is a strong signal which we may understand as appealing to the audience's attention. Subsequently, very much as the *ars dicendi* later on in the Middle Ages prescribes, a brief *exordium* generally introduces the topic: "hu ða æþelingas ellen fremedon" ("how the noble ones developed courage"; *Beo* 3) and "hu þa æðelingas ellen cyðdon" ("how the noble ones displayed courage"; *FAp* 3). The *æþelingas* in *Beowulf*, however, are Danish heroes of the Germanic continental past, while in *Fates of the Apostles*, *æðelingas* refers to the twelve apostles (*torht and tireadige twelfe wæron;* "bright and blessed with glory were the twelve"; *FAp* 4). Here we have a formula or formulaic system in the strict sense of Oral-Formulaic Theory, stretching over two half-lines with the only variation being the last verb with nonalliterating stress.

These opening lines, moreover, contain the voice bringing forward the story to follow. Yet the two beginnings differ substantially. In *Beowulf* it is said that "we . . . gefrunon," while in *Fates of the Apostles* a first-person singular claims that "ic þis sang siðgeomor fand." In view of what I stated earlier about the function of the first-person plural pronoun, one could say that in *Beowulf* a communal tradition is established, while the speaker of *Fates of the Apostles* refers to himself as being "the finder" or "gatherer" of what is subsequently told.

Very much depends here, obviously, on how we interpret the verb *fand* in Cynewulf's poem. The variation *samnode,* which follows in the next line, suggests that the act of "finding" is not to be understood as something which has happened by chance, or in an instant. For us, who have the text as a whole in front of us and hence may shift back and forth with our reading, a later section of the poem confirms the interpretation of *fand* in line 1 as an act of mental (re)collection:

> Her mæg findan   foreþances gleaw
> se ðe hine lysteð   leoðgiddunga
> *hwa þas fitte fedge . . .*
>   (*FAp* 96–98a; my emphasis)

> Here may the one who is wise of thoughts,
> who likes this song, find
> *who made this song . . .*

I do not want to discuss here whether a "back-scanning" interpretation of such texts is legitimate. Nevertheless, this last passage, as others in the poems we call "Cynewulfian," gives evidence of an authorial pride which is alien to tradition. Tradition implies a common, shared knowledge to begin with. With authorial statements, such as the one by Cynewulf, we apparently enter a new universe of poetic communication, where the "I-tell-you" attitude prevails over the "we-all-know."

Cynewulf has intrigued historians of early medieval poetry not so much because he thematizes his poetic doings, but because he has "signed" his poems curiously with runes, whose phonetic values add up acronymically to CYN(E)WULF.[22] Jeff Opland has been the first to situate Cynewulf within a larger phenomenological scope: "The literate poet [like Cynewulf] produces an artifact that takes on a life independent of himself, whereas the oral poet . . . cannot be divorced from his poetry: hence the literate poet can observe his artifact objectively and assume a proprietary right to it" (159).

Cynewulf, as Opland says, was a poet very much aware that what he put in words was not so much tied to what had been sung of old but was newly created, something novel which might, or might not, be handed down. A passage at the end of *Juliana* provides evidence for this:

> bidde ic monna gehwone
> gumena cynne   þe þis gied wræce
> þat he mec neodful   bi noman minum
> gemyne modig   and meotud bidde
> þaet me heofona helm   helpe gefremme . . .
>   (*Jln* 718b–722)

> I pray every man
> of human kind, who may recite this song,
> that he earnestly and fervently remember me,
> the needful, by my name,
> and pray the creator
> that heavens' chief may grant me help . . .

I have translated *wræce* as "may recite," which does not necessarily imply Zumthor's "performance." Even when reading alone, people in the Middle Ages were wont to do so aloud. Nevertheless, I doubt whether one can really agree with this statement by Opland: "Clearly the poems of Cynewulf are designed to be read: it is difficult to understand how else the runic signatures might appeal to an audience" (159). Kenneth Sisam convincingly proved a long time ago that the runic signature could be perceived as such by somebody who only received the poem by listening.[23] Moreover, it is unlikely that an early medieval poet composed poetry for such a small audience as the community of literates of the time.[24]

The strongest argument for vocalic reception is the use of formulaic diction. There is at the core of the long-standing debate about formulaic composition the problem of how a poet's undeniable literacy may harmonize with this method of phrasing.[25] Magoun's suggestion that Cynewulf dictated the heavily formulaic passages to himself appears very artificial. Magoun created this argument, I suppose, to save the idea that formulas are by necessity something inherited, a stock which belonged to and could only be transmitted by orality. Opland, in his turn, has made the point that "formulas referring to books or to Apostles could not possibly derive from a pre-Christian oral tradition" (158f.). For Opland, the Cynewulfian formulas are rather evidence for "the relative rapidity with which a purely Christian formulaic diction arose after the conversion" (158f.). We do not really know how rapid this was, because, after all, we do not know when Cynewulf lived. The conclusion that there is a stock of formulas which we may classify as being "purely Christian" speaks less for the handiness of this device for "fast composition," as Lord would have it, and more for the formula's usefulness in securing successful reception in vocality.

For one thing, poetic success depended on intelligibility, on a way of composition whose product did not require a reader to page back, reread immediately, and so forth. On top of that, reception in vocality demanded that the discourse to be received must follow the semiotic principles of orality. Thus, the "purely Christian formulaic diction" which Opland has articulated should be seen as ensuring that those who listened to the poetry with the "new" message would not be run over by novelties but would be presented with something that could have been received as shared knowledge. The price for this might have been that the poets had to create an impression "as if" what was presented could indeed constitute such shared knowledge.

Cynewulf gives evidence of a certain struggle with this necessity. Given our awareness of the "implications of literacy," we could say that Cynewulf was conscious of the impact of the crossroad situation he was in. His poem *Elene* in particular gives ample evidence of this. In the epilogue about the Invention of the Cross, Cynewulf says:

> ic þæs wuldres treowes
> oft nales æne   hæfde ingemynd
> ær ic þæt wundor   onwrigen hæfde
> ymb þone beorhtan beam   swa ic on bocum fand
> wyrda gangum   on gewritum cyðan
> be ðam sigebeacne
>
> (*Ele* 1251b–1256a)

> the tree of glory
> I had more than once in my mind,
> before I had revealed the wonder
> concerning that bright beam, as I found in books,
> the course of events, made known in writing
> concerning that sign of victory

He has found something *in books*, and that is what he is passing on here. Yet Cynewulf does not depict the access to books as being his exclusive privilege—quite the contrary. The poet apparently took pains to make the point that those books too have their authority, and that they are something which can be shared, if only notice is taken of them.

To establish or confirm this authority, he avails himself of a formulaic diction that appears partly original with him. The often discussed formula "hwæt we gehyrdon þurh halige bec" occurs three times in the story of *Elene,* and each time it constitutes part of one of Helena's fervent speeches to the Jews. Judas, Helena's outspoken Jewish antagonist, in his turn, although not denying the existence of those books, gives authority to his arguments in this fashion:

> swa þa þæt ilce gio   min yldra fæder
> sigerof sægde   þam wæs Sachius nama
> frod frynwiota   fæder minum
> (*Ele* 436–438)

> This also of old my father's father,
> the triumphant, said, his name was Zaccheus,
> the wise prophet, to my father

At another point in the poem, Judas tries to defend himself by saying that he did not know how he could gain knowledge about something (i.e., Christ's crucifixion) so long past. Against that Helena holds that "many a tale of heroic feats performed by the Trojans" were still kept in the minds as well as in the books (643–54). Judas turns this argument around and says that they remember this "for nydþearfe" ("on account of necessity"; 657), as they have put these stories into writing ("on gewritu setton"; 658b); yet as for knowledge about the matter in question (Christ's crucifixion), Judas alleges that the situation of the Jews is that

> þis næfre
> þurh æniges mannes   muð gehyrdon
> hæleðu[m] cyðan   butan her nu ða
> (*Ele* 659b–661)

> this we never
> from any man's mouth heard
> made known through men, save here now.

I wonder whether we would strain the text too much if we saw *Elene* as the depiction of the fight between two concurring modes of tradition, one oral (here depicted as "heathen"), the other written (here shown as the only correct one, Christian). Whatever Cynewulf's intention may have been, Helena seems to say, and with her Cynewulf, that it's all in the books, you just have to look for it.

Wilhelm Busse has recently documented that one of the objectives of the Benedictine reform movement in tenth-century England was to establish the authority of books. From scattered (mainly nonpoetical) evidence, Busse is able to display conclusively that "written traditions were not as securely entrenched in late Anglo-Saxon society as is usually thought" ("Boceras" 27). He sees in Cynewulf's *Elene* more evidence for the Church's concern "to impart a modified code of values, in which other values than, for example, worldly honour or material goods dominate the scale" (36). Although it would be consistent with Busse's argument to see Cynewulf's *Elene* as of the tenth century (a deduction only implicit in "Boceras"; cf. his *Altenglische Literatur*), one could at least say that Cynewulf was quite conscious of the two forms of available knowledge and that he was definitely a partisan of the literate tradition—or was he?

Cynewulf was a partisan of books insofar as he saw himself having to promulgate a "book-religion." From the Cynewulfian texts we can gather that he also knew that the only way of achieving this was to give his poetry a shape that was acceptable and intelligible to those who did not have direct access to books. It was for those people that he gave his poetry its oral guise. How else are we to interpret the beginning of the legend of *Juliana?*

> HWÆT WE ÐÆt hydron   hæleð eahtian
> deman dædhwate   þætte in dagum gelamp
> maximianes . . .
>
> <div align="center">(<i>Jln</i> 1–3a)</div>

> Lo! We heard men/heroes laud this,
> brave men extol that it came to pass
> in Maximian's days . . .

The fact that this is Cynewulf's only poem that does not explicitly mention books should not lead us to the conclusion that he himself got to know this story through some oral tradition. It matches perfectly with the story itself, a martyrology, to cast it into what may well have been the traditional way of telling about heroic deeds.

Cynewulf thus uses formulaicness in a very specific way. The exordial formulas match the following stories insofar as they pay tribute to the genre of the respective stories. With *Fates of the Apostles* the poet chose an introductory formula that complies both with "book-knowledge" (which he "found and gathered widely") and with the need to render the apostles' fates into a memorial tradition to be shared. Hence, he takes for a model "hu þa æðelingas ellen cyðdon / torhte and tireadige" ("how the noble ones developed courage, / bright and glorious"; *FAp* 3–4a). For *Juliana* Cynewulf chose to strike an even more "heroic" keynote, using the "communal *we*" as well as the seemingly oral-traditional apparatus. *Elene*, which brings the question of book versus oral tradition so much to the fore within the story itself, does not present such a formulaic front. As if Cynewulf wanted to make his audience aware of the precision of knowledge one may gain from books, he lets *Elene* begin:

> Þa wæs agangen   geara hwyrftum
> tu hund and þreo   geteled rimes
> swylce XXX   eac þinggemearces
> wintra for worulde   þæs þe wealdend god
> acenned wearð
>
>   (*Ele* 1–5a)

> Then had passed, as the years went by,
> two hundred and three, reckoning in numbers,
> and also thirty of the period of time [?]
> of winters in the world, that the ruling god
> was born.

The metacommunicative function of this opening seems to be to signal the precision which may be arrived at only "þurh halige bec" ("through holy books"; *Jln* 364, 670, 852).

It should be safe to say then that Cynewulf availed himself of the metacommunicative function of formulaicness at the beginnings of *Juliana* and *Fates of the Apostles* in order to establish a certain mode of reception for his stories. It is also revealing to see what Cynewulf refrained from doing. Although he introduces the first-person plural in *Juliana,* he does not maintain it through the course of his story. In this poem, a first-person narrator does not appear until the epilogue (695b), with the revelation of the poet's name, thus referring less to the "poetic" than to the "authorial I." In *Elene* I have found one single instance where we could identify a narrator *within* the story (240b).

It is in *Fates of the Apostles* that we find the narrating first person that most utterly—and most formulaically—conveys tradition as well as traditionality. On the one hand, we have three instances of "we gehyrdon / hyrde." [26] The first time it is plain:

> Hwæt we eac gehyrdon   be Iohanne
> æglæawe menn   æðelo reccan
>   (*FAp* 23 f.)

> Lo, we have heard tell about John,
> a man versed in law, of his family.

Next we get that "book formula" which also occurs three times in *Elene*. While in *Elene,* however, the formula belongs to the internal story, that is, it is uttered by Helena, the formula in *Fates of the Apostles* serves as a linking narrative element:

> Hwæt we þæt gehyrdon   þurh halige bec
> þæt mid Sigelwarum   soð yppe wearð
>   (*FAp* 63f.)

> Lo, we heard through holy books
> that to the Ethiopians truth was made known

Finally, we get another "plain" instance:

> Hyrde we þæt Iacob   in Ierusalem
> fore sacerdum   swilt þrowode
>   (*FAp* 70f.)

> We heard that James in Jerusalem
> in front of the priests suffered death.

It is also in *Fates of the Apostles* that we find the only instance in the Cynewulf corpus of the formula "mine gefræge" ("to my knowledge," "as I got to know"; *FAp* 25). This *gefræge* formula occurs five times in *Beowulf* (776, 837, 1955, 2685, 2837), where it figures in each occurrence as a narrator's insertion.

What do we make of this "Beowulfian ring"? With the formula "hu þa æðelingas ellen cyðdon/fremedon" (*FAp* 3 / *Beo* 3), it is tempting to claim that Cynewulf is imitating the oral diction as we find it in *Beowulf*. But what is the basis for claiming that *Beowulf* itself displays "pure oral diction"? There simply is none. All we may say is that both poems use the same formulaic material. And again it is much safer to suppose that this common inventory tells us something about the reception of both poems rather than about the way those poems were composed.

The first person voicing the epilogues, being much more of an "authorial" than a "poetic I," gives evidence of the struggle to endow poetry in vocality with an appropriate shape. Cynewulf—if this name is to be taken as standing for one and the same person who composed all the poems that carry the runic signature—appears to experiment with all the poetic means at his disposal. He quite successfully makes use of formulaic diction both to provide the metacommunicative marker of "traditionality" and to establish what amounts to a contradiction, a paradox: a new tradition, namely that of the authority of the written. His overall reluctance, however, to yield the vicarious voice in his poetry, which is necessary for reception in vocality, may well have to do with the poet's consciousness that such a voice would lift his poems into the realm of "fictionality." Yet as for formulas mentioning the first-person speaker *within* the poems, Cynewulf seems quite reluctant to inscribe such a narrative voice into his poetry. In the shortest of his narrative poems (which is much more of a catalog than a narration), *Fates of the Apostles,* he uses this outstandingly formulaic reference to mark traditionality, although it is precisely this poem which immediately begins with the "individualizing I." In *Elene* and *Juliana*, on the other hand, the narrator virtually disappears from the story. Other poets, like the poet of *Exodus*, seem to have been much less hesitant to extend the feature of "traditionality" to the narrative persona.

Cynewulf obviously did not care much about the "poetic I," but he tried all the harder to make the "auctorial" person known to his audience.[27] If these signatures really witness that Cynewulf "assumes that he will be unknown to his audience" (Opland 159), then the total absence of a narrator-persona in *Juliana* and *Elene* could be interpreted as symptomatic of Cynewulf's awareness that, once written, poetry gets out of its author's hands and its future life is uncontrollable. This potential of written poems to "take on a life independent of the author and achieve a permanency that outlives their creator" (Opland 159) may have been felt as a virtual threat to the purity of the teaching as well as to its inseparability from the teacher.

Fictionality is imminent whenever writing is involved. Cynewulf may well have been aware of that. And this could have been his ultimate reason for tying his poetry forever to the name of its author: to keep it from lapsing forever into the never-land of fictitious discourse. He himself, however, had no choice but to open the way in that very direction.

Notes

1 "La *performance,* c'est l'action complexe par laquelle un message poétique est simultanément transmis et perçu, ici et maintenant. Locuteur, destinataire(s), circonstances (que le texte, par ailleurs, a l'aide de moyens linguistiques, les représente ou non) se trouvent concrètement confrontés, indiscutables. Dans la performance se recoupent les deux axes de la communication sociale: celui qui joint le locuteur à l'auteur; et celui sur quoi s'unissent situation et tradition" (Zumthor, *Introduction* 32).

2 See the well-known dictum of Derrida: "The exteriority of the signifier is the exteriority of writing in general, and I shall try to show . . . that there is no linguistic sign before writing. Without that exteriority the very idea of the sign falls into decay" (*Of Grammatology* 14). He moreover characterizes the distinction between *signifiant* and *signifié* as that "between the sensible and the intelligible" (13).

3 Gauger 127. This quotation is virtually untranslatable, because *Bedeutung* as well as *Bedeuten* would have to be rendered in English with a form in *-ing,* which would then neutralize the distinction Gauger makes.

4 Here we meet with a problem very similar to the one mentioned in note 3 above, since English *utterance* covers both French *énoncé* and *énonciation* (cf. the comment of Terese Lyons, the English translator of Riffaterre's *Text Production*, with regard to the French notions [283 n 7]); I do not make a distinction here because it is my aim to show that the impossibility of discerning one from the other is exactly

what makes one of the differences between reception via reading and that via hearing.

5 To my knowledge the term *poetic "I"* was introduced by Leo Spitzer. I use it (as do Spitzer and Bäuml) to refer to the first-person speaker both of epic and "lyrical" poetic discourse.

6 See in particular Bäuml's articles "Varieties" and "Medieval Texts."

7 For a competent and enlightening linguistic discussion of the differences between oral and written communication, see Koch and Oesterreicher; a comprehensive study of the notion of *text* is provided by Konrad Ehlich.

8 See also Jauss, "Zur historischen Genese," and Marquard, "Kunst als Antifiktion," in *Funktionen des Fiktiven;* also Iser, *Act of Reading* and "Feigning" (the latter article appeared originally in German in *Funktionen des Fiktiven*).

9 "Die pseudoreferentielle Funktion der Sprache ist nichts anderes als Autoreferentialität in der Form von Pseudoreferentialität" (Stierle 362).

10 My use of the term *open* is, of course, not the same as Eco's in his *Opera aperta*. Eco characterizes the modern literary text as "open" and medieval poetry as "closed." What he refers to is *interpretability;* I, however, speak here about *referentiality,* which I consider "open" when extratextual and "closed" when intratextual.

11 See Diller, who deals with the problem of grammatical reference in *Beowulf.*

12 See the ample documentation given in Foley, *Oral-Formulaic Theory.*

13 I hold this question to be forever undecidable with regard to medieval material because there is no way of escaping the well-known dilemma: Historical linguistic material before the invention of voice recording has only come down to us in writing. We thus always deal with the written word, never with what was actually spoken. Whenever we speak about orality with regard to a past period, we set out to search for this very orality in a material which is not oral. We have no choice: we must seek orality in its contrary.

14 The linguistic features, in particular the syntactic ones that have just been touched on, will have to be assumed as given, without further comment. But see also Foley's remarks on oral features in this volume.

15 "*Formulisme* fait référence à tout ce qui, dans les discours et les modes d'énonciation propres à telle société, a tendence à se redire sans cesse en termes à peine diversifiés, à se reproduire avec d'infimes et infinies variations" (Zumthor, *Lettre* 216f., his emphasis).

16 F H. Whitman has made out such "fillers" in an analysis of the Old English translations of the Psalms, the *Meters of Boethius,* and two Latin riddles. Whitman's main point is that those fillers "add nothing to the meaning" (531). This is undoubtedly the case if we are looking for "communicative meaning." I think, however, that particularly in those cases of "semantic emptiness" or "redundance," the formulas serve exactly the function I am dealing with here, namely that of a metacommunicative signal.

17 The first aspect refers to the "homeostasis" of oral societies depicted by Goody and Watt.

18 I have dealt with this aspect of the "aesthetization" of elements like formulas in "The Instance of the Formula."

19 I leave out here the question of the Church's attitude toward fictionality; for that, see Jauss, "Zur historischen Genese" and *Ästhetische Erfahrung* (142); and Schaefer, "Fictionalized Dilemma."

20 Koch and Oesterreicher suggest the term *elaborate orality* ("elaborierte Mündlichkeit"; 30 f.).

21 Old English quotations generally follow the *ASPR* editions, but I follow MS capitals at beginnings of texts and remove Krapp and Dobbie's punctuation, as this at some points implies an interpretation I cannot follow.

22 See Frese for a detailed discussion of the signatures and the relation between the epilogues and the poems preceding.

23 "Cynewulf uses runes because, while they were obvious to a reader, they made possible the communication of his name to an audience in a way at once memorable and sure. An Anglo-Saxon hearing *cen, yr* would know at once that he was dealing with runes; his attention would be directed at once to the task of solution because runes sometimes played a part in Old English riddles; and he would listen closely for the succession" (25). According to Sisam, this must have been the case because, in contrast with the other six runes, the names for the *c-* and *y-*runes must have only been understood as rune names (26). See also Calder: "By using the names of the runes as sounds in the poem, Cynewulf's name could be *heard* as well as *seen*" (23).

24 In "The Uses of Literacy," Wormald convincingly rejects the view that the relatively extensive corpus of Anglo-Saxon vernacular poetry would "imply a wide reading public" (96).

25 See Benson's reply to Magoun, who follows Parry closely; for a survey, see Foley, *Oral-Formulaic Theory.*

26 Anderson gives a somewhat peculiar interpretation of the occurrence of these formulas in *FAp.* He takes them as being "clue[s] about Cynewulf's *life*" (19, my emphasis): "The 'we gehyrdon' formula, and its variant [?] 'mine gefrege' (*Fates*, 23, 25b, 70), suggest a group of auditors gathered at regular intervals to hear reading-portions from a collection on the apostles. There emerges the picture of a monastic refectory where pious lections were given on a regular basis" (19 f.). Aside from the fact that this picture is not surprising, I think that Anderson overestimates the naturalistic potential of such formulas.

27 Sisam shows that, apart from displaying authorial pride, this reference to Cynewulf's name has to be seen in the context of the institution of "prayer intercession" (*adiuvatio orationibus*), which Sisam defines as "the desire to be remembered by name in the prayers of others" (23). I have dealt with this phenomenon in connection with the comparison of the Old English *Wife's Lament* with a letter from an English nun to Boniface in my article "Two Women"; for the term *prayer intercession* there, see 522 n 38.

Voice and Writing in Augustine and in the Troubadour Lyric

The Anthropology of Performance

In a series of recent books, the medievalist Paul Zumthor argues that the performance of medieval song was not simply a matter of substituting singing for reading. Putting the voice in the word went beyond questions of poetic form to raise issues as much anthropological as musical in scope. Zumthor construes voice not simply in a utilitarian sense, as an instrument for public communication, but as part of the body's "signature" or imprint on poetry through performance. As he sees it, the voice is the vehicle for introjecting qualities of inner life, of the unconscious, in the public performance of lyric poetry.

What matters [in oral lyric performance] must be sought at the point of origin of a given poetic form. The movement of the *canso* proceeds, it seems to me, from a sense, at once insistent and yet obscure, of a kind of unknown, either a hidden promise or a menace inscribed in our destiny: an indefinable element intervenes between voice and language, a barrier forbids their identifying with each other and makes even their interaction far from certain. The discourse of the song narrativizes this perception, at least potentially. It is this latent barrier between voice and language which gives rise to the motif of that erotic obstacle, so often evoked by specialists as the thematic key to this poetry.[1]

By making the singing voice a field of encounter between self and other, Zumthor shifts the symbolic ground from writing to lyric performance. The distinction between written and oral expression lies not in the fact of voiced versus written communication but rather in the role played by the written text as a feature of the performance. In the Middle Ages, Zumthor feels, the performing of the lyric poem differed radically from oral recitation from a written text: "When the poet or his interpreter sang or recited . . . voice alone conferred authority on the text. But when the poet gave an oral recitation from a book, the authority came rather from the book." [2] Public recitation of a written text emphasizes writing to the extent that the manuscript being read from will be visually perceived by the audience, thus testifying to the written source of the performance (Zumthor, *Poésie* 35). "In lyric presentation, on the contrary, writing is occulted even in the case of songs based on written texts." [3]

Situating the link between song and the body in the lyric as voiced, rather than as written expression, Zumthor argues for an anthropology of performance based on vocalization—singing or declaiming. All the constituent elements of song—textual, melodic, aesthetic, ideological—yield to the primacy of the *mise en voix* which connects them and gives them their meaning in the performance. "It is in this sense, rather than in the more obvious meaning," he says, "that I am tempted to understand the verb *cantar* ["to sing"], the expression *far canso* ["to make a song"], and their equivalents." [4] Zumthor firmly believes that the materiality of the voice—"omnipresent," he says, in early medieval lyric—plays an important role first in determining the meaning of lyric texts, then in forcing us to modify the way we read them. [5]

The link between voice and body allows Zumthor to assign a social role to the performative voice. Through the voicing of the song by the performer, a reciprocal consciousness not only connects performer and audience but also makes the audience aware of itself as a corporate body in a way, Zumthor claims, different from an audience listening to a recitation from a book, where the written text interposes itself between audience and reader. In the latter case, the reader is a performer of the writing, simply a medium through which the writing communicates to the individual members of the audience. In the case of the song, however, the performer incorporates and enacts the text. Zumthor argues this forcefully, albeit in a rather neoromantic register:

The poetic voice takes on a cohesive and stabilizing function which the social group needs for its continued existence as such. Paradox: thanks to the movements of its interpreters—in space, in time, in self-awareness—[the poetic voice] is omnipresent, known by everyone, integrated in daily discourses where it stands as a permanent and sure reference. [The poetic voice] confers figuratively [on everyday speech] a kind of extra-temporality. . . . [The poetic voice] holds out to daily language the magic mirror where the image never fades. . . . Everyday voices scatter their words in the bed of time; . . . the poetic voice captures them in a unique moment—that of the performance—which disappears as soon as it falls silent; at least it produces this wonder from a fleeting but total presence. Such is the primary function of poetry, one that writing, by its excessive permanence, fulfills badly. . . . The poetic voice is at once prophecy and memory.[6]

If we were to look for an example of what Zumthor is talking about here, we might find an approximation in the first troubadour, Guillaume IX, who hails his fellow nobles in the audience at the beginning of his songs with greetings like "Companho" ("Gentlemen"), while other troubadours say "Senher" ("Lords") or "Amics" ("Friends"), suggesting that Provençal lyric was not a solitary pursuit but a means of joining people in the immediacy of performance. But Zumthor does not seek to privilege voice simply to make it the instrument of a corporate anthropology; he wants it to be the key to a historical poetics. "The starting point for a poetics, of the twelfth century shall we say, ought to be the study of the inner beauty of the human voice, seized as close to its source as possible. . . . This beauty can, in truth, be conceived as an individual phenomenon belonging to the person responsible for emitting the vocal sound: from this viewpoint and except in rare cases, the voice escapes us over such long intervening periods. But [the voice] may also be conceived as social and historical, in as much as it links individuals to one another, and by the way it is used, it can modulate popular culture."[7]

In saying that the sound of the voice rising in song creates a social bond which takes the form of poetry, Zumthor illustrates his conception of an anthropology of performance which is both personal and corporate.[8] Without denying the importance of the performative voice or the anthropological significance Zumthor finds in it, I think we must resist his displacement of writing from the performative arena of the medieval lyric. We must do so for the simple reason that writing was as much a part of the lyric performance as voice. Lyrics written in manuscripts, especially the earliest ones, encouraged running words together in ways that allowed them to be read in various ways, often equivocally. It was not simply a matter of paronomasia (wordplay based on similar sounds with different meanings), which does abound in troubadour lyric, but whole phrases that could be read in diametrically opposed ways: such as when a line referring piously to the Virgin might be reread with a different grouping of syllables to produce an obscene meaning. This was not a procedure as recondite as anagrams but a phenomenon of manuscript reading and writing recognized as early as the seventh century by the grammarian Virgil of Toulouse. Laura Kendrick's recent book, *The Game of Love: Troubadour Wordplay,* brilliantly demonstrates how the manner of writing troubadour poetry in manuscripts with minimal separation between words encouraged wordplay that reveals the poetic voice to be a dual phenomenon of writing and speaking.

This should not surprise us. Writing and speaking both require the media-

Figure 8.1. The Poet (Folquet de Marseilles) declaiming at his desk. Provençal Chansonnier, Padua, Italy, thirteenth century. New York: Pierpont Morgan Library. MS M819 (Chansonnier N), fol. 63 (detail). (Photograph: Pierpont Morgan Library.)

140

tion of the body, the hand, or the voice. Medieval manuscript illuminations testify to the extent to which writing and singing could and often were viewed as connected activities. Looking briefly at three different representations of performative voice and performative hand from thirteenth- and fourteenth-century songbook (*chansonnier*) manuscripts, we first encounter, in Figure 8.1, a rather literal *bas-de-page* miniature of a poet—perhaps Folquet de Marseilles, whose work is represented on the folio—declaiming or singing (since the context is that of troubadour song) at his writing desk. The stylus in his left hand, incorporated in the declamatory gesture symbolizing vocalization, is held immediately in front of his mouth (and eyes), above the parchment scroll. The scroll itself is portrayed in a rather dynamic fashion.

Figure 8.2 represents the link between performative voice and hand in a somewhat subtler and more commanding manner.[9] To begin with, there is the historiated letter *G* that simultaneously illustrates the anonymous poet declaiming his song from a scroll and initiates the first word of the song, *Grant* (meaning "large," but here used in a temporal expression, *grant pieca q[ue] ne chantai*, "For a long time I did not sing"). The historiated initial at once begins the poem—as its first letter—and also provides an image of the envoicement, the delivery of the song by the poet; the letter *G* literally contains the poet, so that the poet as inventor (*trouvère*) and poetic voice underlie the letter and the word in a visual assertion of voice *and* writing as performative manifestations of poetic identity.

The chansonnier is a complex system. Aside from the text of the songs and the illumination, there is also the musical notation. The space of the music and the space of the lyric are very different, as the folio shows by juxtaposing unnotated stanzas and notated ones on the same folio. The musical staffs are like the historiated letter; they demonstrate another dimension of the word: the writing of the word as sound.

Indeed, it is very difficult to read the verbal text under the notation without trying to sound out the words according to the rise and fall of the notes: "Grant pieca que ne chantai; or chanterai a lentrant dou douz mois de may" ("For a long time I did not sing; now I will sing at the beginning of the sweet month of May"). In effect, the musical notation metaphorizes the performative singing voice: the notation is like a sketch in this sense, visually marking the absent voice of the singer.

The last and most sophisticated of our examples, Figure 8.3, comes from a late fourteenth-century manuscript of Guillaume de Machaut's *Remède de Fortune*. This shows the full-scale system of voice and writing as performances conjoined not just in artistic presentation but also in the lover-poet's public acknowledgment of his passion. The manuscript folio shows the text of the poem in the upper two columns, then a portrait of the lover-poet writing the love-song or "lay," which then follows accompanied by the musical nota-

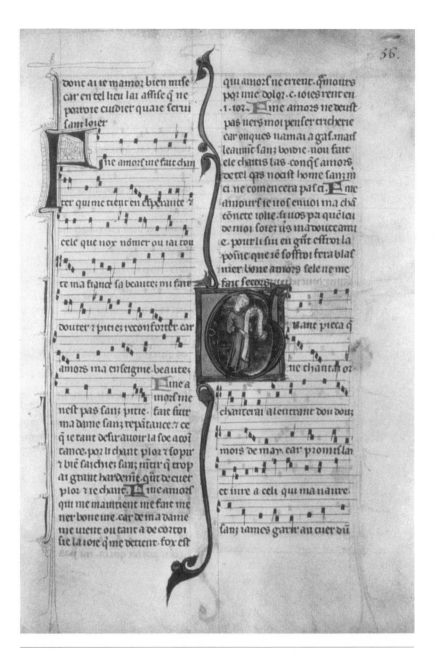

Figure 8.2. Historiated initial *G*. Poet declaiming from a scroll. Paris, Bibliothèque Nationale MS 846 (Chansonnier O), fol. 56. Burgundian, late thirteenth century. (Photograph: Bibliothèque Nationale.)

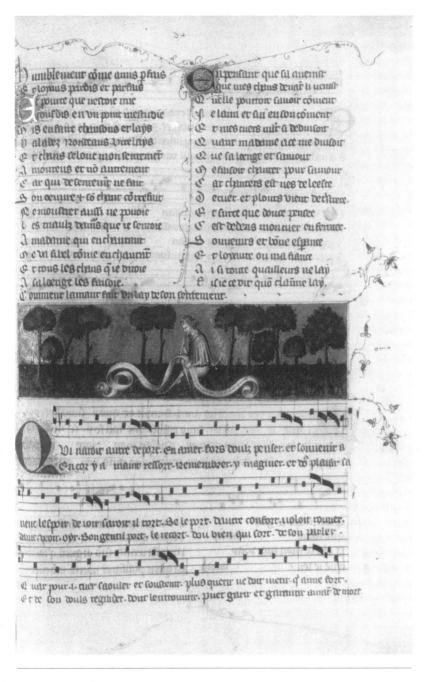

Figure 8.3. Guillaume de Machaut, *Remède de Fortune*. The lover composing his lay. Paris, Bibliothèque Nationale MS 1586, fol. 26 (detail). Paris, c. 1350. (Photograph: Bibliothèque Nationale.)

tion. The label above the painting reads: "Comment l'amant fair un lay de son sentement" ("How the lover makes a lay about his feelings").

This folio incorporates all the elements from figures 1 and 2: a painting of the poet writing on the lyric scroll (which in this case figuratively represents the unfolding and the rise and fall of the music, visually echoed by the notation on the musical staffs below), as well as the juxtaposition of musical notation, lyrics, and nonnotated text that we saw in Figure 2. The caption links all three performative media (singing, writing, visual image) dynamically to the poet's psyche. The key word in the caption is *fait,* which in Middle French may mean oral communication (speaking or saying), written composition, as well as doing or making things. The caption, then, tells us that the painting will link the performative voice and the writing hand of the poet in a quasi-simultaneous representation.

The painting does not quite realize the intentions of the caption on closer inspection. Voice and language, while they must ultimately fuse in performance—the voice is then the music—here retains the marks of their difference. The folio uses three different symbolic languages—writing, painting, and musical notation—representing the challenge that the performer-poet must try to bring together. While it may only be through the mediation of the body that these disparate components can be harmonized, that mediation did not go unquestioned or unchallenged in the Middle Ages.

The issues of music, voice, writing, and the body lay at the heart of major metaphysical and spiritual questions in the early Middle Ages. To understand why the innovation of troubadour love lyric was a major cultural event in the eleventh century *because* it proposed a version of secular culture organized around alternate conventions of voice and writing, we need to understand better why the link between voice, body, and writing proposed by the early troubadours would have been so unsettling.

It certainly was not because the link between voice and body was new. From paleo-Christian times on, certain medieval authorities defined music in terms of the human voice; they too saw a corporate anthropology in the social bond of communal song. Isidore of Seville identified music with the human voice and sought its origin, as preserved in the etymology of the term, by connecting it with such cultural forces as religion, history, and aesthetics, in short with the social "glue" of medieval society. As Noel Swerdlow showed some years ago, medieval etymologies of music linked the Greek concept of the muses—nymphs or aquatic deities—with the Hebrew prophet Moses, so named according to medieval tradition because he was found by the water (Swerdlow 3–9).

The phoneme *mus-* in *music* suggested the mimesis of nature and culture in the act of singing. Isidore of Seville says that "music is so called by its derivation from the muses. The muses are named . . . *from seeking,* because, as the ancients said, the essence of songs and the melody of the voice is sought through them." [10] According to the Carolingian scholar Remigius of Auxerre, "The Muses are called the *Fontigenae* ("Fountain Spirits") because *musica artificialis* was first found in streams, for water is called *moys*." [11] Even earlier than Isidore or Remigius, Cassiodorus had written that "the discipline of music is diffused through all the actions of our life. . . . Music is closely bound up with religion itself." [12]

From these brief examples, we can appreciate how music, voice, and the ethical and religious context of the human being were linked by early medieval thought in ways that may seem strange to us today. The anthropology of voice was philosophically complex, not least because, from Saint Augustine on, vocal symbolic expression, whether music, poetry, or even prayer, was tightly monitored to assure that the human image projected by such expression was, as Cassiodorus would have it, fully harmonious with the divine project:

The discipline of music is diffused through all the actions of our life. First, it is found that if we perform the commandments of the Creator and with pure minds obey the rules he has laid down, every word we speak, every pulsation of our veins, is related by musical rhythms to the powers of harmony. Music indeed is the knowledge of apt modulation. If we live virtuously, we are constantly proved to be under its discipline, *but when we commit injustice we are without music.*[13]

Cassiodorus plays upon the analogy between musical and ethical harmony. Like music, the harmony of human behavior depends upon a justly proportionate disposition of "the numbers"—in this case rule-governed behavior, the golden mean—in relation to actions.[14] "Apt modulation" would be the ability to temper actions with judgment. Cassiodorus raises the specter of "disharmony," and thus of alterity, at the end of the quotation, in the form of a human image discordant with divine intentionality, for example, Adam's in the Fall. Isidore of Seville takes this equation one step further by raising the specter of Cain. Recalling that the Bible had, in Genesis 4.21, linked the invention of music to the race of Cain ("et nomen fratris eius Iubal ipse fuit pater canentium cithara et organo"), he restates the passage in a manner that connects the separate strands of etymology and genealogy to assert music's ambivalent potential: "De inventoribus eius. Moyses dicit repertorem musicae artis fuisse Tubal, qui fuit se stirpe Cain ante diluvium" ("Moses says that the inventor of the art of music was Tubal, who was of the race of Cain, before the flood"; 3.16.1–2).

In other words, the medieval concept of performance was ideological, tied to the genealogy of man in the lapsarian meaning medieval culture gave to the term. And just as the medieval concept of the human was dramatic, because based on a cosmic drama played out at the beginning, middle, and end of time, so was the early medieval concept of lyric performance potentially dramatic. Performance played out permutations of the drama of existence in the fallen world. In this drama, the human image embodied in the song could be one affirming transcendent purpose, the Abel model, or one that attempted to transgress against that norm to assert the Cainonic other.

Saint Augustine was the first to show that, if voice was the marker of the presence of the body in the text of the song, memory was the site of the struggle that determined which of the conflicting images of the body would emerge. Memory embraced a spectrum of possible options from identity to alterity. At one end of the range lay the officially sanctioned image that made memory a vehicle for an anterior text: Scripture. At the other end figured transgressive memory, the recollection of an anterior act of rebellion against authority (e.g., Adam, Cain). These antinomies invest medieval song with a conflictual matrix. Continually balanced between reaffirming norms or challenging them, corporate performance was less removed from writing than Zumthor appears willing to concede. On the contrary, it proclaimed fundamental connections to prior textual traditions. But it did use the human voice, as Zumthor perceived, to represent the body in real human time against an ecclesiastical tradition that set eternity against human time, spirituality against sexuality. The voicing of poetic song could serve as a transgressive gesture intended to counter prevailing orthodoxy founded on written authority. Lyric performance was rendered dramatic by the tensions between normative writing (law) and transgressive voicing, where voicing was a textual mode, a performative gesture, rather than the opposition between writing and orality espoused by Paul Zumthor.

We shall look at how this tension plays out in troubadour lyric in a moment, but first let us glance briefly at Book 11 of Augustine's *Confessions*. Perhaps no other text represents quite so dramatically the far-reaching consequences of performance as the well-known example of the psalm recitation by which Augustine grounds his arguments on the rapport between the dialectics of time and the problem of being for the individual. Paul Ricoeur has recently made *Confessions* 11 the point of departure and focus for his multivolume study, *Time and Narrative*.[15] Ricoeur states:

The fragile example of the *canticus* recited by heart suddenly becomes, toward the end of the inquiry, a powerful paradigm for other *actiones* in which, through engaging itself, the soul suffers distension: "What is true of the whole psalm is also true of all its parts and each syllable. It is true of any longer action [in actione longiore] in which I may be engaged and of which the recitation of the psalm may only be a small part. It is true of a man's whole life, of which all his actions [actiones] are parts. It is true of the whole history of mankind, of which each man's life is a part" (28:38). *The entire province of narrative is laid out here in its potentiality,* from the simple poem, to the story of an entire life, to universal history. (22)

Augustine was perhaps the first to articulate in terms of Christian ideology how performance could play out a confrontation between mind and body, obedience and rebellion, *vox* and *Verbum*.

Orality and Memory in *Confessions* 11

In *Confessions* 11, Augustine ascribes to human memory a major role in a new synthesis of human time whereby its continuous flux might be contained in a distended present through which humans might at least glimpse the nature of eternity.[16] To achieve this comparison of time and eternity, Augustine set out to show that time was being as opposed to nonbeing, as the skeptics argued by asserting that the past was no more, the future not yet, and the present continually passing away. Time exists in the mind, Augustine declares, which manages to contain the past and anticipate the future in an act of conscious distension of the present. By what Ricoeur calls the thesis of the threefold present, Augustine proposes a different present tense, one more linguistically than phenomenologically grounded.[17] In this view of time, past, present, and future exist in a distended present in states something like tropes: memory (*memoria*), present (*continuitus* or *attentio*), and expectation (*expectatio*).[18]

By way of illustrating his concept of the threefold present, Augustine describes the oral recitation of a psalm. This exercise, which for Augustine and his religious contemporaries would have been a commonplace and repeated example, becomes a model for the temporal synthesis of past, present, and future forming the "distended present." *Confessions* 27 and 28 provide a clearly articulated concept of the performative voice leading to contemplation and spiritual illumination through the act of reciting poetry aloud.

Crucial to Augustine's demonstration are the concepts of private contemplation coupled with poetic performance for the purpose of setting human *vox* and (divine) *Verbum* in creative opposition. For Augustine, performance as a step toward spiritual knowledge can only begin when the *vox corporis* (voice of the body) falls silent. Augustine's performative theory embraces the Platonic and especially Pauline mistrust of sensual apprehension, even as it demonstrates unequivocally the crucial role of the voice of the body. The performative subject becomes aware of itself as an autonomous consciousness through hearing its own voice raised in recitation. This is, for Augustine, just the first step in an education which moves progressively toward the discovery of the transcendent ego, a necessary condition for conversion, as he had shown in *Confessions* 8. The contemplative ego could only begin to find itself, however, on condition that the performative subject, the *vox corporis,* fall silent.[19]

One cannot say that Augustine has a negative view of the importance of the body in performance, for the evidence points the other way. We know from *De civitate Dei* 22.24 that he sees music and poetry as fundamental components of human identity. Nonetheless, we can see from the following quotations that he conceives the body in such a way as to limit its sensual impact on the mind. He accepts just enough to stimulate the mind's rational capacities. He says: "ad incandas et suadendas cogitationes quam multitudinem varietatemque signorum, ubi praecipuum locum verba et litterae tenent" ("It was human ingenuity that devised the multitude of signs we use to communicate and express our thoughts—and especially speech and writing").[20] The role of the body is clearly articulated, but in mystical rather than material terms:

Turn now from man's mind to his body. . . . It is a body obviously meant to minister to a rational soul. . . . And if we need further evidence to show to what kind of a mind the body was meant to minister, we have only to think of the *marvelous mobility of the tongue and hands so perfectly suited for speaking and writing, for the arts.* . . . What is more, there is in the man's body such a rhythm, poise, symmetry and beauty, that it is hard to decide whether it was the uses of the beauty of the body that the creator had most in mind. . . . *What I have in mind is the rhythm of the relationships, the "harmonia," as the Greeks would say, whereby the whole body, inside and out, can be looked upon as a kind of organ with a music all its own.* The beauty of this music no one has yet discovered, because no one has dared look for it." (*De civ. D.* 22.24; Walsh et al., trans., 528)

Augustine himself, of course, offers an example of "the beauty of the music of the body" in *Confessions* 11, but both there and in the above passage the body occupies a transient position in which its physical materiality is consistently undercut. The harmony of the body subordinates the *vox corporis* to a superior paradigm, the divine numbers. Augustine's notion of harmony rejects the body's capacity for multiple meanings, for what would amount to an autonomous harmony. I said *rejects,* rather than *envisages,* for we shall see that Augustine conceives all too well of a body free to make its own meanings, its own "music." *Confessions* begins with Augustine's experiences with the body's independent proclivities; the trajectory of the work gradually defines the body away from alterity, or, to use his own term, *dissimilitude,* whose musical counterpart would be disharmony (given the ethical definition by which he construes harmony). The role of the body will be to strive toward the univocal harmony of the human with the divine, which constitutes for Augustine identity or similitude.

In a justly celebrated passage of *Confessions* 11, 28.38, Augustine describes the synthesizing of time in the mind, taking as a model the oral recitation of a psalm which the singer knows by heart. Augustine makes the performative act central to his lesson to illustrate how memory encompasses the different parts of the song during recitation: the part sung, the part being sung, the part remaining—past, present, future. The performative act thereby shows graphically his notion of the "inner and outer harmony of the body working together." Not by accident does it also show the dichotomy between mind and body, performance and contemplation as contrasting kinds of expression: performance tied to the body; contemplation, a purely mental and spiritual activity. The dichotomy serves Augustine's opposition between letter and word, writing and voice.

Strictly speaking, chapter 28 offers a proof for the existence of time in our minds and the consequences of that knowledge for apprehending the relationship between the human and the divine. The chapter itself is rather short, devoted to analysis of the actual recitation of the psalm as a paradigm of memory process. Not surprisingly, it stresses mental activities: the physical act of recitation has no resonance, for the performative transforms itself into its mental equivalent, memory, as we read. Augustine effectively denies the vocal experience, because as we discovered in the previous chapter, he conceives of oral performance as *precognitive:* the work of the mind begins at the moment the voice falls silent, allowing the body to recede.

Little wonder that, in the previous chapter, when he describes oral performance in a brief, but rhetorically forceful, formulation, he refuses any hint of the existence of a performative subject or anything linking performance and body as expression in their own right: "ecce puta vox corporis incipit sonare et sonat et adhuc sonat et ecce desinit, iamque silentium est, et vox illa praeterita est et non est iam vox" ("See, as an example, a bodily voice begins to sound, and does sound, and still sounds, and then, see, it stops. There is silence now: that voice is past, and is no longer a voice"; *Confessions* 11.27.34).

For *voice,* here, we cannot help understanding *body.* Augustine's thrust falls not on outward expression of performance—the concern we shall find with the troubadours—but in the inward turning back on the mind, onto memory. His rhetoric here recalls the imagistic mode of Ovidian metamorphosis. In fact, Augustine subtends both Virgil and Ovid in the strategy of this paragraph to make ironic allusions to Virgil's Dido and Ovid's Echo as "voices" speaking for the repression of the body. The passage just quoted evokes the typical Ovidian transforming *punctum,* or moment. Metamorphosis is always fascinating in Ovid because he casts it visually as the dissolution of past existence by a strange new form which the reader recognizes as the victim's own unconscious reified as a totemic shape. Ovid's rendering of Echo's transformation in *Metamorphosis* 3 serves Augustine as ironic confirmation of the sterility of voice as an end in itself:

> extenuant vigiles corpus miserabile curae
> adducitque cutem macies et in aera sucus
> corporis omnis abit; vox tantum atque ossa supersunt;
> vox manet, ossa ferunt lapidis traxisse figuram
>
> . . . .
> Sonus est, qui vivit in illa.
> $\qquad\qquad$ (Ovid, *Met.* 3.396–99, 401)

[Echo's] sleepless care wastes away her wretched form; she becomes gaunt and wrinkled and all moisture fades from her body into the air. Only her voice and her bones remain: then only voice; for they say that her bones were turned to stone. . . . Sound it is that lives in her.[21]

In a learned play of classical quotations characteristic of *Confessions,* the allusion to Ovid's Echo recalls a Virgilian quotation embedded in the opening line of this chapter (*Confessions* 27) immediately preceding the Ovidian allusion. The quotation, from the fourth book of the *Aeneid* (l. 586), evokes the moment when truth dawns on Dido as she watches the Trojan fleet bearing Aeneas recede over the horizon as the sun comes up. Augustine begins *Confessions* 27.34 with an apostrophe to the mind: "Insiste, anime meus, et adtende fortiter" ("Courage, my mind, and press on boldly"). He links that apostrophe to the mind/body dichotomy by reiterating its key phrase, *adtende fortiter* ("press on boldly"), to a second apostrophe which embeds the Virgilian quotation: "adtende, ubi albescet veritas" ("Press on, where truth begins to dawn").

As though to stress the falling away of the voice as an inexorable moving away from the body and its distracting passions, Augustine ironically inserts the dawning of truth in the narrative of passion in *Aeneid* 4, which for Augustine, as for Dante, is the great subtext of *Confessions.*[22] The second apostrophe, "adtende ubi albescet veritas," also alludes to the moment when Dido looks out from her ramparts in the dawn to discover the receding sails of the Trojan fleet taking Aeneas away from Carthage (*Aeneid* 4.587). For Virgil's Dido, as for Augustine, the light is at first physical, then it becomes the mental light of understanding: "regina e speculis ut primum albescere lucum / vidit" ("The queen looks and sees the first light begin to dawn"; 4.586). The play of quotations links light and truth to the passing away of sensual distraction; for Dido, as for Echo, it leads inevitably to the destruction of the body. As the performative becomes memory, Augustine argues, understanding dawns with the silencing of the voice.

The Augustinian paradigm carried over into the twelfth century. In his allegorical commentary on the *Aeneid,* Bernardus Silvestris glosses Dido's immolation, like the *vox corporis,* as the passing away of the body necessary before thought can begin:

Increpat Mercurius Eneam oratione alicuius censoris. Discedit a Didone esuescit a libidine. Dido deserta emoritur et in cineres excocta demigrat. Desueta enim libido defficit et fervore virilitatis consumpta in favillam, id est *in solas cogitationes,* transit.[23]

Mercury chides Aeneas who leaves Dido and puts passion aside. Having been abandoned, Dido dies, and burned to ashes, she passes away. For abandoned passion ceases and, consumed by the heat of manliness, goes to ashes, *that is to solitary thoughts.*[24]

Augustine subtly but ineluctably establishes a link between oral performance, the body, and its passions. Perceived as transitive markers of material life, they give way once they have transmitted their content to memory. Their import may then be safely recast, by the action of the mind, into the language of identity according to the model of the anterior written text, that is, Scripture. The text to be sung will always, in some way, point back to the psalm, Augustine's paradigm for oral recitation in *Confessions* 11.28.38.

Augustine's and Bernardus Silvestris's attack on the body and its voice reveals a deep suspicion, amounting to hostility toward the free play of vocal expression. Only recitation from sacred texts, or from texts made on their model, can be trusted. In short, Augustine espouses writing. Throughout Augustine's work, the return of the oral to its written scriptural counterpart is a powerful imperative. Is this not the case with the most famous example of oral performance in *Confessions,* the voice like a child crying, "Tolle lege! Tolle lege!" ("Take and *read*")?

What Augustine bequeathed to the clerkly tradition then was a fundamental distrust of orality as an agent of the *vox corporis*. But the constant struggle against the voice and the body in the text made inevitable later challenges to his scriptocentric model. The challenge made itself felt in the very first vernacular lyric manifestation, troubadour song, which mounted one of the most prolonged and successful alternatives to the mystical movement from voice to silence that Augustine propounded.

Voice and Writing in the Troubadour Text

Troubadour song manifests a brilliant tension between the voice and the letter by assigning a dual role to the body. It is, first, the space that engenders desire or in which desire expresses itself most urgently as well as the battleground on which the conflicts of sexual repression and sexual license are carried out. Second, it did not escape the troubadours' sense of irony that the body is also the instrument for both writing and singing, and thus a perfect trope for representing the dynamics of resistance to the sexual and transference to the verbal.

The praxis of troubadour poetry seems to demonstrate what Paul Zumthor appears to downplay in his neoromantic celebration of orality: the importance of the letter, of the *gramma* as a basic element of *hermeneia,* or linguistic signification. But Zumthor is correct in sensing a freedom in troubadour song from the overemphasis on *grammata* ("letters") and *hermeneia* ("interpretation") by which the clerkly tradition contained the *vox corporis*.

Authorization for the blend of voiced music with written textuality can be found, as Giorgio Agamben reminds us, in the "text which determined for centuries, in the ancient world, every reflection on language, that is to say the Aristotelian *De Interpretatione*" (26). In a key passage, Aristotle defines a continuum of signification running from the imagination of the inner being through the voice to the *grammata,* or letters of the written text. Aristotle says: "That which is in the voice is a symbol of affections in the soul and written marks symbols of that which is in the voice. And just as the written marks are not the same for all men, neither are the spoken sounds. But what these are signs of in the first place (the affections of the souls), are the same for all; and what these affections are likenesses of—actual things—are also the same" (*Categories and De Interpretatione* 162.3–7).

Commentators from ancient times to the present have not failed to point out the ambiguities of this passage.[25] It may be taken, as Saint Augustine's demonstration in *Confessions* 11.28.38 does, as arguing that the letter is the sign of the voice that survives the voice once it falls silent. The letter thus contains and interprets the voice; it stands above it as index and surrogate. This emphasis, favored by some ancient grammarians, as Agamben points out (27), ultimately short-circuits the movement from body to voice to letter envisaged by Aristotle. Instead we find self-referentiality where the *grammata* point to themselves in a text which begins and ends with its own letters, eliding the first two stages. Agamben points out that "the *gramma* is the form itself of presupposition and nothing else" (27). This self-reflexivity favors the silent contemplation of mysticism (Agamben 27), and, when we think of it, describes rather accurately the movement from speech to silent meditation that Augustine portrays as the recitation of a psalm.

Whatever its partisans in the ancient world, the above scenario manages to ignore the privileged position accorded to the voice in Aristotle's schema. The body first generates the impulse for and the primary form of symbolic expression. Speech is the first interpreter of what Aristotle calls "the affections of the soul" and Averroes, in his twelfth-century commentary, translates as "the ideas that are in the soul."[26] Writing, in this schema, is secondary, the sign of the voiced images. However problematic his theory of meaning, Aristotle unambiguously accords to the human voice the role of providing meaning to the images arising from the psyche.[27] Only by eliding the body in the ways we have seen can the written text not be referential to the body's dual role of emotion and the envoicement of that emotion. In short, the unconscious receives its initial expression in *spoken* language.

In *Phaedrus* 275e–276a, Plato makes a similar point in arguing the mimetic superiority of speech over writing. He says that written words

seem to talk to you as though they were intelligent, but if you ask them anything about what they say, from a desire to be instructed, they go on telling you just the same thing forever. . . . But now tell me, is there another sort of discourse that is brother to the written speech, but of unquestioned legitimacy? Can we see how it originates, and how much better and more effective it is than the other? . . . [I mean] the sort that goes together with knowledge, and is written in the soul of the learner, that can defend itself, and knows to whom it should speak and to whom it should say nothing?

Phaedrus: You mean no dead discourse, but the living speech, the original of which the written discourse may be fairly called a kind of image. (p. 521)

Plato's point, like Aristotle's, is that speech is contextual with the body. But Plato makes an evaluative judgment against writing.[28] Aristotle is simply trying to analyze the progression from inner being to linguistic expression in speech and thence to the written version of that speech. In so doing, he provides grounds for a specific identity of the speaking subject. By linking voice and writing to a speaking subject who expresses particular variants of universal emotions—the "affections or ideas of the soul"—he invokes the concepts of signature and authority. These key concepts constitute the link between linguistic expression as a mode and the *vox corporis,* the subject in the text who represents his or her psyche as a particular phenomenon.

Guillaume IX (1071–1127), ninth duke of Aquitaine and seventh count of Poitou and the first troubadour, exemplifies Aristotle's concepts.[29] Guillaume makes the body itself—as voice and written text—central to a poetry that takes as its ground the *vox corporis,* a speaking of the body's manifold affective discourses: desire, memory, fantasy, anger, and so on. These discourses define the inner life in terms of the historical role of the poet as social being, as political being, as human being vis-à-vis the sacred, as parent, as lover, and as grand seigneur. The *vox corporis* is both a subject for troubadour song and a metaphysical presupposition for the language and concerns of the song.

Poetic voice, in Guillaume's lyrics, thematizes the emotional range of desire as a correlative of political and secular power. The voice apostrophizes a collectivity or social group which is both audience and peer of the poet. Through the vocalization of direct address between the speaking subject and his audience evoked as immediately present, the song, or *vers,* defines itself as both auditory and visual artifact—sound and image—worked in the *obrador,* or workshop, where the *trobar* (finding/making) takes place. In an exact reversal of Augustine's gesture and a confirmation of Aristotle's concept, Guillaume IX reveals how the poetry originates within the poet's being as inchoate emotion, gradually defined through the action of voice only to be externalized by the intervention of the *grammata,* or letters of writing. In essence, Guillaume defines song as a drama of discovery of language, where language is a vehicle for the independence of the emotions externalized by the dual actions of voice and letters. Each song highlights in its own way a moment of recognition when the speaking subject faces its own inner being, translated not into an incorporeal mystical silence but into an affirmation of a language of the body that calls into question the subject's own self-predication.

Let us look at the first stanza of one of Guillaume IX's songs:

> Ben vueill que sapchon li pluzor
> d'un vers, si es de bona color
> qu'ieu ai trat de bon obrador;
> qu'ieu port d'aicel mester la flor,
> et es vertatz,
> e puesc ne trair lo vers auctor,
> quant er lasatz.
>   (BdT 183.2.1–7)

> I really want the group to know
> about this song (it is a good color)
> that I have fashioned in a good shop
> for I wear the laurels of this métier
> and that's the truth
> and I'll call this song to witness
> when it's finished.[30]

The end of the stanza, "and I'll call this song as *auctor* (authority/author), when it will be 'laced up,' " foresees the moment of separation between poet and the fully textualized (*lasatz*) poem, where the poem offers itself as an independent voice, transforming the desire and sociolect into an aristocratic aestheticized object. The poem has genealogy and beauty: it comes from a good workshop ("qu'ieu ai trat de bon obrador") and has beauty ("si es de bona color"); above all it has authority. The poem distinguishes the functions of poet, the maker of the *vers,* and of the text as *auctor,* authority. Textual authority comes not from the poet but from the body itself, as the *Roman de Flamenca* (thirteenth century) confirms: "Totz cors d'aman es d'aiso autre" ("every lover's body is the authority for this"; 2740).

The last stanzas of the song illustrate the justice of Guillaume's *ars poetica* in the first stanza by showing the universality of poetic signs, specifically their transferability from one context to another. By moving from a courtly or high style in the first stanzas to an eroticized register in the second part of the song, he uses code-switching to illustrate Aristotle's point about the invariance of desire through the Babel of languages. At the same time, he illustrates the protean nature of voice capable of assuming different forms in the same song.

Stanzas 7–9 introduce a dialectic between the poet-as-lover and the beloved. The evolution of the woman in the stanzas, from the passive object of the poem's rhetorical tribute to the ironically witty equal partner in the game of love, highlights the linguistic turn from high culture to bawdy talk. The same metaphoric moves occur in the last stanzas as in the first, but the focus veers dramatically toward the body as sexual and textual subject. Guillaume uses dialogized narrative to switch codes from a courtly to an erotic register, a shift that plays out in sexual language the change of identity experienced by the role of the body from the beginning of the poem. In stanza 1, poetic voice portrays a body identified with the fate of the poem itself: well made, authoritative, handsome, adorned with the colors of rhetoric. By stanza 7, the body—and the poem—have become gendered, speaking and desiring in their own right. They reflect upon and give rise to reflection about the nature of the speaking subject and the authority conceded to it in stanza 1.

> Pero non m'auzez tan gaber
> qu'ieu no fos rahuzatz l'autrer,
> que jogav'a un joc grosser
> que·m fo trop bos al cap primer

tro fo entaulatz;
quan gardei, no m'ac plus mester,
si·m fo camjatz.

(stanza 7)

Well you won't hear me boast so
for I was in trouble the other day
when I was playing a bawdy game
all too pleasant to me at first
till I got into it
when I went at it, I couldn't play
my luck had changed.

While the erotic register may catch the listeners' attention, it is more of a pseudometalepsis of pen to penis than an authentic glimpse into the boudoir. Stanza 7 initiates a debate between the poet and his mistress, in which the woman's voice challenges the potency of the poet's body, his sexual adequacy, in a parodic dialogue which reveals just how closely allied—though carefully masked—are the pretensions of poetic mastery ("I wear the laurels of this métier"; stanza 1) and sexual and knightly prowess: "Tant ai apres del joc dousa / que sobre totz n'ai bona ma" ("I've learned the sweet game so well / that I'm the best hand of all at it"; stanza 4). Sex, poetry, and chivalric prestige all depend on public perception for their accolades. The parodic dialogue of these stanzas uses the woman's voice to impugn the authority of the poet as lover, in a way that must enhance the prestige of the performative, textual voice.

Mas ela·m dis un reprover:
"Don, vostre datz son menuder
et ieu revit vos a dobler!"
Fis·m ieu: "Qui·m dava Monpesler
non er laisatz!"
e levei un pauc son tauler
Ab ams mos bratz.

(stanza 8)

She made me such a reproach
"My lord, kind of small your dice
and I invite you to double!"
But I shot back: "I wouldn't fade
if they gave me Montpellier!"
And I raised her game board some
with both my arms.

The sexual innuendos would not be possible without the "flowers of rhetoric" evoked in stanza 1. Those flowers now control a contest of deflowering, sexual aggression in which the woman leads the attack, that leaves no doubt but that the text is a sign for the material body, the male and female sex organs so graphically elided as "game board" and "dice." The stanzaic form serves as the surrogate for the game board, the sign of the woman's body, while the belated rhetorical tumescence matches that of the poet's organ with which he appears to write the song:

> E quan l'aic levat lo tauler
> espeis los datz:
> e·l dui foron cairat nualler,
> e·l terz plombatz
>   (stanza 9)

> And when I'd lifted that board,
> I threw the dice
> and two were nice 'n' square
> and the third was loaded.

It is this stanza where the text offers the pseudometalepsis from voice to penis, summarizing the tension between the private performance of the erotic and the public performance of the poem. The self-consciously poetic text tries to present itself as spontaneous wit, while visibly demonstrating rhetorical craft, its status as writing dependent on voice. The stanza also contains, in the form(s) that we have it, a reminder of the tight link between the performative context of voice and writing (and memory) in troubadour lyric. Line 59 contains the enigmatic expression rendered by Pasero as "cairat nualler," from the following manuscript readings: C, *carauallier;* N, *cairat ualer;* E, *caramaillier.* The notes to Pasero's edition (185–86), and to Jeanroy's (38) list the various emendations and interpretations proposed for this line in the last hundred years or so. The general sense of the metaphor is clear; the exact sense, or even form, of the word(s) is obscured precisely because of the code-switching into a popular gambling vocabulary whose context has been lost.

In staging this simulacre of verbal foreplay before an audience invited to participate by communal decoding of the innuendo, the stanzas offer a dynamic counter to Augustine's use of memory to decorporealize song. Here each phase—from inner feeling to voiced expression to written text—contains and brings forward its predecessor. Memory provides the matrix organizing and moving the conceits from thought to voice to the collective mind and, presumably, discussion of the audience. The movement outward to writing takes the poem toward the larger social context, the context of politics and power.

We find more than a hint of power politics in the language of these stanzas as political control—"I wouldn't quit if they gave me Montpellier"—is juxtaposed to sexual dominance, itself translated into aristocratic gaming language. We may justifiably feel that the metaphor of the body extends beyond poetic form and sexuality to encompass the body politic—the *pluzors* apostrophized in line 1: "Ben vueill que sapchon li pluzor" ("I really want the group to know"). For Guillaume IX, the most powerful lord of his age, all bodies, whether feminine, textual, or political invite possession and dispossession. This holds true of the noble wives of his vassals whom he takes as mistresses or of his own lands open to depredations by his neighbors as he prepares to leave for the Crusades:

> Qu'era m'en irai en eisil;
> en gran paor, en gran peril,
> en guerra laisserai mon fil;
> faran li mal siei vezi.[31]

> For now I will go into exile
> full of fear, in great danger
> I will leave my son at war;
> his neighbors will do him harm.

By way of conclusion here, I would suggest that the troubadour lyric illustrates the limitations of Augustine's and Boethius's (quite different, but eventually consonant) movements toward a rhetoric of silence in which the *vox corporis* would be effaced. As we have seen in discussing Aristotle's *De Interpretatione* and Plato's *Phaedrus,* troubadour poetry turns out to be more traditional than Augustine's poetics. For the troubadour lyric illustrates what Giorgio Agamben has called "the presupposing structure of language [which] is the structure itself of tradition."[32] By the presupposing structure of language, we mean its continual coming into being through thought, voice, *and* writing, a process that troubadour poetry reasserts for the ear, for the eye, and for the mind.

Notes

1 "Ce qui importe [dans la performance orale lyrique] se situe à la source même d'une forme poétique. Le mouvement en effet de la *canso* procède, me semble-t-il, d'une perception à la fois aiguë et obscure d'une sorte d'inconnue, promesse, sinon menace, cachée, inscrite dans notre destin: un 'quelquechose' intervient entre la voix et le langage, un obstacle interdit leur identification et fait que leur association même ne va pas de soi. Cette perception, le discours de la chanson la narrativise, au moins virtuellement et de façon latente: de là, ce motif de l' 'obstacle' érotique, cent fois et sous des appellations diverses désigné par les spécialistes comme la clé thématique de cette poésie" (Zumthor, *Poésie* 33).

2 "Lorsque le poète ou son interprète chante ou récite . . . sa voix seule confère à celui-ci son autorité. Le prestige de la tradition, c'est l'action de la voix. Si le poète

ou l'interprète, en revanche, lit dans un livre ce qu'entendent ses auditeurs, l'autorité provient plutôt du livre, comme tel, objet visuellement perçu au centre du spectacle performanciel" (Ibid. 35).

3 "Dans le chant ou la récitation, même si le texte déclamé a été composé par écrit, l'écriture reste occultée" (Ibid.).

4 "C'est ainsi que je serais tenté de comprendre (plutôt que dans leur sens obvie) le verbe *cantar*, l'expression du *far canso*, et leurs équivalents français" (Ibid. 34).

5 See ibid. 36; Zumthor *Lettre*, chap. 2.

6 "La voix poétique assume la fonction cohésive et stabilisante sans laquelle le groupe social ne pourrait survivre. Paradoxe: grâce à l'errance de ses interprètes— dans l'espace, dans le temps, dans la conscience de soi—elle est présente en tout lieu, connue de chacun, intégrée aux discours communs, pour eux référence permanente et sûre. Elle leur confère figurément quelque extra-temporalité: à travers elle, ils demeurent et sont justifiés. Elle leur offre le miroir magique d'où l'image ne s'efface pas, lors même qu'ils ont passé. Les voix quotidiennes dispersent les paroles dans le lit du temps, y émiettent le réel; la voix poétique les rassemble dans un instant unique—celui de la performance—aussitôt évanoui qu'elle se tait: du moins se produisit-il cette merveille d'une fugitive mais totale présence. Telle est la fonction primaire de la poésie, et que l'écriture, par son excès de fixité, remplirait mal. . . . La voix poétique est à la fois prophétie et mémoire" (Zumthor, *Lettre* 155).

7 "Le point de départ d'une poétique, mettons du xiiᵉ siècle, devrait être la considération de cette beauté intérieure de la voix humaine, "prise au plus près de sa source," comme disait Paul Valéry. Cette beauté peut, il est vrai, se concevoir comme particulière, propre à l'émetteur du son vocal: à ce titre, et sauf exception difficilement imaginable, elle nous reste insaisissable, par-delà de ses longues durées. Mais elle est concevable aussi comme historique et sociale, en ce qu'elle unit les êtres et, par l'usage qu'on fait d'elle, module la culture commune" (Zumthor, *Poésie* 73).

8 "L'homme écoute, de la multitude des bruits, émerger sa propre voix: autour d'elle se noue le lien social, et prend forme une poésie" (Ibid.).

9 Manuscript O, the so-called Cangé chansonnier, was published in facsimile reproduction by Jean Beck in 1927. See Huot, "The Iconography of Lyricism in the Alphabetical Chansonnier O," in *From Song to Book* 74–80.

10 "Et dicta Musica per derivationem a Musis. Musae autem appellatae α ò τον μασαι, id est a quaerendo, quod per eas, sicut antiqui voluerunt, vis carminum et vocis modulatio quaereretur" (Isidore of Seville 3.15.1). Cassiodorus ascribes a very similar quotation to Clement of Alexandria: "Clemens vero Alexandrinus presbyter, in libro quem *contra Paganos* edidit, musicam ex Musis dicit sumpsisse principium, Musasque ipsas qua de causa inventae fuerint, diligenter exponit. Nam Musae ipsae appellatae sunt *apo tu maso* [α ò τον μωσθαι], id est quaerendo, quod per ipsas, sicunt antiqui voluerunt, vis carminum et vocis modulatio quaereretur" (Cassiodorus 2.5.1). Strunk points out that Cassiodorus misquotes Clement: "Clement reports that Alcman derived the origin of the Muses from Zeus and Mnemosyne; he does not speak of the origin of music. As for the etymology α ò τον μωσθαι, this is due to Plato, *Cratylus*, 406A" (Strunk 87n).

11 *Comm. in Mart. Cap.* 6.286.17. "Fontigenarum id est novem Musarum. Fon-

tigenae enim dicuntur Musae eo quod in undis prius musica artificialis inventa est, nam MOYC dicitur aqua." Remigius of Auxerre, ed. Lutz, 2.126.1–3. Lutz actually corrects the manuscript reading "MOYC" to "MOYCA," a lesson rejected by Swerdlow because "MOYC, not MOYCA is the correct word for water" (Swerdlow 4 n 6). He also points out the distinction, current in the late ninth century, made between *musica artificialis,* music produced with instruments, and *musica naturalis,* defined in part as music produced by the human voice. "Naturalis itaque musica est, quae nullo instrumento musico, nullo tactu digitorum, nullo humano inpulsu aut tactu resonat, sed divinitus adspirata sola natura docente dulces modulatur modos: quae fit aut in coeli motu, aut in humana voce" (Regino Prumiensis VII, Martin Gerbert 1.236b).

12 *Institutiones* 5.1, "De Musica;" quoted by Strunk 88. Cassiodorus also understands music in the strict technical sense: "Musica est disciplina quae de numeris loquitur, qui ad aliquid sunt his qui inveniuntur in sonis" (131.3, Mynors ed.).

13 Strunk 88 (my emphasis). The Latin text runs: "Musica ergo disciplina per omnes actus vitae nostrae hac ratione diffunditur; primum, si Creatoris mandata faciamus et puris mentibus statutis ab eo regulis serviamus. quicquid enim loquimur vel intrinsecus venarum pulsibus commovemur, per musicos rithmos armoniae virtutibus probatur esse sociatum. musica quippe est scientia bene modulandi; quod si nos bona conversatione tractemus, tali disciplinae probamur semper esse sociati. quando vero iniquitates gerimus, musicam non habemus." *Institutiones* 2.5, "De Musica," in Mynors, ed., 143.

14 One hundred twenty-five years or so before Cassiodorus wrote his *Institutiones* between 550 and 562, Saint Augustine had noted the analogy between the musical harmony and the harmony of the human body. In *De civitate Dei* 22.24, he says: "No man has ever dared to try to find those proportions of which I am speaking by which the whole body, within and without, is arranged by a system of mutual adaptation. The Greeks call this adaptation 'harmony,' on the analogy of a musical instrument; and if we were aware of it, we should find in the internal organs also, which make no display of beauty, a rational loveliness so delightful as to be preferred to all that gives pleasure to the eyes in the outward form—preferred that is in the judgment of the mind, of which the eyes are instruments."

15 "The major antithesis around which my reflection will revolve finds its sharpest expression toward the end of Book 11 of Augustine's *Confessions*" (Ricoeur 5).

16 I follow Ricoeur's outline of the problem of time here, although the emphasis on the role of memory, oral recitation, and their consequences is not part of Ricoeur's focus.

17 Ricoeur almost categorically rejects the idea of a phenomenology of time: "First, it must be admitted that in Augustine there is no pure phenomenology of time. Perhaps there never will be" (6).

18 *Confessions* 11.20.26: "Quod autem nunc liquet et claret, nec futura sunt nec praeterita, nec proprie dicitur: tempora sunt tria, praeteritum, praesens et futurum, sed fortasse proprie diceretur: tempora sunt tria, prasens de praeteritis, praesens de praesentibus, praesens de futuris. Sunt enim haec in anima tria quaedam, et alibi ea non video: praesens de praeteritis memoria, praesens de praesentibus contuitus, praesens de futuris expectatio."

19 Augustine will develop the paradox of "silent speech," that is, the *vox mentis* as

opposed to the *vox corporis,* in *Confessions* 11.27–28, as we shall see shortly. In *Confessions* 12.16.23, he employs the full rhetoric of noncorporeal speech, including the striking image that moral suasion aims at silence in imitation of divine speech: "I desire to converse for a little while in your presence, O my God, with these men who grant that all these things, of which your truth is not silent inwardly in my mind, are true. For those who deny these things let them bark as much as they wish, make only a din for themselves [latrent quantum volunt et obstrepant sibi: persuadere conabor, ut quiescant, et viam praebeant ad se verbo tuo]. I will attempt to persuade them, so that they may become quiet and leave open a way into themselves for your Word. . . . I beseech you my God, 'do not be silent to me.' Speak in my heart with truth, for you alone speak thus. I will leave them outside, blowing into the dust and raising up dirt into their own eyes. I will enter into my chamber and there I will sing songs of love to you."

20 Augustine, *De civitate Dei,* Libri 21–22, ed. Green, vol. 7. *The City of God,* abr. ed., trans. Walsh, Zema, Monahan, and Honan, ed. Bourke, 22.24.

21 Ovid describes the beginning of Narcissus's obsession with a similar rhetoric of disjunction:

> dumque sitim sedere cupit, sitis altera crevit,
> Dumque bibit, visae correptus imagine formae
> Spem sine corpore amat, corpus putat esse quod unda est.
>
> *Met.* 3.415–17.

"While he seeks to slake his thirst another thirst springs up, and while he drinks he is smitten by the sight of the beautiful form he sees. He loves a hope (longing) without a body, and takes for body what is shadow."

22 John J. O'Maera initiated this trend in *Confessions* criticism with his article "Augustine the Artist and the *Aeneid,*" 252–61. See also Bennett, "The Conversion of Vergil."

23 Bernardus Silvestris, *Commentary on the First Six Books of the Aeneid,* ed. Jones and Jones, 25 (my emphasis).

24 Bernardus Silvestris, *Commentary on the First Six Books of Virgil's Aeneid,* ed. and trans. Schreiber and Maresca, 27 (my emphasis).

25 See Ackrill's comments, Aristotle, *Categories and De Interpretatione,* p. 113. Isaac comments on the work in general: "La rédaction du *Peri hermeneias* est d'une extrême concision, à tel point qu'on a souvent l'impression d'avoir affaire à de simples notes. Beaucoup de commentateurs, Ammonius et Boèce en particulier, ont souligné ce fait, ainsi que l'obscurité qui en résulte. Il est "enveloppé de multiples obscurités," dit S. Thomas dans sa dédicace, et Cassiodore déjà dans ses *Institutions* cite, d'après un auteur grec, ce dicton qui sera répété bien souvent par la suite: 'Aristote, en écrivant le *Peri hermeneias,* encrait sa plume dans sa pensée.'" Isaac 12.

26 Averroes's translation/commentary of 16[a]4–9 in Butterworth's translation runs as follows: "Thus we say that spoken utterances signify primarily the ideas that are in the soul, while written letters signify primarily these utterances. Just as written letters—I mean, script—are not one and the same for all nations, so too, the utterances by which ideas are expressed are not one and the same for all nations. There-

fore, the meaning of both script and spoken utterances comes from convention rather than nature. And the ideas which are in the soul are one and the same for all people, just as the beings which the ideas in the soul are examples of and signify are one and exist by nature for all people" (Averroes 125).

27 In the notes to his translation, Ackrill, focusing on the question of natural versus conventional signs, faults the theory of meaning propounded by Aristotle, citing as unsatisfactory his argument for the conventional nature of the sign. Aristotle, *Categories and De Interpretatione*, pp. 113–14.

28 Eric Havelock points out that in *Phaedrus* 274, Plato "is fighting 'a rearguard action' . . . his preference for oral methods was not only conservative but illogical, since the Platonic *episteme* which was to supplant *doxa* was being nursed to birth by the literate revolution" (*Preface to Plato* 56n17).

29 On Guillaume IX and the "invention" of the Provençal lyric, see my essay, "The Old Provençal Lyric" 30–36.

30 All translations are my own unless otherwise stated.

31 BdT 183.10, "Pos de chantar m'es pres talenz," 11.5–9.

32 "The presupposing structure of language is the structure itself of tradition: we presuppose and betray (both in the etymological and in the common sense of the Latin verb: *tradere*) the thing itself in language so that language may bear upon something (κατα τινος). The sinking of the thing itself is the foundation upon which— and only upon which—something like a tradition can constitute itself" (Agamben 25).

9 *Laurence de Looze*

Signing Off in the Middle Ages: Medieval Textuality and Strategies of Authorial Self-Naming

The signing of the literary work of art has received less attention from the-oreticians of the text than the tenacious persistence of its appearance from the very beginning of vernacular French literature to the present day might lead one to expect.[1] The *Chanson de Roland,* for example, can be said to be "signed," hence authorized if not actually authored, by a certain Turoldus. Despite the fact that we know nothing about this Turoldus, that we have no idea what his role in the genesis or elaboration of the poem really was, and that we cannot indeed even prove that a Turoldus actually existed, the name bridges the poem's composition and its subsequent reception by both medieval and modern listeners/readers. The inscription of the name places Turoldus in a position of responsibility for having "declined" the work, situating him at the intermediary fringes between reader and work. The last statement shifts the burden of the heroic ethos from the shoulders of the characters "acting" within the work to those of Turoldus, the controlling force who is both part of and also (presumably) outside of the text. The *Chanson de Roland* is also the *Chanson de Turoldus;* text and story will be as good as Turoldus was at his job. The authorial name thus takes responsibility not only for the textual transmission but also for what takes place on the part of the characters.[2]

This issue of the relationship between the authorial name and the responsibility it implies is a delicate one, and it is still very much with us. Medieval authors such as Marie de France and Chrétien de Troyes use their own or their patrons' names in order to assume (or delegate) responsibility for their works, exploiting their selves/names to authenticate the truth of the tales (as in the case of Marie de France) or their patron's name to ward off flak for having exalted what some might see as an ethic of dubious morality (as in Chrétien de Troyes's *Lancelot*). Even modern writers, though quick to declare the author dead, as Roland Barthes polemically did in an influential article ("Mort de l'auteur"), continue nevertheless to sign their works, associating a particular approach or body of writings to a particular sentient being, and they continue to argue about where the limits of their responsibility as writers should properly lie.

The example of an exchange a few years back between the two historians Michel Foucault and Lawrence Stone calls attention to this tension, and the dialogue is all the more revealing since Foucault has, in his famous essay "Qu'est-ce qu'un auteur?" attempted to redefine the nature of authorship. In his landmark article, Foucault argues that the author is more than a simple signatory, for his signature authorizes and/or authenticates certain strategies and groups of discourse. What the precise relationship between the author's actual words and what they necessarily imply—"Foucault's" as opposed to "Foucauldian" thought, for example—is not entirely specified. Interestingly enough, when Foucault complained about what he felt were excesses in Lawrence Stone's article on him in the *New York Review of Books,* Stone based his defense, for better or worse, on the grounds that the body of discourse for which a writer, especially a writer as visible as Foucault, becomes responsible can include more than simply the totality of his actual utterances. Stone rejected Foucault's argument that since he never signed his name to developments from or extensions and interpretations of his ideas, they were not authorized.[3] Thus from the most famous example of anonymous French medieval "orality" to the most recent theories of the twentieth century, both of which would deny (each for its own reasons) individual authors and authorship, there is, perhaps paradoxically, an insistence on the authorial name as a unifying and authorizing feature and an implicit association of the name with an extra-textual being (real or invented) who "stands behind" (in both senses of the expression) the work.

This appeal to referentiality is not hostile, however, to the notions of literary code, to a conception of literary creation as intertextual rewriting, or to Paul Zumthor's seminal teaching that "le poète est situé dans son langage plutôt que son langage en lui" ("the poet is placed in his language rather than his language in him"; *Essai* 68).[4] That there might seem to be a tension between modern literary theory and the idea of an external authorizing existence posited by the authorial signature reveals a certain uneasiness regarding the authorial signature and where to situate it: text, paratext, autotext, metatext, intertext, all of the above, or none of the above?

Now to be sure, many medieval works are not signed at all; they speak to us, as we know, from "la nuit des temps." What is more, any distinctions we might establish between signed and unsigned works are guidelines and nothing more and cannot be taken as adhering to hard-and-fast rules. If epics, for example, are often anonymous, then such exceptions as *Aymeri de Narbonne* and the *Chanson de Roland* are noteworthy. Romance, by contrast, may appear to be more prone to naming its author—at least after the period of the first historical romances (*Roman de Thebes, Roman d'Eneas*)—which suggests that the genre which has less pretensions to historical veracity (that is, to controlling a historiographic tradition) takes greater pains to name its creators; but the rule is by no means strictly held.[5] Nevertheless, the exceptions are few enough to permit a certain degree of generalization.

In capsulized form, then, the thesis we shall explore is as follows. The major writers of courtly narrative in the late twelfth century—Chrétien de Troyes, Marie de France, Benoit de St. Maure, Hue de Rotelande—stitch their names into their texts with surprising consistency, tying self-perpetuation to textual perpetuation and using their posited authorial role to authorize and authenticate their works. In the thirteenth century this tendency undergoes modification, and the authorial name per se is seen as less important as a guarantor of the text's authority than is the authorial experience. Jean de Meun has himself named only indirectly—before (supposedly) he has even been born; Jean Renart may or may not have signed his works; Guillaume de Lorris never mentions his name; and likewise the authors of most sections of the monumental *Grail-Prose Cycle* do not mention theirs.[6] Strategies of nonnaming or indirect naming are molded in the fourteenth century into forms of oblique "naming by not naming." Guillaume de Machaut and Jean Froissart typify their age in their exploration of complex anagrams from which we are required to reconstruct the authors' names. By the fifteenth century, the anagrammic puzzle, though still embedding the name in the text, has discarded its trappings of complexity: as the example of Christine de Pizan's works clearly illustrates, the elaborate search for an "unknown" authorial name is abandoned, and the most important concern is less a matter of finding out (or pretending to find out) who the author is than of discovering the precise way in which the author's name has been anagrammed. In this shift of emphasis from "who" to "how," the scrambled form of the authorial signature—the anagram—takes on new significance in its own right. It now produces meaning independent of the name it also encodes and signifies. The mode and manner of these authorial "signatures" are thus indexical of the development of medieval thinking regarding both textuality and authorship.

It is perhaps worth recalling that medieval notions of the author differ considerably from modern concepts. Marie-Dominique Chenu taught scholars many years ago that the medieval cluster of terms *actor/auctor/aut[h]or* is considerably richer than our corresponding designations and distinguishes several aspects: *auctor*, from *augeo,* meaning "he who produces," and *actor,* from *ago,* meaning "he who does something" (Chenu, "Auctor"). The medieval author is renowned in particular for his authority, for which reason of course the medieval period was fond of false attributions to well-known *auctores.*

In the thirteenth century, however, an important change takes place in the medieval conception of the author: *actor,* of which the French form is *acteur,* comes to be written in place of *auctor* (Chenu, "Auctor" 84), whereas *auctor,* written also as *autor* and *author,* becomes associated with *auctoritas* and Greek *authentin,* designating authority and authenticity. The modulation and division of terms reflect an important shift in mentality and relate the authority of a text to the personal experience of its author, making the authorial *vécu* an authenticating feature. Interestingly, Chenu's findings have recently been corroborated by Alistair J. Minnis in a book on the medieval theory of authorship.[7] In much the same ways as Chenu, Minnis sees the thirteenth century as pivotal. The distant *auctoritas* figure, Minnis argues, even in Latin and religious texts, comes to be authoritative not for the weightiness of his name but for the life he lived, the latter being called upon to authorize the events of the text.

Most interesting to us here is that to demonstrate this thirteenth-century promotion of the *acteur*/author distinction and the new modes of authorizing the text, both Chenu and Minnis single out the *Roman de la rose.* Now, since it is also the same century, indeed the same text, that greatly advances the notion of *écriture* as the guarantor of the work's "truth," the configuration of all three elements is especially intriguing: the text claims as its authorizing agent (*auctor*) the life of its author as that life is in fact depicted in writing within the work (as *acteur*). Guillaume de Lorris tells us that everything that happens within the text corresponds to something in the five-year period after the text's completion, and vice versa. The complete "author-function" (to use modern terminology) comprises therefore both the writer—the authorial *acteur* within the work who explicitly links his role within the *Roman* to an existence outside the text—and his literary offspring, the written text which he claims as authorizing his story, as testament to his tale's authenticity. The author (in the modern sense) creates the text which he then claims as his *aut[h]or* in the medieval sense.

If the system of mutual authorial authorizing is circular, then the reciprocity causes problems when the circle short-circuits. The Guillaume de Lorris text, for example, leads to a paradox, a dead end in more ways than one, and the text is left incomplete. Does textual lack of closure reflect amorous incompletion? Was the love affair never resolved (as the most rigorous application of Guillaume de Lorris's logic would demand), or should we turn the problem around and consider that the love is not fulfilled simply because the text is left unfinished? Moreover, despite the expectation one might have that the authorial signature would be of capital importance in this situation—the self-inscription whereby the author authorizes the authenticity of his work through an act of self-naming that relates *actor* to *autor*—Guillaume de Lorris in fact keeps mum. The problem of the relationship between the authority and authenticity of the text on the one hand and the life of its *acteur* on the other is thus dumped in the lap of the reader.

To our good fortune we have two medieval readers' responses: one in the form of the anonymous completion and the other in Jean de Meun's continuation. The two could of course not be more diametrically opposed. Nevertheless both testify to the hermeneutical role of the reader who, in a synthetic act, both authors and authorizes the novel by completing its "gaps." In this regard, then, the *Roman de la rose* proves a pivotal text as regards the development of the author figure in medieval French texts, his designation as such, and the constitution of the text itself as authoritative and authentic.

In terms of its authorial signing, the *Roman de la rose* manages to have it both ways: it is both signed and anonymous. The Guillaume de Lorris portion, as we have it, for all its circularity of verification (the referential life of the author verifies the text, the text's ending should tell us what happened in the author's "real" life, etc.) textually mimes the plot's lack of completion and closure. *Aut[h]or* as authority and authentification is insisted upon to the exclusion of the author's name—excluding any attempt, that is, actually to link the work up with a life posited as existing in the referential world outside the text. Though the link is insisted upon, the text is left floating free, authorless. What do we do with a work which claims as its source the *source* (fountain) within the text itself? (Baumgartner, "Competence").

The naming of the *acteur* Guillaume de Lorris is, of course, the work of the *Roman*'s greatest reader, Jean de Meun. I do not speak of historical considerations here but simply of the fact that Jean de Meun completes the "author-function" by naming the authors' names and signing both parts of the *Roman* authorially.

The very fact that the reader affixes the first author's name indicates that the signature, rich in paradoxes and reversals, is more problematic than are the straightforward pronouncements of twelfth-century authors. To be sure, if the Guillaume de Lorris signature is marginal to the Guillaume de Lorris text (coming six thousand verses into the Jean de Meun continuation), it is central nevertheless to the composite work as a whole, coming near the very midpoint of the complete *Roman de la rose*. Moreover, Guillaume de Lorris's name is only generated long after he is supposedly dead.

We might describe, then, the movement from the twelfth to the thirteenth century as an evolution from concern for the author as a *name* to concern for the author as a *life*. Play and pun there may well have been in the self-appellation "Chrétien de Troyes," as has often been suggested (Dragonetti, *Vie*, most recently), but the reader's "creation" of the author is something that especially characterizes post–twelfth-century works.[8] Indeed, one can sketch a chiastic relationship between the rise of *écriture* as an authenticating and authorizing agent (as the *autor*) and the naming of the *acteur* directly within the text itself. The diminution of interest in directly naming the author in the thirteenth century should be seen therefore as a relocation of interest in the author. Concern that the author's name will live on "tant con durra cres-tïantez," as Chrétien de Troyes put it (*Erec et Enide*, v. 25), is replaced by an anxiousness regarding whether the author will (even) live his life and a view that completion of his life and completion of his work will be one. To wit Jean de Meun's anxieties regarding castration (see Bloch, esp. chap. 4) and the very matter of his own birth: what happens if Jean de Meun is not born or not born whole, and as a result the work is left similarly truncated?

Jean de Meun's anxieties humorously illustrate the way in which the *corps* of the *auctor* becomes the authorizing feature for the life of the *acteur* and for the literary *corpus*. One's life text is both text and life, and to cut life short (Guillaume de Lorris) or not bring life to birth (the threat allegedly hanging over Jean de Meun) is to cut short the text (the failure to end the first part of the *Roman de la rose;* the danger of never even beginning the second part).

As the old notion of the *auctor* wanes, then, a new complicity between author and reader is forged. If the twelfth-century "complete" text completed itself by naming its author, the thirteenth-century work sees the authorial function as incomplete without the inclusion of the writer's partner, the reader. The reader's consent and accord are sought to authorize the text or determine its course. Renaut de Beaujeu asks his lady-reader to author and authorize a different ending to *Le bel inconnu* by accepting his suit as a lover, upon which he promises to write the different ending she favors. And Guillaume de Lorris clearly implies that his lover can pluck the rose only if the "real" author has been allowed to capture his lady's love in the real world; indeed as much as his text is supposed to be a map of what has already taken place, it is also written to curry favor with its first reader, the lady, to get her to authorize an ending that Guillaume de Lorris will then write into the text. To be sure, it may well be the tension between these conflicting requirements that made nonending the only possible ending adequate to both Guillaume de Lorris's and Renaut de Beaujeu's texts (see Haidu).

Having considered the progression from the twelfth-century "complete" text which completes itself by naming its author to the "incomplete" text in the thirteenth century that looks to its reader for authorizing and authentification, we may now move to fourteenth-century literature which vociferously refuses to name its author directly and calls upon the reader to author the author out of the scrambled text of the anagrammic puzzle. The work in its complete form reveals itself as incomplete and, in a most literal sense, asks the reader to bring to it what Derridean critics would no doubt call a *supplément.*[9] The reader is thus charged with authoring the author and with authorizing and authenticating the text; the reader is made an *auctor* who intertextually rewrites the anagrammed text and creates the author.

This is, on the one hand, self-consciousness pushed to an extreme, and certainly this naming-by-not-naming is typical of the way in which works by Guillaume de Machaut and Jean Froissart display what we could term postmodern concerns for surface and the role of the reader. Still, this refusal of the authors to name names should not be seen as a lack of concern for authors—that is, as a medieval "death of the author." The fourteenth century is a period when courtly writers took an active part in the compilation of grand codices of their works, in editing literary *corpora* which were explicitly or implicitly analogous to their own lives, and even in the articulation of programs of manuscript illumination. If a thirteenth-century work such as the *Roman de la rose* is already moving "vers la société de l'écriture," as a recent article has described it (Hult, "Vers la société"), then fourteenth-century narrative has fully arrived. François Avril has, for example, demonstrated Machaut's active participation in the artistic program of MS Paris, Bibliothèque Nationale, f.fr. 1584 of Machaut's "complete works," and a similar role seems likely in the case of Froissart (Huot, *From Song to Book*). In addition, passages such as Dante's insistence in Canto 33 of the *Paradiso* that his work not be scattered, and Chaucer's testy poem to "Adam Scriveyn" all testify to the delicate balance between *sema* and the dangers of uncontrolled dissemination, the spilled literary seed, if you will.

This consolidation of *écriture* must thus be measured in the role of the reader and the work demanded of him. Despite one's initial expectation that the more overt the textual orientation of medieval literature becomes, the more "work" the text might do for the reader, the opposite in fact is and should be true: the more the written text is conceived as a written text and not as pseudo-orality, the more the reader—now an active participant rather than a passive listener—shall be called upon to do.[10] Chaucer's well-known admonition to the reader to turn the pages and choose another tale, like the nonsequential reading the modern writer Julio Cortázar proposes for *Rayuela,* presupposes that the individual is privately reading the text, not listening to it read aloud.[11]

As concerns the reader's reconstruction of the author and the authorial signature, in the fourteenth century it is no longer done *in* the text *by* another reader, but it becomes the task of the reader of the manuscript: our task, in other words. The author's identity is still presented as authorizing or authenticating the literary work, but the reader is charged with the task of recognizing and re-creating the authorial signature/identity through the *engins* of anagrams and word games. Writing and reading are part of a mutually engendering cycle: the reader must rearrange the text to re-create the author whose identity serves to unify, authorize, and authenticate the literary work the reader is reading.

We have not, however, come full circle back to the anonymity of the earlier Middle Ages. For the "discovery" of the author of a fourteenth-century work is very different from discovering the author of an earlier medieval work. Rather, the fourteenth-century literary text makes great play of doubling back on the past; mock anonymity is a ludic evocation of earlier anonymity, but a ludic evocation only, for one only tries to solve an anagrammic puzzle to which one already has the solution.[12] In a recent article I demonstrated that authorial anagrammic self-naming does not in fact function according to the code of the quest by which it claims to operate (de Looze). Though the works—of Guillaume de Machaut or Jean Froissart, say—admonish the reader to seek and find the name of the author dissimulated among the words of the text, this *inventio* is in fact a witty fiction that depends on the complicity of writer and reader. There is in reality no search, for one only knows which "solutions" to discard and which one to retain if one has prior knowledge of the right answer. The cardinal rule is therefore one of circularity. Ernest Hoepffner unwittingly acknowledged as much, in his edition of Machaut's works, when he remarked that in the case of Mauchaut's first work, the *Dit dou Vergier,* the author was not yet sufficiently famous to permit an anagrammic signature. In other words, readers would not have known whose name to "discover" in the scrambled text. Indeed, a century of literary scholarship on the subject shows very clearly that readers manage to produce "Guillaume de Machaut" regardless of what the text actually gives. The anagrammic passage of the *Dit dou Lyon* is certainly exemplary: it can be made to yield such "solutions" as Victor [H]ugo, Ronsard, Turoldus, C[h]arles d'Orléans, Georges Sand, Gérard Genette, Socrate, Auguste Rodin, Aristote (or Aristoteles), and "Guillaume" de Lorris. None of this dissuades us from rejecting these answers as "wrong." In fact we already have the "right" answer—Guillaume de Machaut—and the only problem is that we cannot produce it from the passage supposedly containing the author's name (see de Looze).

The question arises: If the laborious—and occasionally labyrinthian—task of dissembling the designated verses of a literary work, then rearranging them to spell the author's name, is in fact a completely circular process in which one works backward from the already-determined solution to the puzzle which one then proceeds to solve, what possible purpose is served by this tortuously complex procedure?

The answer, I believe, is multiple. First, this playful return to "anonymity" cleverly knits together the strategies of the previous centuries: what parades as pre–twelfth-century anonymity also claims to contain a signature of the author's name (a twelfth-century feature), and appeals to the reader for completion, as do thirteenth-century writers. Moreover, the anagrammic signature is a feature crucial to fourteenth-century literary self-consciousness in that, behind the fiction of hide-and-seek, it reaffirms notions of the text and textuality which are consonant with a neoplatonic view of the world. Furthermore, the calls to the reader to "discover" or "compose" the author (the word often used is *trouver,* implying both invention and literary composition) are generally confined to the prologue or final verses of the work and hence are threshold features.

The relatively unproblematic threshold naming of twelfth-century texts is gone, however, for it is left to the reader to create the bridge which the authorial name once constructed. The reader is asked to relate the text to the referential world precisely at that point in the text where text and world come into contact. Moreover, what the reader is asked to create is at once a new text and the author of the present text—an act of creation which both looks backward, in terms of textual genealogy, to the "father" text and also creates at the same time a "filial" text in the father's image. Glancing back at the *Roman de la rose* again for a moment, let us remember that the very passage that gave identity to the first author, Guillaume de Lorris, was the same one which declared him prematurely dead and hence opened the possibility for the birth of the filial text. Jean de Meun's obsessional anguish in the *Roman* regarding his own birth is, in this light, highly important and emblematic of the fear on the part of the filial author/text that has killed off the paternal author/text that the same might happen to him/it.

What takes place with great anxiety in the *Roman de la rose* is more cheerfully staged in fourteenth-century works. The text is not complete until "signed" with the author's name, not by the author but by the reader cum author. The reader, in the act of "solving" the anagram, completes and closes one text while at the same time creating a new one, at the very minimum the author's name. In this sense the reader's "response" is more concrete and more active than in many contemporary, even "postmodern" literary works. Assuming a role that is both recreational and re-creational, the reader must author the author, though the author authors the text which endows the reader with this power. Indeed, the complete work is a kind of literary Möbius strip: the reader authors the author who authors the text that authorizes the reader to author the author who authors the text—and so on.

The anagrammic signature thus reaffirms the materiality and the limits of the text and draws attention to the fact that the text is nothing but a web of signification, that meaning is masked by the marks on the page and must be recovered through the hermeneutical act of reading. One must know how this textuality functions in order to read according to this nonsequential code, as well as according to that of sequential narrative; hence knowing *how* to reconstruct the author's name is more important than the actual discovery of the name, which is, in truth, known all along. Therefore, to come up with the solution is proof not of one's capabilities when it comes to conundrums but of a certain kind of literary competence. What Paul Zumthor pointed out some years ago in his essay on the *carmina figurata* has relevance for the anagrammic signature as well: "Le monde sensible n'est . . . qu'un masque dissimulant une réalité différente, de sorte que l'observation importe moins à la connaissance qu'une méthode d'interprétation" ("The sensible world is . . . but a mask dissimulating a different reality, such that observation has less importance for understanding than does a method of interpretation"; *Langue* 28). The only change one might consider making in Zumthor's formulation would perhaps be the temptation in our decade to spell *different* with the Derridean *a*.

For to read according to a different reality is to read in a manner that both differs and defers. The "meaning" of the anagram is deferred to a new text. The anagrammic signature is, in microcosmic form, a restaging of the process of literary genealogy inherent in such thirteenth-century works such as the *Vulgate Cycle of the Arthurian Romances* and the *Roman de la rose* and made explicit a century later in such major cycles of literary texts as Machaut's *Jugement* poems or Jean Froissart's *La espinette amoureuse* and *La joli buisson de Jonece*. In Froissart's most ambitious work, *La prison amoureuse*, this program of the writing out of a reading of a previous text forms the very matter of the work's story. Indeed it is with reference to his lady and his patron—rather than to his own name—that the narrator closes the text, his first reader having become the alpha and omega of the text ("Vous qui estes cause et matere d'avoir che empris"; "You who are the cause and subject of my having undertaken this"; Fourrier 171). The protagonist, Rose, for example, writes a letter to the narrator in which he recounts a dream and asks the narrator to make a book about it. Once the work has been written, Rose then asks the narrator to gloss it with a new text, text and interpretation constituting the "complete" text, at least for the moment. He subsequently asks the narrator to join to the first interpretation an additional, supplemental interpretation of one part.

The evidence of the fifteenth century stands as a confirmation of, and yet effects as well a new permutation of, the extreme textual play of anagrammic authorial self-naming. The direct literary descendent of Machaut and Froissart and the most prolific of all late medieval French poets, Christine de Pizan, shows, like her predecessors, a predilection for anagrammic signatures. There is, however, a subtle shift from her forebears, and it is perhaps worthwhile to consider Christine in some detail.

Machaut's and Froissart's anagrams are, it must be remembered, meticulous in their instructions. The reader is told precisely which letters to retain and which to elide from a particular verse, in order to isolate with exactitude the scrambled form containing the author's name. Machaut's *Confort d'ami*, for example, counsels that

> Si osteras premierement
> Une sillabe entierement
> Au commencier dou ver onsieme
> Et une lettre dou disieme
> Pres de la fin.
> (Hoepffner ed., vv. 35–39)

You will thus first remove one whole syllable from the beginning of the eleventh verse and one letter from near the end of the tenth.

La founteinne amoureuse similarly announces that

> Jusqu'a quarante compteras
> Ces vers ci, et quarante et un.
> . . . .
> Nos noms entiers y trouveras,
> Mais trois lettres en osteras
> Droit en la fin dou ver quarante.
> (Hoepffner ed., vv. 46–51)

You shall count these verses up to number forty, and forty one. . . . There you will find our names in their entirety, but you will have to remove three letters right at the end of the fortieth verse.

The complexity of these instructions is designed precisely to make the reader forget that the search is entirely circular; in the cutting and pasting required of the reader one has the impression of a difficult quest.[13]

The closest Christine de Pizan comes to such a technique is at the end of *Le dit de la rose:*

> De par celle qui ce dictié
> A fait par loyale amitié,
> S'aucun en veult le nom savoir,
> Je lui en diray tout le voir:
> Qui un tout seul cry crieroit
> Et la fin d'Aoust y mettroit
> Se il disoit avec une yne
> Il savroit le nom bel et digne.
> (Maurice Roy ed.,
>   vv. 642–49)

By will of she who composed this work out of loyal affection, if anyone wants to know her name, I will tell that person the whole truth: whoever might cry out a "cry" all alone and then add to it the end of August, if he pronounced it along with an "yne," he would know the name quite nicely and rightly.

What is almost overlooked in the complexity of Christine's instructions is that she does not, in truth, propose an anagram but rather something quite different.[14] Christine doubles back even further in medieval literature than did Machaut or Froissart and creates a "new orality," though one born of textuality. For the instructions are not to cut and paste, as in the case of fourteenth-century authors; rather, this "signature" is entirely phonetic. Christine de Pizan gives detailed directions for the *pronunciation* of her name. The written text thus forces the reader into orality: to utter her name.

The paradoxes and levels of irony are brilliantly captured in the cleverly redundant and almost nonsensical "cry crieroit" and "une yne." As the reader cries out a "cry," onomatopoeia gives way to the first syllable of the author's name. Moreover, the reader is directed toward the end of August, but according to a temporality which is not the experiential or seasonal one to which we are accustomed but entirely linguistic, designating the last two letters: *st.* Finally, one must pronounce "une yne." The language play again appears "postmodern" in its characteristics: the linguistic minimal pair, virtually nonsensical as a purely textual phenomenon, is meaningfully resolved once one grasps *une* as part of a text to be read and *yne* as part of a text to be pronounced aloud, as a phoneme. These elements which might first appear to the eye as scribal error—the "cry cri" quite clearly a visual doubling, echoed two lines later by "une yne"—are in fact neat juxtapositions of the written and the spoken. Christine de Pizan wittily plays off orality and textuality in this signature which is no signature at all but an utterance molded by the text. Paradoxically redundant textual signifiers have second, entirely oral significations: in the oral *cry* and the oral *yne* it is a matter of neither a scream nor of a nonsense syllable, but rather the result is [cry]+[st]+[yne] or Christine.

In other works Christine invents new ways of exploiting her name and the signature of that name. Christine closes *Le débat de deux amans,* for example, by playing the written text off against the contingent world, thereby effecting much the same self-conscious juxtaposition of text and world as she did in the previous example, which forced the reader into utterance in the referential world. Just as she plays off two temporalities in *Le dit de la rose*, she here juxtaposes two spaces—that of the text and that of the referential world:

> Et or est temps de mon oeuvre affiner,
> Mais de trouver, s'aucun au deffiner
>   A volenté,
> Quel est mon nom, sanz y querir planté,
> Si le serche, trouver le peut enté
> En tous lieux ou est cristienté.
>   (Maurice Roy ed., vv. 2018–23)

And now it is time to end my work, but if someone on finishing it wishes to find out what my name is, without having to hunt a lot for it, he can find it

made fast if he looks for it in all the places where "Christianity" ["cristienté"] is.

It is the last word, *cristienté,* which, rearranged, forms the name "Christ-
tinee" or "Christine."[15] In terms of textual space, this statement of course
operates on two levels. On the one hand, Christine is saying that any time the
word *Christianity* pops up, her name will be invoked anagrammically. But the
passage is also a clever intertextual allusion to, and rewriting of, Chrétien de
Troyes's famous boast that *his* name will last as long as Christianity. For
Christine makes every instance of the word *Christianity,* including that of
Chrétien de Troyes's text, an evocation of *her* name. And since the word is
certainly frequent in the Middle Ages, *Christine* comes to represent metonymically the vast textuality of Christianity: every such text is her, and she is
all those texts.

This aspect of course spills over into referential space: wherever there is
Christianity, Christine is. And the passage does not limit her to textual occurrences only: on the contrary, the ambiguity of the reference to *lieux* affords a
much wider application. Christine identifies herself with universal Christian
fellowship of all times and places, associating her name with universal
"Christian" life.

Clearly, the textuality of the anagrammic signature has undergone a considerable change. The point of the signature is no longer simply an amusing
game of hide-and-seek such as that proposed by Christine's predecessors. She
dispenses entirely with telling us precisely which letters house her name and
which do not; this is a covert recognition of the fact that to be able to "solve"
the puzzle, one must already have the solution. But then solving puzzles is no
longer Christine's goal. Rather she exploits the fact that the scrambled form
can constitute a signifier in its own right, and for this reason she takes such
care that the scrambled form of her name is not simply a meaningless hodge-
podge of letters. *Cristienté* is both "Christine" and "christianity."[16] The
creintis ("fearful") authorial signature of *Le dit de Poissy* is both a description of the proper posture of true lovers and an anagram of Christine's name,
though once again the directions make no effort to isolate that word in
particular.[17]

Christine de Pizan's exploitation of the anagrammic signature can thus be
seen as a culminating reflection on medieval textuality and its limits. She carries the Machauldian game of signing without signing to new limits: the signature paradoxically becomes an oral utterance; it can be "fearful" and can even
become all of Christianity. Christine seems supremely aware of that illusive
quality of the authorial signature: it does not in reality bring us any closer to
the flesh-and-blood being that created the work, despite the impression of
doing so, for the signature is but another writing, another text, a trace left by
the writer (or reader) who has "always already" slipped away.

In this respect exploitation of the paradox of presence and absence in anagrammic signatures anticipates much recent post-structuralist thought on the impossibility of recovering a referent outside textuality. In a sense, Christine does modern theory one better, however, by actually forcing the reader to utter her name in the referential world: she breaks the endless cycle of textuality which, like the person who keeps cutting the distance between himself and his goal in half endless times and thus never arrives, will never actually attain its referent. That the author's signature is simply more writing is already clearly inscribed in one of Christine's earliest major works, her *Cent balades*. The final *balade* is devoted entirely to the matter of *écriture*, both of the whole work and of her own name. The first strophe runs:

> Cent balades ay cy escriptes,
> Trestoutes de mon sentement.
> Si en sont mes promesses quites
> A qui m'en pria chierement.
> Nommée m'i suis proprement;
> Qui le vouldra savoir ou non,
> En la centiesme entierement
> En escrit y ay mis mon nom.
>   (Maurice Roy ed., vv. 1–8)

I have written one hundred ballads here, all composed from my sentiment. Thus are my promises fulfilled to the person who earnestly asked this of me. I have correctly named myself. Whoever would like to know it or not, in the hundredth ballad I have put my name in writing in its entirety.

In the second strophe too she mentions that

> Et au dernier ver proprement
> En escrit y ay mis mon nom.
>   (vv. 15–16)

And right in the last verse I have put my name in writing.

And she again mentions it to close the third stanza:

> En escrit y ay mis mon nom.
>   (v. 24)

In writing I have put my name there.

The literary joke is again created by the manner in which the anagram signifies in two distinct ways. It is not merely that Christine has signed her name in writing ("en escrit") but that the "en escrit" is the very signature itself: it unscrambles as "Crestine." The writing of her name becomes a writing of writing: a direct allusion to the whole project of *écriture* and to the identity between the poet's *corps* and the poet's *corpus.* Christine is writing, and "Christine" is the writing of Christine.

Christine thus reveals a new meditation on the notion that text spawns text which spawns text. Or perhaps we should say that text spawns metatext which spawns metametatext. Though she devises ways to force both a return to earlier literary modes and nontextual action in the referential world, she is supremely aware that to write is to be written and rewritten, that the authorial name bridges the chasm between the written and unwritten, "en escrit" in the threshold space where text meets world.

To be sure, we are once more back to the notion of literary creation as intertextual rewriting, of which the re-creational and recreational act of reconstructing the author from the anagrammic passage can be said to be emblematic in fourteenth-century French letters. Thus if, as Harold Bloom remarked in one of his Norton lectures at Harvard University in 1987, the notion of the author, like short skirts, has a way of coming back again and again, so also does the contrasting concept of literary production as intertextual rewriting. Whether or not hemlines can be both high and low at the same time is a matter we can safely leave to the trade of couture. The literary text, at any rate, does manage to have it both ways: the "solving" of the anagrams posits readers as writers, re-creating the authors of the texts they are reading, positing an *acteur* as *aut[h]or,* but one fashioned intertextually by the reader.

Notes

1 Regarding authorial signatures in the visual arts, see Charles Sala's interesting article. Curtius's "Mention of the Author's Name in Medieval Literature" in *European Literature and the Latin Middle Ages* remains one of the best discussions of the subject.

2 That medieval scribes sought to improve their texts when they felt improvement was needed is well known. The medieval scribe had a certain responsibility to the text to copy neither sloppily (making unwanted and unwarranted changes out of ignorance) nor slavishly (leaving unchanged matters which, for one reason or another, the scribe felt could be rectified). See Bruns 113–29.

3 Lawrence Stone writes: "One can, I think, debate the extent to which an original thinker is responsible for the ramifications, or extensions, or perversions of his work by others. Can Marx be held responsible for Marxism?" (Foucault and Stone 43).

4 This and all other translations in this essay are my own.

5 *Partenope de Blois,* for example, must be reckoned an exception. The same basic distinction between "unsigned" epics and "signed" nonepic poetry also characterizes classical literature (Curtius 515).

6 *La mort le roi Artu* of course claims to have been written by Walter Map.

7 See also the review article by Rita Copeland.

8 Jean Renart, rare among medieval writers for having insisted on the novelty of his
  work ("novele chose") may or may not have stitched his name into an *engin*. In
  his recent book *Le mirage des sources*, Roger Dragonetti has shown that Jean Renart's is not the only name that can be reconstructed from the verses supposedly
  containing the authorial anagram. "Lorris," for example, can be as easily produced
  as "Renart." Thus the "solution" Joseph Bédier proposes in his edition of *Le lai
  de l'ombre* may be that of a reader trying—perhaps desperately—to fill the gaps in
  his text. Cf. also Dragonetti, "Qui est l'auteur," and Ehrhart (122). A recent example of how easy it is to "see" ("project") anagrammic signatures is Ferdinand
  de Saussure's "discovery" of anagrams, presented and discussed by Jean Starobinski ("Texte").

9 Curiously this is not a *residu*, but a text inherent in the letters (*residu*), although
  uncrafted.

10 The same has of course been argued regarding modern textuality. See in particular
   Roland Barthes's discussion of what he calls the "texte de jouissance" (*Plaisir du
   texte.*)

11 This is true, despite the fact that the same passage also refers to the possibility of
   reader's "hearing" things he does not like. The rhetoric of orality remains as a
   pseudo-oral feature long after texts are entirely conceived and conveyed in writing.
   Indeed we still regularly write such phrases as "By this I mean to say that," or
   "Now I wish to tell of/speak of/discuss." The presence of "oral" features inter-
   mingled with "written" features can thus be a proof only of writing, unless it be
   proved that the written features are later accretions. No oral work will refer to itself
   as being written, though the opposite obtains. The example from Chaucer is therefore a remarkable instance of textuality not *despite* but *because of* the hear/read
   admixture.

12 Chaucer provides an excellent example of this playful attitude in the *House of
   Fame* by having the Eagle call him by name in a work in which he claims to be
   entirely indifferent to whether or not his reader has his name "in honde."

13 For a detailed study of this phenomenon in Machaut's anagrams, see my article in
   Romanic Review.

14 Maurice Roy, however, calls the signature an anagram (2: 48).

15 Here again Christine plays with the normal rules of anagrams, which permit the
   doubling of letters that occur only once in the anagram. If letters of the anagram
   can be doubled to form the real name, why not use the opposite strategy, whereby
   doubles have to be eliminated to form the real name? Christine wittily calls attention to the process by reversing it.

16 Cf. the end of *Le livre des trois jugemens:*

Mais au dernier ver vueil dire et retraire
Quel est mon nom, qui le voldra hors traire
      Comme il deffine.
Et en la fin, de pensée enterine,
Qui vous ottroit joye parfaitte et fine
Pri Jhesu Crist, qui ne fault ne ne fine.
        (ll. 1526–31)

[Crist]+[ine] gives C[h]ristine, though without any of the Machauldian-Froissartian pretense about the reader needing detailed instructions to be able to figure out who the author is. The double signification of the anagram matters more to Christine than the game of the anagrammic search.

17 So also *Creintis* appears, with no directions at all, as a kind of authorial "Christine" signature at the end of *L'épistre au dieu d'amours.*

PART FOUR
THE THEMATICS OF
ORALITY AND WRITING

Introduction

The shift from a fully oral to a fully literate vernacular and mentality varied from one location to another, but it was always slow and complex. To what degree was this change, which we now see as profound, felt and expressed in the Middle Ages? Stephen G. Nichols, in the previous section, shows its place in a long, literate, philosophical discussion about the priority and relative superiority of the mind's contemplation or the body's voice. The change also shows itself within medieval stories. This section presents modern readings of texts composed in twelfth- and fourteenth-century France. The production of each text involves writing in different ways, and each shows in its thematics a different confrontation with writing. In a text that has as a stated purpose the preservation in writing of ephemeral oral performances, the anxiety of change from oral to written production steps forward under the cover of allegory; a text participating in a widespread written tradition—a prose romance—makes its layers of production, oral and written, a major element of its plot and a topic of explicit discussion.

Like Stephen Nichols, Dolores Warwick Frese sees the twelfth century as a time of battle between voice and text, so that Marie de France's preservation of the oral Breton lais in writing is not simply literary amusement but rather an act in the politics of gender and social change. Frese reads Marie's "Bisclavret" as an allegory of these politics and the female, writing poet's position in them: her story of the werewolf whose wife prevents his return to human form by taking away his clothes from him is also a story of written *textus* being kept from the oral poet, of not allowing him to change from the howl of voice to the silence of letters. Contemporary stories of werewolves and other shape-shiftings image a cultural sense that the boundary between human and beast was all too permeable. At the same time, the vocalizing and gesturing male jongleurs are coming and going and finally disappearing and being replaced by quite a different thing, the figure who writes individually and in silence, a figure that might well be female. Marie yokes into a single allegory these two transformations, making all this available to our interpretation, as only a written text can. In doing so, she shows the liminality of her scripted lais and her own position as female writing poet.

181

By the fourteenth century, the production of history and of literature incorporates the oral into the literary, and interest (according to Huot, "one might even say obsession") stands in the place of anxiety. Sylvia Huot demonstrates the *Roman de Perceforest* to be a *mise en scène* of how history and romances are produced. Through its fiction (a story shaped in writing), the romance puts before us events that stage relationships among "real" incidents, oral lais in Breton, chronicles written in Greek and Latin, the oral activity of interpretation, and French romances. We see the differing hermeneutics required for the diverse genres and their differing relations to time and social context. Through her analysis of *Perceforest* and its place in the romance tradition, Huot shows the French romance to be a grand mediator of orality and writing—of the social classes that generated and were shaped through oral and written productions and of their matter, aesthetics, and mode of communication.

C. B. P.

The Marriage of Woman and Werewolf: Poetics of Estrangement in Marie de France's "Bisclavret"

Documenting and explicating the development of literacy from Greco-Roman antiquity to the High Middle Ages and beyond, recent literary and cultural historians have laid increasing emphasis on those periods—sometimes prolonged for centuries—when literate and nonliterate societal norms coexisted, clashed, and were integrated and transformed through the transition from orality to textuality.[1] Brian Stock has carefully detailed that "there is in fact no clear point of transition from a nonliterate to a literate society" (9). This is so, Stock claims, despite the fact that the transformation of oral culture by writing and textuality had been "irrevocably" determined in the Western world by the twelfth century (18). In this essay, I will argue that the transition from oral to literate culture was not only gradual but also traumatic. One dimension of that traumatic revision involved sexual politics, since, in the practice of poetry at least, oral artists were male, while poets creating written texts could be either male or female.

Marie de France, a twelfth-century woman writer, stands as a tutelary presence in the textual record of such change. In the prologue to her *Lais*, Marie explicitly describes her poetic agenda as involving the preservation of ancient oral performance in the newly written poetic texts she is authoring. For Marie, the shift from oral to written performance is ineluctably associated with the paradigmatic shift from male to female artist. Furthermore, within each of these twelve fictions, there is a persistent emphasis on the female subject. At one point Marie even makes explicit note of her titular change wherein she renames a lai in order to emphasize that the adventure being redacted happened to women: "Kar des dames est avenu" ("Eliduc" 25).

While each one of Marie's lais arguably contains some trace of the shift from oral to written cultural practice, now featuring orality, now literacy by turn, the lai of "Bisclavret" is a key piece whose topic may be seen as nothing less than the transformational process itself. Read as a fable of poetic change, Marie's werewolf fiction speaks with particular force to her own function and self-conception as a female practitioner of the art of poetry at a time when the gradual transition from orality to textuality was observably in process. The gradual nature of this change as well as its irreversibility are both subtly detailed in "Bisclavret," where the generalized cultural anxiety expressed in stories of werewolves takes on particular literary valence which it is my present purpose to explore. The anxiety arises from a terrifying slippage backward, forcing the hero of this lai to perform a wordless pantomime for the king. In this gestural way he successfully communicates his plea for survival. In the sparing of the werewolf we are given important literary information and a touching record of archaic performance undertaken by one whose voice has been silenced.

The silenced werewolf who disappears into the realm of the anonymous daemonic stands in sharp contrast to the literary artist who, quite atypically at this early moment in textual history, insists on signing her name to her written work. As Mickel (143 nn1, 2) and Freeman (878 n1) make clear, there are hazards in oversimplifying the historical questions surrounding the nominal and authorial identity of this woman poet. Nevertheless, someone named Marie clearly intended that her name would survive as long as her poetic texts should live. Her signatory intent is appended in documentary fashion at the end of her translation of Aesop's *Fables* from English into French:

> Al finement de cest escrit,
> Que en romanz ai treité e dit,
> Me numerai pur remembrance:
> MARIE ai nun, si sui de France.
> (Epilogue 1–4)

> At the end of this piece of writing, which I have translated and set into French, I will name myself for posterity: I have the name Marie, and I am from France.

Elsewhere, in the concluding lines of the *Espurgatoire Saint Patrice* (2297–98), and again at the beginning of "Guigemar" (3), first of the twelve *Lais,* we reencounter this Marian act of nominal self-description. Each time, as in the above-mentioned "escrit . . . e dit . . . pur remembrance," the witnessing name, Marie, has been situated in close textual proximity to verbs of "remembering" or "nonforgetting" and to words that record the "speaking" and "writing" crucially implicated in the poetics of oral-to-written performance. These are written texts that intend simultaneously to memorialize and efface their oral counterparts.[2] For a poet who begins the prologue to her *Lais* with references to the sixth-century grammarian Priscian and to other "ancient philosophers" of literature whose custom it was to labor over the construction of ingenious textual effects that would both guard and communicate their literary meaning (1–22), such rhetorically prestigious featuring of her own name is not without poetic point. For beside her name, we typically find Marie's concomitant record of intended poetic piety. Not once but many times, noted and discussed by Burgess and Busby in the introduction to their translation of the *Lais* (8–13), Marie testifies to her pious intention to undertake the cultural work of oral conservation in the midst of emergent literacy.

Oral survival in the new textual environment represents much more than a written record of an oral transaction, however. As Stock has succinctly noted, "Literacy is not textuality"; in the case of Marie's *Lais,* we can point to implicit literary resonance that regularly attends the making and reception of the text, for traceable literary intention will repeatedly certify these narratives as works meant to serve "a dispositive role, which effectively superseded oral arrangements" (Stock 7). In the course of her literary work, Marie will attempt to "translate" the expiring oral performances of her male predecessors into her present act of silent writing. She will "carry out" this work, much as Aeneas had "carried out" Anchises, the mythopoetic male ancestor, when the walls of Troy had been irreversibly breached. Though Aeneas is never overtly named in Marie's text, the repeated characterization of the literary project as a saving of the male precursor causes the reader to see the long shadow cast upon Marie's work by that fictional "first hero," imagined in the memorial work of "carrying out" his own ancestral figure.[3] This memorable image of the male ancestor, slung across the shoulders of his lineal descendant like some precious burden of rote whose unsung memories must now be written down or die, supplies the underlying figuration for Marie's announced project in undertaking to write the *Lais*. From outset to end, and by ingenious literary analogy which works not by foreshadowing but by the penumbra which is its partial and imperfect reverse, Marie de France conspires to make her textual work resemble the post-Homeric undertakings of Virgil's *pius Aeneas.*

Such textual strategies, communicated at the outset of the *Lais*, furnish us with ways of accessing the poetics of literacy which we find encoded in particularly acute form in the lai "Bisclavret." In this lai of the werewolf, as we shall see, the silent woman poet and her equally silent, absent, invisible, and privatized reading audience are brought to life and brought together. With literacy itself hanging in the balance, writer and reader are made imaginatively coextensive in "Bisclavret" by metaphors of shape-shifting estrangement and by metonymies of textual redress. Together, these articulate Marie's parable of literary history.

For the reader's convenience, the following résumé will serve to introduce my analysis of Marie's brief 318-line fiction:

> In Brittany, a happily married baron perplexes his wife by three-day absences each week. After her persistent, urgent requests for explanation, he admits to becoming a werewolf during these periodic excursions into the forest. Further pressed for specifics, he confesses to complete divestiture during these adventures and confides that he hides his clothes in a hollow stone beside an old chapel at the edge of the woods. The man begs the woman to keep his secret, since to lose his clothing would doom him to being a werewolf forever. Shocked and terrified at these disclosures, the wife consents to the suit of another man, one she does not even love, requiring only that he permanently impound the clothing temporarily put aside by her husband.
>
> Now a werewolf, Bisclavret is compelled to remain in the wood, unable to become human again. One year later, pursued by the king and his retinue who are hunting in the forest, the werewolf, brought to bay, begs for mercy in a remarkable pantomimic performance that amazes and moves the king. The king spares the life of this communicatively talented creature, taking him back to court, where he is installed as beloved and constant companion to the whole royal household.
>
> In due time, during a ceremonial visit of all who owe fealty to the king, Bisclavret shocks the court by a savage and seemingly gratuitous attack on the knight who has supplanted him as consort to the traitorous wife. Shortly thereafter—that thoroughly discomfited pretender having been the first to leave court—Bisclavret's wife arranges to greet the king and bring him a present. Spying his traitorous wife, Bisclavret repeats the fearsome attack, this time tearing the very nose from the face of his betrayer. Thanks to the logical skills of a regnal counselor who reminds the king that this werewolf has never attacked any but these two and since the counselor further deduces the significant connection between the second marriage of the wife and the inexplicable disappearance of the baron, the king puts the faithless spouse to the torture until she supplies an oral confession.
>
> Given back his clothes, Bisclavret at first refuses to put them on, declining to change in front of the courtly audience. After according him a private room and a decent interval of time, however, the king and his counselors return to find a movingly beautiful knight, now fully clothed, asleep on the bed. As for the faithless woman and her complicit partner, we learn in a final burst of brilliant wordplay that, having been banished from polite society, these two bred a progeny of noseless females whose descendants can be seen to this day, still exhibiting the singular fault of noselessness: "C'est veritez, senz nes sunt neies / E si viveient esnasees" ("That's the truth; they were born [and bred?] noseless, and so they lived, noseless, [unhappily?] ever after"; 313–14).

Obviously, the fascination with werewolves in the lai "Bisclavret" represents a narrative theme which Marie is exploiting, not inventing. Such fearful adventures in metamorphic reversion were commonly perceived in the Middle

Ages as phenomena of daemonic or diabolical possession and had furnished the subject of prior narratives, including Ovid's tale of Lycaon in the *Metamorphoses* and Petronius's tale of transformation told by Niceros in the *Satyricon* (in Otten 227–33). Husband-and-wife werewolves, moreover, make their appearance in the *Topographia Hibernica* of Giraldus Cambrensis, Marie's contemporary.[4] The epistemological issues of reality and appearance raised by werewolves were regularly subjected to theological debate by medieval philosophers and theologians based on Augustine's discussion of shapeshifting in Book 18 of *The City of God* (chaps. 17–18): "What Varro says of incredible transformations of men" and "What we should believe concerning the transformations which seem to happen to men through the art of demons."

Presumably, too, werewolves had supplied the subject for countless oral horror stories where victimization might alternate between the fate of devourment and the counterhorror of becoming the one transformed, the boundaries of self dissolving as the helpless protagonist felt himself (occasionally herself) falling victim to the terrifying slippage backward. The symptoms of such slippage would typically include bestial reversion, accompanied by the loss of language, and the growing of fur, fangs, and claws.

Scandinavian berserks who donned bearskins for battle, the nocturnal rites of Herne or Cernunnos that included animal cross-dressing (Nicholson 637–69), and even periods of famine in the Middle Ages that drove wolves from the woods into the villages (Otten 2) may be adduced as cultural contexts for this deeply installed topos expressed in numerous narrative analogues. These cognate narratives range from familiar hagiographic accounts of Saint Francis of Assisi taming the Wolf of Gubbio (Habig 697–98) to the obscure and notably misogynistic "Arthur and Gorlagon" (in Otten 234–55).

In this last-named, little-noticed Arthurian text preserved in a late fourteenth-century copy, we find a striking collocation of the themes of faithless female spouse, the transformation of a husband into a werewolf, the affectionate adoption of the beast by a king whose own adulterous wife is then exposed by the werewolf through pantomimic gestural performance, and the combination of logical deduction and physical torture as adjuncts to the final restoration of the werewolf to his human form. Indeed, this werewolf proves to have been none other than King Gorlagon himself, to whose court Arthur has traveled in order to learn the truth concerning "the heart, the nature and the ways of women" (Otten 236). Gorlagon's adoptive protector while in transitional wolf-guise was none other than his own younger brother, King Gargol.

We need not labor the evident connection of this late fourteenth-century text and Marie's twelfth-century "Bisclavret." What must be noted, however, is the status of both texts as poetic fables concerned to represent the prolonged and often anguished phase of adjustment attending the cultural shift from orality to literacy. In "Arthur and Gorlagon," the intent to commemorate oral performance is underscored by the explicit dramatic format of the text, in which speaking parts are assigned to each actor and the recitative skills of King Gorlagon are on dramatic display.

"Arthur and Gorlagon" further conserves the artistic record of oral performance via Arthur's final observation to his host, immediately prior to Gorlagon's revelation that he himself is the former werewolf: "You are like a harper," says Arthur, "who almost before he has finished playing the music of a song keeps on repeatedly interposing the concluding passages without anyone singing to his accompaniment" (248). This striking performative observation suggests something of the oralic drama of repetition and delay enhanced by musical accompaniment as performed by skilled jongleurs. The remark occurs at the end of a feast—the traditional setting for oral performance—where Arthur persistently refuses to take food until the whole truth of Gorlagon's commentary on women has been unfolded.

That final truth, now linked to Gorlagon's identification of himself as the former werewolf, shifts the center of attention to the presence of a hitherto unmentioned weeping woman. Her gruesome portion at this feast involves a human head swimming in a dish of blood. At Arthur's questioning, Gorlagon identifies this sad, silent woman as his former spouse, who had betrayed him for "the son of a pagan king" (238). Like a priest kissing the book, this traitor must now kiss the embalmed head "for whose sake she had committed that crime" (250). She must do so each time that Gorlagon pauses in his recital to kiss the new wife he has taken in her stead. The concluding scene of "Arthur and Gorlagon" furnishes a prophetically remarkable literary icon, one that speaks in a compelling way to enduring centers of textual tension between pagan past and Christian present, between clerical and popular culture, between written and oral formulations of experience, all of which characterized the gradual and traumatic shift to literacy and texuality as cultural norm.[5]

The metamorphic theme that explores the uncertain boundaries between man and beast, between original and evolved behaviors, thus appears to have shown a natural affinity for works of literary fabulation in which the underlying images of lupine baying at the moon and the dramatic presence of claws could suggest poetry's literate transformation from its earlier form as an oral orphic rite. After all, properly performed, oral poetics would call for skillful vocal projection, as well as the biomorphic cultivation of those "sharpened nails" which the art of medieval minstrelsy required. The latter requirement is openly attested in the Middle English romance *King Horn*, in which the titular hero is described in the process of learning "to harpe / wiþ his nayles scharpe" (11. 231–32). In suggesting that Marie's "Bisclavret" intends to present a parable of poetic transformation from earlier oral to later written forms, we must be cautious, as Stock has noted, about drawing direct parallels between the evolution of literary texts and those of law, theology, and historical writing, where the intention to include signs of earlier oral formulas into the newly written record has been more openly recorded. Nevertheless, "literature did not develop in complete isolation," and though "its conventions were different, and authors were often inclined to obey their own instincts rather than general prescriptions" (Stock 81), Marie de France has made it explicit that her *Lais* do intend a literary version of this same incorporation of oral past and written present. In the lai "Bisclavret," if the werewolf carries vestigial traces of orality about him, it is equally true that his clothing is a logical symbol for the written text itself, since *textus* is just as applicable to a piece of writing as it is to a piece of cloth. Having appropriated the metamorphic theme of the werewolf for her poetic fable of orality's sporadic and uncertain demise, Marie then adds her own inventive versions of this attestably common medieval trope of clothing or cloth as a sign of textuality and its associated traditions of learning.[6] It is the clothes, or *textus,* which Marie installs in "Bisclavret" as the "symbolic artifact" whose appearance, under varying guises in each of her twelve lais, Hanning and Ferrante (2) have correctly identified as a fictional constant which serves as a kind of hallmark or poetic signature for Marie's art.[7]

As early as Boethius, we find the commonplace of clothing as text informing the metaphor of the torn garment which the prisoner observes on Lady Philosophy when she visits his cell (4). This shredded hand-me-down is later borrowed by Alain de Lille to clothe Philosophy's kinswoman, Dame Nature, who complains of attempted rape by men who have snatched piecemeal at her fabric, rendering her ragged (15). Such insights help us to penetrate the fictive veil in Chrétien's story of "marital adjustments" between a "mercurial" young man and his "wise" bride, Enide. The torn, worn, threadbare, and strangely attractive dress that Enide wears when Erec first meets her signifies her textual lineage as a daughter of the aforementioned Philosophy, née Nature. Clothing as text thus situates Chrétien's *Erec and Enide* in a lineage that includes *The Marriage of Philology and Mercury,* for in Martian's textual fiction the perfectly matched pair openly represent Wisdom and Eloquence and are faithfully served by seven handmaidens who are the Liberal Arts.[8] To this growing medieval tradition of the textual wardrobe, where garments serve as a sign of the learned tradition, we must add the gorgeous robe with representations of Geometry, Arithmetic, Music, and Astronomy woven into its magical fabric and used to cloak Chrétien's Erec on the occasion of his coronation at Nantes. Mussetter rightly perceives this culminating scene as the enthronement of a "master of the quadrivium" (151).

The foregoing brief digression into the trope of *textus* has been undertaken by way of securely establishing the poetic centricity of the clothes in Marie's lai. The hero's periodic putting off of his clothing for orphic excursions back into the wood imply the text whose shape-shifting is both subject and object of

Marie's literary exercise in "Bisclavret." The wife's poetic catechism—how, when, where, why do such transformations take place?—thus concludes with an allusively textual question, followed by her mate's stunningly direct answer: "Enquis li ad e demaundé / S'il se despuille u vet vestuz. / 'Dame,' fet il, 'jeo vois tuz nuz'" ("She inquired further and asked him if he took off his clothes or kept them on. 'Madame,' he replied, 'I go stark naked'"; 68–70). Ancient history and present praxis are both enclosed in this account of poetic transformation; for in every age, and through remarkably variant circumstances, poetry's own account of its sublime and terrifying act of possession attests to the fact that poets always attempt to lay aside whatever vestiges of civilization or acculturated experience might stand between their individual poetic voices and the encounter with what is truly primal or original in human experiences. "Nudity" or "bareness" before the prepossessing experience is thus at once the poet's greatest strength and greatest vulnerability.[9]

In Marie's fable, the clothing that qualifies Bisclavret to be a man among men is precisely what he must put off in his poetic attempt to become a daemon among daemons. To the uxoriously orphic risk of the wife, then, this panpoetic male figure must add the explicit demand of lifelong mediation between the oral past and the culturally evolving written text which is here signaled by his courtly clothes. It is important to note that Marie has taken pains to suggest such a gradual, potentially lifelong, transitional phase by featuring the sustained time frame during which Bisclavret successfully negotiates these compelled excursions back into primitivity. Her suggestive figure must be taken into account in reassessing Lord's influential assertion that the line between orality and literacy was necessarily a clear-cut one in the career of any given poet practicing during the period of transition between oral and written style: "Once the oral technique is lost," Lord asserts, "it is never regained. . . . It is conceivable that a man might be an oral poet in his younger years and a written poet later in life, but it is not possible that he be *both* an oral and a written poet at any given time in his career. The two by their very nature are mutually exclusive" (*Singer* 129). *Pace* Lord, the extended transitional phase suggested by Marie's poetic fable would seem to validate Stock's counterthesis of gradual change and simultaneous modalities of performance, applicable to literary as well as to legal and administrative expressions of cultural shift, with the textual evidence itself attesting that "the written did not supersede the oral" in any absolute way (Stock 16).

It is not by chance that Marie's werewolf poet employs the verb *jeo vois* ("I go"; 170), when describing his excursions into the more primitive form of expression, for with this verb he simultaneously intrudes the substantive *vois* that also designates the human voice. The poetic rift—that cleft wherein the man returns his "text" to the prelithographic rock by the woodside chapel—translates to an anguished admission whose deepest disclosures confess the

risk of Bisclavret's permanent return to the realm of the anonymous daemonic. Should his textual strategies become unavailable to him, should his
periodically forsworn "text" be permanently denied, he would "become a
werewolf forever": "Bisclavret sereie a tuz jurs" (75).

This fictional heightening of two mutually exclusive poetic impulses—
"pleasing terror" on the one hand and the "counterstress of self-preservation" on the other—can be seen to correspond with striking exactitude to
aspects of the countersublimity described by Bloom in his account of the re-
visionary ratio of daemonization, necessarily undertaken but rarely accomplished by aspiring poets (*Anxiety* 101). The poetic transactions of daemonization are accompanied by such high risks to the poet precisely because the
"finding out" by poetry is frequently accompanied by a subsequent failure to
master the influx of energy associated with the profound experience of such
"discovering and being discovered" (25–26).

But it is not only Bisclavret, an oral male performer attempting to accommodate the anguish of textual displacement, who is figured in Marie's fable of
thwarted poetic evolution. Bisclavret's wife has also been compellingly envi-
sioned by Marie as an arriviste woman poet, caught in the act of prostituting
her own potential by these perverse attempts to deny her precursor/spouse his
entitled right to poetic survival. As Marie-the-poet has already made clear in
the prologue to the *Lais,* her own acts of textual conscription are undertaken
to guarantee the survival of the more primitive poetic form, not to ensure its
demise. This express poetic agenda constrains the meaning of the fictional
woman who initially displays these two nascent but authentic symptoms of
poetic daemonization only to subvert their initial appearance; for "pleasing
terror" and the "counterstress of self-preservation" are described by Bloom
as essential responses to the encounter with poetic sublimity (*Anxiety* 101).
We witness these as the wife of Bisclavret first "turns blood red from fear"
("De poür fu tute vermeille"; 98) and then instantly contrives to save her own
skin by the proffer to another man to whom she feels neither love nor obliga-
tion: "Ele ne l'aveit unc amé / Ne de s'amur aseüré" ("She had never even
loved him, nor offered any assurance of love"; 107–8). What the wife attempts here is not merely marital betrayal; it is textual treason.

Textual treason engenders our instinctually correct censuring of this pragmatic survivalist who is drawn as a false female ephebe. She is a shallow
woman poetaster who dispatches her new, clearly inferior consort to the
woods, pointing him to the precise path that Bisclavret has previously taken.
The husband's original trace is shown to the lesser man who succeeds him, not
that he might follow in those footsteps, join him in the woods, rehabilitate
him, or even put him to death. The wife's sole intent is that Bisclavret be permanently denied those textual strategies necessary to his survival in the time
of traumatic transition. And indeed, Marie's parable of generic demise might

have been nicely concluded at the point at which the nameless wife marries this textually complicit supplanter. A fable limited to depicting the definitive end of orality could even have been concluded with some mention of occasional hauntings by the beast, a typical scenario in generic werewolf fictions.

But such a conclusion would not comport with Marie's implicit concern to represent the sporadic and then final disappearance of oral jongleurs, nor would it accommodate the need to represent the transformation of cultural consciousness which accompanied their gradual demise. In characterizing the communal response to the baronial husband's extenuated absence, Marie supplies a mirror image for that phase of literary history when the public gradually needed to accommodate the occasional, and then absolute, disappearance of the jongleurs: "Pur ceo qu'hum le perdeit sovent, / Quidouent tuit communalment / Que dunc s'en fust del tut alez" ("Because the man had often disappeared, they were all of the common opinion that this time he had gone away for good"; 127–29).

But this is only half the tale. Such closure would not be consonant with Marie's repeatedly stated intention not "to bury the dead," drawing the sheets of her own written text over their fading forms, or—more ruinously—to falsify the record of their pure past with images of negative primitivity, happily obsolescent. Rather, Marie has proposed to save the life of those past performances, working their history, their eloquent art, their very science, into the fabric of her own new textual work. The prologue to the *Lais* announces this explicit commitment to "bon' estoire" (29), "bone eloquence" (2), and "escïence" (1). In her foundational statement, then, Marie solicits the survival of her oral precursors, even as she uses their sacrificial silencing as the foundational event that places her written artifacts into the new genealogy of purely textual constructs. This memorial record of *chanson de geste,* where gestural acting out was an essential part of the aesthetic of performance and reception, becomes the acceptable offering when combined with the oblation of silence. This is how we can understand the werewolf's astonishing performance in the woods when he approaches his sovereign, takes hold of the stirrup, and kisses the leg and foot of the lord in antique ceremonial rites of fealty involved in "becoming [someone's] man." The silenced oralist—now constrained by a rubric of wordless mimetics—successfully communicates his plea for survival through pantomimic gesture alone.

The king and his retinue of hunters combine aspects of the vanishing oral performer and the audience for such performance. Like such artists and their clientele, he seems intuitively to perceive the underlying need for renunciation without yet fully understanding its implications. Thus, in response to the werewolf's performative silence which is both ancient and new, both prevocalic and prototextual, the king announces that he himself "will hunt no more that day": "Kar jeo ne chacerai hui mes" (160). In this notable vow to "leave the wood" and to "forswear the hunt," the woman poet's lai "Bisclavret" inscribes a poetic history of male atavism and its religio-poetic ritual origins even as the feminine act of writing records the ceding of such archaic rituals to new textual rites.

The poetic history of such male atavism can be found elsewhere in medieval conventions of the hunt that similarly conceal the history of textuality within their ceremonial fictive incidents. This poetic theme is subtly exemplified by the "hart-hunt" of Gottfried's *Tristan,* where it is the young harper who instructs the court of King Mark in the proper rubrics attendant upon the "excoriation of the heart" (78–86). The semiotic connection of this "huntsman's" ritual involving the "heart-of-the-hart" and the poetic hypothesis detailed by Mickel (50–54), whereby lyric lais are seen to represent the "heart" of longer narrative lais in which they were once embedded, must not be too quickly dismissed. Indeed, in the speech of Marie's fictive king—a "nobles reis" of literary acuity equal to that of the sovereign whose regnal patronage Marie acknowledges in the dedicatory remarks that preface her *Lais* (43–44)—we find versions of two highly conscious literary terms of art, *antancïon* and *san.* These are terms of art made famous, if not made clear, by Chrétien de Troyes in the prologue to his "Le chevalier de la charrete." Douglas Kelly has made the presence of these and other literary terms in Chrétien's romance the subject of a book-length study, *Sens and Conjointure.* In explicating the poetic presence and critical import of *sens* and *antancïon* in Chrétien, Kelly construes the former term as meaning "signification" or "interpretation" which he takes to mean "saying the same thing in as many different ways as possible" (Kelly 36). *Antancïon,* closely related to *sens* but not synonymous with it, Kelly defines as the poet's ability "to gloss, to interpret, to develop" a given poetic idea conveyed in the *sens* of the text (37).

We need not here digress into a critical history of scholarly debate on the precise and/or shaded meaning of these terms, though that record is a long and distinguished one containing important insights useful for coming to terms with twelfth-century poetics in particular and medieval literary art in general.[10] What we must not overlook in "Bisclavret" is Marie's deliberate incorporation of these documented textual terms and the dramatic attachment of their appearance to the metamorphic process that is symbolized by her iconic accommodation of the human to the bestial: "Ceste beste ad entente e sen" ("This beast has 'intention' and 'sense'" 157).

When Marie installs "entente e sen" in her werewolf and dramatizes the acknowledgment of their presence in this lai by the king's act of identification, such poetic installations serve to announce the matrix of *textuality* whose verbal "overdetermination," as Riffaterre says, "adds its own powerful connec-

tion to the normal links between words—grammar and lexical distribution,"
finally conferring upon the accomplished literary text its dimension of monu-
mentality by virtue of the fact that

> it is so well built and rests upon so many intricate relationships that it is relatively
> impervious to change and deterioration of the linguistic code. Because of the complex-
> ity of its structures and the multiple motivation of its words, the text's hold on the
> reader's attention is so strong that even his absentmindedness, or, in later eras, his
> estrangement from the esthetic reflected in the poem or its genre, cannot quite obliter-
> ate the poem's features or their power to control his decoding. (*Semiotics* 21–22)

Unlike the oral pun, in which the potential of multiple meanings in the
heard phonemes must be swiftly sorted out and the appropriate choice made
without any help from the spelling, the aesthetics of literacy inscribes phonemic ambiguity, with multiple routes of meanings as equal interpretative
possibilities. Such dramatized textual surplus, however, a phenomenon that
Marie elsewhere designates explicitly as a *surplus* of *sen* (prologue to *lais* 16),
is discoverable only through repeated experiences of rereading that presuppose the existence and immediate availability of a stable written artifact. The
traditional word-binding of *sens,* which means to say the same thing in as
many different ways as possible, is thus textually reenforced by this "second
sense," which means to say as many different things as possible within the
structure of a single word or phrase. The intimate art of reading depends on
the ability of writers to construct, and of readers to decipher, such complex
verbal codes, which regularly surpass the bounds of mere literacy to constitute
genuine textual art. Marie de France is just such a textual artist, and her lai
"Bisclavret" offers a specifically textual account of the generic passage from
one version of poetic practice to another. Recent studies by Frederick Ahl
(*Lucan; Metaformations*) have documented the extent and textual depth of
such complex "wordplay and soundplay" as they characterize the work of Lucan, Ovid, Virgil, Statius, and others classical Latin poets and constitute a
poetic infrastructure in their writings. Similar poetic festivities discernable
throughout Marie de France's "Bisclavret" suggest that she, too, had mas-
tered this metaformulaic theory and practice of poetic wordplay.

In the matter of Marie's *sen* and its "surplus," both Tony Hunt (402–3) and
Robert Sturges (248–49) have more recently questioned the long-standing as-
sertions of Spitzer and Robertson that Marie's "lettre," "sen," and "surplus"
represent a straightforward reference to the respective *littera, sensus,* and *sen-
tentia* of conventional scriptural exegesis as practiced by academic theologians who sought to "determine the doctrinal content" of every medieval text,
both sacred and profane (Robertson, "Marie de France" 338). Sturges is especially concerned to develop the secular thematics of textual interpretation as

these appear in the *Lais*, each one of which "continually acknowledges, even emphasizes, the fact that it is a verbal, fictional creation, a text" (244). Sturges lays particular emphasis on those figures within the tales "who act as readers or interpreters analogous to the reader of the *Lais* themselves," adding this important note: "Since the interpreting figures within the *lais* are invariably lovers, a further analogy, between the activities of love and of reading, is also suggested" (244). Though he mentions the lai "Bisclavret" only in passing in this important essay and does not concern himself at all with the "love" between the king and the werewolf, Sturges's observations on the textual self-reflectivity of the *Lais* may serve here as a useful entrée for understanding the remarks of Bisclavret's sovereign when he addresses his companions in the woods.

The king's address, indeed, may be imagined as the opening remarks of a magisterial lecture on twelfth-century contemporary critical theory, replete with references to the attested poetic concepts of "intention" and "sense," here made the more remarkable by virtue of their assignment to a speechless beast. The werewolf and his co-opted garments are best read as *involucra* intended to communicate a veiled account of the generic passage from orality to textuality.[11]

> "Seignurs," fet il, "avant venez!
> Ceste merveillë esgardez,
> Cum ceste beste s'humilie!
> Ele ad sen d'hume, merci crie.
> Chaciez mei tuz ces chiens ariere,
> Si gardez que hum ne la fiere!
> Ceste beste ad entente e sen.
> Espleitiez vus! Alum nus en!
> A la beste durrai ma pes,
> Kar jeo ne chacerai hui mes"
>   (151–60)

> "Gentlemen," he said, "come forward; consider this marvel; note how this creature humbles himself! Possessed of the sense of man, he begs to be spared. Chase all the dogs away for me. Take care that no man interferes; this creature has 'intention' and 'sense.' Make haste! Let's leave the field. I'm offering my peace to this creature; I'll hunt no more today."

In this definitive lai of lais, in which oral rites are being replaced by written rubrics, Marie repeats the orally performative word *Oëz* ("Listen," "Hear this!"; cf. OE "Hwaet!" ME "Hear ye!"; for she invokes the ritual word *Oyez* at precisely those junctural moments when the narrative connections between incidental input and superintending poetic outcome are being called into explicit consciousness: "Oëz aprés cument avint! . . . Oiez cum il est bien vengiez" ("Listen! to how it turned out afterward. . . . Hear this, how well he was avenged"; 185, 234).

And indeed, the justice of Marie's final outcome is superbly poetic as administered by the pen of *midons,* for she arranges a final spectacular display of oral prowess whereby Bisclavret overwhelms his unentitled male replacement, attempting to sink his teeth, not once but twice, into the man's body. The duple structure subtly recollects the fundamental design feature of oral poetics: verse pairs, parataxis, pleonasm, and chiastic repetition and substitution express the very grammar of performance, with these patterns of formulas finally proving more important than any particular formulas themselves (Lord, *Singer* 30–67).

The twice-witnessed "reversion" of the werewolf is prevented from total poetic relapse only by intervention from the king, who here "speaks"—presumably "softly"—but who also "carries a big stick." The poetic purpose of this baton, regardless of any vestigial trace of ritual, phallic origins, now provides us with a performative precursor of what we should recognize as the conductor's wand: "li reis ki l'apela, / D'une verge le manaça ("the king [who] called out to him; threatened him with a stick"; 201–2). When the traitorous wife subsequently attempts to make her own presentation to the king, Bisclavret repeats his performance as a gestural impresario, this time tearing the nose from the face of his literary betrayer.

Marie's semiotics of the nose are exemplary. Radically different but equally sexual resonances of virginity or adultery may be attached to her featuring of this signal female disfigurement. Historically, such nasal effacement, a conventional punishment for adultery, was superficially indistinguishable from those self-mutilations described and documented by Schulenburg (29–72), where deliberate disfigurations were undertaken by certain medieval women determined to preserve their virginity at all costs in the face of male invasion. As such, the definitively marred visage in "Bisclavret" may suggest either adulterous dissipation or deliberate self-curtailment. In either case, it serves to direct aesthetic attention to Marie's underlying issue of reproductive authenticity in the transition from oral to written poetics. In this way, the matrix of textuality—a word unspoken but ever-present throughout the lai "Bisclavret"—operates like the sexuality it countercontrives to resonate, making the matrix of textuality a prime example of Riffaterre's "tamperproof" deposit of meaning, wherein the verbally repressed matrix causes the text to function "something like a neurosis; as the matrix is repressed, the displacement produces variants all through the text, just as suppressed symptoms break out somewhere else in the body" (*Semiotics* 19). Since a matrix is itself only a hypothetical entity, actualized in ongoing grammatical and lexical effects that constantly call for a "double or bilinear deciphering of the single, linear text"

(*Semiotics* 5), the structure of any given matrix, as Riffaterre has noted, "becomes visible only in its variants"; while the "mimesis" of any textual artifact "occupies a lot of space . . . the matrix structure can be summed up in a single word" (*Semiotics* 13). I am suggesting that the summary, single-word matrix in "Bisclavret" is *textuality*.

Throughout "Bisclavret," the locking-in of Marie's textual meaning is accomplished by just such ingenuities of grammatical and lexical choice as Riffaterre describes. So Marie locks in meaning in the four semiotically crucial lines wherein she narrates the castrative disfigurement of her unendorsed female protagonist. As we shall see, the terse description of this imagined event also records a poetic version of the literary translation from male orality to female textuality, and does so precisely by ingenious grammatical and lexical choices that govern Marie's semiosis:

> Vers li curut cum enragiez.
> Oiez cum il est bien vengiez:
> Le neis li esracha del vis!
> Que li peüst il faire pis?
> (233–36)

> He ran toward her in the manner of a madman [a berserk?]. Now hear how
> well he is avenged! He ripped the nose off her face. What worse thing could
> he have done?

The most naive listener will have no trouble reconstructing a vivid scenario of pit bullish horror from these four seemingly unadorned lines whose ostensible purpose is simply to "show and tell" the rough justice inherent in an incident of shocking mutilation. But at the second stage of "retroactive reading"—that "second take" described by Riffaterre (*Semiotics* 4–6) wherein the "truly hermeneutic" constitutions of meaning are accomplished—it is only readers, not listeners, who will be able to retrieve and resupply that denotative meaning derived from the "first, heuristic reading," using it as a base for deliberate modifications now thrust upon them by the poet. In this "transfer of a sign from one level of discourse to another"—in Marie's move from "mimesis" to "significance"—readers will observe that the first word in this key passage is *vers*. Thus, the verse (*vers*) itself can be seen in the act of running its prophetic course toward (*vers*) the end of the oral tradition. The "enraged male poet," the "berserk" werewolf who embodies vanishing oral poetics, involves a male subject running toward the terminus of the *enragiez*, verbally installed at the end of this line: "Vers . . . enragiez."

The featured orality of Marie's poetic representation is further dramatized by the initial word of the next line; *Oiez* calls the reader to strict poetic attention. This line ends with the celebrated "vengeance" whose notably poetic justice will be witnessed in the shocking dismemberment to ensue: "Oiez . . . vengiez." In the following line, perhaps the most mimetically shocking in the entire lai but also one of its most poetically festive accomplishments, Marie constructs a verbal *tour de force.* For in this line, by means of its *neis,* or "nose," literally cut off to spite the traitorous wife's face, we may also detect the verbal trace of birth and accomplished marital status, as in "Madame Frese, née Warwick." At the same time, and with the same nasalized word, signally torn from the woman's *vis,* or "face," the text itself carries out its own castrative punishment upon the female offender of "Bisclavret," now left nameless and noseless, in contrast with her poetic creator, Marie. Indeed, as this traitorous woman is deprived of name and fame, she is also deprived of the literary instrument of the pen-which-is-a-metaphorical-penis, for the final word of this textually consummate line involves the *vis,* which in Old French may mean either "face" or "phallus": "Le neis . . . del vis." the line that begins with the *neis* and ends with the *vis* thus stunningly encodes the fundamental textual/sexual question of female literary production; this is the question which Gilbert and Gubar have addressed at great length, opening their investigation of nineteenth-century women writers with the query: "Is a pen a metaphorical penis?" (3).

In his reading of Marie's scenario of "female castration," Huchet notes certain echoes of this fable in Rabelais's later association of female genital "wounding" with the popular belief—implicitly present in Marie's metonymic scene—that the length of the nose provided a measure of the male sexual organ: "Moreover, as to the infamous mark (the ripped-off nose), does it not exhibit, metonymically, the wound of the feminine sex since the popular belief—and Rabelais will echo it in his *Gargantua*—determines that by the length of the nose one may gauge the (male) sex organ?" [12] The pre-Freudian potencies and Gargantuan *longueurs* noted in Huchet's reading of "Bisclavret" are then explicitly connected by him to the permissible equivocality in Old French between the " 'vis' (visage) et 'vit' (membre viril)" (419). Such playful shape-shifting of lexical referents reproduces the physiology of male sexual process itself, while proving Marie's treacherous wife to be an anti-heroine who must now suffer the shape-shifting, negative fate of a castrated/aborted/congenitally deformed poetic project. [13]

This doomed woman's fate is further overdetermined as a literary one by the verb *escracha,* a word whose "erasures" we may still "hear" as well as "see." The deliberate overdetermination of these four brief lines summarizes their burden of literacy, finalized in the acute rhetorical question which, compressed, becomes a comment: "What worse thing could he have done?" "Quel . . . pis"—"What a shame!" The textual shame becomes unambiguously clear in the final lines of the lai in which Marie definitively "writes off" all such twelfth-century "lady scribblers." The perpetuated symptom of "noselessness" continues to afflict the descendants of the failed female poetic ephebe. All such female castrates, signifying and signified by the continuing generation of disfigured poetic progeny, inscribe Marie's sense of the difference/différance between oral and written poetic discourse. The new literacy is constituted through a practice as available to women writers as to men. "Bisclavret" dramatizes this by casting both men and women in the role of poets, true and false—Marie herself, Bisclavret, the false wife, her notably weak second spouse. Along this continuum of practitioners, the poetically "engendered" sign of sexual/textual (non)success(ion) is contained in Marie's mark of continuing deformity, coproduced by male and female poetic pretenders. These are indicted by her own brilliant burst of homophonic punning at the end. Having the last word, Marie shows herself to be fully empowered as a poet of the new literacy: "C'est veritez, senz nes sunt neies / E si viveient esnasees" ("That's the truth; they were born [and bred?] noseless, and so they lived, noseless, [unhappily?] ever after"; 313–14). With oral/aural sound and lexical sense held in a state of delicate balance, Marie's poetics are suspended between the possibilities of birth ("sunt neies") and birth defect ("senz nes").

In the foregoing analysis, necessarily by example rather than exhaustive, we begin to construct an argument for Marie's consciously textual poetics, laid down here as a foundational chapter in literary history. That chapter, concerned with the moment of translation from oral to written performance, was this magisterial poet's announced undertaking in the *Lais*. In carrying out her work, the imaginative connections established between sexual nose and textual clothes, between sexual and textual consorting and betrayal, all serve to accommodate Marie's unique intersection of meanings in which the changing gender of performing poets and the newly experienced constraints of silence upon sound are given adequate imaginative exercise.

In the end, it is by virtue of Marie's own remarkably accomplished textual designs upon her reader's imagination that we are able to retrieve and reconstruct such a spectacular memory of oral poetic performances, enacted by men in communal situations ranging from the most ancient and archaic to the most contemporary and courtly. At the same time, in Marie's own purely textual performance we see the poet of literacy brilliantly compensating for a certain undeniable rigor mortis setting in upon the silent text. Marie's poetic wordplay celebrates textuality itself, with acts of verbal legerdemain equal to the acrobatic turns and twists and breathtaking leaps of any jongleur. Marie's textual effects serve to divert, even as they deepen, the routes of meaning in a new performance in which words must now stand as the sole semiological substitutes for what Jean Starobinski has called the body's "superlative power of persuasion" ("Rousseau's Happy Days" 163). It is by way of poetic compensation that Marie's written text is thus laid out, in lines whose arduous contortions finally come to appear as spontaneous acts of festivity. These seemingly effortless streams of verbal wordplay are intended to share and supply a constant *jouissance* to the reflective experience of rereading.

"The Werewolf," beautifully but elegiacally translated here into an irreversibly stable and silent form, presents the finalization of the sartorial trope: in the end, clothes, quite literally, do and do not make the man. Privately, in silence, behind the closed doors of the writer's study or the solitary reader's quiet space, the text of the werewolf is constantly being transformed.

In this superb valediction to oral performance, the risks as well as the mysteries are drawn deeply into the embodied image of the sleeping lord. He is fully dressed, arrested in silence, but breathing, still inspired and inspiring, thanks to the period of grace granted to him by Marie, his creator, his savior. "Une grant piece l'i laissums" ("Let's leave him there for a while"; 291). This is salutary advice, given by wise couselors, who urge that the metamorphic creature be accorded such peace and privacy as may be necessary to accomplish his final translations. The "grant piece" which is a sufficient space of time may also designate the "great piece" of work: the *pièce de résistance* which Marie's lai of "Bisclavret" finally proves to be. "Laissums," "Let's leave him there," or "Lais sums," "I am the *Lais*." [14]

Notes

1 See Stock for a thorough discussion of the fundamental issue of oral and written traditions as historically coextensive, and for a useful bibliography through 1983. Havelock's discussion (*Muse*) is especially responsive to the problem of orality and literacy as manifested in the cultural shift of late antiquity; his bibliography extends through 1986. Coleman and Gellrich, not referenced in Havelock, provide further insights, with studies focused on the European Middle Ages, and also have extensive bibliographies. Havelock, *Muse,* chap. 4, "Radio and the Rediscovery of Rhetoric" (30–33), notes the twentieth-century oral form of radio broadcast which "was not a reversion to a primeval past but a forced marriage, or remarriage, between the resources of the written word and of the spoken, a marriage of a sort which has reinforced the latent energies of both parties" (33). My "marital" title intends to capture some of the twelfth-century resonances implicit in Havelock's twentieth-century observations.

2 For recent speculation concerning the oral jongleurs and their poetic influence on later written texts, see Quinn and Hall, who also suggest "word pairs" as a poetic alternative to Parry/Lord "formulas" for the structuring principle of oral poetic composition. For Marie's intention to conserve the oral past in the written present, and to do so with deliberately inclusive versions of wordplay and soundplay, see the lai of "Guigemar," "Oëz, seignurs, ke dit Marie, / Ki en sun tens pas ne s'oblie" (3–4), and *Espurgatoire,* "Jo, Marie, ai mis, en memoire, / le livre de l'Espurgatoire" (2297–98). Noteworthy here is Marie's characteristic skill at the art of verbal shape-shifting, registered in the phrase *en sun tens;* the phonic constitution of this phrase merges the notion of the author's contemporary poetic prac-

tice—"in her [own] time"—with the artifacts of the "ancient times." In the phrase *en sun tens,* which phonically suggests "ancien temps" or "ancient times," the phonics of the present simultaneously appear to designate an opposite moment in the past. It is this memorable past which Marie means to conserve now by her present poetic labors. Quotations from Marie's poetry in this essay are from the editions of Warnke (*Espurgatoire*), Ewert and Johnston (*Fables*), and Rychner (*Lais*), cited in the bibliography under Marie de France. Though I have not had the opportunity to consult BL Harley 978, on which both Ewert and Rychner base their editions of the *Lais,* in 1. 314 of "Bisclavret" I have adopted Ewert's reading "E si viveient esnasees" ("and so they lived on, noseless"), which seems preferable to Rychner's "E sovent ierent esnasees" ("and they often were noseless"). Translations are mine throughout, though for the *Lais* I have regularly consulted the excellent translation by Hanning and Ferrante, and the more recent one by Burgess and Busby. I am particularly grateful to Maureen Boulton for reading an earlier draft of this essay and reviewing my translations.

3 Burgess and Busby (21–22) hypothesize the influence of the *Roman d'Eneas* on Marie's *Lais.* Freeman (877) makes the provocative opposite point, suggesting Marie's deliberate evasion of such "monumental historical pretensions." My present essay attempts to fuse these insights, which I do not consider to be mutually exclusive.

4 Although the identity of Marie and the "nobles reis" to whom she dedicates the *Lais* must remain a subject of scholarly speculation, her connection to the Anglo-Norman Plantagenets is less debatable. For Gerald of Wales, c. 1146–1223, and his similar connection, see Williams 2: 52–61. Thomas Forester's translation of this lycanthropic episode narrated by Gerald is reprinted in Otten (57–61).

5 See note 2, above, regarding the text behind this assertion. The silence of the "clothed" knight is crucial here. In another context, Freeman notes the appearance of the "poetics of silence" in Perceval, Chrétien de Troyes's young hero who must, in a sense, "dissolve the silence" and "make the Grail speak, as it were. (The romance is, after all, called *Le Conte du Graal*)" (866). Concerning the "silent *conte,*" it is hard not to connect such icons of silence and speech to the feminist theorizing of Hélène Cixous; her explorations of "femme écriture" and its connection to the "talking cunt" form the subject of Conley's book-length study of Cixous. Conley recalls Cixous's punning on "cunt/conte"—a punning usage typical of her critical texts—and provides a particularly rich paragraph from Cixous's *Partie,* which includes a reference to the "lubrifission of incuntinuity" (68). It is interesting to compare and contrast Bloom's (male) "anxiety" with Marie's (female) "jouissance," as these conditions are attached to the act of writing poems. As "first writer," and "first woman," Marie appears significantly immune to Bloom's "poetic influenza" (38).

6 For a recent survey of literary works using the trope of cloth as text, see Thundy 19–25.

7 See Stock for the characteristic employment of some symbolic object or artifact— "a physical object, a rod or piece of sod"—which played an analogous role in the legal ritual of oral land contracts under Salic law (47). Stock also notes the later "odd hybrid of a 'dispositive' twig sown to a 'probative' text" and the attested

"parchment, pen and ink . . . placed on the land to be sold" as transitional legal forms that combined written and oral versions of witnessed contractual exchange (48).

8 For Enide's "old," "torn and worn" clothing when Erec first makes her acquaintance, see Chrétien de Troyes, *Erec and Enide,* ed. and trans. Carroll, ll. 401–13 (pp. 18–19). For the text of Martian's poem, see Stahl, Johnson, and Burge, trans., vol. 2 of *Martianus Capella and the Seven Liberal Arts.* Erec's "coronation," "nuptial," and "graduation" dress may be one "textual" artifact.

9 See Bloom (*Anxiety* 25–26) for a recent theoretical analysis of events attending the incarnation of the poetic character.

10 In addition to Kelly, see Spitzer ("Prologue"), Robertson ("Marie de France"), and Foulet and Uitti for discussion of literary terms contained in the Prologue to Marie's *Lais.*

11 For a useful summary of *involucrum* and *integumentum* as these terms were used to designate "veiled" poetic practice in the Middle Ages, see Robertson (*Preface* 316–18, 345–46, 359–60). Also see Chenu ("Involucrum"), Dane, and Jeauneau.

12 "Au-delà, la marque infamante (le nez arraché) n'exhibe-t-elle pas, métonymiquement, la blessure du sexe feminin puisque la croyance populaire—et Rabelais s'en fera encore l'écho en son *Gargantua*—veut qu'a la longueur du nez on mesure le sexe?" (Huchet 419).

13 Bloch provides acute discussions of the textual/sexual connection in medieval poetics; see esp. chap. 4, "Poetry, Philosophy and Desire," in which the subsection "Poetry and Castration" (137–41) explores the same trope of generative curtailment that I am positing at the heart of poetic meaning in Marie's lai "Bisclavret."

14 Freeman (872–76) provides an acute discussion of Marie's "Chievrefoil," in which the key lines—"Ceo fu la summe de l'escrit / Qu'il li aveit mandé e dit" (61–62)—may contain a deliberate homophonic coordinate linking the *lais* implicit in "Laissums" of "Bisclavret" and those *lais* that are more explicitly communicated in the phrase "la summe de l'escrit." This "summary" inscribed on the staff with which the lovers communicate has been reduced to the nominal signature TR-IST-AN. The name itself supplies an image of the genre, according to Freeman, by virtue of its compacting of an experiently extended event into a single word. Even that one word, which is the name of Tristan, involves the "identities of two lovers," for in the signature we actually find the names of both lovers, "the -IST- representing the written (i.e., scribally abbreviated and perfectly conventional) letters of 'Iseut,' her name being surrounded, or encircled, by the similarly abbreviated letters of her lover's. Indeed, the one cannot exist without the other" (874). This, too, as described by Freeman, is state-of-the-art lai and involves a highly intellectualized and nominalized image of the medieval practice of "conjointure," whose artful imperatives are explored by Kelly in *Sens and Conjointure.*

11 *Sylvia Huot*

Chronicle, Lai, and Romance: Orality and Writing in the *Roman de Perceforest*

Old French literary narrative is heir to a rich and diverse heritage, including, among other things, the Latin literary tradition and Breton folklore, often referred to as *matière antique* and *matière de Bretagne*. Examples of the former include the romances of antiquity, such as the *Roman d'Eneas* and the *Roman de Troie;* an example of the latter is Marie de France's *Lais,* in which she tells us that she has set down in writing the stories that lie behind the Breton lais she has heard, so that they won't be forgotten. But even within *matière de Bretagne* we find a mixture of oral and written sources posited by romance authors. Chrétien de Troyes, for example, claims to have found the material for his *Conte du graal* in a book given to him by Count Phillip of Flanders; he also asserts that the story of *Cligés* is to be found in a book at the church of Saint Pierre at Beauvais. The only source he acknowledges for *Erec et Enide,* on the other hand, is "un conte d'avanture" ("a tale of adventure"; Roques ed., v. 13), which evidently belongs to the oral repertoire of the jongleurs, "cil qui de conter vivre vuelent" ("those who want to make their living by telling stories"; v. 22). In *Yvain* he links his story to a Breton lai, commenting that Yvain's wife was "fille au duc / Laududez, dom an note un lai" ("daughter of duke Laududez, about whom there is a lai"; Roques ed., vv. 2154–55). And in the *Charrete* he claims to have received the story directly from the Countess Marie de Champagne—presumably in oral form, as there is no reference to a book.

Old French romance, at its origins, is a coming together of oral and written traditions and claims a diverse cultural heritage: the learned, writerly culture of the Greco-Latin tradition on the one hand, and an indigenous oral culture, rooted ultimately in Breton tales and lais, on the other. This dual heritage resulted in a new sort of literature, partaking of both the written and the oral: unlike Greek and Latin, French was the language of common speech, and unlike Breton it was also a written language. I propose to examine this duality and its implications for the status of romance as literature and French as a literary language in the *Roman de Perceforest,* a voluminous prose romance written in the second quarter of the fourteenth century.[1] Romance had come a long way since Chrétien's time. The *Perceforest* author, aware of this rich tradition, produced a deliberately archaic text, modeled on earlier romances, such as the prose *Tristan.* His tale is set in an even more distant past, that of pre-Christian England. An educated man, probably a cleric, the *Perceforest* author reveals his commitment to a learned tradition linking medieval French literary activity both to a monastic setting and to the Greco-Latin heritage.[2] At the same time, his loving re-creation of the exotic romance world betrays a certain nostalgia for this imagined distant past, governed by chivalric values, replete with magic, and knit together by the unceasing activity of wandering minstrels, perpetrators of a living oral tradition.

The romance begins with a recapitulation of the history of Britain as told by Geoffrey of Monmouth; the events of his story are located just after the death of King Pir, here identified as an incompetent king who allowed chivalry virtually to die out. Before proceeding with his narration, the *Perceforest* author then presents an explanation of the textual history of the romance (Taylor ed., 120–24). This history is undoubtedly fictional, but if it tells us little or nothing about the actual sources of the *Perceforest* author, it does tell us something about how he conceived his work and how he wished it to be thought of by its readers. The author explains that the original book was found, along with a royal crown, on an altar that had been hidden in a secret compartment in the wall of an abbey in England. Both book and crown clearly dated from the distant past. The abbot sent the crown to the king of England and kept the book, which was in a strange language that he could not identify. The language turned out to be Greek. The book, in fact, is a chronicle of events taking place during the time when Britain was under Greek rule: blown off course by a storm, Alexander the Great and his men arrived in Britain one day, and Alexander's brother Betis, under the new name Perceforest, became king of England. It is not until toward the end of Book 2 that we learn how the chronicle came to be compiled: Perceforest founded the Franc Palais, a forerunner of the Round Table, and decreed that all his knights should report their adventures on a regular basis for recording by the court clerk, Cressus, in the great book. The practice continued through several generations, and when (in Book 6) Cressus became too old to serve, his job was taken over by another clerk, Porchon. It is this great book, compiled through the years on the basis of eyewitness accounts, that was eventually walled up in the abbey to preserve it from the invading Danes.

Let us return to the account of the discovery of the chronicle, in Book 1. One day a visiting Greek, who had been studying philosophy in Paris, arrived at the abbey and agreed to translate the book into Latin. It was at about this time that Count Guillaume of Hainaut happened to visit the monastery and learned about the book.[3] The abbot read to him from the Latin translation, providing an explanatory commentary in French as he went: "si en leut luy mesmes par devant le conte, et ce qu'il entendoit il l'exposoit en françois" ("thus he read from it himself before the count, and he explained what he understood of it in French"; Taylor ed., 123). The count was so impressed with the book's contents that he at once wanted to have a copy made for himself. It would, he felt, be highly edifying material for his knights. After some negotiations about the manner and speed of copying, during which the abbot expressed great reluctance to let the book out of his possession, the count had his copy made and took it home with him. There he entrusted it to a monk in a local monastery, who undertook to translate it into French. The resulting French book is, of course, the *Roman de Perceforest;* the narrator poses not as the author but as the translator from Latin into French.

According to the fiction established in its own prologue, then, the *Perceforest* derives from a written tradition reaching back into the far distant past and moving from Greek to Latin to French. The tradition is clearly marked as one in which chivalry is served by men of learning: its participants are two Greco-British court clerics, a Greek scholar, an English abbot, and a monk employed by the count of Hainaut. The process of linguistic translation is appropriately doubled in the transfer of the crown, which presumably shares the book's origins, to the king of England. This double transference represents the process of *translatio studii et imperii,* the translation/transference of learning and imperial authority from Greece to Rome to medieval Europe that is perhaps most clearly enunciated in the prologue of Chrétien's *Cligés* and which is fundamental to the medieval view of cultural history. Book and crown are material relics of past greatness. Though shrouded in mystery, they can be decoded and incorporated into contemporary medieval society, thereby making this glorious past a part of medieval culture.

The attention to the process of translation stresses the way in which the romance serves to open up this past, to bring it into the present and make it a viable force in medieval society. It is due to their status as written text that the stories contained in the book have survived at all, for this is a past that lies beyond the reach of memory. As I said, the book tells of the adventures that took place in Britain between the arrival of Alexander the Great and that of the Danes. It is explained at the end of the romance that the final demise of Britain's Greek culture came with the conquest of Britain by the Danes, who sponsored a revival of Britain's Trojan heritage and suppressed all traces and all memory of Britain's Greek past. If not for the book, all knowledge of these events would have been lost forever. But the original Greek book is a hermetic object, sealed off from even the most learned members of society. It is, first of all, literally hidden, and the narrator stresses this point by reminding us that "le livre est ainsi entitulé: 'En ce livre est contenue l'ystoire celee d'un bon roy Percheforest, roy de Bretaigne'" ("the book is titled thus: 'In this book is contained the hidden story of a good king, Perceforest, king of Britain'"; Taylor ed., 123). Once it has been unearthed, the book is still linguistically impenetrable; and, of course, it treats of a completely obscure, indeed quite forgotten, period of history. The book requires an outsider to decipher it so that it can even be read. Indeed, the marginality of the first translator is stressed through his status not only as foreigner—presumably not even a member of the Roman Catholic Church—but also as fugitive from the law: he had fled from Paris to England because he was wanted for murder. Once the book has been put into Latin, it is accessible to a wider audience, but still limited to the educated class and still, one can gather, in need of frequent explanation. Its translation into French opens it up still further; and its translator, the romance narrator, gives us to believe that he has expanded on the chronicle in order to clarify the account and to render it more entertaining, a point to which I will return later. The story of Perceforest is at last accessible to all, and the adventures of the great heroes of Britain's Greek past can serve as inspiration for the knights of medieval Europe.

From this perspective, French emerges as the direct heir to Greek and Latin, the two languages of learning, of writing, authority. French too is a written language, one capable of expressing the subtleties and the important cultural values of the Greek and Latin texts. The narrator stresses the difficulty he faced in forging a language suitable to the book's noble content. Speaking of himself in the third person, he states that he undertook the task "assez doubtivement" ("with considerable misgiving") because "il faloit a l'œuvre vesture de parolles dont il ne se sentoit pas bien pourveu. Car il convient selon la matiere qu'elles fussent coulourees d'armes et d'amours" ("the work needed to be clothed in words that he did not feel himself equal to. For it was necessary to the subject matter that they be colored by arms and by love"; Taylor ed., 124). This modesty topos, of course, only serves to underscore the author's success. But although French may be the equal in eloquence of Greek and Latin, it differs from them in its status as a spoken language. It is due to this that the French translation can capture the essence of the original text and at the same time unveil it, open it up for a contemporary audience.

This attention to the written tradition in the prologue contrasts with the body of the text, which describes in great detail the formation and dissemination of an oral tradition of lais recording the adventures of various knights and ladies.[4] The growth of the lai repertoire is paralleled by the construction of monuments—both paintings and sculptures, often with short inscriptions—that commemorate these same adventures. In short, the romance is a *mise en scène* of the making and recording of history. When Alexander and his men explore Britain, they encounter various prophecies and magical adventures waiting to happen. Betis acquires the name Perceforest, for example, because it was foretold that the evil sorcerer Darnant, whom Betis kills, would meet his death at the hands of a certain King Perceforest (Taylor ed., 198, 203–4). He further establishes his right to the English throne by his ability to remove a certain shield from its peg (Taylor ed., 249, 428). These prophecies and enchanted artifacts, typical romance fare, are a sort of history of the future; they remain incomprehensible and suspended until the arrival of the knight destined to fulfill the prophecy. As the adventures slowly unfold and spells are cast and broken, the British countryside is covered with new artifacts, monuments, and inscriptions, not prophetic but commemorative: the land is acquiring a history, one which can provide the basis for its cultural renewal. And whereas a monument is localized and by no means always self-explanatory—though less obscure than the prophecies, the commemorative inscriptions nonetheless often puzzle those who read them—the corresponding lais allow news, both public and private, to circulate throughout the kingdom. The performer is always present to supply commentary.

The itinerant minstrel plays an extremely important role in the society portrayed in the *Perceforest;* it is he or she who is responsible for the dissemination of information around the kingdom. Just as Count Guillaume wanted a copy of the book, so people who hear a minstrel perform often want to learn the song themselves. And just as the book bears an elaborate textual history, recounting the processes of translation and copying, so the lai acquires its own history: the minstrel frequently introduces the lai with an account of the circumstances under which it was composed or under which he or she learned it. I offer as example three lais from *Perceforest,* Book 2, involving the knights Lyonnel and Estonné. Since this portion of the romance is unpublished, I begin with a brief summary.[5]

In love with Blanche, daughter of the Fairy Queen, Lyonnel performs a number of exploits designed to win her hand; but he is robbed of his trophies and, grief-stricken and ashamed, feels he cannot now face her. Instead, he composes a lai—the "Lai de la complainte"—describing his deeds and his current predicament. The twenty-two stanzas of the lai are a combination of emotional outpouring and first-person narrative. Lyonnel begins with a nine-stanza lament addressed to the God of Love:

> Plus courroucié qu'oncques hom ne nasquy,
> Commenz mon lay, mais je ne sçay, las, cui

> Pri fors qu'Amors, sy me trairay a luy.
> Je ne sçay plus ou puisse avoir refuy,
> En luy mectz ma besongne.
>   (Lods ed., vv. 1–5)

More distressed than any man ever born, I begin my lai, but I do not know, alas, whom I entreat except Love, and so I turn to him. I do not know where else I could find refuge, I place my need in him.

The next eight stanzas narrate Lyonnel's predicament. Having learned that he can win the maiden he loves by defeating the golden-haired giant, he sets off at once, but victory is followed by disaster:

> Sy n'arrestasse, pour tout l'or d'Abilant
> Que je n'alasse, tout le pays cerchant.
> Tant que conquiz le chief du fort gueant,
> Non par proesse, ains par l'espoir qu'euz grant
>   De l'aÿde a la belle.
> Ha! Dieu d'amours, ceste bonne cheance
> Me vint aprés a tres grant mescheance.
> Le chief perdy, dont ay au coeur grevance,
> Et mon escu, sans ferir coup de lance,
>   Et mon lyon qu'amoie.
>   (Lods ed., vv. 66–75)

So I would not have stopped, for all the gold of Abilant, from going and seeking all over the country, until I conquered the head of the mighty giant, not by prowess, but by the great hope that I had of the lovely maiden's help. Oh! God of Love, this good luck later turned to great misfortune. I lost the head, for which I am heavy-hearted, and my shield, without striking a blow, and the lion that I loved.

The five concluding stanzas continue the lament with which the lai began. Lyonnel feels that dissemination of this lai will alleviate his situation: "Or vouldroie je que tous amans par amours sceussent mon lay. Sy savoient partie de mon meschief. Car il ne porroit estre qu'ilz n'eussent aucune pitié de moy; si prieroient pour moy" ("Now I would like all true lovers to know my lai. Thus they would know a little of my sorrow. For it could not be that they would not take pity on me; and they would pray for me"; BN fr. 346, fol. 235v). Lyonnel accordingly teaches the lai to a minstrel who conveniently appears just as Lyonnel has finished composing the lai. The minstrel composes a melody for the lai and proceeds to perform it. As luck would have it, he is heard one day by Blanche herself, who recognizes that it must have been composed by Lyonnel.

Blanche's first move is to get the minstrel to sing the lai again and again, "tant qu'elle le sceut de point en point" ("until she knew it word for word"; fol. 242v). She then decides to compose a reply: "Mais en la fin s'advisa qu'elle feroit ung lay pour resconforter le chevalier. Car autrement ne sçavoit trouver voie de luy aidier" ("But in the end she decided to make a lai to comfort the knight. For she knew no other way to help him"; fol. 242v). Blanche accordingly composes her own lai—the "Lai de confort"—and teaches it to the minstrel, who adds it to his repertoire; she instructs him to play it far and wide. The lai in fact creates something of a sensation: "Et sachiez que en plusieurs lieux joua le lay ou il y avoit dames et chevaliers qui le lay moult prisierent, car moult doulcement confortoit la pucelle le chevalier" ("And know that he played the lai in many places where there were knights and ladies who greatly admired the lai, for the maiden comforted the knight very sweetly"; fol. 243r). Ultimately, the minstrel happens to perform the lai in the hearing of Lyonnel, who recognizes the lai as a response to his and reveals himself. The minstrel points out to Lyonnel that the lai instructs him to seek his lost trophies in the Temple de la Franche Garde; Lyonnel, much comforted, departs at once to seek the temple.

This is not, however, the last we hear of the "Lai de la complainte" and the "Lai de confort." In spite of the fact that the two lais have served their immediate purpose, the minstrel continues to perform them. We next encounter him at a feast given by the queen of England, who, puzzled by Lyonnel's absence from the festivities, inquires for news of him. Great tales are told of his exploits, but no one can account for his whereabouts. It is at this point that the minstrel comes forward and states that although he does not know who Lyonnel is, he has seen the knight who performed the exploits mentioned, and this knight taught him a lai. Needless to say, the queen wants to hear the lai. The minstrel's performance makes quite an impression: "Lors ala accorder sa harpe et puis joua le lay, et chanta le dit si bien et si piteusement qu'il n'y eut en la compaignie dames ne chevaliers qui ne larmoiassent de pitié" ("Then he went ahead and tuned his harp and then played the lai, and he sang the words so well and so piteously that there were no ladies or knights in the assembled company who did not weep for pity"; fol. 294r). When the minstrel has finished, the queen expresses her wish that the maiden in question could hear the lai, for surely she would find a way to comfort the knight. The minstrel replies with the account of his encounter with Blanche, the composition of the "Lai de confort," and its subsequent performance for Lyonnel. Delighted, the queen requests that he perform this one as well. The minstrel obliges, creating a further sensation:

Sy ala jouer le lay si bien et si doulcement que dames et chevaliers le prisierent a merveille, et moult recommenderent le lay. Et dirent que la pucelle estoit sage et courtoise

et de hault honneur qui le lay avoit fait. Sy devez sçavoir que moult y gaigna le menes-
rel a l'aprendre, car chascun le vouloit sçavoir. (fol. 295r)

Thus he played the lai so well and so sweetly that ladies and knights praised it
wondrously, and they greatly commended the lai. And they said that the maiden who
made it was wise and courteous and of high honor. And you should know that the
minstrel earned quite a lot by teaching it, for everyone wanted to know it.

Finally, the minstrel's story has reminded the queen of yet another lai; he has
referred in passing to a certain monument, the Pillar of Estonné, and she
wants to know more about this monument. He describes it in greater detail and
then proceeds to sing a lai—the "Lai de l'ours"—describing the events com-
memorated by the pillar.

The adventures of Lyonnel and Estonné illustrate the great importance of
the oral tradition for both private and public communication. In the case of
Lyonnel, the minstrel's performances serve to tell the two lovers one another's
stories and to set in motion the series of events that will result in their ultimate
reconciliation and marriage. But the lais take on a public importance as well
when sung for the court. They have helped spread word of Lyonnel's wonder-
ful exploits, resulting in a significant rise in his reputation. The lais also explain Lyonnel's absence from the court festivities: he is preoccupied in an important unfinished adventure. Estonné in turn is present at the minstrel's
public performance, so the performance serves simultaneously to publicize
his adventure and to clarify it for Estonné himself. The lai recounts the same
story that is represented visually on the sculpted pillar: Estonné is transformed
into a bear as punishment for infidelity toward his beloved, a ward of the Fairy
Queen's. In this form he lives at the Fairy Queen's court as a sort of family pet.
One day, he kills two knights who attempted to abduct his beloved and her
companion; in gratitude for this deed, the Fairy Queen restores his human
form. The pillar is near the tombs of the two villainous knights, which bear an
explanatory inscription: "Cy gisent .ii. chevaliers du lignaige Darnant que Estonné, conte des Desers, mist a mort, luy estant en figure d'ours, pour l'ou-
traige qu'ilz vouloient faire a .ii. pucelles" ("Here lie two knights of the lineage of Darnant whom Estonné, count of the Desers, put to death, he being in
the form of a bear, for the outrage that they tried to commit against two maid-
ens"; fol. 291v).

In spite of its visual clarity and explicit inscription, the Pillar of Estonné is
never fully comprehended by anyone without the aid of an oral commentary.
A group of twelve knights who come upon the pillar examine it carefully and
read the inscription; "ils eurent grant merveilles quelle signifiance c'estoit"
("they greatly marveled as to what this might mean"; fol. 251v). When a
preudhomme (wise man) appears on the scene, they ask him "que c'est a
dire" ("what this means"; fol. 252r). The wise man then explains that the

events depicted on the pillar took place recently, summarizes the sequence of events, and confirms that the bear was really Estonné. Only then are the twelve knights satisfied. Estonné, for his part, at first believes this adventure to have been a dream; when he sees the pillar with its images of his "dream," he assumes that the pillar is a hallucination caused by enchantment. He describes his vision to the queen of England, concluding:

Et pour ce le tien a songe et a merveille. Car je tien pour certain que qui seroit ou lieu ou nous veïsmes le pilier et la forest et le tombeau, il n'y trouveroit ne l'un ne l'autre. Songe fut et a songe est tourné. (fol. 292v)

And so I consider it a dream and a marvel. For I am certain that whoever might be in the place where we saw the pillar and the forest and the tomb, he would see neither the one nor the other. Dream it was and to dream it has returned.

It is only when Estonné hears the story told by a minstrel that he accepts it as actual fact, as a part of history. And it is only then that he can consciously repent of the misdeed for which he was being punished during his transformation: "Madame," he tells the queen, "je dy que je suys le plus maleureux chevalier qui soit" ("Madame, I say that I am the most unfortunate knight there is"; fol. 296v).

Episodes like this clearly demonstrate the importance of the oral tradition within the culture described by the romance. In the society portrayed here, the minstrel is the guarantor of truth, the authority from whom history—public and personal, current and past—is learned. The commemorative function of the lai, and its importance in spreading news, is announced in the opening stanza of the "Lai de l'ours":

> N'est tresor tant repus
> Ne soit en fin trouvés,
> Ne fais si bien celés
> Qu'en fin ne soit sceüz,
>   Bien le dist on.
>   (Lods ed., vv. 1–5)

There is no treasure so hidden that it is not found in the end, nor any deed so concealed that it is not known in the end, so it is said.

The language recalls that used nearly two centuries earlier by Marie de France:

> Cele aventure fu cuntee,
> Ne pot estre lunges celee.
> Un lai en firent il Bretun:
> *Le Laüstic* l'apelë hum.[6]

> This adventure was told, it could not be concealed for long. The Bretons made a lai about it: it is called *The Nightingale.*

From their first appearance in Old French literature, lais were associated with the revelation and commemoration of events and the dissemination of knowledge about both current and historical events. Faithful to this tradition, the *Perceforest* author shows us that lais were the first means by which important events were recorded and the minstrels the first to spread the tales: this oral tradition thus grew up alongside Cressus's chronicle. In fact, harp-playing performers of lais belong to a distinguished tradition within French medieval literature and are an essential element of any reconstruction of the Breton world.[7] Descriptions of the minstrels' voices, of the tuning of the harp, and of audience dialogue with the performer stress the immediacy and the pure orality of these musical commemorations. The *Perceforest* author draws on well-established conventions for the description of lai performances; positing an oral tradition of harp-playing minstrels alongside the written chronicle is a way for him to imbue his work with another kind of authenticity, a vivid sense of the distant past as figured in the medieval imagination.

As a given minstrel builds up a repertoire based on his or her personal contacts, a particular oral history is woven around the person of the performer. And as these are transposed into the written format of chronicle or romance, the repertoires of various minstrels are combined, creating an encyclopedic whole that spans several generations. By giving such prominence to the composition and dissemination of lais, the *Perceforest* author pays homage to certain indigenous oral traditions that gave rise to French romance. French is a language that is both spoken and written; French romance incorporates both chronicle and lai.

The distinction between oral and written traditions is further defined through the interpretive processes appropriate to each. I earlier described the Greek chronicle as a hermetic object due to the unknown language in which it was written and the unstudied period of history to which it referred. The unraveling of its mysteries required linguistic competence and historical knowledge, the special domain of the clerk. The lai, on the other hand, can have its own kind of hermeticism. This is especially clear in an episode in Book 3 of *Perceforest,* that of the so-called "Lai secret," which a female minstrel performs for the royal court on the occasion of a feast. When asked if she minds performing this "secret lai" in public, the minstrel replies, not at all, for "il est fait tant celeement que personne n'en puet sçavoir le secret s'il n'en est digne" ("it is made so obscurely that no one can know the secret unless he is worthy of it"; Roussineau ed., 275); its secrets are therefore safe even in public performance. The lai is indeed a hermetic text, built of impenetrable metaphors which are understood by no one except Lyonnel, Estonné, and Le Tor, whose experiences are described there. (The reader likewise understands, having followed the adventures of these knights in the preceding narrative.) The king at once recognizes that the lai relates personal experiences involving difficulties in love; beyond that very general understanding, however, he acknowledges that "il n'est homme vivant qui sceust penser l'entendement sy non celui ou ceulx a qui il touche" ("there is no man alive who would know how to figure out its meaning except the one or ones whom it concerns"; Roussineau ed., 278).

Following the performance, Lyonnel rides off, meditates on the lai—which he has committed to memory—and comes up with a complete *explication de texte* for the lines applicable to him, explaining to himself that all of the images refer to his experiences with Blanche and that the lai instructs him about how he can win her hand. The portion of the lai that applies to Lyonnel is as follows:

> Jadis en l'eaue vit la lys,
> Plus blanche ne fut oncques lys,
> Car sa blancheur paroit en l'onde.
> Le cedre en fut appalis.
> Tant fist que le champ fu alys
> Pour avoir le veüe monde.
> Plus corroucié n'eust puis au monde,
> Car rien ne vey a la reonde,
> Parquoy son espoir fut fallys,
> Puis veit en passant comme aronde.
> Face que voie la seconde,
> Que tenus ne soit pour fallys.
>
> (p. 276)

> Long ago he saw the lily in the water, no lily was ever whiter, for its whiteness appeared in the stream. The cedar was overwhelmed by it. He acted such that the field was cleared, in order to have a clear view. There was never anyone in the world so dismayed, for he saw nothing anywhere, and so his spirit fell. Then he sees a swallow in passing; let him act so as to see a second one, lest he be held for recreant.

Lyonnel begins by realizing that the part concerning him must have been composed by Blanche, and that it begins with a reference to her:

se print a dire en soy mesmes que le lay avoit esté compilé de la bouche de la pucelle qu'il amoit sus toutes riens. "Car la ou ele dist:

> 'Jadis en l'eaue vey la lys
> Plus beau que ne fut onques lys,
> Car sa blancheur paroit en l'onde,'

ce n'est," dist Lyonnel, "autre chose a dire sy non que la pucelle te voeult faire sçavoir que d'elle il te souviengne. . . . Elle te ramentoit comment tu la veis baignier en l'onde, dont se compare a la lys pour sa blancheur. Et pour ce dist elle que oncques la lys ne fut plus belle, car parmy la couverture, c'est a dire parmy l'onde de l'eaue, tu veoies sa char tout plainement, qui passe toutes autres en souveraine blancheur." (pp. 280–81)

He began to say to himself that the lai had been put together from the mouth of the maiden that he loved above all else. "For when she said,

    'Long ago in the water I saw the lily
    More beautiful than any lily ever was
    For its whiteness appeared in the stream,'

that," said Lyonnel, "means nothing other than that the maiden wants to let you know that you should remember her. . . . She reminds you of how you saw her bathing in the water, whereby she compares herself to the lily because of her whiteness. And for this reason she said that the lily was never so beautiful, because through the covering, that is, through the current of the water, you saw her flesh quite clearly, which surpasses all others in resplendant whiteness."

Having identified the lily in the text as Blanche, Lyonnel then goes on to interpret the cedar as an image of himself:

Et encores dist elle: "La cedre en fu appalys." Elle te compare au cedre, qui est l'un des plus haulz arbre du monde. Et par ce cedre, qui de sa beauté fut appalys, elle veult dire que quant tu veis sa beauté, tu en fus moult esmerveillé, mais elle dit vray. (p. 281)

And then she said, "The cedar was overwhelmed by it." She compares you to the cedar, which is one of the tallest trees in the world. And by that cedar that was overwhelmed by her beauty, she means that when you saw her beauty, you were completely amazed by it; and she speaks the truth.

In this manner Lyonnel continues his exposition of the lai, deciphering its images to arrive at a quasi-narrative account of his initial sight of Blanche, the prowess that this inspired in him, his disappointment when she vanished from his sight, and his next fleeting glimpse of her. Blanche's closing lines, he realizes, are an exhortation to seek her out, which he accordingly sets off to do. He is confident of his interpretation and of the secrecy that ensures that this could only be a message from Blanche to him: "Je ne puis comprendre qu'en ces vers ait aucune autre exposition, ne il n'est personne vivant qui sache ceste chose sy non elle et moy tant seullement" ("I cannot imagine that there could be any other interpretation of these lines. Nor is there anyone alive who knows about this, other than myself and her exclusively"; p. 282). Thus, like the earlier "Lai de confort," the "Lai secret" prompts Lyonnel—and Estonné and Le Tor—to direct action.

Clearly the oral tradition as presented here—the medieval cleric's nostalgic vision of a sort of primeval, pure orality—is rooted in experience: the one who can comprehend the lai is not the one who is sufficiently educated but

rather the one who has lived its story. The lai is personal, like so many magical romance adventures: only one knight in the world has had these experiences, and therefore only he can decipher the poetic code. Just as the lai requires the personal memory of the minstrel and his or her actual presence to
perform it, so also it is rooted in personal history and mediates between the
private and public realms—presenting one aspect to the public at large, another to the select few in the know—and slowly becomes clearer as more
pieces of the story become known.

   The book, for its part, is a collective, public document. Though grounded
in individual experience, it transcends personal memory; it presents a collective history, explicating what is hidden, making public what was private.
Though specialized, the linguistic knowledge needed to penetrate its text and
the sophistication needed to understand ancient customs and to locate the
reign of Perceforest on the time line of British and world history are nonetheless available through study; and by means of successive translations the book
reaches a wider and wider audience. The minstrel always has only a partial
knowledge of the events of which he or she sings. The one who encounters
Lyonnel, for example, freely acknowledges that he does not know who this
knight is; he knows only the two lais and the story of their composition and
performance. Similarly, although he knows the lai of Estonné, he does not
know who Estonné is and does not even realize that Estonné himself is present
at the performance. The key to the "Lai secret" may have been known to the
maiden who took it upon herself to disseminate it. But it probably is not
understood by the other minstrel who, having learned the lai himself, provides
a second performance of it a little later for Lyonnel and Estonné. In contrast,
the authors of the chronicle, due to their personal interviews with the pro-
tagonists, are able to record the most private moments in the lives of its doz-
ens of characters. In the book, the fragmented, frequently mysterious historical record scattered about Britain in the form of monuments and lais is unified
and clarified; its many events are ordered and contextualized.

   If the oral tradition is presented as alive and evolving, generated directly
from experience and in turn generating further actions, then the chronicle is
associated with a certain kind of closure and stasis. A lai triggers memories
for those who hear it, raises interpretive questions, starts discussions, inspires
chivalrous action, prompts the composition and dissemination of new lais. It
can be a source of entertainment, of news, of self-knowledge. The chronicle,
on the other hand, functions more as repository, indeed as final resting place
for knightly exploits. Once an adventure has been recorded in the book, it is
preserved from oblivion; but for this very reason, it no longer needs to be
remembered or retold. The chronicle itself is never closed as long as the society keeping it is in existence. Like the oral tradition as a whole, the book
continues to grow through a process of accretion, for there are always new

adventures to record, new deeds to sing of. But the vitality of the lai seems denied to the chronicle, which, within the context of its own society, does not appear to participate in any ongoing process of private or public interpretation, does not engage in dialogue with other texts, does not erupt into the life of a knight or a lady and refocus that character's attention, redirect utterly his or her activity.

It is here, in this space between the simultaneously composed oral and written records of the age of Perceforest, that the French romance comes into being. The elaborate fictions surrounding its preparation leave no doubt that the romance is conceived as a written work. Yet the narrator, though posing as a translator, also takes credit for having altered the narrative as he found it in the Latin translation of the chronicle; and the motive behind these revisions, as he states it, is to render the work more fitting for oral delivery. As Taylor points out, the narrator calls attention to his craft by claiming to have embroidered on his source.[8] He justifies this procedure thus:

> combien que je florisse les fais et prolonge par paroles ung pou plus long que je ne les treuve en latin *pour estre un petit plus plaisans a oyr*, sans rien adjouster aux fais ne nouvel. Car se je disoie: "Cellui tua celluy, et cellui navra l'autre, et cellui ost desconfy cel autre," et m'en passasse ainsy briefvement que fait le latin, on vous auroit tantost tout compté et *sy n'y auriez ja eu plaisance a l'oyr, ne deduit.* (BN fr. 345, fol. 225r; my emphasis)

> However much I embroider the deeds and prolong with words a little longer than I find them in the Latin, *in order to be a little more pleasant to listen to,* without changing any of the facts. For if I said: "This one killed that one, and this one wounded the other, and this one defeated that other one," and I passed over it as briefly as the Latin does, soon it would all have been told to you *and yet there would have been no enjoyment in the listening, no delight.*

The narrator also claims to have restructured the narrative in places in order to make it more interesting to listen to. He interpolates adventures, for example, between each of a series of twelve tournaments that take place in Book 3, arguing that it would be difficult to sustain the listener's attention if the tournaments were simply recounted one after another: "la matiere ne seroit point tant agreable aux escoutans" ("the material would not be as pleasant for the listeners"; Roussineau ed., 238). And the narrator intervenes from time to time with explanatory material designed to help the fourteenth-century audience understand the events and customs of the distant past; or again, as a moralizer, he draws comparisons between the glorious knights of Perceforest's England and those, more degenerate, of his own day. His role, in short, recalls that of the abbot reading to Count Guillaume, who provided a spontaneous oral commentary or translation into French of the Latin text. There is no illusion that the romance allows for unmediated access to either the Latin or the Greek original. Rather, the persona of the narrator/translator is interposed between the chronicle and the romance audience. The events recorded in the chronicle come to us filtered through his consciousness, very much as though he were reading it to us, pausing to comment, expanding on the narrative outlines, constantly adjusting his material in response to our interests and expectations.

We are now in a better position to grasp the complex interrelationship of writing and orality as conceived by our anonymous fourteenth-century romancer. The Greek chronicle, though directly rooted in oral, eyewitness accounts, was, we are given to understand, a somewhat dry, perfunctory document: it contained "just the facts" and nothing more. The orally composed and transmitted lai, on the other hand, was the medium for the expression of sentiment: it was in this form that knights and ladies recorded their grief, their joy, their hopes and desires. It is in the lais, too, that we encounter a poetic language, capable both of hiding and of transmitting meaning, of communicating on different levels to different members of the audience, and—perhaps most important—possessing an aesthetic value quite independent of its communicative functions. The "Lai secret," after all, is enjoyed as a performance piece even by those who do not understand its message. And because the lais could be encountered only through the person of the performer, they always unfolded in a context of dialogue, giving rise to questions, comments, or further lais.

The French romance reverses the process that originally produced the chronicle: whereas Cressus and Porchon received oral reports and put them into writing, the romance narrator claims to have taken a written text and recast it for oral delivery. This involves, in part, a recuperation of the special qualities of the oral tradition: the implied presence of a persona from whom the stories are received, a series of asides to the implied audience and a concern with their pleasure and understanding, an ongoing attention to the aesthetics of the text. At the same time, the repeated insistence on the romance's written source and its clerkly associations reminds us that the romance owes its very being to the phenomenon of writing and that it is imbued with the kind of learning and authority that come from the study of books. Yet even in its very status as book, the romance escapes the isolation of the original chronicle; for just as a given lai exists in a sort of intertextual relationship with monuments or other lais, so also the romance is inscribed in a larger intertextual system.

In order to appreciate this last point, we must briefly look at the larger picture of Old French romance as it had developed by the mid–fourteenth century. The *Perceforest* is not unique in its attention to the writerly process. If it presents a sophisticated meditation on the poetic and linguistic bases of romance, and on written and oral modes of expression, it is partly because it

comes late in the romance tradition and its author was a careful reader of earlier romances. An interest—one might even say obsession—with real and
fictional origins, with processes of oral and written transmission, with transcription, translation, compilation, and interpretation, runs like a leitmotiv
throughout the corpus of Old French romance. The ongoing formation of romance cycles, for example, is described in *Guiron le courtois,* composed
around 1235.[9] The author, who identifies himself as Hélie de Boron, begins
with a lengthy account of the many French books that have been produced by
translating portions of the mythical Latin book of the Holy Grail:

> Car bien est veritez que aucun saint homme, clerc et chevalier s'en sont ja entremis de
> translater ce livre de latin en langue françoise. Mesires Luces de Gau s'en entremist
> premierement; ce fu li premiers chevaliers qui s'estude y mist et sa cure, bien le sa-
> vons; et cil translata en langue françoise partie de l'estoire mon seigneur Tristran, et
> mains assez que il ne deust. . . . Aprés s'en entremist mesires Gasses li blons, qui
> parens fu le roi Henri. Aprés s'en entremist maistres Gautiers Map, qui fu clers au roy
> Henri et devisa cil l'estoire de mon seigneur Lancelot du Lac que d'autre chose ne
> parla il mie gramment en son livre. Mesires Robert de Borron s'en entremist aprés.
> (Lathuillère 176)

> For it is certainly true that several holy men, clerks, and knights have already under-
> taken to translate this book from Latin into French. Sir Luce del Gat first took it up.
> And he was the first knight who devoted his study and bent his will to it, as we well
> know. And he translated into French part of the story of Lord Tristan, and indeed
> less than he should have. . . . Next Sir Gace the Blond took it up, who was a rela-
> tive of King Henry. Next Sir Walter Map took it up, who was clerk to King Henry.
> And he worked on the story of Lord Lancelot du Lac, for he did not speak much
> about anything else in his book. Sir Robert de Boron took it up next.

And so it continues, until Hélie arrives at his own part in the collective
project of French romance production. So abundant a source is this Latin Ur-
text that even after all of the aforementioned translations, King Henry realizes
that "ne encore n'estoit dedens tous ses livres mis ce que li livres du latin
devisoit, ains en remest a translater molt grant partie" ("all his books still did
not contain that which the Latin book told of, for there remained a large part
of it still to translate"; Lathuillère 177). It is from this untranslated portion of
the Latin book, of course, that *Guiron le courtois* is supposedly produced.
Like the *Perceforest* author, Hélie inscribes himself in a historical movement
from Latin to French literary expression. What is also clear from the *Guiron*
prologue is that the production of French literature is a collective enterprise
involving both knights and clerics, and that each individual romance, far from
standing alone, is an integral part of the overall corpus.

Consistent with his interest in literary history, Hélie de Boron produces an
explanation for the origin of the lai as a poetic-musical genre suitable to the

expression of individual sentiment and its dissemination both to one's beloved and to an audience at large. The first lai, we learn here, was composed by King Meliadus out of love for the queen of Scotland. Meliadus had made many "chançons" about his love for the queen, but none of these equaled his new piece:

Et au derrenier treuve .i. dit de ses amours plus merveilleus et plus subtilz que nul n'avoit esté devant. Et suer celui treuve chant tel que on le pooit chanter en harpe. . . . 'Lai' l'appelle en signe qu'il vouloit laissier tous autres chans. Et sachiez que celui lai fu le premier qui onques fust chanté en harpe. Devant celui n'avoit onques lai esté dist. (BN fr. 355, fol. 161v)

And at last he makes up a poem about his love that is more marvelous and more subtle that any other had been before. And he makes up a tune for it such that it can be sung to the accompaniment of the harp. . . . He calls it "lai" to signify that he wanted to leave behind all other songs. And know that that lai was the first ever to be sung to the harp. Before that one, no lai had ever been sung.

The newness of the genre is stressed in the reaction of the knight for whom Meliadus first performed his lai: "Et pour ce que il n'avoit onques mais oÿ tel dit, demanda au roy, 'Comment s'appelle cestui dist?' Et li roys li dist, 'Il s'appelle "lay."' " ("And since he had never before heard such a poem, he asked the king, 'What is this poem called?' And the king said to him, 'It is called "lai"'"; fol. 162r). The knight obligingly offered to perform the lai at Arthur's court, where the queen of Scotland was visiting. The performance impressed Arthur's court, and Arthur ordered that all knights should learn and sing the lai because it was made by the greatest knight in the world. It also impressed the visiting queen, who was persuaded to look upon Meliadus's plea for love rather more favorably. The new verse form, we may conclude, was off to an auspicious beginning.

While *Guiron le courtois* purports to explain the origins of the lai as a genre, the idea of placing lais in a prose romance actually originates with the slightly earlier prose *Tristan*. Like the other prose romances, the *Tristan* offers itself as a translation from the Latin, while also presenting a similar view of a society in which traveling minstrels are the bearers of an oral history.[10] As in the *Perceforest*, the orality of the lai is stressed by detailed accounts of harp-tuning, of the singing voice, and of interaction between minstrel and audience. It is in the prose *Tristan*, for example, that we learn of the resident minstrel at Arthur's court, Heliot the Gay:

Tous les lais et toutes les chançons que les compaignons de la table ronde trouvoient, il savoit, quar chascun lui disoit le dit et le chant qu'il faisoit. Et il le chantoit puis devant les compaignons de la table ronde. Et avoit nom ce harpeur Heliot l'envoisié. (BN fr. 335, fol. 415v)

He knew all the lais and all the songs that the companions of the Round Table made
up, for each one would tell him the words and the tune that he made. And then he
would sing it before the companions of the Round Table. And this harpist was named
Heliot the Gay.

Heliot's performances were not limited to the company of the Round Table,
however, for it was Heliot to whom Dynadan taught his notorious "Lai voir
disant," a scathing attack on the character of King Marc. Heliot performed
this lai at Marc's court; and "cestui lay fu puis compté et chanté par toute la
Grant Bretaigne" ("this lai was then recounted and sung all over Great Britain"; BN fr. 336, fol. 3r), thereby effectively ruining that unfortunate king's
reputation.

   Finally, it is in the epilogue of the *Tristan* that the great romance corpus is
invoked in an image that is subtly echoed at the beginning of the *Perceforest,*
that of the crown. Having incorporated considerable additional material, including a detailed Grail quest, into the romance of Tristan, the author called
Hélie de Boron nonetheless acknowledges that he has not yet exhausted the
material present in the famous Latin source.[11] He promises to translate this
material in his next book and stresses the close relationship of this new book
to the other exemplars of Old French romance, which he characterizes as so
many flowers:

> Et de toutes ces flors ferai je une corone a mon grant livre, en tel maniere que li livres
> de monsoingneur Luces de Gant et de maistre Gautier Map et de monsoingneur Robert
> de Berron . . . s'accourderont au mien livre(s), et li miens s'accorderont en meintes
> choses as lour. (Curtis 322–23; from BN fr. 104)

> And from all these flowers, I will make a crown for my great book, in such a way
> that the book of Lord Luce del Gat and [those] of Master Walter Map and Lord
> Robert de Boron . . . will be in accordance with my book, and mine will be in
> accordance with theirs in many ways.

As Emmanuèle Baumgartner has pointed out, the crown is a metaphor at once
for the circle formed by the knights of the Round Table, hence for the
Arthurian world, and for the cyclical books in which this world is recorded.[12]
The textual circle is one which is continually reopened and reclosed with the
addition of each new translation from King Henry's ever-expanding Latin
book and each new discovery—be it visionary, as in the *Estoire del Saint
Graal,* or archaeological, as in the *Perceforest*—of another piece of the story.

   The book is crowned by the preexisting romance cycle, which it completes
and illuminates and by which it is completed and illuminated in turn: what is
only a fleeting image at the end of the *Tristan* is concretized at the beginning
of the *Perceforest* with the discovery of the book and the crown. The crown, a
concrete relic of past splendor, lends authority and historical verity to the

book, while the book in turn explains—glosses, as it were—the crown. A similar relationship of mutual glossing, mutual confirmation, obtains between the romance of *Perceforest* and the romance tradition. To begin with, the *Perceforest* fills in a previously unnoticed gap in Geoffrey of Monmouth's chronicle of Britain. Moreover, the *Perceforest,* itself a cycle of considerable dimensions, reopens and conjoins in a new, more comprehensive circle the cycles of Alexander, Tristan, and the *Lancelot-Graal.* It provides ancestors for the great Arthurian heroes, linking them to Alexander's entourage: Tristan, for example, is descended from Lyonnel and Blanche; Estonné is the ancestor of none other than Merlin; Arthur is descended from Alexander himself. It establishes a sociopolitical precedent for the golden age of chivalry under Arthur. And it lays the spiritual foundations for the Christianization of Britain and the inauguration of the Grail quest, through the cult of the "unknown god," a monotheistic forerunner of Christianity invented by the author, to which Perceforest, the Fairy Queen, and various other heroes convert.[13] Indeed, the romance closes with a prophecy of the Grail quest that will someday be the culminating adventure of British chivalry.[14]

Placed on a secret, hidden altar as though it were a sacred relic, accompanied by a crown, the mythical book that is the *Roman de Perceforest* comes endowed with the double authority of sanctity and royalty; the story that it tells is itself rooted at once in oral performance and written documentary. It is a learned work, born of literary study and labor, remaining true (more or less!) to British and European history as defined in the romance corpus; it is artfully crafted, geared to the tastes of an audience who will receive it orally, as edifying entertainment. That a romance author would present his work in this fashion reveals his concept of Old French as a literary language. It is thanks to the collective project of French knights and clerics that a new, extraordinarily fertile textual system is forged, one that subsumes and integrates scriptural, classical, and Breton sources; one that combines the learning and durability of writing with the aesthetic and imaginative qualities of oral entertainment. As a literary language, French mediates between the hypothetical poles of pure orality and pure writing, able to fix and preserve the old tales and songs while giving new life to the books of antiquity.

Notes

Preliminary work on this study was supported by a grant from the Exxon Education Foundation for research at the Newberry Library, Chicago. Subsequent work was supported by Faculty Summer Stipends from the Graduate School, Northern Illinois University. Early versions of this study were presented at meetings of the Illinois Medieval Association, Chicago, Feb. 1987, and the Modern Language Association, San Francisco, Dec. 1987. All translations from the Old French are mine.

1　Much of the *Perceforest* remains unedited. In this study, I concentrate on the first three of its six books. The first part of Book 1 has been edited by Jane H. M. Taylor. For the second part of Book 1, I have used the MS Paris, Bibliothèque Nationale fr. 345; for Book 2, BN fr. 346; for Book 3, *Perceforest: Troisième partie*, ed. Roussineau. Book 4 has also been edited by Roussineau, *Perceforest: Quatrième partie*. In addition, I have consulted the complete *Perceforest* in two sixteenth-century printed editions at the Newberry Library, Chicago: *La Treselegante, Delicieuse, Melliflue et tresplaisante Hystoire du tresnoble, victorieux et excellentissime roy Perceforest . . .* , 6 vols. (Paris: N. Cousteau pour Galiot du Pré, 1528; Paris: Gilles de Gourmont, 1531). The lais (none of which are preserved with music) have been published in Lods, ed., *Pièces lyriques*. See also Lods, *Roman de Perceforest;* and Taylor, "Fourteenth Century." According to Taylor, the romance was probably composed some time between 1330 and 1350 (*Perceforest: Première partie* 24–29); Roussineau suggests an even more precise dating of 1337–44 (*Perceforest: Quatrième partie* 1: xiv).

2　Jane H. M. Taylor discusses the *Perceforest* author's possible level of education, concluding that he was probably a cleric, in "Reason and Faith." Her opinion is seconded by the romance's other modern editor, Gilles Roussineau, in the introduction to his edition of Book 4 (p. xiv).

3　Book 3 of the *Perceforest* describes the conquest of the Low Countries, referred to as the "Selve Carbonniere." That the count of Hainaut would commission a work linking the history of his territories to that of Britain is understandable in view of the marriage in 1328 of his daughter Phillipine to King Edward III, resulting in a strengthening of the alliance between Hainaut and England. See Taylor's introduction to her edition of the *Perceforest* (26–27).

4　Although no music survives for the lais of the *Perceforest*, these poems are clearly songs. They are not the narrative poems in octosyllabic couplets that came to be known as lais through the work of such poets as Marie de France. Rather, they are quasi-narrative stanzaic poems, similar to those found in the prose *Tristan*. We have no way of judging to what extent these French compositions resemble actual early medieval Breton lais, but it is clear that they represent a medieval French author's attempt to re-create the Breton lais on which the tales of Marie de France and others were based.

5　I have briefly discussed the genesis of the "Lai de la complainte" and the "Lai de confort" in my *From Song to Book* 297–99. The pertinent passages of the *Perceforest* are edited from MS BN fr. 346 as appendix C, pp. 347–50.

6　Marie de France, "Laüstic," in *Les Lais,* Rychner, vv. 157–60.

7　On descriptions of lai performance in the prose *Tristan,* see Maillard. For a more general discussion of such passages as a literary convention, see Page 92–107.

8　On the *Perceforest* narrator, see Taylor, "Fourteenth Century" 281–86. Interestingly, Luce del Gat, in the prologue to the prose *Tristan,* also speaks of "reading and rereading" the Latin source book but refers to the audience of his "translation" as listeners.

9　*Guiron le courtois*—sometimes also referred to as *Le roman de Palamède* or *Le roman de Meliadus*—remains unedited. The edition printed in Paris c. 1501 by A. Vérard has been reprinted, with an introductory note by C. E. Pickford, as *Gy-*

ron le courtoys, c. 1501 (1977). On the medieval text and its manuscript tradition, see Lathuillère. Modern critics have been unable to identify the author or to determine whether his name really was Hélie de Boron and what relationship, if any, he bore to the second author of the prose *Tristan,* who also called himself Hélie de Boron. Renée L. Curtis argues that the second author of the prose *Tristan* and the author of the *Guiron* were almost certainly not the same person, and that probably neither of them was really named Hélie de Boron. But since we have no other name for him, I will refer to the author of the *Guiron* as Hélie de Boron. Lathuillère prints two versions of the prologue: one from BN fr. 338 (pp. 175–80) and one from BL Add. MS 36673 and Turin, Biblioteca Nationale L.I.7 (pp. 181–83); I cite the prologue according to his edition of the Paris manuscript. In addition, I have consulted *Guiron* in the manuscripts BN fr. 355 and BL Add. MS 12228.

10 On the prose *Tristan,* see Löseth, and Baumgartner, *Tristan en prose.* On the lais, see Maillard, and Baumgartner, "Remarques." On the pervasive association of lais with the figure of Tristan, see Schmolke-Hasselmann. The lais have been edited and published by Fotitch and Steiner. I cite the prose *Tristan* from MSS BN fr. 335–336, as these episodes do not appear in the version edited by Renée Curtis.

11 This epilogue is published in Curtis; I cite from her transcription. The prologue and epilogue of the prose *Tristan* are treated by Emmanuèle Baumgartner in her article "Première Page," and in her book *Tristan en prose* 94–95.

12 Baumgartner comments on the crown as metaphor for the Round Table and the textual cycle in "Ecriture romanesque" 141; and "Couronne" 200.

13 The cult, founded by the hermit Dardanon, involves belief in a single, trinitarian god of perfect goodness who is invisible, omnipresent, and eternal, is the creator *ex nihilo* of the universe, and is expected some day to manifest himself in human form. See Taylor, "Reason and Faith." The primary heroes of the romance are kept alive on the island of Life until the dawn of the Christian era, so that it is possible for them to be baptized and to die Christians; see Taylor, "Fourteenth Century" 277.

14 The Grail quest is prophetically described as "la plus belle adventure et la plus sainte du roiaulme de la Grant Bretaigne" ("the most beautiful and the holiest adventure of the kingdom of Great Britain"); cited by Taylor, "Fourteenth Century" 277.

PART FIVE
ORAL PRINCIPLES
IN MANUSCRIPT FACTS

Introduction

Hovering behind the preceding discussions is the textuality of the manuscripts themselves; here their presence comes into focus. Not simply books constructed by a more primitive technology, manuscripts demand their own theories of semiotics. How does oral theory assist our understanding of manuscripts, and how do manuscripts aid our understanding of orality? Part III, "Staging the Poet's Presence," discussed what happens particularly to concepts and practices related to the poet's presence when writing enters into the text's semiotics. The articles here discuss the manuscripts themselves, their medieval reception, and the implications of these facts in the production of modern editions. Tim William Machan and John Dagenais concentrate on fourteenth-century England and Spain, respectively, cultures in which manuscript production is well established. In their discussions, oral theory, especially the concepts of *mouvance* and the nonrepeatability of a performance, contribute to insights about the manuscript's physical and semiotic dimensions and modern representations of manuscript materials. These discussions force us to question within yet another realm the concepts of authorship, originality, and the inviolability of the text.

Tim Machan distinguishes between the textuality of three different cultural matrices—medieval vernacular, medieval Latin, and modern print—in order to understand the influence of orality on the manner in which late Middle English texts were written down and in turn how that understanding might influence modern editorial and critical practices. One thing that becomes clear is that the physical facts of texts are related to cultural definitions of language, authorship, and text production, but they do not determine them entirely. Latin's universal, stable, and authoritative cultural position contrasted with English's local variations and temporal instability. Although in the fourteenth century both Latin and English texts were transmitted in manuscripts, orality continued to influence the aesthetics and textuality of the English texts. The vernacular scribe retained some of the freedom of oral poets to re-create the text in its transmission. Hence, differences among manuscripts represent improvisation, not corruption of an original. Machan makes clear how much oral theory illuminates this situation and, even more important, its contrariness to modern editorial practices, which are based on a print culture that developed in the Renaissance in concurrence with a new project of fixing English on the Latin model.

John Dagenais takes us past the words of the texts contained in books to the margins and the physicality of ink, smudges, and tears in manuscripts. He places his discussion in the context of Derrida's metaphysics of writing, revealing Derrida's attempt to elide writing's physical existence, its physical trace, in favor of a *différance* that has no physical existence but is the condition for plenitude and in favor of *archi-écriture*. Dagenais's point is that the text's physical existence, the "residue" of writing, cannot be "effaced" either from Derrida's system or from other theories of textuality. Directing our attention, then, to that residue, he points to the uniqueness of each manuscript and dismisses the idea that manuscripts represent, badly, some sort of original. Looking at various manuscripts of the *Libro de buen amor,* he shows the particularities of presentation that each exhibits as well as their separate semantic resonances. Dagenais finally brings us, however, to the similarities between the manuscript and what seems to be its opposite, the oral performance, to see that the manuscript too is an event, with all that term implies about temporality, uniqueness, and relationships to participants. His essay concludes with an ending appropriate to this book as well; namely, that what all the book's participants have been discussing is not a theory of orality or of written texts per se but a theory of textuality in all its specificity, physicality, and humanness.

C. B. P.

Editing, Orality, and
Late Middle English Texts

The orality of the Middle Ages has recently been of special interest to schol-ars. With the recognition that the cultural shift from orality to literacy is not a discrete and decisive shift but rather a continuum of change which transforms a predominately oral culture into a predominately literate one, critics of the late Middle Ages in particular have sought to identify the existence and conse-quences of orality well after the introduction of written language. The English late Middle Ages are particularly appropriate for an examination of the sur-vival and consequences of orality, both because the orality of the fourteenth and fifteenth centuries has been little examined and because the diversity and number of late Middle English texts provide a suitably rich context against which to assess any theory. Indeed, the context is too rich for detailed exami-nation in a single essay, but an exploration of even a few aspects of late medi-eval English orality can suggest whether recognition and utilization of orality are as important for the interpretation of Middle English texts as they are for texts in other medieval languages. The focus of the present discussion, conse-quently, is intentionally narrow: the practical consequences for the modern critic if orality helped to determine the ways in which late Middle English texts existed. I am thus not here concerned with the psychology or poetics of orality, nor with the *mouvance* of oral compositions in its broadest sense. Rather, I intend to ask: What textual and cultural evidence indicates that or-ality influenced how late Middle English texts were recorded and transmitted?

What effect might such influence have on how medieval manuscripts are interpreted and edited? Throughout my discussion I assume that the attempt to recover a medieval past, whatever the hermeneutical limitations of and on such a recovery, is a worthwhile endeavor, for, as I will suggest by way of a conclusion, such is necessarily the assumption of every edition which attempts to present a medieval text.

Language, Culture, and Text Production

The most important evidence for a discussion of orality in any medieval culture is always lacking, for whatever was then spoken and heard, of course, cannot now be studied directly. We must depend, rather, on manuscripts as witnesses of medieval uses of languages and texts and of contemporary attitudes toward them. Consequently, barring the discovery of a primary document which explicitly discusses the orality of medieval England—and for reasons to be considered shortly, such a document almost certainly never existed—we can at best establish only the probability of the influence of orality, not the certainty. The issues with which I am immediately concerned are the conceptual and cultural differences between medieval English, or indeed any medieval vernacular, and Latin. Since orality both defines and is defined by language and its use, the nature of orality in a given culture will in part emerge from the culture's attitudes toward language. An examination of late medieval attitudes toward language may suggest, therefore, whether written English had, or was perceived to have, qualities associated with orality.

Broadly stated, for medieval England linguistic attitudes were always twofold (at least): Latin was the language of tradition, authority, and power; the vernacular was the language of the people, impermanence, and change.[1] In pragmatic terms these differences derive from the fact that Latin, in comparison with Middle English, embodied different conceptions of language, literary style, authorship, and text production. Since there were no native speakers of Latin and since from antiquity Latin had had a highly codified prescriptive grammar, it was in a very real sense a dead language. Indeed, in a world of continual flux, the "necritude," so to speak, of Latin was evidently a cherished quality, and it was in part to assure the geographic and chronological transcendence which this quality enabled that Latin grammars proliferated throughout the Middle Ages. Hence, Dante speaks of

the art of grammar, which is nothing else but a kind of unchangeable identity of speech in different times and places. This, having been settled by the common consent of many peoples, seems exposed to the arbitrary will of none in particular, and consequently cannot be variable. They therefore invented grammar in order that we might not, on account of the variations of speech fluctuating at the will of individuals, either fail altogether in attaining, or at least attain but a partial knowledge of the opinions and exploits of the ancients, or of those whom difference of place causes to differ from us. (420–21)

As Dante and others were well aware, Latin of course did change, both in respect to its development into Vulgar Latin and thence the Romance languages, and in respect to Latin as the spoken medium of the Church and the universities. But the language of the *texts* of the ancients and the Church fathers was fixed because it had already been written, and the dissemination of the grammars of Donatus and Priscian (among others) and the evaluation of grammar as the first of the seven liberal arts testify to the universal perception of this fixity (Curtius 42). At stake was not simply the intelligibility of ancient *auctores* like Virgil and Ovid, though after the twelfth century these writers had become increasingly more important. Rather, the whole of medieval culture might well be considered at issue, for Latin was also the language of Christianity. In Vivien Law's words, "By the fifth century Latin was unchallenged in the West, both in Church and in State. To play any part in the life of the Church—to gain access to the Scriptures, to read the writings of the Church Fathers, even to comprehend the liturgy—a knowledge of Latin was essential" (3). Within this cultural framework, thus, prescriptive grammatical studies of Latin were far more than linguistic diversions: right or wrong grammar meant right or wrong understanding of tradition, culture, and God.

Given the importance of Latin as a linguistic medium in the Middle Ages, it follows that there should have been interest in the stylistics of writing in Latin—that is, in better or worse ways of speaking and writing correctly. Like the grammatical tradition, this rhetorical tradition extended backward to Quintilian, Cicero, and other Roman rhetoricians, but in the high and late Middle Ages, as scholasticism spread throughout the universities, there seems to have been particular interest in the question of how to use Latin well. Indeed, codification of rules for preaching, letter-writing, and the composition of poetry are essential characteristics of Latin as a language in the Middle Ages. What is important to emphasize here is that the work of writers like Matthew of Vendôme, Geoffrey of Vinsauf, and John of Garland, their differences notwithstanding, assumes the legitimacy of Latin as a medium of communication and thereby underscores its linguistic fixity (Murphy, *Rhetoric* and *Medieval Eloquence*). In stylistics as well as grammar, that is, the permanence of Latin as a written language was recognized and in fact cultivated.

The conceptions of authorship and text production which emerge from this linguistic background are in many ways consistent with it. "In a literary context," Alistair J. Minnis notes, "the term *auctor* denoted someone who was at once a writer and an authority, someone not merely to be read but also to be respected and believed" (10). Consequently, the title *auctor* was reserved for Latin writers made venerable by their antiquity and proved excellent either by, in the case of Virgil or Lucan, their style, or by, in the case of the Church

fathers, their morality. "The term *auctor,*" Minnis continues, "may profita-
bly be regarded as an accolade bestowed upon a popular writer by those later
scholars and writers who used extracts from his works as sententious statements or *auctoritates,* gave lectures on his works in the form of textual commentaries, or employed them as literary models" (10). The authority of
authorship was thus not easily acquired, and a text with *auctoritas,* as a lexical and thematic construct, was to be reverenced and studied and therefore
not willfully altered. To my knowledge, there is no large-scale comparison
between authorial and nonauthorial texts in terms of the preservation or alteration of texts during the course of transmission. Whatever the results of such a
comparison, the important issue in the present discussion would not be simply
the fact that Terence, for instance, experienced less alteration than Langland
did.[2] Rather, the essential theoretical point here is that the identification of a
writer with his writings and the cultural status of Latin compositions harmonized with the prescriptive grammar and stylistics of the language itself. The
results of this conjunction were texts which were imbued with the qualities of
prestige, stasis, and, insofar as they had been produced in accordance with
various linguistic and poetic rules, regularity. In other words, even if a manuscript text of an *auctor* is, by modern standards, inaccurate, as an authorial
text in the Middle Ages it would have elicited recognition and expectation of
the possibility of textual correctness or incorrectness.

To the modern reader familiar with postromantic notions of authorship,
there is nothing troubling about this theoretical point. But if the use of Latin as
a linguistic medium and the critical attitudes toward it point to an *a priori*
lexically regular and prestigious text, the various corresponding aspects of
Middle English language and literature do not. In contrast with Latin, Middle
English was a living, changing language; if Saint Jerome's Latin, for instance,
was the same whether read in London or in the Northern Midlands, the language of the readers thereof was not. Speakers of Middle English were of
course well aware both of synchronic linguistic difference and also, as Chaucer makes clear in the proem to Book 2 of *Troilus and Criseyde,* of diachronic
change:

> Ye knowe ek that in forme of speche is chaunge
> Withinne a thousand yeer, and wordes tho
> That hadden pris, now wonder nyce and straunge
> Us thinketh hem, and yet thei spake hem so,
> And spedde as wel in love as men now do.[3]

Several other well-known passages or texts, moreover, bespeak an interest
in the nature of the Middle English language: Trevisa's excursus in his translation of the *Polychronicon* about the diversity of English dialects; the dialectal
exercise of Chaucer's "Reeve's Tale"; and Caxton's remarks on English dia-

lects in his preface to the *Eneydos*. For the most part, however, such passages are born more of idle curiosity than of rigorous inquiry. When truly probing linguistics was practiced, such as by the *modistae,* it was concerned with the authorial language: Latin. As the language of daily transactions and popular diversions—as a language culturally less prestigious than Latin—English offered no intrinsic reason to stay even temporarily this ephemerality by means of prescriptive or descriptive grammar. Thus, while systematic grammars of Latin proliferated throughout the Middle Ages, no similar interest was displayed in Middle English grammar outside of passing remarks by Latin grammarians (like John Leylond) who wrote in Middle English (see Thomson). The very idea of linguistic fixity and correctness may have been imported from Latin, for in Middle English (as well as Old French and Middle Welsh) a common word for a grammar book is, significantly, *donet* (MW *dwned*), a derivative of the name of the Latin grammarian Donatus. In any event, English was not described in any systematically self-conscious way until the early and middle parts of the sixteenth century, when grammarians like Roger Ascham and Thomas Wilson began to argue about English rhetoric and usage, while others, like Sir John Cheke and William Bullokar, offered prescriptive discussions of orthography.

Since as a linguistic medium Middle English thus was imbued with ephemerality, it is not surprising that, again in contrast with Latin, English elicited little stylistic discussion: if a language is not informed by a sense of correctness and incorrectness, then questions of style are of course inappropriate. Indeed, while early in the fourteenth century Dante composed an influential vernacular *ars poetica* when he wrote *De vulgari eloquentia,* a more representative medieval view is that of Petrarch, who in a letter to Boccaccio admits that on occasion he is inclined "to give all my time to writing in the vernacular" but stresses that the vernacular has only the *potential* for excellence: "Latin is of course the loftier language, but it has been so developed by ancient geniuses that neither we nor anyone else can add much of anything to it. The vulgar tongue however has only recently been formulated. It has been mishandled by many and tended by only a few; rough as it is, it could be much beautified and enriched, I am sure" (244).

Though there were some early attempts to stabilize English grammar and style, the linguistic regularity of the group of early thirteenth-century religious texts known as the Katherine Group, for instance, or the linguistic self-consciousness of the late twelfth-century homilist Orm, who precisely articulates his own orthography, are exceptions to the general absence of concern for such matters as they relate to English. A vernacular writer was of course free to use the techniques of Latin rhetoric, and in fact it was in part through the incorporation of such techniques that written English gradually acquired codes of stylistic correctness. Perhaps the most influential figure in this regard was Chaucer, whose eloquence was praised and style imitated by fifteenth-century writers as diverse as Lydgate, Henryson, and Caxton. But Chaucer is not representative of prevailing late medieval literary theory and practice. The stylistics of poetic composition in English, for instance, apparently did not receive extended treatment similar to Dante's of Italian until George Gascoigne's *Certain Notes of Instruction Concerning the Making of Verse or Rhyme in English,* written in 1575.

Indeed, while throughout medieval Europe the vernacular was in general less prestigous than Latin, England in particular seems to have lagged behind other cultures in recognizing its value, inasmuch as grammatical and stylistic discussions of English were preceded by similar discussions of several other vernaculars. The Icelandic *First Grammatical Treatise* of the mid–twelfth century discusses phonology and orthography, and in addition to *De vulgari eloquentia* a number of stylistic works survive: for Icelandic, *Skáldskaparmál* and *Háttatal* of Snorri Sturluson's *Prose Edda* of the mid–thirteenth century; for Welsh, the *Bardic Grammar* of the early fourteenth century; and for French, the various manifestations of the *seconde rhétorique* of the late fourteenth century. In a different vein, the anagrammic signatures of Froissart and Machaut reveal that in the fourteenth century French poets could comfortably assume the posture of an author, as could Chaucer's Welsh contemporary Dafydd ap Gwilym, whose verse contains none of the authorial self-consciousness that appears in, for example, Chaucer's utilization of Lollius in the *Troilus.*

As I noted earlier, according to medieval literary theory a vernacular author was an impossibility, and whatever the notoriety of a Chaucer or a Gower, most surviving Middle English texts are, indeed, anonymous. Since Middle English lacked the stabilizing factors of prescriptive grammar and stylistics and often the identification of writer with text, the texts themselves presumably could not contain the *a priori* assumption of permanence. That is, as a work in the vernacular, any Middle English text necessarily lacked the lexical and thematic prestige associated with a text produced by an *auctor* in the language of *auctoritas.* The key point, again, is not what a comparison of individual authorial and nonauthorial texts would reveal; indeed, the Middle English *Seinte Katerine,* perhaps in some way because of the regularized literary dialect in which it is written, would seem to show less alteration than the works of Terence, mentioned earlier. Rather, what emerges from the present discussion is the fact that the cultural situation of the vernacular rendered the language, style, and structure of a Middle English text as, in effect, non-issues. At the conclusion of the *Troilus* or in the short poem "Adam Scriveyn," of course, Chaucer does express a concern for the fixity of his texts, but as Derek Pearsall notes, such a concern is nonmedieval by nature (*Canterbury Tales* 24). It is the accurate reproduction of authorial texts which is the widespread concern of the late Middle Ages, as is suggested by, for instance, Studie's observation in the C text of *Piers Plowman* that Clergie is "ouer

Skripture þe skilfole and screueynes were trewe" (Pearsall, *Piers Plowman* 11. 97), or by, in a different vein, the concern of the author of the preface to the second Wycliffite Bible for the accurate translation of Scripture.

The essential difference between the written and spoken word is that the former is theoretically fixed while the latter, in Franz H. Bäuml's words, "is heard, and, as sound, it is ephemeral. It therefore is limited to two modes of existence: its utterance and its remembrance" ("Varieties" 247). Spoken language, of course, has its own grammatical and pragmatic rules, but they differ in kind and function from those of written language, which are designed to produce texts which communicate in the absence of the writer. The distinctive feature of written language is less the fact of a text's absolute correctness or incorrectness than the *potential* for such evaluations. This potential is inherent in the written medium and essentially absent from spoken language, since the latter, once it has been uttered in performance, cannot be studied and evaluated (save electronically—an option not open to the Middle Ages) as a discourse phenomenon. Consequently, medieval attitudes toward Latin and English suggest that the latter did indeed embody certain qualities associated with orality. The prestige of Latin was reflected and supplemented by the standards of grammatical and stylistic correctness associated with it, and as primarily the language of written tradition, the Latin of the ecclesiastical and pagan *auctores* was a fixed language. In contrast, even as a written language the vernacular, in a state of continual flux, lacked the grammatical and stylistic regularity which Latin had and which was used to assess the quality and correctness of any piece of writing.

In fact, as has often been noted, throughout the Middle Ages orality was as essential as textuality as a determinant of the stylistics and aesthetics of vernacular texts in a variety of ways. Such is the case, indeed, with the simplistic plot reduplication in the thirteenth-century romances *King Horn* and *Havelok,* and with the manipulation of [u] in the lyric "Sumer is icumen in" and the antiphonal quality of the macaronic poem "Of on þat is so fayr and briȝt," both of which also date to the thirteenth century:

> Of on þat is so fayr and briȝt
> > *velud maris stella,*
> Briȝter þan þe day-is liȝt,
> > *parens & puella,*
> Ic crie to þe, þou se to me,
> Leuedy, preye þi sone for me
> > *tam pia,*
> Þat ic mote come to þe,
> > *maria.*[4]

But more significantly, orality also conditions the poetics of a writer as late and self-consciously textual as Lydgate, whose *Temple of Glas* in part re-

writes Chaucer's *House of Fame* (among other texts) but nonetheless includes
passages as tautological and syntactically loose as the following portion of the
unnamed lady's complaint to Venus:

> For I am bounde to þing þat I nold:
> Freli to chese þere lak I liberte,
> And so I want of þat myn herte would
> The body knyt, alþouȝe my þouȝt be fre;
> So þat I most, of necessite,
> Myn hertis lust outward contrarie—
> Though we be on, þe dede most varie.
>   (Lydgate 76)

The centrality of orality to vernacular aesthetics is also revealed by the fact
that in the metrical romances in particular the illusion of orality was increasingly cultivated through repeated references to a listening audience and
through the employment of tags and formulaic diction.[5] Such textual cultivation of orality in fact nicely reveals the sometimes tenuous distinction between
orality and textuality in Middle English literature. For instance, the Middle
English counterparts to Old English "*ic hyrde*" as rhetorical demarcations of
discourse communities are the various references to the "*boke*" and the reading thereof; and yet while such phrases might seem to reflect unambiguous
textuality, they are used, as in the opening of "Lai le freine," to further the
illusion of a listening audience.[6] Even the physical act of writing could have a
basis in orality, inasmuch as a common scribal copying error involves homophonic confusion, which suggests that scribes articulated their texts at least
silently, if not orally, as they copied them (Chaytor, "Medieval Reader").

Interest in the written vernacular per se of course increased throughout the
Middle Ages (see Parkes), but by medieval and modern standards the cultural
position of late Middle English still in effect paradoxically denied the written
vernacular the status of written language. Like spoken language, to return to
Bäuml, written Middle English could thus in effect be uttered and remembered but not retrieved exactly and evaluated, and without the cultural prestige
of Latin, English could never acquire fixity as a linguistic medium.

Textual Transmission and Oral Improvisation

Having examined the cultural evidence for the existence of certain qualities of
orality in written Middle English, it is appropriate to consider the evidence of
Middle English texts. Specifically, using Lord's model as a reference point I
wish to examine a number of parallels between the transmission of oral compositions and the transmission of a variety of late Middle English texts. My
intention here is not to suggest that Middle English writers thought of themselves as oral poets or even that they would have understood what modern

scholars mean by the concept of orality. Rather, I intend only to show that a variety of the conscious alterations effected by scribes as they "copied" texts are similar to the changes made by oral poets as they re-create songs—that a model of improvisation can describe the performance qualities of both oral poets and scribes.

For popular works like romances, the relevance of orality is well known; alliterative formulas and tag phrases like *herkneth lordinges* have long suggested to scholars that the poems could have been recited aloud (Crosby; Baugh, "Improvisation" and "Middle English Romances"; Maldwyn Mills). Even if this was not always the case, as I noted above, such devices at least create the illusion of orality. One need not claim, moreover, that the poems were composed extemporaneously to recognize that for such works the conception of copying as composition or performance had widespread currency. Derek Pearsall, for instance, notes that "the surviving manuscripts of a poem like *Beves of Hamptoun* make it clear that each act of copying was to a large extent an act of recomposition, and not an episode in a process of decomposition from an ideal form" ("Texts" 126–27; see Waldron). A pertinent example comes from *Sir Orfeo,* which survives in three copies from the early fourteenth, early fifteenth, and late fifteenth centuries. When Orfeo returns to his kingdom from captivity among the fairies, he tests his steward's loyalty before revealing his identity. Having found the steward loyal, Orfeo identifies himself, and the poem in Edinburgh, National Library of Scotland MS Advocates 19.2.1, the earliest copy commonly known as the Auchinleck manuscript, continues:

> Þo al þo þat þer-in sete
> Þat it was King Orfeo vnderȝete,
> & þe steward him wele knewe:
> Ouer & ouer þe bord he þrewe,
> & fel adoun to his fet;
> So dede auerich lord þat þer sete,
> & al þai seyd at o criing:
> "ȝe beþ our lord, Sir, & our king!"
>   (Bliss, ll. 575–82)

In London, British Library MS Harley 3810, the early fifteenth-century copy, the last half of Orfeo's identification speech is absent, as is all of the above passage. In the remaining copy, Oxford, Bodleian MS Ashmole 61, this passage appears as:

> All þe lordys þat ther sette
> That was þer kyng þei vnderȝete,
> And wyth þat word þe stewerd hym knew,
> And ouer þe bord a-non he threw,

And fell anon dounne to hys fete,
And so dyd all þat þer sate;
And all þei seyd with a cryeng:
"Welcum, our Orfew þe kyng!"
(ll. 570–77)

As A. J. Bliss indicates, "The divergences between the three texts are so great that it is impracticable to print H [Harley 3810] and B [Ashmole 61] either in the form of variant readings or in parallel columns with A [the Auchinleck MS]" (xvii). The three copies can in fact be regarded as variations on the Orfeo theme, so to speak, for the differences which characterize Harley 3810 and Ashmole 61 as distinct from the Auchinleck manuscript recall differences inherent in improvisation. Thus, Harley 3810 is throughout an abbreviation of the version preserved in the Auchinleck manuscript, and the truncation of the ending in particular, including the above passage, recalls Lord's observation that "the endings of songs are less stable, more open to variation, than their beginnings" (*Singer* 119). On the other hand, the semantically trivial differences (e.g., "þe lordys" for "þo") between the Auchinleck copy and Ashmole 61, which Bliss describes as "the work of an idiosyncratic scribe freely adapting a sound copy" (xvii), mirror the semantically insignificant stylistic variations which will emerge from a comparison of any two versions of a song, for which, Lord notes, we should not "expect verbal identity" (*Singer* 119).

The improvisational qualities of the *Orfeo* manuscripts very likely derive at least in part from the fact that these manuscripts reflect actual performance texts, but other features suggestive of improvisation appear in the manuscripts of *Piers Plowman,* which clearly was never meant to be performed aloud. This late fourteenth-century dream-vision is traditionally ascribed to William Langland and classified in three distinct versions labeled A, B, and C by modern scholars. The fifty-one manuscripts of the poem are classified in these versions on the theory that Langland wrote and then twice lengthened and revised the poem. As is well known, however, six of the seventeen A manuscripts, including Cambridge, Trinity MS R.3.14, the base manuscript for the most recent critical edition (Kane), supplement (at least in part independently) the A text with the portions of the C text which Langland is thought to have added to the original version of the poem. The scribes thus clearly knew of the longer version of *Piers,* and in melding the early version with the conclusion of the longer one they created composites in precisely the same way as improvisational singers. In Lord's analysis, at the end of a song "the tension between themes that arises from habitual association comes into operation. It may help to provide an ending when either there was none in the singer's experience of a given song or what there was seemed vague and hazy in his mind. The process may involve more than a mere ending to a song and actually lead the singer to mix songs, passing from one song pattern to another at a point at which the two patterns coincide" (*Singer* 119–20).

A different characteristic of improvisation occurs frequently in the *Piers* manuscripts when scribes, due to the controversial themes of the poem, highlighted or repressed views with which they agreed or disagreed (Kane 115; Russell). Such alterations are especially common in London, British Library MS Harley 875.[7] When Lady Meed offers bribes to the Mayor in the beginning of the third *passus* of the A text, for example, Langland counsels the reader with a Latin question from Job 15.34 and then observes:

> Among this lewede men • this latin amounteth,
> That fuir schal falle • and brenne atte laste
> The houses and the homes • of hem that desyreth
> For to haue ȝiftes • in ȝouthe or in elde.
> (Skeat 3.87–90)

The allegory continues with a discussion between Lady Meed, the King, and Conscience, but in Harley 875 alone the above passage is followed immediately by a further admonition to the "masters of the law" about virtue:

> Now beoth ȝe war, if ȝe wole • ȝe maysturs of the lawe;
> For the sothe schale be souȝt of ȝoure soules • so me god helpe,
> The suffraunce that ȝe suffre • such wrongus to be wroust;
> While the chaunce is in ȝoure choyse • cheose ȝe the best.[8]

This sort of textual embellishment, to be sure, is reminiscent of the thematic elaboration which Lord has noted is characteristic of improvisation. Such elaboration, however, is not "pure ornamentation; it has meaning in terms of the tradition from which it stems" (Lord, *Singer* 119). In the passage from *Piers*, indeed, the elaboration stems from the apocalyptic tradition which informs the poem, and it consequently gives the passage in Harley 875 both a more somber tone and a greater eschatological emphasis than Langland's hypothetical original A text has.

It might be argued that as broadly "popular" poems both *Sir Orfeo* and *Piers Plowman* would naturally have experienced, if not invited, such scribal involvement, so that the cogency of the parallels with improvisational composition might appear questionable. Yet such parallels also appear in works like Chaucer's *Boece*, which clearly was not "popular." A close translation of a uniquely Chaucerian combination of *De consolatione philosophiae* and Jean de Meun's Old French translation, the *Boece* also incorporates, in the best academic fashion of the late fourteenth century, material from Nicholas Trevet's commentary on the *Consolatio* and, perhaps, some of the so-called Remigian glosses. Despite the technical nature of the composition, however, and despite the fact that it is a translation of an authorial text, the scribes of the *Boece* did on occasion re-create—in effect improvise on—the text they were copying. Some supplemented the Middle English with new translations from the Latin and French, for instance, while others attempted to clarify the dialogue structure by indicating with abbreviations which were the speeches of Lady Philosophy and which were those of Boethius. In one case—Oxford, Bodleian MS Auct. F.3.5—the scribe wrote an interpretive paraphrase of Book 1 using the *Boece* for his lemmata, though he acknowledges neither Chaucer nor the work itself (Machan, "Scribal Role"). In a different vein, the scribe of Oxford, Bodleian MS Bodley 797, written approximately fifty years after Chaucer's death, extensively modernized the syntax and lexicon of the work. Among the variants unique to this manuscript are: "hold" for "leten" (2p3.25), "to be desyred" for "requerable" (2p6.29), "forseyd" for "purposede" (3p2.75), "willingly" for "his thankes" (3p11.86), "ben corect" for "ben coriged" (4p4.84), and "corectith" for "corrigith" (4p7.38). These alterations are of the same semantically trivial sort made by the scribe of Ashmole 61 to his presumed exemplar of *Sir Orfeo,* and here as there the absence of "verbal identity" between manuscripts parallels the transmission of improvisational compositions.

A parallel with the elaboration noted in the *Piers Plowman* manuscripts occurs in another work which clearly was not "popular." The late fourteenth-century treatise *The Cloud of Unknowing* is intended, in the words of its prologue, to be read by or spoken to no one "bot ʒif it be of soche one or to soche one þat haþ (bi þi supposing) in a trewe wille by an hole entent, purposed him to be a parfite folower of Crist" (Hodgson 1–2). The treatise discusses the mystical way in which an individual can come to know God through contemplation. Given the intensely personal nature of its subject, it is perhaps not surprising that its scribes, like the *Piers* scribes, should occasionally have re-created the text in accordance with their own views. For example, during a discussion of how an individual must exercise self-governance in eating and sleeping, the anonymous writer observes:

God woldest þou haue, & synne woldest þou lacke. God wanteþ þee; & synne arte þou sekir of.[9]

In one copy, Sussex, St. Hugh's Charterhouse MS Parkminster D.176, this passage appears as:

God woldest þou haue, & synne woldest þou lacke. & if God wanteþ þee, synne arte þou sekir of.

In this version, the passage no longer simply asserts that the individual lacks God and is sinful; rather, by arranging the final two clauses as a conditional, the scribe offers a more optimistic view of human nature. Similarly, in a discussion of the need to love one's enemy, the phrase "to haue so moche mercy & so moche pite of his enmye" (76) appears in London, British Library MS Harley 2373 as "pite of his euen cristyn or of hys enmye."[10] The emphasis of the passage is thus quite displaced, for the difficulty of loving one's enemy is mitigated by introducing a parallel between the enemy and another Christian.

Editorial Models

It remains to consider what effect the orality of written Middle English and the parallels between Middle English textual transmission and improvisational composition might have on how medieval manuscripts are interpreted and edited. To a large extent, the editing of Middle English literature currently depends on the distinction between authors, who creatively compose texts, and scribes, who transmit or corrupt them. For many texts such as *Seinte Katerine* or the Wycliffite sermons, this is an entirely adequate interpretive and editorial model.[11] But it is important to recognize that this model is predicated on written language; indeed, it is a model which views manuscript production as an (ineffective) prototype of text production in a print culture. Such a model accounts well and consistently for classical and Renaissance texts, since both are infused with (albeit different) conceptions of linguistic fixity and authorship. But while Middle English literature is necessarily written language, it nonetheless lacks several of the essential characteristics of such language. Late medieval culture, moreover, precluded vernacular writers from earning the title *auctor,* and without a conception of textual correctness or the implicit or explicit identification of a writer with a text, for an individual reader the vernacular manuscript he was reading necessarily was the text of that work. Since the movement from primary orality to primary literacy is gradual, it is to be expected that for various ideological reasons certain texts, like the Wycliffite sermons, should be best explained by a model of written language and print culture. But what of others texts, including those discussed above, wherein characteristics of improvisation are apparent? How are these manuscript traditions to be interpreted and edited in light of Middle English orality? Without implying in any way that late Middle English writers knew anything of orality as it has been discussed herein, I would like to consider the possibilities that the cultural attitudes toward late Middle English language and literature may well have preserved an oral residue from earlier English literature, which was at some point unarguably oral, and that adapting a model of oral composition may be a profitable way to interpret the transmission and reception of some late Middle English texts.

The essential feature of oral composition, of course, is the fluidity of the "text" with all the consequent ramifications for style and authorship. In oral literature, John Miles Foley points out, "What presents itself is not the usual phenomenon of an object text, but rather a continuous *tradition* of text-making and -remaking which has, in effect, no texts (as we understand them) until the performance of this or that moment in time is written down and the process is, for better or worse, frozen" ("Oral Theory" 26). Consequently, Foley observes elsewhere, "to establish any one text or textual feature as standard is to mistake the ontology of oral traditional structure" ("Editing Oral Epic Texts" 81; also see Lord, *Singer* 100–102). Within such a living tradition, there can be better or worse composers but not right or wrong ones, for there is no correct text but only a number of versions. The song as performance, rather than the singer as an individual, is the primary aesthetic determinant; even if the latter's identity is known, he is less important than the moment of his composition (see Lord, *Singer* 279). The singer's performance is in part determined by the general features of the theme or story he inherits, but once these features become not general but specific—once a song is memorized rather than composed—traditional orality disappears. In Lord's words, "Those singers who accept the idea of a fixed text are lost to oral traditional processes" (*Singer* 137; also see Foley, "Oral Theory").

In an adaptation of a model of oral composition the general and particular structural changes consciously made by scribes would be seen as parallel to the compositional techniques of oral poets. Just as the oral poet, however, is to some extent limited by the known features of his song, so is the scribe limited by the text he is copying. But the scribe remains, to paraphrase Lord, "at once the tradition and an individual creator" (*Singer* 4), and while he could supplement the *Boece* with additional translation, for instance, he could not completely reorder the arguments. It is important to note here that identification of manuscript variation for the various texts is possible only by evaluation of these texts against some other texts from which they have "deviated," and so in this regard the latter appear to have some authority. But the latter texts are authoritative only in the sense that at certain times certain scribes used them to copy—or improvise—certain texts and not in any larger literary, cultural, or legal sense. Moreover, a view of the entire surviving manuscript tradition is available only to the modern editor. All vernacular texts acquired this kind of authority, that is, on an ad hoc basis whenever they were copied. Within such an orality model an editor would need to reject the traditional distinctions between author and scribe and text and variant: all copies of the work would have equal medieval legitimacy as versions of what might be called a textual theme. It would be the intentions of the writer of the text which must be recovered and not the intention of the hypothetical writer whose words were being transmitted. Rather than isolate A, B, and C versions of *Piers Plowman*, for example, the objective would be to isolate however many "scribal" versions there are.

Within such a model it would be important not to overstate the literary theory of the Middle Ages at the expense of the evidence of given textual traditions. Zumthor, for instance, claims: "The concept of textual authenticity, as the philologists use it, seems very much to have been unknown, particularly with regard to the vernacular, at least until toward the end of the fifteenth century." [12] But a text like *Seinte Katerine,* as I noted earlier, does indeed reflect the "concept of textual authenticity," as do the Wycliffite sermons. In determining whether a model of oral composition is useful for interpreting a manuscript tradition it would be important to take into consideration the cultural and literary ideologies which inform the manuscripts as they are reflected in their production, transmission, and reception (Machan, "Middle English Text Production"). If these do not indicate that the author/scribe distinction of written culture informs the various manuscripts of a given text, then an orality model might well be the most appropriate editorial method.

The general usefulness of such a model can be determined only on the basis of an individual case, but its *a priori* suitability is suggested by its avoidance of the historically problematic distinction between vernacular authors and scribes, by the primacy it gives to actual manuscript texts as moments of composition and interpretation, and by the diversity of texts (popular romances and academic treatises) and the diversity of alterations (large structural changes, as in *Sir Orfeo* or *Piers Plowman,* or ad hoc thematic elaboration, as in *The Cloud of Unknowing*) which it can explain. Similar changes, of course, appear in the transmission both of medieval Latin works and of modern compositions, for oral poets, scribes, printers, and editors can all meld texts, to which Albert Bigelow Paine's treatment of Mark Twain's *Mysterious Stranger* manuscripts attests. But the key point, again, is not simply the evidence of a given Latin or English textual tradition but also the medieval perception of that tradition as a function of culture in a way which predetermines the existence and nature of the evidence. As Paul Kiparsky has suggested in a discussion of the Vedas and the Finnish Kaleva poems, "Contrary to Parry and Lord it is not the *technique* (writing versus speech) that determines the fixity of a text, but rather the *function* which that text has in the society" (101). Thus, while both Latin and English texts obviously exist in written manuscripts, they nonetheless differ significantly in function and kind: Latin was the codified, prestigious language of authors, and texts written in Latin, even when subject to scribal alteration, would be perceived as extensions of a Christian cultural tradition informed in part by the aesthetics of Rome. On the other hand, in the fourteenth and fifteenth centuries the English language was not generally perceived to have linguistic and stylistic fixity, and vernacular texts as lexical constructs would not by nature elicit from readers the expectation of correctness or incorrectness.

An adaptation of an orality model would also harmonize with the changes English language and literature underwent in the transition from the medieval to the Renaissance period. That is, just as extemporaneous oral composition ceases when the text becomes fixed, so would the oral residue cease when Renaissance humanism privileged English language and literature at almost the same time the printing press allowed for the proliferation of identical— hence fixed—texts. Though the movement in English culture from oral primacy to textual primacy has been carefully discussed elsewhere and is well outside the scope of the present discussion (see Chaytor, *From Script to Print;*

Eisenstein), it is worth reiterating the importance the advent of print played in this movement. As the attention of the humanists gradually elevated the cultural status of English, the printed book provided visible evidence of this elevation. Even if a printed text of Renaissance English was as inaccurate (in absolute terms) as a manuscript text of Middle English, the former brought with it the cultural and iconographic *idea* of linguistic and literary regularity which the latter lacked.

At the outset I suggested that the implicit goal of any edition which attempts to recover a medieval text is the recovery of a medieval past. That is, whatever interpretive strategies a reader might employ, an editor attempting to present the "correct" text of a medieval work is necessarily engaged in historical criticism. But a potential paradox is consequently involved, for as I have indicated herein, it is certain that there was no correct written Middle English, and it is questionable whether there ever were correct texts of vernacular compositions. As an exercise in historical criticism, editing thus risks recovering a textual past that unequivocally never existed. A deconstructive edition is theoretically possible—Barthes's *S/Z* may well be such a text—but so long as medieval editions are historical in orientation, they ought also to be historical in method and theory. The issue, perhaps, is one of perspective. As Tennyson's Ulysses observes,

> all experience is an arch wherethrough
> Gleams that untravelled world, whose margin fades
> For ever and for ever when I move.
> (Ricks 563)

If the experience from which editors and interpreters construct their arches is postmedieval, then the margins of Middle English literature will necessarily fade into those of a modern printed page; if the experience is in a sense premedieval, then, as I have suggested herein, the margins in fact fade quite another way. The primary advantage of the orality model I have discussed is that it eliminates the paradox mentioned above: it is a model derived from cultural and textual evidence and self-conscious about the ways in which it is determinative of it. Consequently, I would argue that an orality model is theoretically more consistent than a print model. The latter can make medieval texts more modern in appearance, and therefore in meaning, than they actually are, for it seeks to harmonize medieval culture and text production with modern interpretive and editorial goals. Whether or not a model derived from oral composition is the most appropriate way to explain the ontology of late medieval English texts can be determined only by further textual and cultural research. Whatever the results of such research, it would seem that the orality of late Middle English texts needs to be better recognized and utilized in editorial procedure than it has been heretofore.

Notes

1 At least until the close of the fourteenth century, French also was more culturally prestigious than English. The law courts, as is well known, were not officially opened in English until 1362.

2 On Terence, see Grant, especially the table of variants on pp. 177–214.

3 Ll. 22–26. All quotations of Chaucer's works are taken from *The Riverside Chaucer,* ed. Benson.

4 Carleton Brown 26. Though no music survives, this lyric may well have been intended to be sung, and in fact by the fifteenth century it had developed into a carol with a burden. See Greene 125–26, 398–99.

5 While some of the romances at some time certainly were recited aloud by *disours,* the sixfold repetition of "liþeþ and lestneth" (or variants thereof) in *Gamelyn,* for example, which is a poem of only 902 lines, seems motivated more by rhetorical strategy than by the need to call the audience's attention. A different textual motivation for the cultivation of orality appears in *Floris and Blancheflour,* wherein the oral atmosphere derives from translation of a French original. See Fewster 1–49.

6 Similar blendings of the oral and the textual occur both in *Sir Gawain and the Green Knight* (ll. 687–90) and in Chaucer's introduction to the "Miller's Tale" (1.3173–77).

7 All the presumed alterations peculiar to this manuscript are recorded in Kane 45–47.

8 Skeat, ll. 91–94. Skeat accepts the quatrain as authorial, but Kane did not, nor do Knott and Fowler.

9 Hodgson 81. The edition prints only single variants, not complete manuscript copies, and so the quotation from the Parkminster manuscript is an amalgamation of the edited text and the relevant variants.

10 The quotation from Harley 2373 is again my own reconstruction.

11 For a discussion of the evidence that the sermons were prepared and corrected in a central area, see Hudson 189–202.

12 "La notion d'authenticité textuelle, telle que l'utilisent les philologues, semble bien avoir été inconnue, spécialment en ce qui concerne la langue vulgaire, au moins jusque vers la fin du XVe siècle" (Zumthor, *Essai* 71).

13 *John Dagenais*

That Bothersome Residue: Toward a Theory of the Physical Text

Qui vol encercar la natura de la poma, . . . en la poma mateixa
ho encerc.
—Ramon Llull

"Written words are residue," says Walter Ong in his study *Orality and Literacy.* "Writing makes 'words' appear similar to things because we think of words as the visible marks signaling words to decoders: we can see and touch such inscribed 'words' in texts and books. Written words are residue. Oral tradition has no such residue or deposit" (11). The sense of this statement seems clear enough in context, and yet we may ask ourselves, first, how something that is a residue, something left over, can be so useful as to serve as a "signal to decoders." If written words are residue, what process are they the residue of (writing? copying? printing? reading?), and what will explain the apparently enduring ability of this residue to function in future acts of decoding? "Writing," the written word on the written page, what I will call here the physical text, seems always caught in this paradox: it is superfluous, a by-product of writing (the activity) and reading, something always existing after writing and before reading, and yet its presence is essential if these twin acts, writing and reading, are to take place. It is at once left over and absolutely necessary. And just to mention now a point I will return to at the close of this study, if we grant that this residue is an essential part of written textuality, might it also be possible, contrary to Ong's affirmation here, that "orality" too possesses such an essential and superfluous residue?

If written words are residue, what exactly is the nature of this residue? And

246

what is its place in the study of "literature," all of which coincides at some point or another with a physical text? Especially, what is its place in the study of the literature of the Middle Ages? Do we need some sort of a theoretical understanding of the physical text, and what might such a theory be? Could a theory of the written word on the written page which suppresses, closes off, such basic concepts as author, text, textual tradition, and intertextuality actually open up, by focusing on a unique, concrete physical occurrence of a written object, a different set of concepts which might prove equally basic to our ideas of what writing is: noise, dialogue, interruption, fading, blanks, margins?

I come to these questions not as a theoretician but as someone who has spent a good deal of time over the past ten years or so looking at physical texts of the Middle Ages. I have been intrigued by the veneration which the difficult access to these materials seems to imply as well as by the lack of ceremony with which they are finally dumped on my *pupitre* after what always seems an unfathomably long delay. Like everyone who works with manuscripts, I suppose, I have felt that special excitement which comes when we first open a new manuscript—as if we are entering a previously unexplored world. And I have gone back to familiar manuscripts and found them as I would find an old friend.

These impressions may serve to explain why I am interested in trying to understand better the nature of the physical text, but they can hardly serve as the foundation for a theory of the physical text. Nevertheless I feel that such strong and often contradictory impressions are symptomatic of a genuine need for those of us who "do" manuscripts to understand the relation of the physical text to what we do with and to it, whether it be transcription, editing, literary criticism, art history, bibliographic description, or simply reading. What exactly is this object we hold for a time in our hands and then abandon when our task is finished? What is its place or role, if any, in what we are doing? There is but one certainty in this: that physical text will remain (though modified by our passage through it) even when we have completed our task.

I think the problem of the physical text must be recognized as a largely unexplored part of that much larger question which has so preoccupied students of literature in this century: Where exactly do we situate our object of study, the literary text? There have been many answers to this question, but nearly all these approaches can be plotted on a line that runs from divine afflatus through authorial intention (by way of intertextuality) to implied readers. This line ends somewhere in an individual human reader (or a world) transformed by his reading of a text. It seems, in fact, that we have found a place for the literary text everywhere except in the one place where it undeniably resides: in the physical text. We have failed to come to grips with this bothersome residue which is not writing as an abstract phenomenon existing in uneasy opposition to speech or orality but writing (or even printing) as the physical word on the physical page.

Parts of my opening discussion seem to have a distinctly Derridean flavor: this business of essential superfluities. But what I want to argue here as a starting point for a theory of the physical text is that one of the central blind spots in *De la grammatologie* is this physical text. Derrida's deconstruction of writing and speech as cultural and metaphysical phenomena, as systems, leaves our physical text largely untouched. Derrida is concerned with *archi-écriture,* which he sets up in opposition to "le concept vulgaire de l'écriture." He never descends below this vulgar concept of writing to consider the, presumably, even more "vulgar" written object. And yet I think it is possible to show that *De la grammatologie* and particularly Derrida's exposition of the supplement and trace are haunted by this bothersome residue which is the physical text.

Origins

Not all of what Derrida has to say is without import for our study of the physical text, however. I think it is worthwhile, before we examine Derrida's evasion of the physical text, to examine how his writings may help to illuminate some of the basic, unspoken premises of those of us who work with manuscripts.

At the center of Derrida's work is the critique of the Western metaphysics of presence, a metaphysics which, according to Derrida, seeks always to restore a lost presence, to discover origins. Central to this metaphysics of presence is a set of oppositions: soul/body, inside/outside, man/woman, heaven/earth, speech/writing. In these oppositions, however, the first term is always given privilege over the other. The second is seen as, more than an opposite, a debasement of the former, always further away from perceived origins.

The prime paradox in all this, of course, is that the "presence" which this metaphysics would try to recover is absent. And I think that there are some ideas of interest in this paradigm for those of us who work with editions and with oral performances. For one thing, it strikes me just how much the act of producing critical editions participates in this "metaphysics of presence." The idea of the critical edition is to work back from the manuscript texts to some originary authentic text (of which the various manuscript witnesses are but debasements).

I am not denying that this is a worthwhile endeavor. What intrigues me, however, is how much the vocabulary of textual criticism participates in the idea of origins and debasement set forth by Derrida. Thus, central to textual criticism is the idea of scribal error (in all its variations: dittography, elision, the hyper- and hypometric lines often blamed on scribes), *recentiores deterio-*

res, lectio facilior (where difficulty is privileged). Then there are other words of the textual critic's vocabulary which are also based on an idea of debasement or fall: lacunae, contamination, loss of folios, and so on. In other words, the very work of textual criticism involves the creation of a hierarchy which inevitably situates the manuscripts and their readings in an inferior and negative position vis-à-vis a generally absent "archetype" or "original." In fact, the *stemma codicum* graphically illustrates this progressive descent and debasement. The paradox is curious. An absent text, a text whose existence cannot be verified, is elevated, set up as a lost "presence" superior to the physical manuscript text which is, I think, for all but the radically skeptical, undeniably present.

To shift temporarily to Saussurian terms, for the textual critic the manuscripts represent a system of signs which signify, represent the lost authentic text.[1] And in the purest of Saussurian ways, these manuscripts constitute only a system of significant differences pointing to a unique, originary text in which these differences are effaced. As signs they are already situated at a debased level with respect to the text they signify.[2]

I would suggest that a similar paradigm obtains in most discussions of oral traditions. Here the individual, unique performances are viewed as signifiers of some authentic text which is actualized in performance, either through manipulation of formulas or through memorization. I think students of oral culture would be less likely than textual critics to devalue the individual oral performance, and yet I do not think they would be willing to set it free of a system of representation and differences, to say that it was not one of many possible performances of some underlying text. Once again, we find the paradox of a descent from presence in what is in fact an oral *present*ation. One of the intriguing things about the metaphysics of presence is that it seems to treat both the stolidly physical and enduring manuscript and the ephemeral oral moment (each in its own way a presence) as equally absent.

Residencia en la tierra

But if Derrida's work serves to illuminate the work of textual critics as a flight from presence in the guise of a search for presence, it also participates with us in that flight. Perhaps what I refer to as a flight or evasion is really the move philosophy or metaphysics must always seem to be making when seen from the point of view of the sort of "particularist" approach I am proposing. I believe, however, that this is not the case. In much the same way that Derrida shows that Rousseau and Saussure cannot talk about speech without making reference to writing, I think it is possible to show that Derrida cannot talk about *archi-écriture* without referring specifically to that very physical text we seek here. In the end his *archi-écriture*, that form of writing which he sets above speech and above that writing he calls "le concept vulgaire de l'écriture," is haunted by that bothersome residue which is present before the act of reading can take place and which lingers long after it is over.

I want to work out briefly the places where I think Derrida's deconstruction of the works of Plato, Rousseau, and Saussure begins to repeat their evasions of the physical text. These are also the places where a theory of the physical text might begin. I will focus on one paragraph in the chapter from *De la grammatologie* entitled "Genèse et structure de l'*Essai sur l'origine des langues*," the place where Derrida works out his theory of "that dangerous supplement." Rousseau uses the word *supplément* in reference both to writing and to masturbation, the former as a supplement to speech, the latter as a substitute for "natural" sex with a woman.[3]

> In both cases [writing and onanism], the possibility of auto-affection manifests itself as such: *it leaves a trace of itself in the world. The worldly residence of a signifier becomes impregnable. That which is written remains, and the experience of touching-touched admits the world as a third party.* The exteriority of space is irreducible there. Within the general structure of auto-affection, within giving-oneself-a-presence or a pleasure, the operation of touching-touched receives the other within the narrow gulf that separates doing from suffering. And the outside, the exposed surface of the body, signifies and marks forever the division that shapes auto-affection.[4]

Perhaps the first thing that strikes us about Derrida's account of the supplement here is his referral to the *résidence mondaine* of the trace left behind by the supplement (in the sense of either writing or onanism). Derrida himself might be intrigued to find here the residuum of that very concept of residue referred to by Ong and which we have seized on, for reasons now obvious, as our lemma for the physical text.[5]

Writing "leaves a trace of itself in the world." Here Derrida introduces the difference key to our theory of the physical text: the supplement, writing the activity, is distinct from writing the product of writing. The one is merely a physical (worldly) trace of the other. The supplement leaves a trace of itself in the world. But this trace is not the supplement, as the following phrase makes clear again: there is a clear distinction between the signifier and its worldly residue. Thus Derrida keeps his supplement and signifier safe from a too-physical existence. Writing, even the "vulgar concept of writing," is distinct from "l'écrit" which remains; and in the second part of this sentence Derrida quickly shifts his attention back from the world which receives this trace to an experiencing subject which "admits the world as a third party." But that world which is admitted is not the same world in which the "trace de soi" now resides, unassailably. It is the world in which the supplement is experienced as an activity. The trace, "residence," is no longer a part of the paradigm. It is left free, residing in the world, and Derrida does not return to it in the remainder of the paragraph cited here, nor indeed in the rest of *De la grammatologie*. The "trace de soi" emerges at the point of contact between subject and world ("giving oneself a presence [through writing] or a pleasure") and is cast into that world, no longer a part of experience and yet "inexpugnable." That bothersome residue which will not go away, cannot be disposed of easily.

And yet I think the bothersome residue reenters Derrida's system at the very place he would dispose of it: in his choice of the word *trace* to designate it here. *Trace,* of course, is one of Derrida's words, often merging with another key term, *archi-écriture*. It is worthwhile to compare the "unassailable" "trace de soi" which takes up earthly residence with what Derrida says about the trace in the course of his deconstruction of Saussure's studies of speech and writing:

It is not the question of a constituted difference here, but rather, before all determination of the content, of the *pure* movement which produces difference. *The (pure) trace is differance.* It does not depend on any sensible plentitude [*sic*], audible or visible, phonic or graphic. It is, on the contrary, the condition of such a plenitude. Although it *does not exist,* although it is never a *being-present* outside of all plenitude, its possibility is by rights anterior to all that one calls sign (signified/signifier, content/expression, etc.), concept or operation, motor or sensory. This differance is therefore not more sensible than intelligible and it permits the articulation of signs among themselves within the same abstract order—a phonic or graphic text for example—or between two orders of expression. It permits the articulation of speech and writing—in the colloquial sense—as it founds the metaphysical opposition between the sensible and the intelligible, then between signifier and signified, expression and content, etc.[6]

At first it seems evident that the two "traces" are in many ways contrary. One trace is pure movement which produces difference, the other is the superfluous residue of the movement (writing, masturbation) which produces difference. One trace is independent of "any sensible . . . , audible or visible, phonic or graphic [plenitude]"; the other, the "résidence mondaine d'un signifiant," exactly that plenitude. The one is anterior to all signs, the other posterior to all signs. The one is nonexistent, the other unassailably resident.

All this suggests to me not that Derrida's theory of the trace is fraught with contradictions but that perhaps that trace, and indeed *archi-écriture* itself, may coincide in part with that physical text which is the object of this study. Is it possible that this physical trace, posterior to the already supplemental act of writing, *is* also that archtrace, *archi-écriture,* which is at once produced and effaced in the process of generating meaning?

It would be gratifying to be able to argue that in all the ponderous pages of abstraction on trace and archtrace and *archi-écriture* Derrida is really talking about that physical text which we can all hold in our hands. I'm not sure I could pull this off. But what I do want to suggest as a starting point for a theory of the physical text is that we recognize within Derrida's system of supplement and trace another feature, largely unacknowledged by him, which we may call "residue." This residue, which we equate with the physical text, is that bothersome by-product of auto-affection or writing (the activity) which cannot be effaced, not even from Derrida's system.

As residue it participates in the "danger" of the supplement which produces it and, by its very nature, which is physical and enduring, is a continuing testimony to the shame and guilt of the supplement. In this way (cf. Nietzsche's deconstruction of cause and effect) it is also the origin of the supplement. This by-product is also the plenitude and origin that both Derrida and the Western metaphysics of presence which he challenges at once seek and deny.

Applications

Such are the ways we might begin to explore the bothersome residence of the physical text at the very heart of Western metaphysics. If we can agree, at least for the moment, that there is such a thing as a physical text and that it is a worthy object of critical attention, our next problem becomes that of finding a way to handle this slippery object which exists after writing and before reading (and which exists before we can begin to speak about writing and remains even after we have finished reading).

There are several levels at which we might attack the problem of the physical text. I think the first thing we have to do in order to get at this physical text is to free it from relations of representation, that is, from the idea that it represents, badly, an originary, authentic text. What I would propose as the first level is a simple shift in the unit we study from "text" to (for medievalists, at least) the individual, unique, concrete manuscript codex. This would mean, for example, that instead of studying the *Poema de mio Cid* we would study Madrid, Biblioteca Nacional, MS Vitrina 7–17. Instead of the *Libro de buen amor* by Juan Ruiz, Archpriest of Hita, we would study Salamanca, Biblioteca Universitaria, MS 2663 (MS S), Madrid, Biblioteca Nacional, MS Vitrina 6–1 (MS T), and Madrid, Academia Española, MS 19 (MS G). At this first level, although we might continue to view the various manuscript witnesses as part of a system of differences, it would be necessary to suppress the idea that these manuscripts "represent" an authentic literary text which is, say, the *Libro de buen amor.*[7]

There are, in fact, three quite distinct *Libros de buen amor.* One of them, MS G (late fourteenth century), *treats *the *text as a source of moral exempla, signaling "insiemplo" in the margins or simply breaking the text with a space for an initial where a new exemplum begins.[8] Neither G nor T (also of the fourteenth century) recognizes physically what has been for modern readers the most interesting part of the book, the autobiographical frame, the story of the love misadventures of the Archpriest of Hita, into which these exempla (taken from diverse classical, Western, and Oriental sources) are woven.

MS T, otherwise the most *fragmentary of the three manuscripts, includes *in *addition *to the *Libro de buen amor, a Castilian *translation of the *Visio Filiberti, a debate between the body and the soul after death witnessed by the monk Filiberto. It is curious that this latter *text has figured not at all in the thousands of pages which have been written about the *Libro de buen amor in the past hundred years, not even in studies, such as Walker's, which have seen death as the dominant theme of the work. The metaphysics of presence, the search for the authentic *Libro de buen amor as seen through the glass of the manuscript witnesses, darkly, has totally suppressed the remarkable meditation on death which is MS T in its medieval physicality. The *addition of the *Vision to the *Libro de buen amor *continues the imprecation against death as seen from the mortal perspective which begins in the final half of the *Libro (see Walker), *adding an eschatological element not present in the *Libro itself.

MS S (early fifteenth century), by far the most *complete of the three manuscripts, presents a *Libro radically different from those found in G and T. The numerous rubrics stress the autobiographical frame as well as the exempla ("De lo que contesçio al arçipreste."; stanza 1006).[9] A burlesque sermon prologue precedes the text of the *Libro, and an equally burlesque "Cántica de los clérigos de Talavera" (in which the clerics protest an archbishop's mandate that they abandon their concubines) follows, together with numerous popular and devout lyrics not found in G and T. Although MS S is usually chosen as the base text by editors (in effect setting up an originary *Libro de buen amor* which is a burlesque autobiography rather than a bitter satire on death), the focus has been that of determining which of these *additional elements are "authentic," that is, were written by Juan Ruiz, and which are *spurious. If the majority are spurious, the underlying assumption of critics seems to be that this will detract from our appreciation of Juan Ruiz's *Libro,* not that they serve to or help to constitute a medieval text worthy of study in its own right, a text (along with MSS G and T) to which we may apply the same spectrum of critical approaches we have been bringing to that nonexistent, originary *Libro de buen amor.* To put all this another way, MSS S, G, and T are medieval books, the *Libro de buen amor* is not.

The foregoing may seem to be simply an extension of a series of critical strategies which have served gradually to efface the author from the text. Perhaps it is that. It is also, I would hasten to point out, following a path already marked out by scholars such as Bruno Roy, Sylvia Huot, and, to some extent, David Hult. But the vocabulary itself of such a move (which I have begun starring in the preceding paragraphs) suggests that freeing individual physical texts from the language of representation (of lost origin and debasement) may not be as easy as it first appears.

It is in this area that I think our most profitable work with the physical text can be done. The very act of suppressing such concepts as "scribal error" (and the rest of the vocabulary which goes with it: carelessness, distraction, ignorance, contamination) invites us to reevaluate medieval texts on their own terms. Why do the scribes of the *Libro de buen amor* consistently *insert *nonrhyming *synonyms into the monorhymed quatrains of the *cuaderna vía* form? Surely they were as capable of recognizing rhyme and verse form in their own language as are modern editors who have never heard Old Castilian spoken.[10]

Why do the scribes of the *Libro de buen amor* seem *so *little *concerned about the gender of nouns referring to persons or object pronouns in the course of direct addresses to the audience or in the application to it of didactic messages contained in the text? Modern scholars have devoted a great deal of attention to determining whether this is a book for women or for men or for both. The scribes of S, G, and T *disagree among themselves and are even individually inconsistent in their use of gender, forcing modern editors, who seek coherence on this point, into arbitrary choices.[11] Surely, the copyists of S, G, and T were as aware of gender differences as we and were more in tune with their text's potential didactic message. It seems to me that there is something of significance in these phenomena which we miss if we relegate them to the realm of *error or *carelessness.

This brings me to one more point I would like to make about the uses of a theory of the physical text: an awareness of the things we do to physical texts to *correct *error, to *recover *lost *meaning or *origins, to *fill *in *lacunae, to establish the *beginning and *end of texts, and to determine if they are *complete reveals, more than anything else, the set of assumptions we bring to the texts we study. The points we identify as differences (*variants, *lacunae) are hot spots which focus critical attention and expose, not an underlying originary text, but the critic. One brief example. The unique manuscript of the *Poema de mio Cid* is considered *incomplete at the *beginning. The manuscript as we have it begins with the line: "De los sos oios tan fuerte mientre lorando" ("Weeping so strongly from his eyes"). Examining the ways various critics have dealt with this *fragmentary *beginning, we find them caught between two very modern needs. On the one hand is the historicist, positivist desire to explain, to *complete (using contemporary chronicles, ballads, and documentary sources) the series of betrayals which leads to the Cid's weeping. On the other is the Romantic impulse to let the emotional impact of the moment unfold slowly over the next few stanzas, stanzas which explain the fact of but not the reasons for the Cid's exile from Castile. This second reading allows the physical text, in effect, to establish its own beginning, but only because we find within our own set of "beginnings" a type to which this *accidentally Romantic beginning corresponds.

But there is a second level to a theory of the physical text. On this level we push beyond a theory which leaves the physical text freed of representation but still caught up in a system of differences. Thus, so far I have sought to do away with the idea that MSS S, G, and T are three representatives of, witnesses to, an originary text to which we give the name *Libro de buen amor.* But I have retained the idea that the three physical texts together articulate a system of significant differences (variations in rhyme words, gender of pronouns).[12] But at the second level we free S, G, and T from the bonds of relation to one another through difference and are left with three concrete physical objects whose concrete and individual presence we must now attempt somehow to master. How can we come to grips with the worldly residence of the physical text, with that peculiar plenitude which is the written word on the written page? Can we achieve an appreciation of the physical text independent of notions of textual origins or authenticity, an appreciation which would not fall into an opposite error of mere antiquarianism or even fetishism? How can we begin to speak about that physical object after writing and before reading which is also the beginning, place of residence, and residue of both processes? That favorite mode of medieval and postmodern thought, analogy, may help to illuminate the place in which I think we need to work. One way of getting a grip on the physical text is, paradoxically, by viewing the manuscript text as a variety of oral performance. Curiously, that most ephemeral of literary events, an oral performance, comes closest to imitating that solidly physical text we seek: in its uniqueness, in the impossibility of its iteration, in its vulnerability to accidents of time and environment. A physical text, a manuscript of, say, the *Poema de mio Cid* is in fact an oral performance.

Once we admit the possibility of this analogy, it becomes fairly easy to work out the various parallels. Certain manuscript texts, we know, are in fact "presentation" manuscripts. Both the oral performance and the manuscript text are unique, as we have said. No oral performance of a *text (here I begin to suppress words which have to do with difference as well as those having to do with representation) is the *same as *another; no manuscript is an exact *copy of *another. The manuscript is subject to interferences of various types, to "noise": the application of chemical reagents, simple exposure to light, water stains, deliberate and accidental acts of destruction, fire, worm holes. In the same way, an oral performance can be interfered with by ambient noise, wind, weather (it can be rained out). Both oral performance and manuscript have a tendency to grow fainter with distance: in oral performance it is physical distance from the speaker, in the case of the manuscript, temporal distance from the scribe.

More interesting for me is the fact that both exist in constant dialogue with an audience. The audience of an oral performance may sit in absolute silence, but its presence is absolutely essential. More often, the audience participates actively, reacting to the presentation, even intervening, correcting, amplifying, challenging the performer or affirming what he has said. In the same way a manuscript is a dialogue which may take place across centuries: marginal and interlinear comments, emendations, glosses.[13] The audience may even talk among themselves, ignoring the "text" of the performance, as in the case of Madrid, MS 10073, fol. 45v, in which a reader has written in the top margin, "yo, amigo, tengo te por fodido, amen." No one would deny, I believe, the role of the audience in shaping an individual oral performance. In the same way, these "audience responses" in the margins modify the manuscript performance significantly. Even our own silent finger on the page, as librarians love to remind us, leaves behind potentially destructive residues of its own. It is a part of the dialogue.

I could probably go on with this, but I hope I have made my main point. If we accept the analogy between the physical text and oral performances as valid, we might be tempted to turn to the work of students of orality for guidance. When we do so (I refer to the work of Professor Tedlock here), we find them wrestling with precisely the same problem: how do we recover the plenitude of the oral moment itself? And if we could recover that plenitude, how would we make it an object of critical study? Does its very quality as plenitude preclude its becoming an object of critical attention? This suggests to me that what began as an analogy might be something much more, that within a theory of the physical text we may be drawing close to an idea of what "textual fields," both oral and literate, are about. Is there, in fact, some essential unity to those phenomena scholars have been working so hard to distinguish: "orality" and "literacy"? Perhaps the very constitution of a "textual field" does not depend on some absent and authentic origin (be it in the mind of the divine or human author or the reader, or in the "mythology" of a culture or a collection of formulas) or on a system of similarity with and difference from other textual fields. Perhaps it can be found in the physicality that is parchment and sound, in the possibility of noise and dialogue, and in the residence on earth and residue in time (be it only an instant or a thousand years) which allow noise and dialogue to happen.

Notes

1 Or better, this is true in Saussurian terms as deconstructed by Derrida. Saussure attempts to establish language and meaning as a system of signs composed of purely arbitrary differences, free of the relation to some originary signified. But Derrida shows that at the moment Saussure divides the sign into signifier and signified he allows representation back into his analysis. Something which contains this division can no longer be said to exist independent of meaning. The point Der-

rida makes is that this division is as true of speech as it is of writing, that the traditional hierarchy speech/writing cannot stand. From this point Derrida begins his own arbitrary choice of "writing" (or *archi-écriture*) to name this infinite divisibility of signifying systems.

2 We might also wish to see this problem in terms of Zumthor's *mouvance*. The very concept of *mouvance* is grounded in the same set of assumptions: that individual manuscripts are somehow representative of an archetypal text and that the system of differences set up by the manuscript witness of this archetype (or the oral performance of a medieval song) *move* about, deviate, differ from this center (*Essai* 65–75).

3 This theory rests on the double meaning of *supplément* in French as either "supplement" or "substitute." Derrida pursues the contradiction contained in this dual meaning: *supplément* may merely serve as an addition to something already present (already a contradiction, since something fully present has no need to be supplemented), or it may replace fully a thing which is, in the act of being replaced, made absent. The supplement becomes necessary. The idea of the supplement as a thing both superfluous and essential is echoed in the discussion of Ong's description of the residue above.

4 Derrida, *Of Grammatology* 165; my emphasis. "Dans les deux cas [l'écriture *and* l'onanisme], la possibilité de l'auto-affection se manifeste comme telle: elle laisse une trace de soi dans le monde. La résidence mondaine d'un signifiant devient inexpugnable. L'écrit reste et l'expérience du touchant-touché admet le monde en tiers. L'extériorité de l'espace y est irréductible. Dans la structure générale de l'auto-affection, dans le se-donner-une-presence ou une jouissance, l'opération du touchant-touché accueille l'autre dans la mince différence qui sépare, l'agir du pâtir. Et le dehors, la surface exposée du corps, signifie, marque à jamais la division qui travaille l'auto-affection" (Derrida, *De la grammatologie* 235).

5 Nor should we let it pass unnoticed that Derrida here employs his favorite suffix, the suffix which is the hinge of his entire system of *différence/différance*. In the same way that *différance* contains the sense of its homophone *différence* while including as well the idea of deferring, perhaps a full theory of the physical text would have to include a word *résidance,* a word that would embrace *résidence,* the plenary inhabitation of a physical location and "the quality or state of being residue," that which is left over as a result of a process.

6 Derrida, *Of Grammatology* 62–63; Derrida's emphasis. "Il ne s'agit donc pas ici d'une différence constituée mais, avant toute détermination de contenu, du mouvement *pur* qui produit la différence. *La trace (pure) est la différance.* Elle ne dépend d'aucune plénitude sensible, audible ou visible, phonique ou graphique. Elle en est au contraire la condition. Bien qu'elle *n'existe pas,* bien qu'elle ne soit jamais un *étant-présent* hors de toute plénitude, sa possibilité est antérieure en droit à tout ce qu'on appelle signe (signifié/signifiant, contenu/expression, etc.), concept ou opération, motrice ou sensible. Cette différance n'est donc pas plus sensible qu'intelligible et elle permet l'articulation des signes entre eux à l'intérieur d'un même ordre abstrait—d'un texte phonique ou graphique par exemple—ou entre deux ordres d'expression. Elle permet l'articulation de la parole et de l'écriture—au sens courant—comme elle fonde l'opposition métaphysique entre

le sensible et l'intelligible, puis entre signifiant et signifié, expression et contenu, etc." (Derrida, *De la grammatologie* 92).

7 I want to stress that I am not suggesting that we cease from editing texts but that we begin to explore as well what we are left with, or should I say, what we may gain, when we free the physical text from its bondage to the metaphysics of presence. I am asking that we merely suspend for a moment the traditional attitudes of critical editing and try to understand what this object of our affection is when thus set free.

8 The initials themselves have not been filled in. MSS S, G, and T have all been published in facsimile. I am not sure precisely where the manuscript facsimile fits into my theory of the physical text.

9 In addition to emphasizing, through rubrics, the personality of the pseudo-auto-biographical narrator of the *Libro*, MS S tends to include matter which stresses this narrator's role as preacher or teacher as well; that is, it situates the didactic material of the text within the *Book of the Archpriest of Hita* itself, rather than in the larger world of exempla available for use by *any* preacher, teacher, or reader, as does MS G. Thus S:892 is preceded by the rubric "Del castigo quel arçipreste da a las dueñas." Stanza S:892 proper includes the narrator's introduction to the fable which follows: "dueñas aved orejas, oyd buena liçion, / entendet bien las fablas, guardat vos del varon, / guardat vos no vos contesca commo con el leon / al asno syn orejas e syn su coraçon." In MS G, the division occurs one stanza later, at 893, with the beginning of the fable proper: "[E]l leon fue doliente e doliele la tiesta." Similar examples may be found at S 44/G:47, S 407/G:408, S:474a/G474c, S:950/G:951.

10 Thus in MS S, the scribe uses the nonrhyming *engañes* in rhyme position in the fourth line of the stanza in a place where *enlases* (as in MSS G and T) is clearly demanded: "Tal eres commo el lobo, rretraes lo que fazes, / estrañas lo que ves E Non el lodo en que yazes, / eres mal enemigo a todos quantos plases, / fablas con grant synpleza por que muchos *engañes*" (S:372; my emphasis). The case is even clearer in G:446. Here, not only the rhyme but also the sense of the line demand the obvious word *acuerda:* "en la cama muy loca, en casa muy cuerda, / non oluides tal dueña mas della te *enamora;* / esto que te castigo con ouidio concuerda, / e para aquesta cata la fyna avancuerda" (my emphasis). See also G:507, where *pellejo* appears for the obvious rhyming synonym *cuero*.

11 In MS S, stanza 391 reads: "Non as miedo nin verguença de Rey nin Reyna, / mudas te do te pagas cada dia Ayna, / huesped eres de muchos, non duras so cortina; / como el fuego andas de vesin*a* en vesin*a*" (my emphasis). In MS G, the fourth line reads: "commo el fuego te andas de vesin*o* en vesin*a*" (my emphasis). The majority of critical editions choose the version in MS S, if only because they take S as the base; thus Blecua, Cejador, Chiarni, Gybbon-Monypenny, Joset. Willis, who takes G as the base, naturally has the reading of G, as does Coro-minas. As it is Don Amor himself who is being addressed here, there seem to be at least two reasons for choosing the reading of G, however: the fact that the fire of heterosexual love is the obvious theme of the *Libro* and the nice parallelism that is established with "Rey nin Reyna" in the first line of the stanza. Another example may be found in stanza 393. Still talking to Don Amor, the narrator says, in the version of MS S: "fazes como folguym en tu mesma manera, atalayas de lexos e

caças *la* primera, / *al* que quieres matar sacas *los* de carrera, / de logar encobyerto sacas çelada fiera." In G, the two middle lines of the stanza read: "ataleas de luene, tu tomas *la* primera, / a *la* que matar quieres sacas *la* de carrera." Thus, in MS S, Love hunts the first *woman* to come along, and then also a *man* (using a masculine pronoun with no explicit referent) whom he wishes to kill and takes *them* (again a plural pronoun with no referent) from the "path." There is an obvious grammatical inconsistency here, and most editors either accept the reading of G (Blecua, Cejador, Corominas, Joset, and Willis) or take the reading of S and correct *los* to *lo* (Chiarini, Gybbon-Monypenny): "as for the man you wish to kill, you take him from the path." In MS G, it is a single woman whom love "takes," "wishes to kill," and "snatches from the path." (*La primera* does not necessarily mean "the first woman," however, as Blecua explains [66n393b]: "Podría entenderse como una frase adverbial, 'a la primera'; o bien 'que caza la pieza que dirige el grupo para que éste se disperse y así sacar del camino a la mejor pieza'; o, finalmente, 'la mejor pieza.'") Joset chooses the reading of G, saying that the reading of S "muestra que [the scribe?] no ha entendido el texto. Se trata de una caza de doncella" (1: 150, content note 393c). Gybbon-Monypenny defends the reading of S: "La lección de *G* . . . cuadra mejor con el contexto, a primera vista. Pero una manera de 'matar' a los *neçios locos* sería juntarlos con una joven caprichosa, y así arruinar a los dos, como se dice en 398b. Conservo la lección de *S*, pues" (191n393c). But the following stanzas (394–97) deal specifically with the seduction of a young woman by Don Amor. My point in these examples is that both readings are genuine medieval readings (both by the scribes and by those who read the manuscripts they transcribed) of the passages in question. Any reading we privilege, for whatever reasons, ignores the physical validity of the medieval book before us. This is not to say that medieval scribes never rendered legible texts incomprehensible to medieval readers. Indeed, this is a frequent complaint among medieval authors. But again, my point is that these "errors" or "variants" (on what basis can we ultimately distinguish the two?) are an integral part of the physical system of medieval texts and that medievalists must find the way to deal with these features in all their scruffiness. The theory of the physical text proceeds, not by *eliminatio,* but by *amplexus.*

12 It is interesting that at the first level it is the fact that the differences among S, G, and T are few, not that they are many, which allows us to talk about them as a "system." That is, there are fewer differences among S, G, and T than there are between any of these and Madrid, Biblioteca Nacional MS Vitrina 7–17 (the *Cid*). The system of difference can only function through its opposite: similarity.

13 Burgo de Osma, MS 92 (S. 14), fol. 85r, defines various types of glosses in a way which suggests the very activities of amplification, correction, and affirmation which are part of the oral performance: "[G]losula alia est de continuatione sensus, alia de continuatione littere, alia suppletionis si quid minus dictum est, alia explanationis ubi obscura, alia conditionis quando auctoritatibus quod dictum est confirmatur. Ordinem predictum obserua in legendo. Ordo multum operatur ad intelligentiam."

Works Cited
Index

Works Cited

Aebischer, P. " 'Le fragment de La Haye': Les problèmes qu'il pose et les enseignements qu'il donne." *Zeitschrift für Romanische Philologie* 73 (1957): 20–37.

Ælfric. "Hortatorius Sermo de Efficacia Sanctae Missae." *Ælfric's Catholic Homilies: The Second Series.* Ed. Malcolm Godden. Early English Text Society e.s. 5, London: Oxford UP, 1979.

Agamben, Giorgio. "The Thing Itself." *Sub-Stance* 16.53 (1987): 18–28.

Ahl, Frederick. *Lucan: An Introduction.* Ithaca: Cornell UP, 1976.

Ahl, Frederick. *Metaformations: Soundplay and Wordplay in Ovid and Other Classical Poets.* Ithaca: Cornell UP, 1985.

Alain de Lille. *The Complaint of Nature.* Trans. Douglas M. Moffat. Hamden: Archon, 1972.

Ammianus Marcellinus. *Romische Geschichte.* Ed. W. Seyfarth. Vol. 4. Schriften der Alten Welt 21.4. Berlin: Akademie, 1971.

Anderson, Earl R. *Cynewulf: Structure, Style and Theme in His Poetry.* Rutherford: Fairleigh Dickinson UP, 1983.

Anderson, John R. *Cognitive Psychology and Its Implications.* 2nd ed. New York: W. H. Freeman, 1985.

Andersson, Theodore M. "Blood on the Battlefield." *Neophilologus* 56 (1972): 12–16.

Andersson, Theodore M. "Cassiodorus and the Gothic Legend of Ermanaric." *Euphorion* 57 (1963): 23–43.

Anglo-Saxon Poetic Records: A Collective Edition. Ed. George P. Krapp and E. Van Kirk Dobbie. 6 vols. New York: Columbia UP, 1931–53.

Aristotle. *Aristotelis Categoriae et Liber de interpretatione.* Ed. L. Minio-Paluello. Oxford: Clarendon, 1961.

Aristotle. *Categories and De interpretatione.* Trans. J. A. Ackrill. Oxford: Clarendon, 1979.

Augustine. *The City of God.* Trans. Marcus Dods. New York: Modern Library, 1950.

Augustine. *The City of God.* Trans. Gerald G. Walsh, Demetrius B. Zema, Grace Monahan, and Daniel Honan. Ed. Vernon J. Bourke. Abr. ed. New York: Doubleday, 1962.

Augustine. *De civitate Dei.* Libri 21–22. Ed. William M. Green. Vol. 7. Cambridge: Harvard UP, 1972.

Augustine. *Confessions.* Trans. William Watts. 2 vols. Cambridge: Harvard UP, 1979.

Augustine. *The Confessions of Saint Augustine*. Trans. John K. Ryan. New York: Doubleday, 1960.

Averroes. *Averroes' Middle Commentaries on Aristotle's "Categories" and "De Interpretatione."* Trans. Charles E. Butterworth. Princeton: Princeton UP, 1983.

Avril, François. "Les manuscrits enluminés de Guillaume de Machaut: Essai de chronologie." *Guillaume de Machaut: Poète et compositeur.* Paris: Klincksieck, 1982. 117–33.

Bakhtin, M. M. *The Dialogic Imagination: Four Essays.* Ed. Michael Holquist. Trans. Caryl Emerson and Michael Holquist. Austin: U of Texas P, 1981.

Bakhtin, M. M. *Speech Genres and Other Late Essays.* Ed. Caryl Emerson and Michael Holquist. Trans. Vern W. McGee. Austin: U of Texas P, 1985.

Barthes, Roland. "Introduction à l'analyse structurale des récits." *Communications* 8 (1966): 1–27.

Barthes, Roland. "La mort de l'auteur." *Manteia* 5 (1968): 12–17.

Barthes, Roland. *Le plaisir du texte.* Paris: Seuil, 1973.

The Battle of Brunanburh. Ed. Alistair Campbell. London: Heinemann, 1938.

The Battle of Maldon. Ed. E. V. Gordon. London: Methuen, 1968.

Baugh, A. C. "Improvisation in the Middle English Romance." *Proceedings of the American Philosophical Society* 103 (1959): 418–54.

Baugh, A. C. "Middle English Romances: Some Questions of Creation, Presentation, and Preservation." *Speculum* 42 (1967): 1–31.

Baumgartner, Emmanuèle. "La competence de l'écrivain [médiévale]." Talk delivered at Boston College, Newton, MA. 13 Oct. 1987.

Baumgartner, Emmanuèle. "La couronne et le cercle: Arthur et la Table Ronde dans les manuscrits du Lancelot-Graal." *Texte et image: Actes du colloque international de Chantilly (13 au 15 octobre 1982).* Centre de Recherche de l'Université de Paris 10. Paris: Belles Lettres, 1984.

Baumgartner, Emmanuèle. "L'écriture romanesque et son modèle scriptuaire: Ecriture et réécriture du Graal." *L'imitation, aliénation ou source de la liberté?* Rencontres de l'Ecole du Louvre, septembre 1984. Paris: Documentation Française, 1985.

Baumgartner, Emmanuèle. "La 'Première Page' dans les manuscrits du *Tristan en prose.*" *La présentation du livre.* Ed. Emmanuèle Baumgartner and Nicole Boulestreau. Littérales: Cahiers du Département du Français 2. Nanterre: Centre de Recherches du Département de Français, 1987. 51–63.

Baumgartner, Emmanuèle. "Remarques sur les pièces lyriques du *Tristan en prose.*" *Etudes de langue et de littérature du moyen âge offertes à Félix Lecoy.* Paris: Champion, 1973. 19–25.

Baumgartner, Emmanuèle. *Le Tristan en prose: Essai d'interprétation d'un roman médiéval.* Publications Romanes at Françaises 133, Geneva: Droz, 1975.

Bäuml, Franz H. "Medieval Literacy and Illiteracy: An Essay toward the Construction of a Model." *Germanic Studies in Honor of Otto Springer.* Ed Stephen J. Kaplowitt. Pittsburgh: K & S Enterprises, 1978. 41–54.

Bäuml, Franz H. "Medieval Texts and the Two Theories of Oral-Formulaic Composition: A Proposal for a Third Theory." *New Literary History* 16 (1984–85): 31–49.

Bäuml, Franz H. "Transformations of the Heroine: From Epic Heard to Epic Read." *The Role of Woman in the Middle Ages.* Ed. Rosemarie T. Morewedge. Albany: State U of New York P, 1975. 23–40.

Bäuml, Franz H. "Der Übergang mündlicher zur *artes*-bestimmten Literatur des Mittelalters: Gedanken und Bedenken." *Oral Poetry: Das Problem der Mündlichkeit mittelalterlicher epischer Dichtung.* Ed. N. Voorwinden and M. de Haan. Darmstadt: Wissenschaftliche Buchgesellschaft, 1979. 238–50.

Bäuml, Franz H. "The Unmaking of the Hero: Some Critical Implications of the Transition from Oral to Written Epic." *The Epic in Medieval Society: Aesthetic and Moral Values.* Ed. Harald Scholler. Tübingen: Niemeyer, 1977. 86–99.

Bäuml, Franz H. "Varieties and Consequences of Medieval Literacy and Illiteracy." *Speculum* 55 (1980): 237–65.

Beck, Jean, ed. *Les Chansonniers des troubadours et des trouvères, publiés en facsimilé et transcrits en notation moderne.* Vol. 1, *Reproduction phototypique du chansonnier Cangé (Paris, Bibliothèque Nationale, MS français no. 846).* Corpus Cantilenarum Medii Aevi, ser. 1, no. 1. Paris: Champion; Philadelphia: U of Pennsylvania P, 1927.

Becker, Alfons. *Papst Urban II (1088–1099).* Schriften der Monumenta Germaniae Historica 19.1–2. Stuttgart: Hiersemann, 1964, 1988.

Bede. *Ecclesiastical History.* Ed. and trans. Bertram Colgrave and R. A. B. Mynors. Oxford: Clarendon, 1969.

Bédier, Joseph. *Le lai de l'ombre.* Paris: SATF, 1913.

Bennett, Camille. "The Conversion of Vergil: The *Aeneid* in Augustine's *Confessions.*" *Revue des études Augustiniennes* 34 (1988): 47–69.

Benson, Larry D. "The Literary Character of Anglo-Saxon Formulaic Poetry." *PMLA* 81 (1966): 334–41.

Beowulf and the Fight at Finnsburg. Ed. Frederick Klaeber. 3rd ed. Lexington, MA: Heath, 1950.

Bernardus Silvestris. *The Commentary on the First Six Books of the Aeneid of Virgil Commonly Attributed to Bernardus Silvestris.* Ed. Julian Ward Jones and Elizabeth Frances Jones. Lincoln: U of Nebraska P, 1977.

Bernardus Silvestris. *Commentary on the First Six Books of Virgil's Aeneid.* Ed. and trans. Earl G. Schreiber and Thomas E. Maresca. Lincoln: U of Nebraska P, 1979.

Beumann, Helmut. *Die Ottonen.* Stuttgart: Kohlhammer, 1987.

Bliss, A. J., ed. *Sir Orfeo.* 2nd ed. Oxford: Clarendon, 1966.

Bloch, R. Howard. *Etymologies and Genealogies: A Literary Anthropology of the French Middle Ages.* Chicago: U of Chicago P, 1983.

Bloom, Harold. *The Anxiety of Influence: A Theory of Poetry.* London: Oxford UP, 1973.

Bloom, Harold. "Poetry and Belief: The Hebrew Bible." Charles Eliot Norton Lectures. Harvard University, Cambridge, MA. 7 Oct. 1987.

Boethius. *The Consolation of Philosophy.* Trans. Richard Green. Indianapolis: Bobbs, 1962.

Böhmer-Zimmermann. See Zimmermann, Harald.

Brault, Gerard J. *The Song of Roland: An Analytical Edition.* Vol. 1, *Introduction and Commentary.* University Park: Pennsylvania State UP, 1978.

Braune, Wilhelm. *Althochdeutsches Lesebuch.* 16th ed. Rev. by Ernst A. Ebbinghaus. Tübingen: Niemeyer, 1979.

Brooks, Nicholas, ed. *Latin and the Vernacular Languages in Early Medieval Britain.* Leicester: Leicester UP, 1982.

Brown, Arthur. "The Transmission of the Text." *Medieval and Renaissance Studies* 2 (1968): 3–20.

Brown, Carleton, ed. *English Lyrics of the XIIIth Century.* Oxford: Clarendon, 1932.

Brown, Sterling A. "Background of Folklore in Negro Literature." *Mother Wit from the Laughing Barrel: Readings in the Interpretation of Afro-American Folklore.* Ed. Alan Dundes. Englewood Cliffs: Prentice, 1973, 39–44.

Bruns, Gerald L. "The Originality of Texts in a Manuscript Culture." *Comparative Literature* 32 (1980): 113–29.

Buchner, R. *Quellen des 9. und 11. Jahrhunderts zur Geschichte der Hamburgischen Kirche und des Reichs.* Ausgewählte Quellen zur deutschen Geschichte des Mittelalters 11. Darmstadt: Wissenschaftliche Buchgesellschaft, 1978.

Burgess, Glyn, and Keith Busby. Introduction. *The Lais of Marie de France.* By Marie de France. Trans. Glyn Burgess and Keith Busby. Middlesex: Penguin, 1986.

Burns, Allan. *An Epoch of Miracles: Oral Literature of the Yucatec Maya.* Austin: U of Texas P, 1983.

Busse, Wilhelm G. *Altenglische Literatur und ihre Geschichte: Zur Kritik des gegenwärtigen Deutungssystems.* Dusseldorf: Droste, 1987.

Busse, Wilhelm G. "*Boceras:* Written and Oral Traditions in the Late Tenth Century." Erzgräber and Volk 27–37.

Calder, Daniel G. *Cynewulf.* Twayne's English Authors 327. Boston: Twayne, 1981.

Cambridge Medieval History. Ed. H. M. Gwatkin and J. P. Whitney. Vols. 3–5. Cambridge: Cambridge UP, 1922–26.

Cassiodorus. *Cassiodori senatoris institutiones.* Ed. R. A. B. Mynors. Oxford: Clarendon, 1963.

Chaucer, Geoffrey. *The Riverside Chaucer.* Ed. Larry D. Benson et al. 3rd ed. Boston: Houghton, 1987.

Chaytor, H. J. *From Script to Print.* Cambridge: Heffer, 1945.

Chaytor, H. J. "The Medieval Reader and Textual Criticism." *Bulletin of the John Rylands Library* 26 (1941–42): 49–56.

Chenu, M. D. "Auctor, actor, autor." *Bulletin du Cange: Archivum Latinitatis Medii Aevi* 2 (1927): 81–86.

Chenu, M. D. "*Involucrum:* Le mythe selon les théologiens médiévaux." *Archives d'histoire doctrinale et littéraire du Moyen Age* 32 (1956): 75–79.

Chrétien de Troyes. *Le chevalier au lyon (Yvain).* Ed. Mario Roques. Classiques Français du Moyen Age. Paris: Champion, 1968; rpt., 1971.

Chrétien de Troyes. *Erec et Enide.* Ed. Mario Roques. Classiques Français du Moyen Age. Paris: Champion, 1954; rpt., 1981. English version, ed. and trans. Carleton W. Carroll. Garland Library of Medieval Literature 25. New York: Garland, 1987.

Chrétien de Troyes. *Lancelot; or, The Knight of the Cart (Le chevalier de la charrete).* Ed. and trans. William W. Kibler. Garland Library of Medieval Literature 1. New York: Garland, 1981.

Clark, C. "Byrhtnoth and Roland: A Contrast." *Neophilologus* 51 (1967): 288–93.

Coleman, Janet. *Medieval Readers and Writers: 1350–1400.* New York: Columbia UP, 1981.

Conley, Verena Andermatt. *Hélène Cixous: Writing the Feminine.* Lincoln: U of Nebraska P, 1984.

Coomaraswamy, Ananda K. "The Bugbear of Literacy." *Am I My Brother's Keeper?* Freeport, NY: Books for Libraries, 1967.

Copeland, Rita. "Literary Theory in the Later Middle Ages." *Romance Philology* 41 (1987): 58–71.

Crosby, Ruth. "Oral Delivery in the Middle Ages." *Speculum* 11 (1936): 88–110.

Curtis, Renée L. "The Problems of the Authorship of the *Prose Tristan.*" *Romania* 79 (1958): 314–38.

Curtius, Ernst Robert. *European Literature and the Latin Middle Ages.* Trans. Willard R. Trask. Princeton: Princeton UP, 1953.

Dane, Joseph A. "*Integuementum* as Interpretation: A Note on William of Conches' Commentary on Macrobius (I, 2, 10–11)." *Classical Folia* 32 (1978): 201–15.

Dante Alighieri. *De vulgari eloquentia.* Trans. A. G. Ferrers Howell and Philip H. Wicksteed. *Classical and Medieval Literary Criticism, Translations and Interpretations.* Ed. Alex Preminger, et al. New York: Ungar, 1974. 412–46.

Dauenhauer, Nora Marks, and Richard Dauenhauer. *Haa Shuká, Our Ancestors: Tlingit Oral Narratives.* Seattle: U of Washington P, 1987.

Decretales Pseudo-Isidorianae et Capitula Angilramni. Ed. Paul Hinschius. Leipzig: Tauchnitz, 1863.

de Looze, Laurence. "'Mon nom trouveras': A New Look at the Anagrams of Guillaume de Machaut—The Enigmas, Responses, and Solutions." *Romanic Review* 79 (1988): 537–57.

Derrida, Jacques. *De la grammatologie.* Paris: Editions de Minuit, 1967. English version, *Of Grammatology.* Trans. Gayatri Chakravorty Spivak. Baltimore: Johns Hopkins UP, 1974; rpt. 1976.

Derrida, Jacques. "Différance." *Speech and Phenomena, and Other Essays on Husserl's Theory of Signs.* Trans. David B. Allison. Evanston: Northwestern UP, 1973. 129–60.

Diller, Hans-Jürgen. "Literacy and Orality in *Beowulf.* The Problem of Reference." Erzgräber and Volk 15–25.

Dragonetti, Roger. *Le mirage des sources: L'art du faux dans le roman médiéval.* Paris: Seuil, 1987.

Dragonetti, Roger. "Qui est l'auteur du comte d'Anjou?" *Médiévales* 11 (1986): 85–98.

Dragonetti, Roger. *La vie de la lettre au Moyen Age (le Conte du Graal).* Paris: Seuil, 1980.

Dronke, Ursula. *The Poetic Edda.* Vol. 1, *Heroic Poems.* Oxford: Clarendon, 1969.

Eagleton, Terry. *Literary Theory: An Introduction.* Minneapolis: U of Minnesota P, 1983.

Eco, Umberto. *L'opera aperta.* Milan: Bompiani, 1962.

Eco, Umberto. *The Role of the Reader: Explorations on the Semiotics of Texts.* Bloomington: Indiana UP, 1979.

Edda: Die Lieder des Codex Regius nebst verwandten Denkmälern. Ed. Gustav Neckel, I. Text, 4th rev. ed. by Hans Kuhn. Heidelberg: Winter, 1962.

Eddukvæði. Ed. Guðni Jónsson. Reykjavík: Íslendingasagnaútgáfan, 1949.

Ehlich, Konrad. "Text und sprachliches Handeln: Die Entstehung von Texten aus dem Bedürfnis nach Überlieferung." *Schrift und Gedächtnis: Beiträge zur Archäologie der literarischen Kommunikation.* Ed. A. Assmann, J. Assmann, and Christof Hardmeier. Munich: Fink, 1983. 24–43.

Ehrhart, Margaret J. "Machaut's *Dit de la fonteinne amoureuse,* the Choice of Paris, and the Duties of Rulers." *Philological Quarterly* 59 (1980): 119–39.

Eisenstein, Elizabeth L. *The Printing Press as an Agent of Change.* Cambridge: Cambridge UP, 1979.

Ellis, John M. *Against Deconstruction.* Princeton: Princeton UP, 1989.

Erdmann, Carl. *Studien zur Briefliteratur Deutschlands im elften Jahrhundert.* Schriften der Monumenta Germaniae Historica 1. 1938. Rpt. Stuttgart: Hiersemann, 1962.

Erdmann, Carl, and Norbert Fickermann, eds. *Briefsammlungen zur Zeit Heinrichs IV.* Monumenta Germaniae Historica, Die Briefe der deutschen Kaiserzeit 5. Weimar: H. Bohlaus Nachfolger, 1950.

Ermold le Noir. *Poème sur Louis le Pieux.* Ed. and trans. E. Faral. Classiques de l'Histoire de France au Moyen Age 14. Paris: Champion, 1932.

Erzgräber, Willi, and Sabine Volk, eds. *Mündlichkeit und Schriftlichkeit im englischen Mittelalter.* ScriptOralia 5. Tübingen: Narr, 1988.

Fenske, Lutz. *Adelsopposition und kirchliche Reformbewegung im östlichen Sachsen.* Veröffentlichungen des Max-Planck-Instituts für Geschichte 47. Göttingen: Vandenhoeck und Ruprecht, 1977.

Fewster, Carol. *Traditionality and Genre in Middle English Romance.* Cambridge: Brewer, 1987.

Fidjestøl, Bjarne. "Die Saga vom Heiligen Olaf." Lecture delivered at the meeting of the Swiss Scandinavian Society, Lenzburg. 14 June 1986.

Finnegan, Ruth. *Oral Poetry: Its Nature, Significance, and Social Context.* Cambridge: Cambridge UP, 1977.

Fleckenstein, Josef. *Grundlagen und Beginn der deutschen Geschichte.* 3rd ed. Deutsche Geschichte 1. Göttingen: Vandenhoeck und Ruprecht, 1985.

Fleckenstein, Josef. "Problematik und Gestalt der ottonisch-salischen Reichskirche." *Reich und Kirche vor dem Investiturstreit.* Ed. Karl Schmid. Sigmaringen: Thorbecke, 1985. 83–98.

Fleckenstein, Josef. "Zum Begriff der ottonisch-salischen Reichskirche." *Geschichte, Wirtschaft, Gesellschaft: Festschrift für Clemens Bauer.* Ed. Erich Hassinger, et al. Berlin: Duncker und Humblot. 1974. 61–74.

Foley, John Miles, ed. *Comparative Research on Oral Traditions: A Memorial for Milman Parry.* Columbus: Slavica, 1987.

Foley, John Miles. "Editing Oral Epic Texts: Theory and Practice." *Text* 1 (1984): 75–94.

Foley, John Miles. "Formula in Yugoslav and Comparative Folk Epic: Structure and Function." *The Heroic Process.* Ed. Bo Almqvist et al. Dublin: Glendale, 1987. 485–504.

Foley, John Miles. *From Structure to Meaning in Traditional Oral Epic.* Bloomington: Indiana UP, 1991.

Foley, John Miles. "Literary Art and Oral Tradition in Old English and Serbian Poetry." *Anglo-Saxon England* 12 (1983): 183–214.

Foley, John Miles. *Oral-Formulaic Theory and Research: An Introduction and Annotated Bibliography.* New York: Garland, 1985.

Foley, John Miles. "The Oral Theory in Context." *Oral Traditional Literature: A Festschrift for Albert Bates Lord.* Ed. John Miles Foley. Columbus: Slavica, 1980. 27–122.

Foley, John Miles, ed. *Oral Tradition in Literature: Interpretation in Context.* Columbia: U of Missouri P, 1986.

Foley, John Miles. "Reading the Oral Traditional Text: Aesthetics of Creation and Response." Foley, ed., *Comparative Research* 185–212.

Foley, John Miles. *The Theory of Oral Composition: History and Methodology.* Bloomington: Indiana UP, 1988.

Foley, John Miles. "Tradition and the Collective Talent: Oral Epic, Textual Meaning, and Receptionalist Theory." *Cultural Anthropology* 1 (1986): 203–22.

Foley, John Miles. *Traditional Oral Epic: The Odyssey, Beowulf, and the Serbo-Croatian Return Song.* Berkeley: U of California P, 1990.

Fotitch, Tatiana, and Ruth Steiner, eds. *Les lais du roman de Tristan en prose.* Münchener romanistische Arbeiten 38. Munich: Fink, 1974.

Foucault, Michel. "Qu'est-ce qu'un auteur?" *Bulletin de la Société française de Philosophie* 63.3 (1969): 73–104. English trans. "What Is an Author?" *Language, Countermemory, Practice.* Ed. Donald F. Bouchard. Ithaca: Cornell UP, 1977. 113–38.

Foucault, Michel, and Lawrence Stone. "An Exchange with Michel Foucault." *New York Review of Books* 31 Mar. 1983: 43.

Foulet, Alfred, and K. D. Uitti. "The Prologue to the *Lais* of Marie de France: A Reconsideration." *Romance Philology* 35 (1981): 242–49.

Fourrier, Anthime, ed. *Jean Froissart: La prison amoureuse.* Paris: Klincksieck, 1974.

Freeman, Michelle A. "Marie de France's Poetics of Silence: The Implications for a Feminine *Translatio.*" *PMLA* 99 (1984): 860–83.

Frese, Dolores Warwick. "The Art of Cynewulf's Runic Signatures." *Anglo-Saxon Poetry: Essays in Appreciation for John C. McGalliard.* Ed. Lewis E. Nicholson and D. W. Frese. Notre Dame: U of Notre Dame P, 1975. 312–34.

Frutolf von Michelsberg. *Frutolfs und Ekkehards Chroniken und die Anonyme Kaiserchronik.* Ed. and trans. F. J. Schmale and I. Schmale-Ott. Ausgewählte Quellen zur deutschen Geschichte des Mittelalters 15. Darmstadt: Wissenschaftliche Buchgesellschaft, 1972. 47–121.

Fuhrmann, Horst. *Deutsche Geschichte im hohen Mittelalter von der Mitte des 11. bis zum Ende des 12. Jahrhunderts.* 2nd ed. Göttingen: Vandenhoeck und Ruprecht, 1985.

Gauger, Hans-Martin. "Zum Bedeutungsbegriff der strukturellen Semantik." *Sprachbewusstsein und Sprachwissenschaft.* Ed. Hans-Martin Gauger. Munich: Piper, 1976. 108–40.

Gellrich, Jesse M. *The Idea of the Book in the Middle Ages.* Ithaca: Cornell UP, 1985.

Gennep, Arnold van. *La question d'Homère.* Paris: Mercure de France, 1909.

Gerbert, Martin. *Scriptores ecclesiastici de musica sacrapotissimum.* 3 vols. 1784. Rpt. Hildesheim: Olms, 1963.

Gilbert, Sandra M., and Susan Gubar. *The Madwoman in the Attic: The Woman Writer and the Nineteenth-Century Literary Imagination*. New Haven: Yale UP, 1979.

Goody, Jack. *The Interface between the Written and the Oral*. Studies in Literacy, Family, Culture and the State. Cambridge: Cambridge UP, 1987.

Goody, Jack. *The Logic of Writing and the Organization of Society*. Studies in Literacy, Family, Culture and the State. Cambridge: Cambridge UP, 1986.

Goody, Jack, and Ian Watt. "The Consequences of Literacy." *Comparative Studies in Society and History* 5.3 (1963): 304–45. Rpt. in *Literacy in Traditional Societies*. Ed. Jack Goody. Cambridge: Cambridge UP, 1963. 27–68.

Gottfried von Strassburg. *Tristan*. Trans. A. T. Hatto. Middlesex: Penguin, 1960.

Grant, John N. *Studies in the Textual Tradition of Terence*. Toronto: U of Toronto P, 1986.

Greene, Richard Leighton. *The Early English Carol*. 2nd ed. Oxford: Clarendon, 1977.

Greenfield, Stanley B. "The Formulaic Expression of the Theme of 'Exile' in Anglo-Saxon Poetry." *Speculum* 30 (1955): 200–206.

Grimm, Wilhelm. *Die deutsche Heldensage*. 4th ed. Darmstadt: Gentner, 1957.

Grimstad, Kaaren. "The Revenge of Volundr." *Edda: A Collection of Essays*. Ed. Robert J. Glendinning and Haraldur Bessason. [Winnipeg]: U of Manitoba P, 1983. 187–209.

Gschwantler, Otto. "Ermanrich, sein Selbstmord und die Hamdirsage: Zur Darstellung von Ermanrichs Ende in Getica 24, 129f." *Die Volker an der Mittleren und unteren Donau im fünften und sechsten Jahrhundert*. Ed. Herwig Wolfram and Falko Daim. Philosophisch-Historische Klasse Denkschriften 145. Vienna: Osterreichischen Akademie der Wissenschaften, 1980. 187–204.

Guillaume IX d'Aquitaine. *Guglielmo IX: Poesie*. Ed. Nicolò Pasero. Modena: STEM, 1973.

Guiron le courtois. MS fr. 335. Bibliothèque Nationale, Paris.

Guiron le courtois. Add. MS 12228. British Library, London.

Gurevi, Elena A. "The Formulaic Pair in Eddic Poetry: An Experimental Analysis." *Structure and Meaning in Old Norse Literature*. Ed. John Lindow, Lars Lönnroth, and Gerd Wolfgang Weber. Odense: Odense UP, 1986. 32–55.

Gyron le courtoys. Paris: A. Vérard, c. 1501; rpt., London: Scolar, 1977.

Habig, Marion A., ed. *St. Francis of Assisi: Writings and Early Biographies: English Omnibus of the Sources for the Life of St. Francis*. Trans. Raphael Brown et al. Chicago: Franciscan Herald, 1973.

Haidu, Peter. "Realism, Convention, Fictionality and the Theory of Genres in *Le Bel Inconnu*." *L'ésprit createur* 12 (1972): 37–60.

Halle, Adam de la. *Le Jeu de Robin et de Marion*. Ed. Ernst Langlois. Paris: Champion, 1965.

Hanning, Robert, and Joan Ferrante. Introduction. *The Lais of Marie de France*. Trans. Robert Hanning and Joan Ferrante. New York: Dutton, 1978.

Harris, Joseph. "Eddic Poetry." *Old Norse-Icelandic Literature: A Critical Guide*. Islandica 45. Ithaca: Cornell UP, 1985. 68–156.

Harris, Joseph. "Eddic Poetry as Oral Poetry: The Evidence of Parallel Passages in the Helgi Poems for Questions of Composition and Performance." *Edda: A Collection of Essays*. Ed. R. J. Glendinning and Haraldur Bessason. [Winnipeg]: U of Manitoba P, 1983. 210–42.

Harvey, R. "The Provenance of the Old High German *Ludwigslied*." *Medium Aevum* 14 (1945): 1–20.

Hauck, Karl. "Bilddenkmäler: Zur Religion." *Reallexikon der germanischen Altertumskunde*. 2nd ed., vol. 2. Ed. Kurt Ranke et al. Cols. 577–91. Berlin: de Gruyter, 1972.

Haugen, E. "First Grammatical Treatise: An Edition, Translation and Commentary." Supplement to *Language* 26 (1950): 1–65.

Havelock, Eric A. *The Literate Revolution in Greece and Its Cultural Consequences*. Princeton: Princeton UP, 1982.

Havelock, Eric A. *The Muse Learns to Write: Reflections on Orality and Literacy from Antiquity to the Present*. New Haven: Yale UP, 1986.

Havelock, Eric A. *A Preface to Plato*. Cambridge: Belknap–Harvard UP, 1963, rpt. 1982.

Haverkamp, Alfred. *Aufbruch und Gestaltung: Deutschland, 1056–1273*. Munich, 1984. English trans. *Medieval Germany, 1056–1273*. Trans. Richard Mortimer and Helga Braun. Oxford: Oxford UP, 1988.

Healey, Antonette DiPaolo, and Richard L. Venezky. *A Microfiche Concordance to Old English*. Rev. ed. Toronto: Pontifical Institute of Mediaeval Studies, 1985.

Hermann the Lame. *Chronicon*. Ed. G. H. Pertz. Monumenta Germaniae Historica, *Scriptores* 5. Hannover, 1844. 67–133.

Heusler, Andreas. *Die altgermanische Dichtung*. 2nd rev. ed. Darmstadt: Wissenschaftliche Buchgesellschaft, 1957.

Highet, Gilbert. *The Classical Tradition: Greek and Roman Influences on Western Literature*. Oxford: Oxford UP, 1967.

Hodgson, Phyllis, ed. *The Cloud of Unknowing and the Book of Privy Counselling*. EETS o.s. 218. Oxford: Oxford UP, 1944.

Hoepffner, Ernest, ed. *Oeuvres de Guillaume de Machaut*. 3 vols. Paris: SATF, 1908–21.

Hofmann, Dietrich. "Vers und Prose in der mündlich gepflegten mittelalterlichen Erzählkunst der germanischen Länder." *Frühmittelalterliche Studien* 5 (1971): 135–75.

Hoops, Johannes. *Reallexicon der germanischen Altertumskunde*. 2nd ed. Rev. H. Arbman, ed. Heinrich Bech. Berlin: De Gruyter, 1973.

Huchet, Jean-Charles. "Nom de femme et écriture féminin au Moyen Age: Les *Lais* de Marie de France." *Poétique* 48 (1981): 407–30.

Hudson, Anne. *English Wycliffite Sermons*. Vol. 1. Oxford: Clarendon, 1983.

Hult, David F. *Self-Fulfilling Prophecies: Readership and Authority in the First "Roman de la Rose."* Cambridge: Cambridge UP, 1986.

Hult, David F. "Vers la société de l'écriture." *Poétique* 50 (1982): 155–72.

Hunt, Tony. "Glossing Marie de France." *Romanische Forschungen* 86 (1986): 396–418.

Huot, Sylvia. *From Song to Book: The Poetics of Writing in Old French Lyric and Lyrical Narrative Poetry*. Ithaca: Cornell UP, 1987.

Huot, Sylvia. "The Scribe as Editor: Rubrication as Critical Apparatus in Two Manuscripts of the *Roman de la Rose*." *L'ésprit createur* 27 (1987): 67–78.

Isaac, J. *Le Peri Hermeneias en Occident de Boèce à Saint Thomas: Histoire littéraire
d'un traité d'Aristote*. Paris: Vrin, 1953.

Iser, Wolfgang. *The Act of Reading: A Theory of Aesthetic Response*. Baltimore: Johns
Hopkins UP, 1978.

Iser, Wolfgang. "Feigning in Fiction." *The Identity of the Text*. Ed. Mario Valdes.
Toronto: Toronto UP, 1985. 204–28.

Iser, Wolfgang. *The Implied Reader*. Baltimore: Johns Hopkins UP, 1974.

Isidore of Seville. *Etymologiarum sive originum*. Ed. W. M. Lindsay. Vol. 1. Oxford:
Oxford Classical Texts, 1985.

Jauss, Hans-Robert. *Ästhetische Erfahrung und literarische Hermeneutik*. Munich:
Fink, 1977.

Jauss, Hans-Robert. "Theorie der Gattungen und Literatur des Mittelalters." *Alterität
un Modernität der mittelalterlichen Literatur: Gesammelte Aufsätze, 1956–1976*.
Ed. Hans-Robert Jauss. Munich: Fink, 1977. 327–58.

Jauss, Hans-Robert. "Zur historischen Genese der Scheidung von Fiktion und Realität." *Funktionen des Fiktiven*. Ed. D. Henrich and W. Iser. Poetik und Hermeneutik
10. Munich: Fink, 1982. 423–31.

Jeauneau, Eduard. "L'usage de la notion d'*integumentum* à travers les gloses de
Guillaume de Conches." *Archives d'histoire doctrinale et littérarie du Moyen Age*
24 (1958): 35–100.

Jordanes. *Jordanis de origine actibusque Getarum*. Ed. T. Mommsen. Monumenta
Germaniae Historica: Auctores Antiquissimi 5, 1. Berlin: Weidmann, 1882, rpt.
1961. 53–138.

Kane, George, ed. *Piers Plowman: The A Version*. London: Athlone, 1960.

Kelber, Werner H. "The Authority of the Word in St. John's Gospel: Charismatic
Speech, Narrative Text, Logocentric Metaphysics." *Oral Tradition* 2 (1987):
108–31.

Keller, Hagen. *Zwischen regionaler Begrenzung und universalem Horizont, 1024–
1250*. Propyläen Geschichte Deutschlands 2. Berlin: Propyläen, 1986.

Kellogg, Robert. *A Concordance to Eddic Poetry*. East Lansing: Colleagues Press,
1988.

Kelly, F. Douglas. *Sens and Conjointure in the Chevalier de la Charrette*. The Hague:
Mouton, 1966.

Kendrick, Laura. *The Game of Love: Troubadour Wordplay*. Berkeley: U of California
P, 1988.

Kernan, Alvin. *Printing Technology, Letters, and Samuel Johnson*. Princeton: Princeton UP, 1987.

King, K. C. "On the Naming of Places in Heroic Literature: Some Examples from the
Nibelungenlied." *Oxford German Studies* 2 (1967): 13–24.

King Horn: A Middle-English Romance. Ed. Joseph Hall. Oxford: Clarendon, 1901.

Kinneavy, James L. *A Theory of Discourse: The Aims of Discourse*. 1971. Rpt. New
York: Norton, 1980.

Kiparsky, Paul. "Oral Poetry: Some Linguistic and Typological Considerations."
Oral Literature and the Formula. Ed. Benjamin A. Stolz and Richard S. Shannon

III. Ann Arbor: Center for the Coordination of Ancient and Modern Studies, 1976. 73–106.

Kleinhenz, Christopher, ed. *Medieval Manuscripts and Textual Criticism.* Chapel Hill: U of North Carolina P, 1976.

Knab, Tim. "Three Tales from the Sierra de Puebla." *Alcheringa/Ethnopoetics,* n.s. 4, no. 2 (1980): 2–36.

Knott, Thomas A., and David C. Fowler, eds. *Piers the Plowman: A Critical Edition of the A-Version.* Baltimore: Johns Hopkins UP, 1952.

Koch, Peter, and Wulf Oesterreicher. "Sprache de Nahe-Sprache der Distanz: Mündlichkeit und Schriftlichkeit im Spannungsfeld von Sprachtheorie und Sprachgeschichte." Romanistisches Jahrbuch 36 (1986 for 1985): 15–43.

Kristeva, Julia. "Word, Dialogue, and Novel." *The Kristeva Reader.* Ed. Toril Moi. New York: Columbia UP, 1986. 34–61.

Lathuillère, Roger. *Guiron le courtois: Etude de la tradition manuscrite et analyse critique.* Publications Romans et Françaises 86. Geneva: Droz, 1966.

Law, Vivien. *The Insular Latin Grammarians.* Woodbridge: Boydell, 1982.

Leyser, Karl. *The Crisis of Medieval Germany.* Raleigh Lectures on History 1983. London: British Academy, 1984.

Liber de unitate ecclesiae conservanda. Ed. W. Schwenkenbecher. Monumenta Germaniae Historica: Libelli de Lite 2. Hannover: Impensis Bibliopolii Hahniani, 1892. 173–284.

Lindblad, Gustaf. "Poetiska Eddans förhistoria och skrivskicket i Codex regius." *Arkiv för Nordisk Filologi* 95 (1980): 142–67.

Lods, Jeanne, ed. *Les pièces lyriques du Roman de Perceforest.* Société de Publications Romanes et Françaises 36. Geneva: Droz; Lille: Giard, 1953.

Lods, Jeanne. *Le "Roman de Perceforest": Origines, composition, caractères, valeur et influence.* Société de Publications Romanes et Françaises 32. Geneva: Droz; Lille: Giard, 1951.

Lönnroth, Lars. "Hjalmár's Death Song and the Delivery of Eddic Poetry." *Speculum* 46 (1971): 1–20.

Lönnroth, Lars. "Iorð fannz æva né upphiminn: A formula analysis." *Speculum Norroenum: Norse Studies in Memory of Gabriel Turville-Petre.* Ed. Ursula Dronke et al. Odense: Odense UP, 1981. 310–27.

Lord, Albert. "Perspectives on Recent Work on the Oral Traditional Formula." *Oral Tradition* 1 (1986): 467–503.

Lord, Albert. *The Singer of Tales.* Cambridge: Harvard UP, 1960; rpt. New York: Atheneum, 1978.

Löseth, E. *The roman en prose de Tristan, le roman de Palamède et la compilation de Rusticien de Pise, analyse critique d'après les manuscrits de Paris.* Paris: Bouillon, 1890.

Louise, René. *Girart, Comte de Vienne dans les chansons de geste. Girart de Vienne, Girart de Fraite, Girart de Roussillon.* 2 vols. Auxerre: Bureaux de l'Imprimerie Moderne, 1947.

Lydgate, John. *John Lydgate, Poems.* Ed. John Norton-Smith. Oxford: Clarendon, 1966.

Machan, Tim William. "Middle English Text Production and Modern Editorial Procedure." *Currents and Controversies in Medieval English Textual Criticism*. Ed. A. J. Minnis and Charlotte Brewer. Oxford: Oxford UP (forthcoming 1992).

Machan, Tim William. "Scribal Role, Authorial Intention, and Chaucer's *Boece*." *Chaucer Review* 24 (1989): 150–62.

Magoun, Francis P., Jr. "The Oral-Formulaic Character of Anglo-Saxon Narrative Poetry." *Speculum* 28 (1953): 446–67.

Maillard, Jean. "Coutumes musicales au moyen âge d'après le *Tristan en prose*." *Cahiers de civilisation médiévale* 2 (1959): 341–53.

Marie de France. *Espurgatoire Saint Patrice*. Ed. Karl Warnke. Halle: Niemeyer, 1938.

Marie de France. *Fables*. Ed. Alfred Ewert and R. C. Johnston. Oxford: Blackwell, 1942.

Marie de France. *Lais*. Ed. Alfred Ewert. Oxford: Blackwell, 1944.

Marie de France. *Les Lais*. Ed. Jean Rychner. Classiques Français du Moyen Age 93. Paris: Champion, 1973.

Marquard, Odo. "Kunst als Antifiktion-Versuch über den Weg der Wirklichkeit ins Fiktive." *Funktionen des Fiktiven*. Ed. D. Heinrich and W. Iser. Poetik und Hermeneutik 10. Munich: Fink, 1982. 35–54.

Martianus Capella. *The Marriage of Philology and Mercury*. Trans. William Harris Stahl and Richard Johnson with E. L. Burge. New York: Columbia UP, 1977. Vol. 2 of *Martianus Capella and the Seven Liberal Arts*. 2 vols. 1971–77.

Meletinsky, Eleazar M. "Commonplaces and Other Elements of Folkloristic Style in Eddic Poetry." *Structure and Meaning in Old Norse Literature*. Ed. John Lindow, Lars Lönnroth, and Gerd Wolfgang Weber. Odense: Odense UP, 1986. 15–31.

Menéndez Pidal, Ramón. *"La Chanson de Roland" et la tradition épique des Francs*. Trans. I. M. Cluzel. 2nd ed. Paris: Picard, 1960.

Meyer von Knonau, Gerold. *Jahrbucher des deutschen Reiches unter Heinrich IV und Heinrich V*. Jahrbucher der deutschen Geschicht 4. 1903. Rpt. Berlin: Duncker and Humblot, 1965.

Mickel, Emanuel J., Jr. *Marie de France*. Twayne's World Authors 306. New York: Twayne, 1974.

Miller, D. Gary. *Improvisation, Typology, Culture, and "The New Orthodoxy": How Oral is Homer?* Washington, D.C.: University Press of America, 1982.

Miller, J. Hillis. "The Triumph of Theory, the Resistance to Reading, and the Question of the Material Base." *PMLA* 102 (1987): 281–91.

Mills, Maldwyn. "A Medieval Reviser at Work." *Medium Aevum* 32 (1963): 11–23.

Mills, Margaret. "An Afghan Folktale." *The Harvard Advocate* 117.3a (1983): 58–66.

Minnis, Alistair J. *Medieval Theory of Authorship: Scholastic Literary Attitudes in the Later Middle Ages*. London: Scolar, 1984.

Mueke, Stephen, Alan Rumsey, and Banjo Wirrunmarra. "Pidgeon the Outlaw. History as Texts." *Aboriginal History* 9 (1985): 81–100.

Murphy, James J. *Medieval Eloquence: Studies in the Theory and Practice of Medieval Rhetoric*. Berkeley: U of California P, 1978.

Murphy, James J. *Rhetoric in the Middle Ages: A History of Rhetorical Theory from St. Augustine to the Renaissance*. Berkeley: U of California P, 1974.

Mussetter, Sally. "The Education of Chrétien's Enide." *Romanic Review* 73 (1982): 147–66.

Nichols, Stephen G. "Aesthesis and the Power of Marginality in Medieval Women Writers." *The Politics of Tradition: Placing Women in French Literature.* Ed. Joan de Jean and Nancy K. Miller. Yale French Studies 75. New Haven: Yale UP, 1988. 77–94.

Nichols, Stephen G. "The Old Provençal Lyric." *A New History of French Literature.* Ed. Denis Hollier et al. Cambridge: Harvard UP, 1989. 30–36.

Nichols, Stephen G. *Voices in the Text.* Forthcoming.

Nicholson, Lewis E. "*Beowulf* and the Pagan Cult of the Stag." *Studi Medievali* 27 (1986): 637–69.

Notker Labeo (Notker der Deutsche). *Boethius, De consolatione Philosophiae, Buch I/II.* Ed. Petrus W. Tax. Altdeutsche Textbibliothek 84. Tübingen: Niemeyer, 1986.

Octavio de Toledo, Jose M. "Vision [*sic*] de Filiberto." *Zeitschrift für Romanische Philologie* 2 (1878): 40–69.

Ohly, Friedrich. "Die Zerreissung als Strafe für Liebesverrat in der Antike und im Alten Testament." *Sprache und Recht: Beiträge zur Kulturgeschichte des mittelalters: Festschrift für Ruth Schmidt-Wiegand zum 60.* Berlin: De Gruyter, 1986. 554–624.

Ohly, Friedrich. "Zu den Ursprungen der *Chanson de Roland.*" *Mediaevalia literaria: Festschrift für Helmut de Boor.* Ed. Ursula Henning and Herbert Kolb. Munich: Beck, 1971. 135–53.

Olson, David. "From Utterance to Text: The Bias of Language in Speech and Writing." *Harvard Educational Review* 47 (1977): 257–81.

O'Maera, John J. "Augustine the Artist and the *Aeneid.*" *Mélanges offerts à Mlle. Christine Mohrmann.* Utrecht: Spectrum Editeurs, 1963. 252–61.

Ong, Walter J. "Before Textuality: Orality and Interpretation." *Oral Tradition* 3 (1988): 259–69.

Ong, Walter J. *Interfaces of the Word: Studies in the Evolution of Consciousness and Culture.* Ithaca: Cornell UP, 1977.

Ong, Walter J. "Latin Language Study as a Renaissance Puberty Rite." *Rhetoric, Romance, and Technology: Studies in the Interaction of Expression and Culture.* Ithaca: Cornell UP, 1971. 113–41.

Ong, Walter J. *Orality and Literacy: The Technologizing of the Word.* London: Methuen, 1982.

Ong, Walter J. *The Presence of the Word: Some Prolegomena for Culture and Religious History.* New Haven: Yale UP, 1967.

Ong, Walter J. "Text as Interpretation: Mark and After." In Foley, *Oral Tradition* 147–69.

Ong, Walter J. "The Writer's Audience Is Always a Fiction." *PMLA* 90 (1975): 9–22.

Ong, Walter J. "Writing Is a Technology That Restructures Thought." *The Written Word: Literacy in Tradition.* Ed. Gerd Baumann. Wolfson College Lectures 1985. Oxford: Clarendon, 1986. 23–50.

Opland, Jeff. *Anglo-Saxon Oral Poetry: A Study of the Tradition.* New Haven: Yale UP, 1980.

Otfrid von Weissenburg. *Evangelienbuch.* Ed. L. Wolff. 3rd ed. Altdeutsche Textbibliothek 49. Tübingen: Niemeyer, 1957.

Otten, Charlotte, ed. *A Lycanthropy Reader: Werewolves in Western Culture.* Syracuse: Syracuse UP, 1986.

Ovid. *Metamorphoses.* Trans. Frank Justus Miller. 3rd ed. Cambridge: Harvard UP, 1977.

Page, Christopher. *Voices and Instruments of the Middle Ages: Instrumental Practice and Songs in France, 1100–1300.* Berkeley: U of California P, 1986.

Parkes, M. B. "The Literacy of the Laity." *The Medieval World.* Ed. David Daiches and Anthony Thorlby. London: Aldus, 1973. 555–77. Vol. 2 of *Literature and Western Civilization.*

Parks, Ward. "Interperformativity and *Beowulf.*" *Narodna umjetnost* 26 (1989): 25–35.

Parks, Ward. "Orality and Poetics: Synchrony, Diachrony, and the Axes of Narrative Transmission." In Foley, ed., *Comparative Research* 511–32.

Parks, Ward. "The Traditional Narrator and the 'I Heard' Formulas in Old English Poetry." *Anglo-Saxon England* 16 (1987): 45–66.

Parks, Ward. "The Traditional Narrator in *Beowulf* and Homer." In *De Gustibus: A Festschrift for Alain Renoir.* Ed. John Miles Foley. New York: Garland (forthcoming).

Pàroli, Teresa. *Sull'elemento formulare nella poesia germanica antica.* Rome: Istituto de glottologia, Università de Roma, 1975.

Parry, Milman. *L'épithète traditionnelle dans Homère: Essai sur un problème de style homérique.* 1928. Trans. Adam Parry in *The Making of Homeric Verse.* 1–190.

Parry, Milman. *Les formules et la métrique d'Homere.* 1928. Trans. Adam Parry in *The Making of Homeric Verse* 191–239.

Parry, Milman. *The Making of Homeric Verse: The Collected Papers of Milman Parry.* Ed. and trans. Adam Parry. Oxford: Clarendon, 1971.

Parry, Milman. "Studies in the Epic Technique of Oral Verse-Making: I. Homer and Homeric Style; II. The Homeric Language as the Language of an Oral Poetry." *Harvard Studies in Classical Philology* 41 (1930): 73–147; 43 (1932): 1–50. Rpt. in *The Making of Homeric Verse* 266–324, 325–64.

Pearsall, Derek, ed. *The Canterbury Tales.* By Geoffrey Chaucer. London: Allen, 1985.

Pearsall, Derek. *Piers Plowman by William Langland: An Edition of the C-Text.* Berkeley: U of California P, 1978.

Pearsall, Derek. "Texts, Textual Criticism, and Fifteenth-Century Manuscript Production." *Fifteenth-Century Studies.* Ed. Robert F. Yeager. Hamden: Archon, 1984. 121–36.

Petrarch, Francis. *Letters from Petrarch.* Comp. and trans. Morris Bishop. Bloomington: Indiana UP, 1966.

Plato. *The Collected Dialogues of Plato.* Ed. Edith Hamilton and Huntington Cairns. Bollingen Series 71. Princeton: Princeton UP, 1982.

Quinn, William A., and Audley S. Hall. *Jongleur: A Modified Theory of Oral Improvisation and Its Effect on the Performance and Transmission of Middle English Romance.* Washington, D.C.: University Press of America, 1982.

Remigius of Auxerre. *Remigii Autissiodorensis commentum in Martianum Capellam.* Libri III–IX. Ed. Cora E. Lutz. Vol. 2. Leiden: Brill, 1965.

Renoir, Alain. *A Key to Old Poems.* University Park: Pennsylvania State UP, 1988.

Reuter, Timothy. "The 'Imperial Church System' of the Ottonian and Salian Rulers: A Reconsideration." *Journal of Ecclesiastical History* 33 (1982): 347–74.

Ricketts, Peter T., ed. *Acts du premier congrès international de l'Association Internationale des Études Occitanes.* London: AIEO, 1987.

Ricks, Christopher, ed. *The Poems of Tennyson.* London: Longman, 1969.

Ricoeur, Paul. *Time and Narrative.* Trans. Kathleen McLaughlin and David Pellauer. Vol. 1. Chicago: U of Chicago P, 1984.

Riffaterre, Michael. *Semiotics of Poetry.* Bloomington: Indiana UP, 1984.

Riffaterre, Michael. *Text Production.* Trans. Terese Lyons. New York: Columbia UP, 1983.

Riquer, Martin de. *Les chansons de geste françaises.* Trans. I. M. Cluzel. 2nd ed. Paris: Nizet, 1957.

Robertson, D. W., Jr. "Marie de France, *Lais,* Prologue 13–16." *Modern Language Notes* 64 (1949): 336–38.

Robertson, D. W., Jr. *A Preface to Chaucer: Studies in Medieval Perspectives.* Princeton: Princeton UP, 1962.

Robinson, Ian Stuart. *Authority and Resistance in the Investiture Contest: The Polemical Literature of the Late Eleventh Century.* Manchester: Manchester UP, 1978.

Le Roman de Perceforest. MSS fr. 345–47. Bibliothèque Nationale, Paris.

Ross, D. I. A. "L'originalité de Turoldus: Le mandement de la lance." *Cahiers de civilisation médiévale* 6 (1963): 127–38.

Ross, Margaret Clunies. *Skáldskaparmál: Snorri Sturluson's Ars poetica and Medieval Theories of Language.* Odense: Odense UP, 1987.

Roussineau, Gilles, ed. *Perceforest: Quatrième partie.* 2 vols. Textes Littéraires Français. Geneva: Droz, 1987.

Roussineau, Gilles, ed. *Perceforest: Troisième partie.* Textes Littéraires Français. Geneva: Droz, 1988.

Roy, Bruno. "A la recherche des lecteurs médiévaux du *De Amore* d'Andre le Chapelain." *Revue de l'Université d'Ottawa / University of Ottawa Quarterly* 55 (1985): 45–73.

Roy, Maurice, ed. *Oeuvres Poétiques de Christine de Pisan.* 3 vols. Paris: Didot, 1886–96.

Ruiz, Juan. *Libro de buen amor.* MS 19 (Fourteenth century) (MS. G). Academia Española, Madrid. *Libro de buen amor: Edicíon facsímil del manuscrito Gayoso (1389) propiedad de la Real Academia Española* Fac. ed. Madrid: Real Academia Española, 1974.

Ruiz, Juan. *Libro de buen amor.* MS 10073 (Fourteenth century). Biblioteca Nacional, Madrid.

Ruiz, Juan. *Libro de buen amor.* MS Vitrina 6–1 (Fourteenth century) (MS T). Biblioteca Nacional, Madrid. *Libro de buen amor.* Ed. Manuel Criado de Val and Eric W. Naylor. Fac. ed. 3 vols. Madrid: Espasa-Calpe, 1977.

Ruiz, Juan. *Libro de buen amor.* MS Vitrina 7–17. Biblioteca Nacional, Madrid.

Ruiz, Juan. *Libro de buen amor.* MS 2663 (Fifteenth century) (MS S). Biblioteca Universitaria, Salamanca. *Libro de buen amor: Edicíon facsímil del códice de Salamanca.* Fac. ed. 2 vols. Madrid: EDILAN, 1975.

Ruiz, Juan. *Libro de buen amor.* Ed. Julio Cejador y Frauca. Clasicos Castellanos 14 and 17. 2 vols. Madrid: Espasa-Calpe, 1913.

Ruiz, Juan. *Libro de buen amor.* Ed. Giorgio Chiarini. Milan: Riccardo Ricciardi, 1964.

Ruiz, Juan. *Libro de buen amor.* Ed. Juan Corominas. Madrid: Gredos, 1967.

Ruiz, Juan. *Libro de buen amor.* Ed. Raymond S. Willis. Princeton: Princeton UP, 1972.

Ruiz, Juan. *Libro de buen amor.* Ed. Jacques Joset. Clásicos Castellanos 14 and 17. 2 vols. Madrid: Espasa-Calpe, 1974.

Ruiz, Juan. *Libro de buen amor.* Ed. Alberto Blecua. Barcelona: Planeta, 1983.

Ruiz, Juan. *Libro de buen amor.* Ed. G. B. Gybbon-Monypenny. Madrid: Castalia, 1988.

Russell, G. H. "Some Aspects of the Process of Revision in *Piers Plowman.*" *Piers Plowman: Critical Approaches.* Ed. S. S. Hussey. London: Methuen, 1969. 27–49.

Sala, Charles. "La signature à la lettre et au figuré." *Poétique* 69 (1987): 119–27.

Schaefer, Ursula. "The Fictionalized Dilemma: Old English Poems at the Crossroads of Orality and Literacy." Erzgräber and Volk 39–51.

Schaefer, Ursula. "The Instance of the Formula: A Poetic Device Revisited." *Papers on Language and Mediaeval Studies Presented to Alfred Schopf.* Ed. Richard Matthews and Joachim Schmole-Rostosky. Neue Studien zur Anglistik und Amerikanistik 37. Frankfurt: Lang, 1988. 39–57.

Schaefer, Ursula. "Two Women in Need of a Friend: A Comparison of *The Wife's Lament* and Eangyth's Letter to Boniface." *Germanic Dialects: Linguistic and Philological Investigations.* Ed. Bela Brogyanyi and Thomas Krommelbein. Amsterdam: Benjamins, 1986. 491–524.

Schieffer, Rudolf. *Die Entstehung des päpstlichen Investiturverbots für den deutschen König.* Schriften der Monumenta Germaniae Historica 28. Stuttgart: Hersemann, 1981.

Schieffer, Rudolf. " 'Priesterbild': Reformpapsttum und Investiturstreit. Methodische Anmerkungen zu einer Neuerscheinung." *Archiv für Kulturgeschichte* 68 (1986): 479–94.

Schmolke-Hasselmann, Beate. "Tristan als Dichter: Ein Beitrag zur Erforschung des *lai lyrique breton.*" *Romanische Forschungen* 98 (1986): 258–76.

Schneider, Hermann. *Germanische Heldensage.* 2nd ed. Vol. 1. Berlin: De Gruyter, 1962.

Scholes, Robert. *Textual Power: Literary Theory and the Teaching of English.* New Haven: Yale UP, 1985.

Schulenburg, Jane Tibbetts. "The Heroics of Virginity: Brides of Christ and Sacrificial Mutilation." *Women in the Middle Ages and the Renaissance: Literary and Historical Perspectives.* Ed. Mary Beth Rose. Syracuse: Syracuse UP, 1986.

Seitel, Peter. *See So That We May See: Performances and Interpretations of Traditional Tales from Tanzania.* Bloomington: Indiana UP, 1980.

Sigurðsson, Gisli. "On the Classification of Eddic Heroic Poetry in View of the Oral Theory." *Poetry in the Scandinavian Middle Ages* (Proceedings of the Seventh

International Saga Conference). Spoleto: Centro italiano di studi sull'alto medioevo, 1990. 245–55.

Sir Gawain and the Green Knight. Ed. J. R. R. Tolkien and E. V. Gordon. 2nd ed. Rev. Norman Davis. Oxford: Clarendon, 1967.

Sisam, Kenneth. "Cynewulf and His Poetry." *Studies in the History of Old English Literature.* Oxford: Clarendon, 1953. 1–28.

Skeat, Walter W., ed. *The Vision of William concerning Piers the Plowman in Three Parallel Texts together with Richard the Redeless.* Oxford: Oxford UP, 1886.

Southern, Richard W. *The Making of the Middle Ages.* New Haven: Yale UP, 1953.

Spitzer, Leo. "Note on the Poetic and the Empirical 'I' in Medieval Authors." *Traditio* 4 (1946): 414–22.

Spitzer, Leo. "The Prologue to the *Lais* of Marie de France and Medieval Poetics." *Modern Philology* 41 (1943): 96–102.

Starobinski, Jean. "Rousseau's Happy Days." *New Literary History* 11 (1979): 147–66.

Starobinski, Jean. "*Le texte dans le texte:* Extraits inédits des cahiers d'anagrammes de Ferdinand de Saussure." *Tel Quel* 39 (1969): 3–33.

Stevenson, Matilda Coxe. "The Zuñi Indians." *Annual Report of the Bureau of American Ethnology* 23 (1904): 73–88.

Stierle, Karlheinz. "Was heisst Rezeption bei fiktionalen Texten?" *Poetica* 7 (1975): 345–87.

Stock, Brian. *The Implications of Literacy: Written Language and Models of Interpretation in the Eleventh and Twelfth Centuries.* Princeton: Princeton UP, 1983.

Strunk, Oliver. *Source Readings in Music History, from Classical Antiquity through the Romantic Era.* New York: Norton, 1950.

Sturges, Robert. "Texts and Readers in Marie de France's *Lais.*" *Romanic Review* 71 (1980): 244–64.

Swerdlow, Noel. "Musica Dicitur A Moys, Quod est Aqua." *Journal of the American Musicological Society* 20 (1967): 3–9.

Tacitus. *Cornelii Taciti Annalium ab excessu divi Augusti libri.* Ed. C. D. Fisher. Oxford: Clarendon, 1963.

Tacitus. *Germania.* Ed. E. Fehrle. 2nd ed. Munich: Lehmann, 1935.

Tannen, Deborah. "The Oral/ Literate Continuum in Discourse." *Spoken and Written language: Exploiting Orality and Literacy.* Ed D. Tannen. Norwood, N.J.: ABLEX, 1982. 1–16.

Taylor, Jane H. M. "The Fourteenth Century: Context, Text, and Intertext." *The Legacy of Chrétien de Troyes.* Ed. Norris J. Lacy, Douglas Kelly, and Keith Busby. Vol. 1. Amsterdam: Rodopi, 1987. 267–332.

Taylor, Jane H. M. "Reason and Faith in the *Roman de Perceforest.*" *Studies in Medieval Literature and Languages in Memory of Frederick Whitehead.* Ed. W. Rothwell, et al. Manchester: Manchester UP, 1973. 303–22.

Taylor, Jane H. M., ed. *Le roman de Perceforest: Première partie.* Textes Littéraires Français. Geneva: Droz, 1979.

Tedlock, Dennis. *Finding the Center: Narrative Poetry of the Zuni Indians.* 1972. Lincoln: U of Nebraska P, 1978.

Tedlock, Dennis. *The Spoken Word and the Work of Interpretation.* Philadelphia: U of Pennsylvnia P, 1983.

Tedlock, Dennis. "Toward an Oral Poetics." *New Literary History* 8 (1977): 507–19.

Tellenbach, Gerd. *Libertas, Kirche und Weltordnung im Zeitalter des Investiturstreits.* Forschungen zur Kirchen und Geistesgeschichte 7. Stuttgart, 1936. English version. *Church, State and Christian Society at the Time of the Investiture Contest.* Trans. R. F. Bennett. Studies in Medieval History 3. Oxford: Blackwell, 1940.

Tellenbach, Gerd. *Die westliche Kirche vom 10. bis zum fruhen 12. Jahrhundert.* Die Kirche in ihrer Geschichte. Ein Handbuch. Ed. Bernd Moller. Vol. 2, F 1. Göttingen, 1988.

Thietmar von Merseburg. *Die Chronik des Bischofs Thietmar von Merseberg und ihre Korveier Überarbeitung.* Ed. Robert Holzmann. Monumenta Germaniae Historia, SS rer. Germ., n.s., vol. 9. Berlin: Weidmannsche Buchhandlung, 1935.

Thietmar von Merseburg. *Chronik.* Ed. W. Trillmich. Ausgewählte Quellen zur deutschen Geschichte des Mittelalters 9. Darmstadt: Wissenschaftliche Buchgesellschaft, 1962.

Thomson, David. *An Edition of the Middle English Grammatical Texts.* New York: Garland, 1984.

Thundy, Zacharias P. "Intertextuality, Buddhism, and the Infancy Gospels." *Religious Systems and Religious Writings: Systematic Analysis.* Ed. Jacob Neusner et al. Atlanta: Scholar's Press for Brown Judaic Studies, 1989. 1: 71–73.

Titon, Jeff. *Powerhouse for God: Speech, Chant, and Song in an Appalachian Baptist Church.* Austin: U of Texas P, 1988.

Toelken, Barre, and Tacheeni Scott. "Poetic Retranslation and the 'Pretty Languages' of Yellowman." *Traditional Literatures of the American Indian: Texts and Enterpretations.* Ed. Karl Kroeber. Lincoln: U of Nebraska P, 1981. 65–116.

Tómasson, Sverrir. *Formálar íslenskra sagnaritara á miðöldum.* Reykjavík: Stofnun Árna Magnússonar, 1988.

La Treselegante, Delicieuse, Melliflue et tresplaisante Hystoire du tresnoble, victorieux et excellentissime roy Perceforest. . . . 6 vols. Paris: N. Cousteau pour Galiot du Pre, 1528; Paris: Gilles de Gourmont, 1531.

Tristan en prose. MSS fr. 335–36. Bibliothèque Nationale, Paris.

Tripp, Raymond P., Jr. *More about the Fight with the Dragon: Beowulf 2208b–3182, Commentary, Edition and Translation.* Lanham, MD.: U of America P, 1983.

Tyler, Stephen A. *The Unspeakable: Discourse, Dialogue, and Rhetoric in the Postmodern World.* Madison: U of Wisconsin P, 1987.

Virgil. *P. Virgili Maronis Opera.* Ed. Frederick A. Hirtzel. Oxford: Clarendon, 1942.

Vogel, Jorgen. "Zur Kirchenpolitik Heinrichs IV. nach seiner Kaiserkrönung und zur Wirksamkeit der Legaten Gregors VII. und Clemens' III. im deutschen Reich 1084–85." *Frühmittelalterliche Studien* 16 (1982): 161–92.

Waldron, R. A. "Oral-Formulaic Technique and Middle English Alliterative Poetry." *Speculum* 32 (1957): 792–804.

Walker, Roger M. " 'Con miedo de la muerte la miel non es sabrosa': Love, Sin and Death in the *Libro de buen amor.*" *Libro de buen amor Studies.* Ed. G. B. Gybbon-Monypenny. London: Tamesis, 1970. 231–52.

Warning, Rainer. "Staged Discourse: Remarks on the Pragmatics of Fiction." *Dispositio* 5 (1980): 35–54.

Wehrli, M. "Gattungsgeschichtliche Betrachtungen zum *Ludwigslied*." *Formen mittelalterlicher Erzählung.* Zurich: Atlantis, 1969. 73–87.

Whitman, F. H. "The Meaning of 'Formulaic' in Old English Verse Composition." *Neuphilologische Mitteilungen* 76 (1975): 529–37.

Williams, A. H. *The Middle Ages.* Cardiff: U of Wales P, n.d. Vol. 2, Pt. 1 of *An Introduction to the History of Wales.* 2 vols. 1941–[1944].

Wilson, Edward O. *Sociobiology: The New Synthesis.* Cambridge, MA: Belknap–Harvard UP, 1975.

Wolf, Alois. "Der Abend wiegte schon die Erde und an den Bergen hing die Nacht." *Bild und Gedanke: Festschrift für Gerharts Baumann zum 60.* Ed. Gunter Schnitzler et al. Munich: Fink, 1980. 187–206.

Wolf, Alois. "Altisländische theoretische Äußerungen zur Verschriftlichung und die Verschriftlichung der Bibelungensagen im Norden." *Zwischen Festtag und Alltag.* Ed. Wolfgang Raible. ScriptOralia 6. Tübingen: Narr, 1988. 167–89.

Wolf, Alois. "Frühmittelalterliches Erzählen im Spannungsfeld von Vers, Abschnitt und Strophe: Versuch einer Bestandsaufnahme." *Script Oralia,* Tübingen. Forthcoming.

Wolf, Alois. "Das literarische Leben Österreichs im Hochmittelalter." *Geschichte der österreichischen Literatur,* ed. Herbert Zeman. Forthcoming.

Wolf, Alois. "Mittelalterliche Heldensagen zwischen Vergil, Prudentius und raffinierter Klosterliteratur: Beobachtungen zum Waltharius." *Sprachkunst* 7 (1976): 180–212.

Wolf, Alois. "Nibelungenlied—Chanson de geste—hofischer Roman: Zum Problem der Verschriftlichung der deutschen Nibelungensagen." *"Nibelungelied" und Klage: Sage und Geschichte, Struktur und Gattung.* Ed. F. P. Knapp. Passauer Nibelungen-Gespräche 1985. Heidelberg: C. Winter, 1987. 171–201.

Wolf, Alois. "Die Verschriftlichung der Nibelungensage und die französisch-deutschen Literaturbeziehungen im Mittelalter." *Hohenemser Studien zum "Nibelungenlied."* Ed. Achim Masser. Dornbirn: Vorarlberger, 1981. 53–71.

Wolf, Alois. "Die Verschriftlichung von europäischen Heldensagen als mittelalterliches Kulturproblem." *Heldensage und Heldendichtung im Germanischen.* Ed. H. Beck. Berlin: De Gruyter, 1988. 305–28.

Wolf, Alois. "Volkssprachliche Heldensagen und lateinische Monchskultur: Grundsatzliche Überlegungen zum Waltharius." In *Geistesleben um den Bodensee im frühen Mittelalter.* Literatur und Geschichte am Oberrhein 2. Freiburg, 1989. 157–83.

Wormald, C. P. "The Uses of Literacy in Anglo-Saxon England and Its Neighbours." *Transactions of the Royal Historical Society.* 5th Ser. 27 (1977): 95–114.

Yates, Frances A. *The Art of Memory.* Chicago: U of Chicago P, 1966.

Zimmermann, Harald, ed. *Papstregesten, 911–1024.* Vol. 5 of *Regesta Imperii II: Sächsische Zeit.* Ed. J. F. Böhmer. Vienna: Bohlaus, 1969.

Zumthor, Paul. *Essai de poétique médievale.* Paris: Seuil, 1972.

Zumthor, Paul. "Intertextualité et mouvance." *Littérature* 41 (1981): 8–16.

Zumthor, Paul. *Introduction à la poésie orale.* Paris: Seuil, 1983.

Zumthor, Paul. *Langue, texte, énigme.* Paris: Seuil, 1975.

Zumthor, Paul. *La lettre et la voix: De la "littérature" médiévale.* Paris: Seuil, 1987.

Zumthor, Paul. "Médiéviste ou pas." *Poétique* 31 (1977): 306–21.

Zumthor, Paul. *La poésie et la voix dans la civilisation médiévale.* Collège de France: Essais et Conférences. Paris: PUF, 1984.

Zumthor, Paul. "Spoken Language and Oral Poetry in the Middle Ages." *Style* 19 (1985): 191–98.

Zumthor, Paul. "The Text and the Voice." *New Literary History* 16 (1984–85): 67–92.

Index

Acteur. *See* author
Actor. *See* author
Agamben, Giorgio, 151, 152, 157
Ahl, Frederick, 194
Alain de Lille, 189
Ammianus Marcellinus, 69, 87*n8*
Anagram, 168, 169
Anaphora, 43, 44
Anderson, Earl R., 136*n26*
Andersson, Theodore M., 70
Anonymity, 169
Antancïon, 193
Archi-écriture. See Derrida
Aristotle, 151, 161*n27;* "option" of the veri-
  similar, 124; voice and body, 152, 153; and
  invariance of desire, 154; in troubador
  lyric, 157
"Arthur and Gorlagon", 187, 188
Attila, 69, 72
Auctor(es) 231, 232, 234, 235, 241. *See also*
  Author
Audience, 138; in metrical romances, 236
Auditive reception, 120
Augustine: effect on vocal symbolic expres-
  sion, 145; and memory, 146, 147, 148,
  156; and the body, 148; and oral perfor-
  mance, 149, 151; and the voice, 149–52;
  reversed by Guillaume IX, 153; and rheto-
  ric of silence, 157; and harmony, 159*n14;*
  silent speech, 159*n19;* and shapeshifting,
  187
Authenticity, 165, 166
Author, 165–68 *passim;* 176
Author function, 165, 166
Authorial "I", 132, 133
Authorial signature, 169, 176, 176*n1;* of
  Cynewulf, 127, 128, 136*nn23,27;* in
  Chanson de Roland, 162; of Chrétien

de Troyes, 163; of Marie de France,
  163, 184, 185; of Christine de Pizan,
  164, 171–76, 177*nn15,16,* 178*n17;* of
  Guillaume de Machaut, 164, 172, 177*n13,*
  234; of Jean de Meun, 164; of Jean
  Froissart, 164, 234; of Jean Renart, 164;
  and romance, 164; situation of, 164; and
  authority, 164; and authenticity, 166; anagrammic, 170, 171, 174, 175, 176,
  177*nn8,15,* 234; as trace, 174
Authority, 153, 165; in the epic, 7; in
  Guillaume IX, 154; and authorial signature, 164; and authenticity, 166; and
  readers, 167; of the minstrel, 211; of
  authorship, 232; establishment of, in manuscripts, 242
Authorship: definition, 163, 165; and authorial signature, 164; as emergent concept, 231; authority of, 232; and linguistic
  fixity, 241
Autonomy: of medieval poetry, 117, 118; of
  literary texts, 119, 120
Autor, 166, 167
Avril, François, 168

Bakhtin, M. M., 6, 13, 33*n;* and epic, 7, 56,
  61*n19;* heteroglossia, 32, 56; and dialogics, 53; "unmediated reality", 55
Battle of Brunanburh: compared to *Ludwigslied,* 80; tradition of naming in, 81
Battle of Maldon: and Old French Epic, 81,
  88*n23;* poetic style, 81; epic patterns, 82;
  and hagiography, 82, 83; the heroic in, 83,
  88*n24*
Baumgartner, Emmanuèle, 220
Bäuml, Franz H., 119, 235, 236
Bédier, Joseph, 177*n8*
Beowulf: oral heroic matter, 79; signs of oral